ŚŪDRAS IN ANCIENT INDIA

ŚŪDRAS IN ANCIENT INDIA

A social history of the lower order down to circa A.D. 600

RAM SHARAN SHARMA

MOTILAL BANARSIDASS PUBLISHERS
PRIVATE LIMITED • DELHI

2nd Reprint: Delhi, 2014
Third Revised Edition: Delhi, 1990
First Edition: Delhi, 1958

ISBN: 978-81-208-0706-8 (Cloth)
ISBN: 978-81-208-0873-7 (Paper)

MOTILAL BANARSIDASS
41 U.A. Bungalow Road, Jawahar Nagar, Delhi 110 007
8 Mahalaxmi Chamber, 22 Bhulabhai Desai Road, Mumbai 400 026
203 Royapettah High Road, Mylapore, Chennai 600 004
236, 9th Main III Block, Jayanagar, Bengaluru 560 011
Sanas Plaza, 1302 Baji Rao Road, Pune 411 002
8 Camac Street, Kolkata 700 017
Ashok Rajpath, Patna 800 004
Chowk, Varanasi 221 001

Printed in India

by RP Jain at NAB Printing Unit,
A-44, Naraina Industrial Area, Phase I, New Delhi–110028
and published by JP Jain for Motilal Banarsidass Publishers (P) Ltd,
41 U.A. Bungalow Road, Jawahar Nagar, Delhi-110007

PREFACE TO THE SECOND EDITION

Since the publication of the book in 1958, the critical edition of the *Mahābhārata* has been completed, and a couple of studies on the text of the *Arthaśāstra* of Kauṭilya have appeared. Proto-historical and historical archaeology has also made considerable advance, and new dimensions have been added to the anthropological studies of social differentiation and to the historical studies of several ancient societies. In the light of all this as well as in the light of published reviews and comments, certain portions have been modified. Some explanation has been offered for the proliferation of servile castes in the form of two appendices. Most chapter headings have been changed, and several chapters heavily recast. The concluding chapter has been rewritten, and the bibliography updated.

An important consideration for bringing out the book has been its absence from the market for a long time. A more thorough revision would have delayed publication without improving the book materially. All that has been done in the present edition may not satisfy the expectations of readers, but something is always better than nothing.

I would like to express my sincere thanks to Dr Mohanchand for help in preparing the index and bibliography.

Department of History,
University of Delhi — R. S. Sharma
26 June 1980

PREFACE TO THE FIRST EDITION

I took up the study of this subject about ten years ago, but the pressing duties of an Indian university teacher and lack of proper library facilities prevented me from making any appreciable progress. The major part of the work was done in two academic sessions (1954-56) at the School of Oriental and African Studies, made possible by the generous grant of study leave by the Patna University. This book, therefore, substantially represents my thesis approved for the degree of Ph.D. at the University of London in 1956.

I wish to thank Dr. F. R. Allchin, Professor H. W. Bailey, Dr. T. N. Dave, Dr. J. D. M. Derrett, Professor C. von Furer-Haimendorf, Professor D. D. Kosambi, Professor R. N. Sharma, Dr. A. K. Warder and numerous friends, from whom I have received various kinds of help in the course of this work. I am grateful to Dr. L. D. Barnett for his valuable suggestions and encouragement from time to time. I must express my thanks to my esteemed friend Dr. Dev Raj, but for whose help in proof-reading and allied matters the publication of the book would have been further delayed. I have also to acknowledge my debt to Dr. Upendra Thakur, who has prepared the index and helped me in proof-reading. Above all, I consider myself fortunate in having worked with Professor A. L. Basham, whose exacting standards of scholarship, love of intellectual independence on the part of his students and friendly guidance have contributed much to the making of this work. But I am responsible for any errors of fact and judgment, or technical irregularities, that may have remained unnoticed. I have been, however, helpless in the case of some printing mistakes, which could not be removed in spite of my best efforts.

R. S. SHARMA

ABBREVIATIONS

AI—*Ancient India*, Delhi.

AICL—*Ancient India as Described in Classical Literature by* J. W. McCrindle.

AIE—*Ancient Indian Education by* R. K. Mookerji.

AIMA—*Ancient India as Described by Megasthenes and Arrian by* J. W. McCrindle.

Ait. Br.—*Aitareya Brāhmaṇa.*

AK—*Amarakośa.*

Aṅg. N—*Aṅguttara Nikāya.*

Anu. P.—*Anuśāsana Parva.*

Antag.—*Antagaḍa Dasāo.*

AO—*Archiv Orientalani*, Prague.

Āp. Dh. S.—*Āpastamba Dharmasūtra.*

Āp. Gṛ. S.—*Āpastamba Gṛhyasūtra.*

Āp. Śr. S—*Āpastamba Śrautasūtra.*

AŚ—*Arthaśāstra of Kauṭilya.*

ASR—*Archaeological Survey (of India) Reports.*

ĀSS.—*Ānandāśrama Sanskrit Series.*

Āśva. Gṛ. S.—*Āśvalāyana Gṛhyasūtra.*

Āśva.Śr. S.—*Āśvalāyana Śrautasūtra.*

Āyār.—*Āyāraṅga Sutta.*

AV—*Atharva Veda.*

Bau. Dh. S.—*Baudhāyana Dharmasūtra.*

Bau. Gṛ. S.—*Baudhāyana Gṛhyasūtra.*

Bhār. Gṛ. S.—*Bhāradvāja Gṛhyasūtra.*

Bhāg. P.—*Bhāgavata Purāṇa.*

Bhav. P.—*Bhaviṣyat Purāṇa.*

BI—*Bibliotheca India.*

Bṛ.—*Bṛhaspati Smṛti.*

Bṛ. Saṃhitā—*Bṛhat Saṃhitā.*

Bṛ. Up.—*Bṛhadāraṇyaka Upaniṣad.*

Chā. Up.—*Chāndogya Upaniṣad.*

Cal.—*Calcutta Edition of the Mahābhārata.*

CHI—*Cambridge History of India, i, Ed.* E. J. Rapson.

CII—*Corpus Inscriptionum Indicarum.*

Cr. Edn.—Critical Edition of the *Mahābhārata* published by the Bhandarkar Oriental Institute, Poona.

Digha N.—*Digha Nikāya.*

Divya.—*Divyāvadāna.*

DKA—*Dynasties of the Kali Age. by* F. E. Pargiter.

Ed.—Edited by, Edition.

EI—*Epigraphia Indica,* Calcutta and Delhi.

Gaut. Dh. S.—*Gautama Dharmasūtra.*

GOS—*Gaikawad Oriental Series.*

HIL—*History of Indian Literature by* M. Winternitz.

Hin. P.L.—*Hindu Public Life by* U. N. Ghoshal.

Hist. Dh. S.—*History of Dharmaśāstra by* P. V. Kane.

Hist. & Essays—*Historiography and other Essays by* U. N Ghoshal.

HOS—*Harvard Oriental Series.*

HPL—*History of Pali Literature by* B. C. Law.

HSL—*History of Sanskrit Literature by* S. N. Dasgupta and S. K. De.

IA—*Indian Antiquary,* Bombay.

IC—*Indian Culture,* Calcutta.

IHQ—*Indian Historical Quarterly,* Calcutta.

Ind. Alt.—*Indische Alterthumskunde by* Christian Lassen.

Jai. Mi. S.—*Jaimini-Mimāṃsā Sūtra.*

JAHRS—*Journal of Andhra Historical Research Society,* Rajmundry.

JAOS—*Journal of the American Oriental Society,* Baltimore.

JASB—*Journal of the Asiatic Society of Bengal,* Calcutta.

JBBRAS—*Journal of the Bombay Branch of the Royal Asiatic Society,* Bombay.

JBORS—*Journal of the Bihar and Orissa Research Society,* Patna.

JBRS—*Journal of the Bihar Research Society,* Patna.

JESHO—*Journal of the Economic and Social History of the Orient,* Leiden.

JOR—*Journal of Oriental Research,* Madras.

JRAS—*Journal of the Royal Asiatic Society of Great Britain and Ireland,* London.

JRASB—*Journal of the Royal Asiatic Society of Bengal,* Calcutta.

Kā. Śr. S.—*Katyāyana Śrautasūtra.*

Kām. N. S.—*Kāmandaka Nitisāra.*

Kāma S.—*Kāmasūtra of Vātsyāyana.*

Kap. S.—*Kapiṣṭhala Saṃhitā.*
Kātyā—*Kātyāyana Smṛti.*
KS—*Kāṭhaka Saṃhitā.*
Kumb.—Kumbkonam Edition of the *Mahābhārata* (also indicated as *SE*).
Lāṭyā. Śr. S—*Lāṭyāyana Śrautasūtra.*
Majj. N.—*Majjhima Nikāya.*
Manu—*Manu Smṛti.*
Mārk. P.—*Mārkaṇḍeya Purāṇa.*
Mat. P.—*Matsya Purāṇa.*
Mbh.—*Mahābhārata.*
Milinda—*Milinda-pañho.*
MR—*Modern Review*, Calcutta.
MS—*Maitrāyaṇi Saṃhitā.*
Nār—*Nārada Smṛti.*
NE—Northern Edition of the *Mahābhārata* (also indicated as Cal.)
NF—Neue Folge.
NS—New Series.
Pā—*Pāṇini's Grammar.*
Pañc. Br.—*Pañcaviṃśa Brāhmaṇa.*
Pār. Gṛ. S.—*Pāraskara Gṛhyasūtra.*
Pat—Patañjali's *Mahābhāṣya.*
Paipp.—*Paippalāda recension of the Atharva Veda.*
P.E.—Pillar Edict of Aśoka.
Petv. A.—*Petavatthu Aṭṭhakahā.*
PHAI—*Political History of Ancient India by* H. C. Raychaudhuri
PTS—*Pali Text Society.*
Rām.—*Rāmāyaṇa.*
R.E. Rock Edict of Aśoka.
RV—*Ṛg Veda.*
Saṃy. N.—*Saṃyutta Nikāya.*
Sāṃ. Br.—*Sāmavidhāna Brāhmaṇa.*
Śāṅkh. Gṛ S.—*Śāṅkhāyana Gṛhyasūtra.*
Śāṅkh. Śr. S.—*Śāṅkhāyana Śrautasūtra.*
Śat. Br.—*Śatapatha Brāhmaṇa.*
Satyā. Śr. S.—*Satyāṣāḍha Śrautasūtra.*
SBB—*Sacred Books of the Buddhists.*
SBE—*Sacred Books of the East.*

SE – Southern Edition of the Mahābhārata.
(also indicated as Kumb.)
ŚP – Śānti Parvan.
SONI – Social Organisation of North-Eastern India by R. Fick.
SS—Shamasastry.
Sut. Nipāt – Sutta Nipāta.
Sūya.—Sūyagaḍam.
Tai. Br.—Taittirīya Brāhmaṇa.
TGS – T. Gaṇapati Śāstri's edition of the *Arthaśāstra.*
Tr.—Translated by, Translation.
TS – Taittirīya Saṃhitā.
Uttarā—Uttarādhyayanasūtra.
Uvāsaga – Uvāsage-Dasāo.
VA—The Vedic Age, Ed. R. C. Majumdar.
Vā. P. – Vāyu Purāṇa.
Vas. Dh. S. – Vasiṣṭha Dharmasūtra.
Ved. S. – Vedāntasūtra.
VI – Vedic Index by A. A. Macdonell *and* A. B. Keith.
Vin. – Vinaya Piṭaka.
Vin.A. – Vinaya Piṭaka Aṭṭhakathā.
Viṣ. P. – Viṣṇu Purāṇa.
Viṣṇu – Viṣṇu Smṛti.
VS – Vājasaneyi Saṃhitā.
Yāj. – Yājñavalkya Smṛti.
ZDMG – Zeitschrift der Deutschen Morgenlandischen Gesellschaft, Berlin.
ZII – Zeitschrift fur Indologic und Iranistik, Leipzig.

In addition to the journals mentioned in the list of abbreviations given above, the following journals and periodicals have also been consulted :

Journal of Indian History, Trivandrum.
Journal of the Economic and Social History of the Orient, Leiden.
Past and Present, London.
Proceedings of the Indian History Congress.
The Indian Historical Review, New Delhi.
Transactions of the Philological Society, London.
Bulletin of the School of Oriental and African Studies, London.

Roman Equivalents of Nāgarī Letters

अ	a	ए	e	क्	k	च्	c
आ	ā	ऐ	ai	ख्	kh	छ्	ch
इ	i	ओ	o	ग्	g	ज्	j
ई	ī	औ	au	घ्	gh	झ्	jh
उ	u	ऋ	ṛ	ङ्	ṅ	ञ्	ñ
ऊ	ū						
ट्	ṭ	त्	t	प्	p	य्	y
ठ्	ṭh	थ्	th	फ्	ph	र्	r
ड्	ḍ	द्	d	ब्	b	ल्	l
ढ्	ḍh	ध्	dh	भ्	bh	व्	v
ण्	ṇ	न्	n	म्	m	श	ś
	ष्	ṣ	Anusvâra	ṃ			
	स्	s	Visarga	: ḥ			
	ह्	h					

CONTENTS

CHAPTER I

HISTORIOGRAPHY AND APPROACH

The modern study of the ancient Indian social order owed its inception to the efforts of the East India Company, which could not govern an alien people without some knowledge of their institutions. The preface to *A Code of Gentoo Laws* (1776), one of the first English works which have some bearing on the early social history of India, states that "the importance of the commerce of India and the advantages of a territorial establishment in Bengal" could be maintained only by "an adoption of such original institutes of the country, as do not intimately clash with the laws or interests of the conquerors."[1] In his preface to the translation of the *Manu Smṛti* (1794) Sir William Jones, the father of modern Indology, adds that, if this policy is pursued, "the well-directed industry" of "many millions of Hindu subjects" "would largely add to the wealth of Britain".[2] Four years later, on the basis of these sources, Colebrooke wrote an essay on the "Enumeration of Indian classes",[3] which appeared to him among the most remarkable institutions of India.[4] Soon after, in 1818 these sources were utilised by Mill to describe the caste system in his *History of India*. Discussing the disabilities of the śūdras he came to the conclusion that the vices of caste subordination were carried to a more destructive height among the Hindus than among any other people,[5] and remarked that the hideous society of the Hindus continued in his times. But

1. *Vivādārṇavasetu*, Translator's preface, p. IX. This work was translated from English into German in 1778.

2. *Institutes of Hindu Law*, Preface, p. XIX. Cf. Discourse of Colebrooke in the first general meeting of *RAS*(15 March, 1823), *Essays*, i, 1-2.

3. *Essays*, ii, 157-70.

4. *Ibid.*, ii, 157.

5. *The History of India*, ii, 166; i, 166-9; 169 fn. 1. It seems that Mill's generalizations about the history of India exercised the most dominant influence on later British historians.

from the same sources Elphinstone (1841) deduced that the condition of the śūdras "was much better than that of the public slaves under some ancient republics, and, indeed, than that of the villains of the middle ages, or any other servile class with which we are acquainted".[1] He also perceived that such a servile class did not exist any longer in his time.[2]

But there is no doubt that many age-old social practices continued into the 19th century. The glaring contrast between the rising industrial society of England and the old decaying society of India[3] attracted the attention of the educated intelligentsia, who were being permeated with the spirit of nationalism. They realised that the practices of *sati*, lifelong widowhood, child marriage, and caste endogamy were great obstacles to national progress. Since these practices were supposed to derive sanction from the Dharmaśāstras, it was felt that necessary reforms could be effected easily if they could be proved to be in consonance with the sacred texts. Thus in 1818 Rammohan Roy published his first tract against *sati*, in which he tried to show that, according to the śāstras, it was not the best way for the salvation of a woman.[4] In the fifties of the same century Ishwarchandra Vidyasagar ransacked Smṛti literature in order to make out a case for widow remarriage.[5] In 1879 Swami Dayanand, the founder of the Ārya Samāj, brought out a collection of original Sanskrit texts called the *Satyārthaprakāśa* to support widow remarriage, rejection of caste based on birth,[6] and the śūdras' right to Vedic education.[7] We do not know how far the early social reformers drew inspiration from the contemporary works of the British scholar Muir,[8] who tried to prove that the belief in the origin of the four varṇas from the primeaval man did not exist in ancient times,[9] and from those of the

1 *The History of India*, i, 34.
2. *Ibid.*, 107.
3. In 1902 an old Indian writer laments that the brāhmaṇas should be made to take their place below Eurasian (Anglo-Indian) industrialists. J. C. Ghosh, *Brahmanism and Sudra*, p. 46.
4. *The English Works of Rammohan Roy*, i, Introd., pp. XVIII; ii, 123-192.
5. R.G. Bhandarkar, *Collected Works*, ii, 498.
6. *Satyārthaprakāśa*, 4th samullāsa, pp. 83-92, 113-122.
7. *Ibid.*, 3rd samullāsa, pp. 39, 73-74.
8. *Original Sanskrit Texts*, i.
9. *Ibid.*, 159-60.

German scholar Weber, who presented the first important critical study of the caste system on the basis of the Brāhmaṇas and the Sūtras.[1]

On the occasion of the introduction of the Age of Consent Bill in 1891, Sir R. G. Bhandarkar brought out a well-documented pamphlet citing Sanskrit texts to establish that a girl should be married only when she attains maturity. On the other hand B.G. Tilak, to whom any stick was good enough to beat the alien rulers, cited texts against this Bill.[2]

This tendency to quote ancient scriptures in support of modern reforms can be well summed up in the words of R. G. Bhandarkar (1895): "In ancient times girls were married after they had attained maturity, now they must be married before; widow marriage was in practice, now it has entirely gone out. ... Interdining among the castes was not prohibited, now the numberless castes...cannot have intercommunication of that nature."[3]

But the attempt of the Indian scholars to present their early social institutions in a form more palatable to the modern mind did not always commend itself to western writers. Thus Senart (1896) pointed out that the castes are compared by Hindus of English upbringing with the social distinctions that exist among Europeans, but that they correspond only very remotely to western social classes.[4] Similarly Hopkins (1881) stated that the position of the śūdra was not different from that of the American house slave before 1860.[5] Reviewing Hopkins' generalizations, Hillebrandt (1896) held that the position of the śūdras should be judged in comparison with the slaves of the ancient world and not in the context of developments in later times.[6]

1. *Indische Studien*, x, 1-160.

2. R.G. Bhandarkar, *Collected Works*, ii, 538-83.
Also see Bhandarkar's criticism of Jolly's article on the "History of Child Marriage", *Ibid.*, 584-602.

3. *Collected Works*, ii, 522-23.

4. *Caste in India*, pp. 12-13.

5. *Mutual Relations of the Four Castes*, p. 102.

6. Hillebrandt, "Brāhmaṇen und Śūdras", *Festschrift für Karl Weinhold*, p. 57.

Criticising Hopkins, Ketkar (1911) complains that European writers are influenced by their ideas of racial discrimination against the Negroes, and hence unduly exaggerate this in their treatment of the caste system.[1] The main trend noticeable in the works of recent Indian writers such as Ketkar, Dutt, Ghurye and others is to present the system in such a way as may help to recast it in response to present requirements.[2] Thus it would appear that problems of ancient Indian society have been largely studied against the background of struggle between the reformist and orthodox schools. The dominant motives of reform and nationalism have undoubtedly produced valuable works on India's early social life; but what appeared to be seamy and ugly in comparison with modern standards came to be either ignored or explained away unconvincingly. For instance, it has been argued that the disabilities of the śūdras did not reduce their happiness or well-being.[3]

It is this tendency to concentrate on favourable aspects of early social life that accounts for the almost complete absence of works on the position of the śūdras in ancient India. Even European writers gave their attention mainly to the study of the upper classes of Hindu society. Thus Muir devoted 188 pages to the legends of struggles between brāhmaṇas and kṣatriyas,[4] and Hopkins (1889) presented a comprehensive study of the "Position of Ruling Caste in Ancient India."[5] The admirable work of Fick (1897) on the social organization of north-eastern India also mainly confined itself to the treatment of kṣatriyas, brāhmaṇas and gahapatis or seṭṭhis. It is difficult to explain these writers' lack of interest in the fortunes of the lower orders unless we suppose that their vision was circumscribed by the dominant class outlook of their age.

The first independent work on the śūdras was a short article by V. S. Śāstri (1922), who discussed the philosophical basis of

1. Ketkar, *History of Caste*, p. 78, fn. 3.

2 Ketkar, *op. cit.*, p. 9; Radhakrishnan's foreword to Valavalkar's *Hindu Social Institutions*. The works of Dutt and Ghurye display a better historical sense, but see Dutt, *op. cit.*, Preface, p. VI.

3. On the basis of the *Śukranīti-sāra*, Sarkar, *Hindu Sociology*, p. 92-95. cf. K. V. Rangaswami Aiyangar, *Indian Comeralism*, p. 85.

4. *Original Sanskrit Texts*, i, Ch. IV.

5. *JAOS*, xiii, 57-376.

the term *śūdra.*[1] In another article (1923) on this subject he tried to show that the śūdras could perform Vedic rituals.[2] In a paper published in 1947 Ghoshal dealt with the status of the śūdras in the Dharmasūtras.[3] A valuable article was by a Russian writer G. F. Ilyin (1950),[4] who, on the basis of the Dharmaśāstra evidence,[5] demonstrated that śūdras were not slaves. The only monograph on śūdras (1946) was published by a well-known Indian politician, who confined himself to the question of their origin.[6] The author was entirely dependent for his source-material on translations,[7] and, what is worse, he seems to have worked with the fixed purpose of proving a high origin for the śūdras, a tendency which has been very much in evidence among the educated sections of the lower caste people in recent times. A single passage of the *Śānti Parvan*, which states that the śūdra Paijavana performed sacrifice, is sufficient to establish the thesis that śūdras were originally kṣatriyas.[8] The author did not bother himself about the complex of various circumstances which led to the formation of the labouring class known as the śūdras. A publication[9] (1957), allied to our subject, brings together scattered information on labourers in ancient India, but does not make any significant addition to our knowledge. The main object of this book is to explore the field of Labour Economics in ancient India, and in doing so the author notices in the past parallels to modern wage-boards, arbitrators, social security etc., with the result that this work suffers from much

1. *IA*, li, 137-9.
2. "The Status of the Śūdra in Ancient India", *Viswa Bharati Quarterly*, i, 268-278.
3. *IC*, xiv, 21-27.
4. Śūdras und sklaven in den altindischen Gesetzbüchern" in *Sowjetwissenschaft*, 1952, 2 tr. from *Vestnik drevnei istorii.* 1950, No. 2, pp. 94-107.
5. Kane's compilation of the Dharmaśāstra extracts regarding śūdras provide valuable raw material for an historical study of their position. Chitra Tiwari's *Śūdras in Manu* (1963) does not add to our understanding.
6. Ambedkar, *Who w re the Shudras ?*
7. *Ibid.*, Preface, p. IV.
8. It is to be noticed that in recent caste movements many śūdra castes claim to be kṣatriyas. Thus the Dusādhas claim to be the descendants of Duḥśāsana, and the Goālās those of the Yadus.
9. K. M. Saran, *Labour in Ancient India.*

modernism. Moreover, the book mainly draws on the *Arthaśāstra* of Kauṭilya, is sketchy, and lacks historical sense.

The present work has been undertaken not only to provide an adequate treatment of the position of the śūdras in ancient times, but also to evaluate their modern characterizations, either based on insufficient data, or inspired by reformist or anti-reformist motives. An attempt will be made to present a connected and systematic account of the various developments in the position of the śūdras down to *circa* A. D. 600.

Since the śūdras were regarded as the labouring class, in this study particular attention has been paid to the investigation of their material conditions and the nature of their economic and social relations with the members of the higher varṇas. This has naturally involved the study of the position of slaves, with whom the śūdras were considered identical. The untouchables are also theoretically placed in the category of śūdras, and hence their origin and position has also been discussed in some detail.

The position of the lowest order in ancient Indian society cannot be studied without raising a few questions. What led to the formation of the śūdra community ? If the śūdras were meant for serving the three higher orders, can they be categorised as slaves ? Was ancient Indian society a slave society ? How far does the ritual status of the śūdras correspond to their economic status ? Did the reforming religious sects bring about any fundamental change in the position of the lower orders or did they try to contain and stabilise the changes that had occurred on account of other factors ? Did the role of the lower orders in the economic system undergo any change over the centuries? How is it that the twice-born vaiśyas came to be reduced to the level of the śūdras and śūdras placed on a par with the vaiśyas ? How do we explain the proliferation of the servile orders towards the end of the period of our study ? How did the śūdras react to their servility and disabilities ? Why are social revolts comparatively absent in ancient India ? We have tried to tackle these and similar other problems.

This study has to be mainly based on literary sources, the precise dating of which or of their various parts has been a baffling problem. We have adopted the generally accepted chronology of the literary texts, but in the case of differences of opinion we have indicated our own reasons for adopting an unconventional dating.

Although the texts belong to different periods, they repeat *ad nauseam* the same formulae and terminologies, which make it difficult to detect changes in society; hence special attention has been paid to the study of variants. Many of these texts cannot be understood without the aid of the commentators, who not unoften project the ideas of their own times into earlier periods.

Further, the literary texts, brāhmaṇical and non-brāhmaṇical, seek to establish the supremacy of the brāhmaṇas or of the kṣatriyas, or of both, but they hardly show any sympathy for the śūdras. It is argued that the Dharmaśāstras and other treatises are books written by the enemies of the śūdras and as such have no evidential value.[1] But the law-books of other ancient societies also follow the principle of class legislation as the Dharmaśāstras do; unfortunately for lack of sufficient data we cannot definitely say how far the Dharmaśāstra laws were followed.

Myths and rituals with which ancient texts are replete form an important source for the reconstruction of social history. Recently under the influence of some sociologists a few Western Sanskritists have started questioning the validity of this method. They attribute all kinds of symbolical meanings to rituals and connect many of them with the creation processes. We cannot ignore fertility rites, but it should be noted that they underscore the importance of the production of plants, animals and human beings. The operation of rituals in day-to-day life shows that they originate in reality, and change with change in real life. Hence studies in rituals cannot be discarded by social historians. Some shreds of reality cannot be denied to myths. It was in response to certain social needs that the original 8800 verses of the *Mahābhārata* were first raised to 24000 and then finally to 100000.

Since the history of social classes cannot be followed in isolation from developments in material life, changes in material culture in time sequence have been indicated on the basis of archaeology and inscriptions. At various stages the impact of settled agricultural life, flourishing trade and land grants on the

1. Ambedkar, *op. cit.*, p. 114.

social formation has been examined, and its implications for occupational and territorial mobility discussed.

In order to explain and illustrate certain developments in the position of the śūdras, wherever possible comparisons have been made with similar developments in other ancient societies and among primitive peoples known to anthropology.

CHAPTER II

ORIGIN

In 1847 it was suggested by Roth that the śūdras might have been outside the pale of the Āryan society.[1] Since then it has usually been held that the fourth varṇa of brāhmaṇical society was mainly formed by the non-Āryan population, who were reduced to that position by the Āryan conquerors.[2] This view continues to derive support from the analogy of conflict between the white-coloured Europeans and the non-white population of Asia and Africa.

In such a postulate the Āryan conquerors are codsidered to be identical with the Ārya race, and the non-Āryans with the Dāsa and Dasyu races. But it has been shown by H. W. Bailey that the racial import cannot be drawn uniformly from the term *ārya* in all the Ṛg Vedic references in which it is used. The term can be derived from the base *ar*, which means to get.[3] In the Iranian references the term *ārya* stands for possessor or noble,[4] and its extension *ārya* does not have a different sense in the Vedic texts,[5] not to speak of its use in the sense of noble or civilised in post-Vedic Sanskrit and Buddhist and Jain texts.[6] "The *ārya* are the party of the poets, and certainly it is a laudatory epithet".[7] From all this it may be inferred that the leaders

1. *ZDMG*, i, 84.
2. *VI*, ii, 265, 388; R.C. Dutt, *A History of Civ. in Anc. India*, i, 2; Senart, *Caste in India*, p. 83; N. K. Dutt, *Origin and Growth of Caste in India.* pp. 151-52; Ghurye, *Caste and Class*, pp. 151-52; D. R. Bhandarkar, *Some Aspects of Ancient Indian Culture*, p. 10.
3. H.W. Bailey, "Iranian *Arya* and *Daha-*", *Transactions of the Philological Society*, 1959, 71-83.
4. The relevant passages to which these meanings suit have been quoted in *Ibid.*, 70-94.
5. *Ibid.*, 103-104.
6. *Ibid.*, 102-103.
7. *Ibid.*, 102.

of the Ṛg Vedic people or gods who are extolled in the hymns as *ārya* were either possessors of wealth or noble or both. But too much cannot be made of their wealth. In a predominantly pastoral society the existing forms of property could not be accumulated on any scale.[1] Therefore the Ṛg Vedic society was organised neither on the basis of social division of labour nor on that of differences in wealth. The Ṛg Vedic society was primarily organised on the basis of kin, tribe, and lineage. The terms used for various types of kin-based units occur frequently. Thus *jana* is mentioned about 275 times and *viś* about 170 times. Similarly *gaṇa* and *vrāta* repeatedly occur. These units seem to be fairly large, because *kula*, which stands for family and later for noble family, is mentioned only once in the *Ṛg Veda*, and that too as a part of the term *kulapā*. However if the term *gṛha* is taken in the sense of family, it is mentioned many times in the *Ṛg Veda*, although these occurrences are less than 100 and therefore far less frequent than those in the case of *jana* and *viś*. The '*Āryan*' tribes mentioned in the *Ṛg Veda* may not have belonged to the same ethnic stock, but they were united by a common language and a common style of life. The term Āryan therefore used by us may be understood in this sense.

Although it has been argued that the Dāsas and Dasyus were racially not non-Ārya,[2] in our opinion this is far more true of the Dāsa. As will be shown later, the Dasyus are represented as speaking probably a different language and having a different life-style, which does not seem to be the case with the Dāsa. Further the Dāsas were organised into tribe called *viś*, which is a term used for Vedic people or tribes. Seen in this light the conflict between the Ārya and the Dāsa would appear to be the one within the fold of the Vedic tribes leading more or less the same type of life. In the numerous hymns of the *Ṛg Veda*, which are repeated in the *Atharva Veda*, the Āryan god Indra appears as the conqueror of the Dāsas, who mostly appear to have been human

1. R. S. Sharma, "Forms of Property in the Early Portions of the *Ṛg Veda*," *Essays in Honour of Prof. S.C. Sarkar*, pp. 39-50.

2. Muir, *Original Sanskrit Texts*, ii, 387.

beings. It is said that Indra consigned the base Dāsa varṇa to the cave.[1] As the controller of the world, he takes upon himself the task of bringing the Dāsas into subjection,[2] and is asked to prepare himself for their destruction.[3] The recurring theme of the Ṛg Vedic prayers to Indra is the request for the overthrow of the Dāsa tribes (*viśas*).[4] Indra is also represented as having deprived the Dasyus of all good qualities, and as having subjugated the Dāsas.[5]

There are more references to the destruction or subjugation of the Dasyus by Indra than of the Dāsas. It is stated that having killed the Dasyus he protected the Āryan varṇa.[6] Prayer is made to him to fight against the Dasyus in order to increase the strength of the Āryans.[7] It is significant that there are at least twelve references to the slaughter of the Dasyus, mostly by Indra.[8] On the contrary, although there are references to the killing of individual Dāsas, the word *dāsahatyā* does not occur anywhere. This indicates that the two were not identical and may suggest that the Āryans followed a policy of ruthless extermination towards the Dasyus, which, in the case of the Dāsas, was tempered with moderation.

1. *yenémā vī'śvācyávanā kṛtā́ni, yó dā́saṃ várṇamádharaṃ guhā́kaḥ*. *RV*. II. 12. 4. *AV*, XX. 34. 4.
2. ...*yathāvaśáṃ nayati dā́samā́ryaḥ* *RV*, V. 34. 6.
3. ...*dāsáveśā́ya cā́vaḥ*. *RV*, II. 13.8. Sāyaṇa interprets this as the destruction of the dāsas, but *VI*, i, 358 takes it as the name of a Dāsa.
4. *RV*, II, 11.4; VI. 25.2; and X. 148.2.
5. *RV*, IV. 28.4.
6. ...*hatvī'dásyūnprā́ryaṃ várṇamāvat*. *RV*, III. 34.9; *AV*, XX. 11.9 (not in the Paippalāda recension).
7. I. 103.3; *AV*, XX. 20.4.
8. The term *dásyu-hátyā* occurs in *RV*, I. 51.5-6, 103. 4; X. 95.7, 99.7. *Dásyu-ghnā́* occurs in *RV*, IV. 16. 10 and *dásyu-hán* in *RV*, X. 47. 4. *Dásyuhántama* occurs in *RV*. VI. 16.15, VIII. 39.8, and is reproduced in *VS*, XI. 34. There are many other references to the hostility between the Āryans and Dasyus, viz. *RV*, V. 7. 10, VII. 5.6. etc. Indra is called *dásyu-hā́* in *RV*, I. 100. 12; VI. 45.24; VIII. 76. 11, 77. 3. There are similar references to the slaughter of Dasyus by Indra in *AV*, III. 10 12; VIII. 8. 5, 7; IX, 2.17 & 18; X. 3.11; XIX. 46.2; XX. 11.6, 21.4, 29.4, 34.10, 37.4, 42.2, 64.3, and by Agni in *AV*, I. 7.1; XI, 1.2. Manyu is called *dásyu-hā́* in *AV*, IV. 32.3.

The fight between the Āryans and their opponents mainly took the form of the destruction of the fortresses and walled settlements of the latter. Both the Dāsas and Dasyus were in possession of numerous fortified settlements,[1] which are also associated with the enemies of the Āryans in a general way.[2] This naturally reminds us of the later discoveries of fortifications in the Harappā settlements,[3] although so far we have not been able to get any clear archaeological evidence of mass-scale confrontation between the Āryans and the Harappans. It seems that the nomadic Āryans coveted the wealth of their enemies accumulated in the settlements, for the possession of which there went on a regular warfare between them.[4] The worshipper expects that all those who make no oblation should be killed and their wealth should be given to the people.[5] The Dasyus are described as rich (*dhaninaḥ*) but without sacrifice.[6] Mention is made of two Dāsa chiefs who are called wealth-seeking.[7] Desire is expressed that through Indra[8] the might of the Dāsa be subdued, and his collected wealth be divided among the people. The Dasyus also possessed jewels and gold, which probably excited the greed of the Āryans.[9] But to a people of cattle culture such as the Āryans it was primarily the cattle of their enemies which held the greatest temptation. Thus it is argued that the Kīkaṭas, who probably lived in Haryana, do not deserve to have cows because they make no use of milk products in the sacrifice.[10] On the other hand it is likely that the enemies of the Āryans valued the horses and chariots of the latter. A Ṛg Vedic legend tells us that the Asuras had captured the city of a royal sage named Dadhīti, but on their retreat were

1. *RV*, I. 103.3; II, 19.6; IV. 30.20; VI. 20.10, 31.4.
2. *RV*, I. 33.13, 53.8; VIII. 17.14.
3. Wheeler, *The Indus Civilization*, pp. 90-91.
4. *RV*, IV. 30.13; V. 40.6, X. 69.6.
5. *asmábhyamasya védanaṃ daddhí sūriścido hate*. *RV*, I. 176.4.
6. *RV*, I. 33.4.
7. *áhandāsá uṛṣabhó vasnayántodávraje varcínaṃ śámbaraṃ ca*. *RV*, VI. 47.21.
8. *vayáṃ tád asya sámbhṛtaṃ vásu índreṇa vībhajemahi*. *RV*, VIII. 40.6.
9. *RV*, I. 33. 7-8.
10. *kíṃ te kṛṇvanti kíkaṭeṣu gávo nā́śiraṃ duhré ná tapanti gharmám*. *RV*, III 53.14.

intercepted and defeated by Indra, who recovered cattle, horses and chariots and restored them to the prince.[1]

The Dasyu way of life further antagonised the Āryans. Apparently the tribal and semi-settled life of the Āryans based on cattle keeping was incompatible with the sedentary and urban life of the people of the indigenous culture.[2] The predominantly tribal life of the former expressed itself through several communal institutions such as the *gaṇa*, *sabhā*, *samiti* and the *vidatha* in which sacrifice played a very important part. But the Dasyus had nothing to do with sacrifice. This was true of the Dāsas as well, for Indra is described as coming to the sacrifice distinguishing between the Dāsa and the Ārya.[3] A whole passage occurring in the seventh book of the *Ṛg Veda* consists of a string of adjectives such as *akratūn*, *aśraddhān* and *ayajñān* applied to the Dasyus emphasise their non-sacrificing character.[4] Indra is asked to discriminate between the sacrificing Āryans and non-sacrificing Dasyus.[5] They are also called *ayajvānaḥ*.[6] The word *anindra* (without Indra) is used at several places,[7] and presumably refers to the Dasyus, Dāsas and perhaps some Āryans dissenters. In the Āryan view the Dasyus practised black magic.[8] Such a belief is especially found in the *Atharva Veda*, in which the Dasyus appear as evil spirits to be scared away from the sacrifice.[9] It is said that an all-powerful amulet enabled the sage Aṅgiras to break through the Dasyus' fortresses.[10] The evil character of the Dasyus in the *Atharva Veda* seems to have been based on their fighting record in the Ṛg Vedic period. According to the *Atharva Veda* the god-blaspheming Dasyus are to be offered as victims.[11] It is believed that the Dasyus are treacherous, do not practise the Āryan observances, and are hardly human.[12]

1. *RV*, II. 15.4.
2. Wheeler, *The Indus Civilization* pp. 90-91.
3. *RV*, X. 86.19; *AV*, XX. 126.19.
4. *RV*, VII. 6.3.
5. *RV*, I. 51.8.
6. *RV*, I. 33.4.
7. *RV*, I. 133.1; V. 2.3.; VII. I. 8. I 6; X. 27.6; X. 48.7.
8. *RV*, IV. 16.9.
9. *AV*, II. 14.5.
10. *AV*, X, 6.20.
11. *AV*, XII. 1.37.
12. *RV*, X. 22.8.

The difference between the Āryan and the Dasyu way of life was further brought out by indicating the relation in which the Dasyus stood to the Āryan *vrata*, generally meaning law or ordinance.[1] If it be possible to establish some connection between this word and *vrāta*, which means tribal troops or groups, it may be suggested that the term *vrata* probably means tribal law or usage. The Dasyus are generally described as *avrata*[2] and *anyavrata*.[3] The word *apavrata* is used at two places and perhaps applies to the Dasyus and dissenting Āryans.[4] It is notable that such adjectives are not applied to the Dāsas, which again indicates that they were more amenable to the Āryan way of life than the Dasyus.

There are reasons to think that there was difference of colour between the Āryans and their enemies. It appears that the Āryans, who are called human (*mānusi prajā*), worshipping Agni Vaiśvānara, on occasions set fire to the settlements of the dark-hued people (*asiknīviśaḥ*), who deserted their possessions without fighting.[5] The Āryan deity Soma is described as killing people of black skin, who apparently were Dasyus.[6] Further, Indra had to contend against the Rākṣasas of black skin (*tvacamasiknīm*),[7] and at one place he is credited with the slaughter of fifty thousand 'blacks' (*kṛṣṇas*) whom Sāyaṇa regards as Rākṣasas of black colour.[8] The god is also described as tearing off the black skin of the Asura.[9] An important exploit of Indra, which may have some historical basis, refers to his fight against a hero known as Kṛṣṇa. It is stated that, when Kṛṣṇa encamped on the Aṃśumatī or Yamunā with ten thousand soldiers, Indra

1. P.V. Kane, *JBBRAS*, NS. xxix. 12.
2. *RV*, I. 51.8-9; I. 101.2; I. 175.3; VI. 14.3; IX. 41.2. The term *avrata*, however, has nowhere been applied to the Dāsas.
3. *RV*, VIII. 70.11; X. 22.8.
4. *RV*, V. 42.9; in V. 40.6 the term *apavrata* is identified with darkness.
5. *RV*, VII. 5.2-3. Geldner's tr. The end of Harappā culture at Rānā Ghuṇḍai III is marked with 'a great conflagration'. B.B. Lal, *AI*, 9, p. 88.
6. *ghnántaḥ kṛṣṇā́m ápa tvácaṃ...sāhvā́ṃso dásyumavratám. RV*, IX. 41. 1-2.
7. *RV*, IX. 73.5.
8. *RV*, IV. 16.13. Geldner, however, does not introduce the Rākṣasas in this context.
9. *RV*, I. 130.8.

mobilised the Maruts (the Āryan *viś*) and fought against the *adevīḥ viśaḥ* with the help of the priest-god Bṛhaspati.[1] *Adevīḥ viśaḥ* are explained by Sāyaṇa as Asuras of black colour (*kṛṣṇarūpāḥ asurasenāḥ*). It is suggested that Kṛṣṇa was the non-Āryan dark hero of the Yādava tribe.[2] This seems likely because later traditions speak of hostility between Indra and Kṛṣṇa. There is also reference to the killing of the *kṛṣṇgarbhā*, doubtfully interpreted by Sāyaṇa as pregnant wives of an Asura named Kṛṣṇa.[3] Similarly mention is made of the overthrow of the *kṛṣṇayoniḥ dāsīḥ* by Indra.[4] Sāyaṇa fancifully takes them as the lowest demon-like troops (*nikṛṣṭajātiḥ...āsurīḥ senāḥ*), but Wilson takes *kṛṣṇa* in the sense of black. If the latter meaning be correct, it would appear that the Dāsas were black in colour. But the description 'black' may have been applied indiscriminately to them as it was to the Dasyus and other enemies of the Āryans. The above-mentioned references however, leave little doubt that the Āryan followers of Indra, Agni and Soma had to fight against the black people of India. In one reference, the Ṛg Vedic hero Trasadasyu, son of Purukutsa, is described as the leader of the 'dark-complexioned' men.[5] This may indicate that he had established his hold over them.

If the word *anāsa*[6] applied to the Dasyus is taken in the sense of 'noseless' or one with a flat nose, and the term *vṛṣaśipra* applied to the Dāsas[7] as 'bull-lipped' or having big protruding lips, it would appear that the enemies of the Āryans were physiognomically different.

The term *mṛdhravāk*, which occurs in its different forms at several places in the *Ṛg Veda*,[8] gives some idea of difference in the

1. ...*ádha drapsó aṃśumátyā upásthe dhārayattanvám titviṣāṇáḥ; víśo ádevirbhyá carantir bṛhaspátinā yujéndráḥ sasāhe*. *ṚV*, VIII. 96. 13-15.
2. Kosambi, *JBBRAS*, NS, xxvii, 43.
3. *yáḥ kṛṣṇágarbhā niráhann ṛjiśvānā*. *RV*, I. 101.1.
4. *sá vṛtrahéndraḥ kṛṣṇáyoniḥ purandaródāsīrairyadvi*...*RV*, II. 20.7. Sāyaṇa's comm. But Geldner suggests that *dasīḥ* implies understood *púraḥ*, and that the poet is thinking in terms of pregnancy.
5. *RV*, VIII. 19. 36-37.
6. *RV*, V. 29.10. Sāyaṇa explains *anāsa* as one without speech (*āsyarahita*).
7. *RV*, VII. 99.4.
8. *RV*, I, 174.2.; V. 29.10, 32.8; VII. 6.3, 18.13. Not at only four places, as in *Who were the Shudras*, p. 71.

manner of speech between the Āryans and their enemies. It qualifies Dasyus at two places.[1] Sāyaṇa explains it as 'of hostile speech', and Geldner renders it as 'of wrong speech'.[2] Unless the term *mṛdhravācaḥ* is taken in the sense of 'unintelligible speech' it does not give any evidence of linguistic difference between the Āryans and the Dasyus, but only shows that the latter hurt the sentiments of the Āryans by their improper speech. Thus although the main issue in the war between the Āryans and their enemies was the possession of cattle, chariots and other forms of wealth, differences in race, religion and mode of speech also served to exacerbate relations.

If inferences can be drawn from the relative occurrences of the terms *dāsa* and *dāsyu* in the *Ṛg Veda*, it would appear that the Dasyus, who are mentioned eighty-four times, were obviously numerically stronger than the Dāsas, who are mentioned sixty-one times.[3] The struggle against the Dasyus was attended with much bloodshed. The Āryans, who in the early stage of their expansion coveted cattle for their upkeep, naturally did not understand the value of urban settlements and organised agriculture.[4] The Āryans seem to have played some part in the destruction of the pre-Āryan urban settlements, although the evidence for intrusive elements in late Harappā culture is not very strong. While the spoils of war, especially cattle, must have added to the power of the warriors and priests, raising them above the *viś*, it was slowly realised that the peasants of the older culture could provide labour power with which the Āryans could carry on agriculture.

Alongside the conflict between the Āryans and their enemies there went on the internal conflict in the Āryan tribal society. Through a battle song addressed to Manyu (personified Wrath), his aid is invoked for covercoming the two kind of enemies,

1. *RV*, V. 29.10, VII. 6.3.
2. In *RV*, I. 174.2 Geldner translates *mṛdhravācaḥ* as 'missrederd'.
3. Computed on the basis of refs. given in Viśvabandhu Śāstri's *Vedic Kośa*.
4. Wheeler suggests the complete break-up of organised agriculture on account of the invasion of uncivilised nomads (i.e. Āryans) *op. cit.*, p. 8.

Āryans and Dāsas.[1] Indra is asked to fight against both the godless Dāsas and Āryans who are described as the enemies (*śatravaḥ*) of his followers.[2] It is said that Indra and Varuṇa killed the Dāsas and Āryans who were the adversaries of Sudās and thus protected him.[3] On behalf of the good and righteous people prayer is made to the two chief Ṛg Vedic deities Agni and Indra to counteract the hostile activities and oppressions of the Āryans and Dāsas.[4] Since Āryans were one of the chief enemies of their fellow men, it is no wonder that along with the Dāsas they also are said to have been destroyed by Indra.[5] If Wilson's translation of a Ṛg Vedic passage be accepted, Indra is lauded for having saved the people from the Rākṣasas and Āryans on the bank of the seven rivers, and is further called upon to deprive the Dāsas of their weapons.[6]

Of thirty-six occurrences of the word *ārya* in the *Ṛg Veda* nine make clear mention of hostility among the Āryans themselves.[7] At one place the Āryan enemies are lumped together with the Dasyus, and at five places with the Dāsas, which again suggests that the Dāsas were on better terms with a section of the Āryans than were the Dasyus. They were cons dered natural allies of the Āryans in their inter-tribal conflicts, which gradually undermined the tribal basis of their society, and helped the process of fusion between the Āryans and Dāsas. Five of these references occur in the earlier portions of the *Ṛg Veda*, which shows that the internal conflict was a fairly old process.

The most important evidence for internal conflict within the Āryan fold at an early date is the record of the *Dāśarājña* battle,

1. *sāhyáma dásamáryaṃ tváyā yujá sáhaskṛtena sáhasā sáhasvatā*, *RV*, X. 83.1 identical with *AV*, IV. 32.1.
2. *RV*, X, 88.3; cf. *AV*, XX. 36.10.
3. *dásā ca vṛtrá hatámáryāṇi ca sudásam indrāvaruṇávasávatam*. *RV*, VII. 83.1.
4. *RV*, VI. 60.6.
5. *RV*, VI. 33.3; cf. X. 102.3.
6. *yá ṛkṣádámhaso mucádyóvāryāt saptásindhuṣu;*
vádhardāsásya tuvinṛmṇa nīnamaḥ. *RV*, VIII. 24.27. Geldner takes the passage in the sense of Indra's turning aside the weapon of the Dāsa from the Āryan.
7. *RV*, VI. 33.3, 60.6; VII. 83.1; VIII. 24.27 (a disputed passage); X. 38.3, 69.6, 83.1, 86.19, 102.3. Four of these refs. have been correctly quoted by Ambedkar, *op. cit.*, pp. 83.4.

which is the only important historical event in the *Ṛg Veda*, Geldner thinks that *RV*, VII. 33, which speaks of this battle, belongs to an early period.[1] The Battle of Ten Kings was primarily a conflict between two main branches of the Ṛg Vedic Āryans, namely the Pūrus and the Bhāratas, in which the non-Āryans may have joined as auxiliaries.[2] While the Bhāratas were led by the famous Ṛg Vedic hero Sudās and assisted by their priest Vasiṣṭha, their enemies comprised ten kings belonging to the five well-known tribes — Anus, Druhyus, Yadus, Turvaśas and Pūrus, along with five less known tribes — Alina, Paktha, Bhalānas, Śiva and Viṣāṇin. The opposing confederacy was organised by the priest Viśvāmitra and led by the Pūrus.[3] It appears that the battle was, in fact, a memorable attempt of the lesser Āryan tribes to maintain their separate identities, but they were completely routed by the Bhāratas under Sudās on the Paruṣṇi. There is no indication of the treatment of these conquered Āryans, but essentially it might have been the same as in the case of the non-Āryans.

It is not unlikely that there were many other inter-tribal conflicts of this kind, of which we have no records. Indications of such struggles are found in references which represent the Āryans as violators of *vratas* established by the gods. Five such passages quoted by Kane from the *Ṛg Veda* can be interpreted in this light.[4] In a dialogue between the primeval priest Atharvan and Varuṇa, the priest boasts: "No Dāsa by his greatness, not an Āryan, may violate the law that I will establish."[5]

Muir quotes as many as fifty-eight passages from the *Ṛg Veda*, which he interprets as containing denunciations of religious hostility or indifference shown by the members of the Āryan community.[6] Many of these passages belong to the kernal (Book II — VII) of the *Ṛg Veda* and may be taken as

1. *VI*, i, 356, fn. 4 of *s.v.* Dāśa-rājña.
2. *RV*, VII. 33.2-5, 83.8. The actual battle hymn occurs in *RV*, VII. 18.
3. *VA*, p. 245. On account of their hostility to other Āryans the Pūrus are called *mṛdhravācaḥ* in *RV*, VII. 18.13.
4. *JBBRAS*, NS, xxix, 11.
5. *ná me dāsó nā́ryo mahitvā́ vratám mīmāya yádahám dhariṣyé*. *AV*, V. 11.3; *Paipp.*, VIII. 1.3.
6. *JRAS*, NS, ii, 286-294.

reflecting the conditions prevailing in the earliest period of the Āryan settlements. Several of these are directed against the illiberal people who are called *arādhasam*,[1] *apṛṇaṇatam*[2] or *apṛṇataḥ*.[3] At one place Indra is described as the enemy of the prosperous (*edhamānadvit*) probably of Āryans who rendered him no service;[4] since Dāsas and Āryans who concealed their treasure from the people were considered objects of attack.[5] For the sake of his people Agni is said to have captured property whether situated in the plains or the hills, and to have overcome their Dāsa and Āryan enemies.[6] These passages suggest that even the Āryan enemies were deprived of their possessions (presumably cattle) and consequently reduced to the status of impoverished non-Āryans.

Many passages show a general hostility towards the people known as Paṇis.[7] Muir understands them as niggards.[8] According to the authors of the *Vedic Index* Paṇi in the *Ṛg Veda* denotes a person who is rich, but who does not give offerings to the gods, or bestows *dakṣiṇās* on the priests, and who is therefore an object of intense dislike to the composers of the Saṃhitā.[9] In one passage they were described as *bekanāṭas* or 'usurers' (?) subdued by Indra.[10] The fact that the Paṇis were capable of making sacrifices and entitled to wergeld shows that they were members of the Āryan fold.[11] Hillebrandt identifies them with the Paṇis[12] who formed part of "the Dahae, a great group of

1. *RV*, 1.84.8.
2. *RV*, I. 125.7
3. *RV*, VI. 44.11.
4. *RV*, *VI*.47. 16; *JRAS*, NS, ii, 286-294.
5. *yásyāyáṃ víśva áryo dắsaḥ śevadhipā́ aríḥ*. *RV*, VIII. 51.9. Sāyaṇa's comm. to this passage, and also that of Uvaṭa and Mahīdhara to a similar passage in *VS*, XXXIII, take *dāsa* as an adjective of *ārya*, but Geldner (*RV*. VIII. 51.9) takes *ārya* and *dāsa* as two independent nouns. In any case it is clear that the Āryan was also an object of attack.
6. *sámajryā́ parvatyā́ vásūni dā́sā vṛtrā́ṇyā́ryā jigetha*. *RV*, X. 69.6.
7. *RV*, I. 124.10; 182.3; IV. 25.7, 51.3; V. 34.7. VI. 13.3, 53.6-7.
8. *JRAS*, NS, ii, 286-294.
9. *VI*, i, 471.
10. *Ibid*. *RV*, VIII. 66.10.
11. *VI*, i, 472.
12. *Ibid*.

Scythian tribes of horsemen and warriors".[1] The authors of the *Vedic Index* think that the term is wide enough to cover either the aborigines or hostile Āryan tribes.[2]

Of the passages which represent Paṇis as niggards, and condemn illiberal people in general, some may have been inspired by greedy priests eager for gifts, but on the whole they seem to reflect the tendency among certain Āryans to accumulate wealth at the cost of their fellow tribesmen, who naturally expected some share in their acquisitions through sacrifices made to Indra and other gods,[3] thus providing frequent occasions for the common feasts of the community. Failure to check this process was bound to give rise to economic and social inequalities.

It remains to be examined how the extra-tribal and inter-tribal struggles of the Āryans led to the disintegration of tribal society and the formation of social classes. Although the word *varṇa* is applied to the Āryan[4] and Dāsa[5] in the *Ṛg Veda*, it does not indicate any division of labour, which became the basis of the broad social classes of later times. *Ārya*- and *Dāsa-varṇas* represent two large tribal groups, which were in the process of disintegration into social classes. There is sufficient evidence for this in the case of the Āryan people. Criticising Senart Oldenberg rightly points out that caste does not exist in the *Ṛg Veda*,[6] but the collection does give the impression of slowly emerging social classes in their embryonic stage. The word *brāhmaṇa* occurs fifteen times and *kṣatriya* nine times. Nevertheless, as would appear from the repeated occurrences of words such as *jana* and *viś*,[7] and from the nature of its institutions, Ṛg Vedic society was basically tribal in character. We do not know whether the Āryans possessed slaves at the time of their first advent in India.

1. Ghirshman, *Iran*, p. 243.
2. i, 472.
3. *RV*, VII. 40.6.
4. *RV*, III. 34.9.
5. *devā́so manyúṃ dā́sasya ścamnanté na ā́ vakṣantsuitā́ya várṇam RV*, I. 104.2; III 34.9.
6. *ZDMG*, ii, 272.
7. *Jana* is mentioned about 275 times and *viś* about 170 times.

The Vedic Indians were primarily pastoral;[1] at least this holds good of the Āryans known from the early parts of the *Ṛg Veda.* Anthropological investigations show that some pastoral tribes also keep slaves although in a relative sense slavery is more developed among agricultural tribes.[2]

For lack of data it is difficult to get a precise idea of the effects of the Āryan impact on chalcolithic society and *vice versa.* Spoils of war must have added to the wealth and social status of the tribal leaders, who could afford to patronise priests by making gifts of cattle, and in some cases of women slaves. Thus a sacrificer is described as moving with his chariot "first in rank and wealthy, munificent and lauded in assemblies".[3]

Despite the paucity of information reasonable hypotheses may be made about the social adjustment between the Āryans and members of pre-Āryan chalcolithic societies and other peoples. In the first flush of the Āryan expansion the destruction of the settlements and the peoples such as the Dasyus seems to have been so complete that very few people in north-western India would remain to be absorbed into the new society. But this may not have been the case in the succeeding stages of their expansion. While the majority of the survivors and especially the comparatively backward peoples would be reduced to helotage, the natural tendency would be for the *viś* of the Āryan society to mix with the lower orders and for the Vedic priests and warriors to mix with the higher classes of earlier societies. That in some cases the enemies of the Āryans were given high status in the new composite society is clear from two references. At one place Indra is described as converting the Dāsas into Āryas.[4] Sāyaṇa explains this as teaching them the Āryan way of life. At another place Indra is said to have deprived the Dasyus of the title of the *ārya.*[5] May this suggest that some

1. R.S. Sharma, "Forms of property in the Early Portions of the *Ṛg Veda*" *Essays in Honour of Prof. S.C. Sarkar*. A hymn devoted to agricultural operations (Bk. IV. 57) is considered to be an interpolation by Hopkins.

2. Landtman, *The Origin of the Inequality of Social Classes*, p. 230.

3. *RV*, II. 27.12.

4. *yáyād ắsānyắryāṇi vṛtrắkáro vajrintsutúkā nắhuṣāṇi. RV*, VI. 22.1.

5. *ahám̐ śúṣṇasya śnáthitā vádharyamaṃ ná yó rará ắryaṃ nāma dásyave. RV*, X. 49.3.

Dasyus were raised to Āryan status and then deprived of it, presumably on account of their anti-Āryan activities ? We may also consider the suggestion that *arya* or its extension (*vṛddhi*) *ārya* means a man of substance;[1] on this basis some Dasyus seem to have been dispossessed of their property. All this leads us to suppose that some of the surviving priests and chiefs from the enemy peoples were given corresponding positions (possibly of inferior nature) in the new Āryan society.

It has been contended that Brāhmaṇism is a pre-Āryan institution, and there may be some element of truth in it.[2] The equation of the word *brāhmaṇa* with the Latin *flāmen*, the designation of a type of priest whose office was created during the period of the Roman kings,[3] seems to be a far-fetched philological exercise. However we have the well-known similarity between the Atharvan priests of Vedic Indian and Athravans of Iran. But nevertheless a major objection remains to be answered. Keith says that the state of Ṛg Vedic belief and the comparative magnitude of the Vedic pantheon must have been the product of much priestly effort and the outcome of wholesale syncretism.[4] Further, sufficient evidence has been adduced from Vedic and epic traditions to show that Indra was a brahmicide, and that his chief enemy Vṛtra was a brāhmaṇa.[5] This also confirms the hypothesis that developed priesthood was a pre-Āryan institution, and implies that all the conquered peoples were not reduced to the position of the dāsas and śūdras. And hence, though it is difficult to trace the origin of the brāhmaṇa as an institution, the priestly class of the Āryan conquerors may have been largely recruited from the conquered.[6] Though there is nothing to indicate the proportion, it seems

1. H. W. Bailey, "Iranian Arya—and Daha—," *Transactions of the Philological Society*, 1959, 84.
2. Pargiter, *Ancient Indian Historical Tradition*, pp. 306-08.
3. Dumezil, *Flāmen-Brahman*, Chs. II & III. For another view see Paul Thieme, *ZDMG*, NF. 27, pp. 91-129.
4. *CHI*, i, 103.
5. W. Ruben "Indra's Fight against Vṛtra in the Mahāhbārata," *S.K. Belvalkar Commemoration Volume* (in press; shown by the courtesy of Dr. A.S. Altekar), pp. 116-88; D. Kosambi, *Bhagavān Buddha*, p. 24.
6. Kosambi, *JBBRAS*, NS, xxii, 35.

that some of the pre-Āryan priests found their way into the new society. It would be wrong to think that all the 'blacks' were reduced to the status of the śūdra helots, since there are some references to black seers. In the *Ṛg Veda* the Aśvins are described as presenting fair-skinned women to black (śyāvāya) Kaṇva,[1] who probably is named *kṛṣṇa* 'black' at another place[2] and is the poet of the hymns (*RV*, VIII. 85 and 86) addressed to the twin gods. It is perhaps again Kaṇva who is mentioned as *kṛṣṇa ṛṣi* in the first book of the *Ṛg Veda*.[3] Similarly Dīrghatamas, mentioned as a singer in one hymn of the *Ṛg Veda*, may have been of dark colour, if his name was given to him on account of his complexion.[4] It is significant that in several passages of the *Ṛg Veda* he is known by his metronymic Māmateya alone, and a later legend says that he married Uśij, a slave girl, and begot Kākṣīvant.[5] Again in the first book of the *Ṛg Veda* priestly Divodāsas, whose name suggests a dāsa origin,[6] are described as composing new hymns,[7] while in the tenth book the Aṅgiras author of the *RV*, X. 42-44 is called 'black'.[8] Since most of such references occur in the later portions of the *Ṛg Veda* it would appear that towards the end of the Ṛg Vedic period some of the black seers and Dāsa priests were worming their way into the newly organised Āryan community.

Similarly it appears that some of the conquered chiefs received high status in the new society. Priestly acceptance of gifts from the Dāsa chiefs such as Balbūtha and Tarukṣa earned them unstinted praises, and validated their status in the new order. That the Dāsas were in a position to make gifts and were looked upon as liberal donors can be deduced from the very meaning of the roots *das* from which

1. *RV*, I. 117.8, but Sāyaṇa explains *śyavāya* as *kuṣṭarogeṇa syāmavarṇāya*.
2. *RV*, VIII. 85.3-4. Kaṇva is also mentioned in *RV*, VIII. 50.10.
3. *RV*, I. 116.23; cf. I. 117.7. Pargiter thinks that the Kāṇvāyanas are the only proper brāhmaṇas. *DKA*, p. 35.
4. *RV*, I. 158.6; Ambedkar, *Who were the Śūdras ?*, p. 77.
5. *VI*, i, 366. In the *Sat. Br.*, XIV. 9.4.15, there is the case of a mother wishing for a black son who possesses the knowledge of the Veda.
6. Hillebrandt's suggestion, *VI*, i, 363.
7. *RV*, I. 130.10.
8. Kosambi, *JBBRAS*, NS, xxvi, 44.

the noun Dāsa is derived.[1] The process of assimilation went on in later times, for the later literature records the tradition that Pratardana Daivodāsi went to the world of Indra,[2] who was historically the titular ruler of the Āryan invaders.

Early literature throws hardly any light on the process of assimilation between the Āryan commoners (*viś*) and those of the survivors of earlier societies. It is likely that most of them were reduced to what came to be known as the fourth varṇa in Āryan society. But, if we leave out the *Puruṣasūkta*, there is no evidence of the existence of the śudra varṇa in the age represented by the *Ṛg Veda*. In the early Ṛg Vedic period there existed, however, a small servile class of women slaves. It seems that, when the male members of the enemies of the Āryans were killed, their wives were reduced to slavery. Thus it is stated that Trasadasyu, the son of Purukutsa, gave away fifty women as gifts.[3] Further evidence for the existence of women slaves is to be found in the earlier portions of the *Atharva Veda*. Therein the woman slave is described as wet-handed, smearing the pestle and mortar,[4] and also as throwing lye on the droppings of the cow,[5] which shows that she was engaged in domestic work. This collection provides the earliest reference to a black *dāsi*.[6] References, therefore, suggest that in the early Vedic society women slaves were employed in domestic work. The use of the word *dāsi* makes it obvious that these were the womenfolk of the conquered Dāsas.

The use of the word *dāsa* in the sense of slave is to be found mostly in the later portions of the *Ṛg Veda*. Two cases occur in the first book,[7] one in the tenth book,[8] and one in the supplementary hymns (called *vālakhilya*) inserted

1. *s. v.* dāś, dās, Monier-Williams, *Sansk-Eng. Dict.*
2. *Kauṣītaki Upa.*, III. 1. quoted in *VI*, ii. 30.
3. *RV*, VIII. 19.36.
4. *yádvā dāsyā́rdrâhastā sámaṃtá ulúkhalaṃ músalaṃ śumbhatāpaḥ. AV*, XII. 3.13; *Paipp.*, XVII. 37.3.
5. *AV*, XII. 4.9; in the parallel passage in the *Paipp.* XVII. 16.9 the term *dāsī* is replaced by *devī*.
6. *AV*, V. 13.8.
7. *RV*, I. 92.8, 158.5. after Geldner's tr.
8. *RV*, X. 62.10.

in the eighth book.[1] The only early reference of this type is found in the eighth book.[2] In the *Ṛg Veda* there seems to be no other word which could mean slave, and it is thus clear that men slaves hardly existed in the early Ṛg Vedic period.

Of the number and nature of slaves in the later Ṛg Vedic period, references give only a vague idea. The *vālakhilya* mentions a hundred slaves, who are placed in the same category as asses and sheep.[3] The word *dāsa-pravarga* in another later reference may mean wealth or assemblage of slaves.[4] This would suggest that towards the end of the Ṛg Vedic period slaves were increasing in number, but there is no evidence of their being engaged in productive activities. They seem to have been in the nature of domestic servants attending on their priestly or warrior masters. These masters were usually warriors; only one reference mentions a priest Dīrghatamas as owning slaves.[5] They could be freely given away along with the cattle.[6] It seems that failure to pay debts resulted in the enslavement of the defaulter.[7] But the very name dāsa shows that war was the most important source of slavery during the Vedic period.

Who were the Dāsas? They have been generally confused with the Dasyus. But the absence of the word *dāsa-hatyā* (slaughter of the Dāsas), in contrast to *dasyu-hatyā* (slaughter of the Dasyus), the appearance of Dāsas as auxiliaries in the inter-tribal wars of the Aryans,[8] the absence of their description as *apa-vrata*, *anya-vrata*, etc., the mention of *dāsa viśas* (clans) at three places,[9] and above all their identification with the Iranian

1. *RV*, VIII. 56.3.

2. *RV*, VII. 86.7. Hillebrandt regards this as of doubtful nature. He wrongly adds 'villeicht' to VII. 86.3. which should be VII. 86.7. *ZII*, iii, 16.

3. *śatáṃ me gardabhā́nāṃ śatámūrnāvatīnāṃ; śatáṃ dāsā́ áti srájaḥ*. *RV*, VIII. 56.3. It is possible that 100 may be a conventional number.

4. *úṣasiámaśyāṃ yaśā́saṃ suviraṃ dāsápravargaṃ raytmáśva budhyam*. *RV*, I.92.8.

5. *RV*, I. 158.5-6.

6. *utá dāsā́ pariviṣe smáddiṣtī góparināsā; yádusturváśta māmahe*. *RV*, X. 62.10.

7. *RV*, X. 34.4.

8. *Supra*, pp. 16-17.

9. *RV*, II. 11.4, IV. 28.4, and VI. 25.2. B.N. Dutt thinks that the mention of Dāsa viś in *RV*, VI. 25.2, means that the Dāsa gets the vaiśya rank (*Studies in Indian Social Polity*, p. 334). But since the vaiśyas did not exist then as a social class *viś* can be better interpreted here as clan.

Dahae,[1] a Scythian tribe, sharply distinguish the Dāsas from the Dasyus, who seem to have had hardly anything in common with the Āryans.[2] There is no common word for Dasyu in Indo-European languages. We have the term *dahyu* in the Old Persian and Avestan languages, but it means a place of habitation of peoples, the 'district, counry, land';[3] this is in contrast to the Old Indian *dasyu* which is used of persons, not of a place.[4] On the other hand several languages share a common term for Dāsa. Thus the Greek *doulos* 'servus', now attested in Mycenaean *doero*, may belong with the Iranian *daha*,[5] and points to an Indo-European *dos*.[6] In all these languages the term means man or hero, which eventually came to have ethnic significance. The Greeks knew a people called variously as Daai, Daoi, Doai.[7] It is held by H. W. Bailey that the term *dāsa* is hardly a proper name in the Indian texts.[8] But numerous references in the *Ṛg Veda* speak of the Dāsa as those opposed to the Āryans or as their allies. The term *dāsa* is derived in old India from the base *das*, which means 'to treat violently.[9] They may not have been a homogenous racial stock, but they were undoubtedly a group of peoples in Vedic times. Professor Bailey himself points out the existence of a people called by the ethnic name Iranian *daha*, later found in Old Persian *dahā* placed before *saka* in an inscription of Xerxes.[10] It has been rightly suggested that in Old Indian the base *das* became pejorative on account of later environment.[11]

1. The Dahae may have been closely allied in race and language with the Iranians, but this is not very clearly proved. (VI, i, 357, fn. 20). Zimmer calls the Daoi or Daai of Heredotus, i, 126, a Turanian tribe. (*Ibid.*)
2. It is suggested that the Dāsas and Āryas were on a social level, above the Dasyu-Bhils. Shafer, *Ethnography of Anc. India*, p. 32.
3. H.W. Bailey, "Iranian *Arya*— and *Daha*—", *Transactions of the Philological Society*, 1959, 110.
4. *Ibid.*, p. 112.
5. *Ibid.*, p. 109.
6. *Ibid.*
7. *Ibid.*
8. *Ibid.*, p. 102.
9. *Ibid.*, 114.
10. *Ibid.*, p. 109.
11. *Ibid.*, p. 113.

Possibly the Dāsas were an advance guard of mixed Indo-Āryan peoples who came to India at the time when the Kassites appeared in Babylonia (*c.*1750 B.C.). This can be linked up with the archaeological hypothesis which assumes either a continuous movement or two main movements of peoples from Northern Persia towards India and places the first movement fairly soon after 2000 B.C.[1] Since the Dāsas shared language and some other elements of culture with the Ṛg Vedic people the latter followed a policy of conciliation towards them and easily assimilated into their fold such Dāsa chiefs as Divodāsa, Balbūtha and Tarukṣa. It is because of this that the Dāsas appear as frequent allies of the Āryans in their inter-tribal conflicts. Thus it would appear that the name *dāsa* in the sense of slave was derived not from the non-Āryan inhabitants of India but from a people allied to the Indo-Āryans. The people who were lauded in Iran were condemned in India probably because as an earlier wave of Indo-Āryans they stood in the way of the later wave of the same people. In the later period of the *Ṛg Veda* the term dāsa may have been employed indiscriminately not only to cover the survivors of the original Indo-European *dāsas* but also pre-Āryan peoples such as Dasyus and Rakṣasas and also such sections of the Āryans as were impoverished or reduced to subjection on account of internal conflicts within their ranks.

Had the number of the Āryans been small, they could have imposed themselves as a new ruling minority consisting of the upper classes on the conquered peoples as did the Hittites in Anatolia and the Kassites and Mitannis in Mesopotamia. But in the case of both Iran and India, the linguistic position suggests mass migrations. The Ṛg Vedic evidence is fatal to the hypothesis that the Āryans imposed themselves as a minority in India.[2] In the Vedic texts we encounter movements and settlements of numerous Āryan tribes.[3] Excavations and explorations carried

1. Stuart Piggott, *Antiquity*, Vol. XXIV, No. 96, 218. Lal suggests the influx of peoples at Shahi Tump (modern Baluchistan) in the first half of the second millennium B.C., and at Fort Munro (Afghanistan) in the second half of the second millenium B.C. *AI*, No. 9, pp. 90-91.
2. s. v. varṇa, *VI*, ii, p. 225, fn. 67.
3. For *RV* tribes see *VA*, pp. 245-48 and for later Vedic tribes, pp. 252-62.

out since 1947[1] have produced a rich crop of theories regarding the identification of the Āryans. Several of these theories can be reconciled if we postulate successive waves of newcomers, who have left abundant traces of their material culture in the whole of northwestern India from about 1500 B.C. to 500 B.C. Although the earliest Ṛg Vedic survivals are difficult to identify, the Gāndhāra graves might herald the arrival of the first Āryans around 1800 B.C. In any case numerous Painted Grey Ware sites found in eastern Punjab, Haryana, western Uttar Pradesh, Rajasthan and the adjoining areas of Pakistan do suggest the mass-scale settlement of new peoples between *circa* 1000 and 500 B.C. We can count 315 PGW sites, mostly located in the Upper Gaṅgā and Sutlej basins and also in the Ghaggar valley.[2] Recent explorations have brought to light nearly 300 PGW sites on the banks of the Sarasvatī and Dṛṣadvatī in Haryana, and by this time the number of all such sites may have exceeded 500. Those which have been excavated show that they were inhabited for two or three centuries.

Again, the distribution of the Āryan languages over the greater part of India presupposes mass migration of their speakers. In spite of the occurrence of many words of proto-Munda and 'Dravidian' stock in Sanskrit from Vedic times onwards the pre-Āryans living in north India were so swamped by the newcomers that they could not retain their language. As will be shown later, in northern India the śūdras, along with the vaiśyas, accounted for the overwhelming majority of the population, but there is nothing to show that they spoke non-Āryan language. On the other hand, in the later Vedic period the śūdras understood the Āryan speech, as is clear from the formula of address used for them on the occasions of the sacrifice.[4] In this connection a tradition from the *Mahābhārata* is significant: "Sarasvatī, consisting of the Veda, was formerly designed by Brahmā for all the four varṇas; but the śūdras having through cupidity fallen into 'ignorance', a

1. B.B. Lal. 'Protohistoric Investigation', *AI*, No. 9, 97.
2. On the basis of Vibha Tripathi, *The Painted Grey Ware*, Appendix I.
3. Information from Dr. Suraj Bhan and his colleagues,
4. *Śat. Br.*, I. 1.4.11-12.

condition of darkness, lost the right to the Veda."[1] Weber understands this passage to mean that in ancient times the śūdras spoke the language of the Āryans.[2] It is possible that some of the autochthonous tribes abandoned their speech in favour of Āryan dialects, as in modern times several tribal peoples in Bihar have given up their languages and adopted Āryan dialects such as Kurmālī and Sadānā, but their number must have been small as compared to that of the people whose language they adopted. Even in modern times, when the Āryan-speaking people enjoy much better facilities for spreading their language and culture, they have not been able to oust the non-Āryan languages which, in some cases, have shown capacity for vigorous growth.

On the basis of the foregoing discussion it would not be overbold to state that the Āryans came to India in large numbers. With some possible admixture from the enemy tribes, warriors and priests could account only for a small minority of the Āryan population. In course of time the majority of the Āryans could not escape the fate of being reduced to the position of commoners and semi-helots. But in the Ṛg Vedic period the process of economic and social differentiation was still in its very early stage. In a predominantly tribal, pastoral society the military leaders had hardly any fixed and regular source of surplus cereals or even cattle, on which they and their priestly supporters could live and flourish. Their most important source of income lay in the occasional exaction of tribute and spoils of war from the conquered peoples, which also, presumably, they had to share with the members of the tribe.[3] *Bali* is the only term which indicates the practice of collecting or receiving some sort of surplus in the *Ṛg Veda.* Generally it means a tribute or offering made to a god,[4] but it is also used in the sense of tribute paid to the king.[5] Probably the payment of

1. *varṇāścatvāra ete hi yeṣāṃ brāhm sarasvatī, vihitā brahmaṇā pūrvā lobhāttvajñānatāṃ gataḥ. SP*, 181.15.
2. *Indische Studien*, ii, 94 fn.
3. R.S. Sharma. *JBRS*, xxxviii, 434-35; xxxix, 418-19.
4. *RV*, I. 70.9; V.1.10; VIII. 100.9.
5. 'Balihṛt' (paying tribute) in *RV*, VII. 6.5; X. 173.6.

bali was voluntary[1] as there was neither any regular machinery collection nor any collector such as the *balisādhaka* of post-Vedic times to collect it from the people. Apparently the tribal kinsmen gave trust and voluntary presents to their chief, who in return led them from victory to victory and allowed them a share in the spoils of war. Only defeated hostile tribes may have been compelled to pay *bali* or tributes. At best, princes and priests could exploit the labour of women slaves for domestic purposes, or possibly for looking after their cattle. It seems that the Ṛg Vedic families cultivated their lands themselves, there being no common word for wages in Indo-European languages. The *Ṛg Veda* does neither know of agricultural slaves nor of wage-earners and hired labourers (*karmakara*), who appear as an important element in agricultural operations in post-Vedic times.[2] We have no instance of the grant of land by the tribal chiefs to their warrior or priestly followers, presumably because the land belonged to the tribe as a whole. The near egalitarian character of Ṛg Vedic society is further evident from the prescription of the same wergeld for everybody, man or woman,[3] the compensation amounting to a hundred cows.[4]

In essence the Ṛg Vedic Āryan society was characterised by the absence of sharp class divisions amongst its members, a feature which is usually found in early tribal societies.[5] It was possible to have different ranks but not different social classes. Perhaps the Purāṇic speculation regarding the origin of the varṇas refers to this stage, when it states that until the advent of the Tretā age there was no varṇa division and nothing like greed or the tendency

1. Zimmer's view quoted in *VI*, ii, 62.

2. For a detailed discussion of the Ṛg Vedic economy see R.S. Sharma, "Forms of Property in the Early Portions of the *Ṛg Veda*", *Essays in Honour of* Prof. S.C. Sarkar, pp. 39-50.

3. Max Müller's tr. of *RV*, V. 61.8, *SBE*, xxxii, 361.

4. VI, ii. 331.

5. Landtman, *The Origin of the Inequality of Social Classes*, instances quoted on pp. 5-12. He also refers to the absence of classes among the Nāgas and Kookies of Eastern India (p. 11).

to steal.[1] But even in the earliest period, in addition to the slowly emerging military leaders and priests, there were husbandmen, and artisans who practised a number of crafts. Common words for weaver, tanner, carpenter and painter suggest their Indo-European origins.[2] The existence of a widespread Indo-European word for chariot shows that the chariot-maker may have been known to the Indo-Europeans.[3] The *rathakāra* (chariot-maker), however, does not appear in the *Ṛg Veda*, where the carpenter's work is referred to in several early passages.[4] It appears from the *Atharva Veda* that chariot-makers (*rathakāra*) and metal workers (*karmāra*) enjoyed a position of importance in society. In the early portion of that collection a newly elected king prays to a plant amulet (*parṇa-maṇi*) to help him to strengthen his position among the skilful builders of chariots, and the ingenious workers of metal, who constitute the folk around him. These artisans are to be made his helpers,[5] and in this sense seem to be on a par with the kings, king-makers, charioteers (*sūta*) and troopleaders (*grāmaṇi*),[6] who constitute the folk round about the king and are likewise to be made his helpers.[7]

Obviously the crafts mentioned above were practised by the members of the Āryan community (*viś*), and no social stigma was attached to them. A later passage from the *Ṛg Veda*

1. *varṇāṣramavyavasthāśca na tadāsanna saṃkaraḥ; na lipsanti hi te'nyonyannānugṛhṇanti caiva hi. Vā.* P., i, VIII. 60. cf. *Dīgha Nikāya*, Aggaññasutta.

2. Carl Darling, *A Dictionary of Selected Synonyms in the Principal Indo-European Languages*, for leather (*carman*) see p. 40, for weaving, p. 408, for *takṣan* pp. 589-90, and for plaiting pp. 621-622. Cf. Childe, *The Aryans* p. 86

3. Childe, *The Aryans*, pp. 86 and 92.

4. *RV*, IV. 35-6, 36.5; VI. 32.1.

5. *yé dhivāno rathakārā́ḥ karmā́rayé manīṣíṇaḥ; upastínparṇa máhyaṃ tvā́ṃ sárvānkṛṇvabhíto jánān. AV*, III. 5.6.

Bloomfield's tr. is followed here. Whitney gives the same tr. as Bloomfield, but takes *upastīns* in the sense of subjects after Sāyaṇa. Sā. takes *dhivānaḥ* and *manīṣiṇaḥ* as separate nouns meaning fishermen and intellectuals. The *Paipp.* text is slightly different; *ye takṣāṇo rathakārā karmārā ye manīṣiṇaḥ; sarvāṃs tān parṇa randhayopastiṃ kṛṇu medinam.* III. 13.7.

6. Presumably he was the head of the village both for civil purposes and military operations. *VI*, i, 247.

7. *AV*, .5.7.

describes the carpenter as one who usually bends over his work till his back aches.[1] This may convey some idea of the difficult nature of his work, but implies no contempt for it. That the carpenters were a low caste, or formed a separate class of the people is certainly not true of Vedic times.[2] But the smith (*karmāra*), the carpenter (*takṣan*), the tanner (*carmamna*),[3] the weaver and others, whose occupations were quite dignified in the *Ṛg Veda* and apparently practised by respected members of the *viś*, came to be reckoned as śūdra in the Pāli texts.[4] It is likely that non-Āryans also pursued these crafts independently,[5] but there is no doubt that many descendants of Āryan artisans, who stuck to their old professions, were relegated to the position of the śūdras.

The earliest speculation regarding the origin of the four varṇas is to be found in the mythical story of creation embodied in the *Puruṣasūkta* (hymn of man) of the *Ṛg Veda*. This is considered as an interpolation in the tenth book of that collection. But it is reproduced with slight changes in the later Vedic literature,[6] and in the traditions of the epic,[7] Purāṇas[8] and Dharmaśāstras.[9] It states that the brāhmaṇa emanated from the mouth of the primeval man, the kṣatriya from his arms, the vaiśya from his thighs and the śūdra from his feet.[10] Either it shows that the śūdras were supposed to belong to the same stock, and hence were a section of the Āryan community, or else it represents an attempt to find a common mythical origin for the heterogenous brāhmaṇical society. In point of time the *Puruṣa-sūkta* version may be ascribed to the end of the period of

1. *RV*, I. 105.18.
2. *VI*, i, 297.
3. *RV*, VIII. 5.38.
4. *VI*, ii, 265-6.
5. cf. Fick, *The Social Organization in N. E. India*, pp. 326-27.
6. *Pañc. Br.*, V. I. 6-10; *Vājasaneyi Saṃhita*, XXXI, 11; *Taittirīya Āraṇyaka*, III. 12,5. & 6.
7. *Mbh*, XII. 73.4-8.
8. *Vāyu P.*, i, VIII. 155-9; *Mārk. P.*, ch. 49; *Viṣṇu P*, i. Ch. VI.
9. *Vas. Dh. S.*, IV. 2; *Bau. Dh. S.*, I. 10.19.5-6; cf. *Āp. Dh. S.*, I. 1. 1.7; *Manu*, I. 31; *Yāj.*, III. 126.
10. *RV*, X. 90.12.

the *Atharva Veda*,[1] in which it occurs in the latest portion which may be as late as 800 B.C.[2] It seems to provide a theoretical justification for the disintegration of tribal society into classes. Already in the Ṛg Vedic period division of labour had gone a long way. But although members of the same family worked as poet, physician and grinder,[3] this did not involve any social differentiation. Towards the end of the period of the *Atharva Veda*, however, differentiations of functions tended to develop into differentiations of rank, and tribes and clans gradually disintegrated into social classes. It appears that the Śūdra tribe, or sections of the Āryans employed in servile work, were given the position of the fourth varṇa, and in this sense the tradition of the common origin of the four varṇas may have an element of truth. But it does not represent the whole truth. It is possible that in subsequent times the descendants of the Āryan śudras went on multiplying in the new fertile Gangetic settlements, but from the Vedic period onwards large numbers of aborigines of varying stocks were successively incorporated in the śūdra varṇa.[4] Obviously the old tradition of the common origin of the varṇas could not explain the accession of the non-Āryan tribes to the brāhmaṇical fold, but it could serve as a useful fiction. It could help to assimilate and keep the hetrogenous elements together, and, in so far as the śūdras were supposed to have been born from the feet of the first man, it could justify their servile position in brāhmaṇical society.

When do the śūdras first appear as a social class charged with the service of the three higher varṇas ? Ṛg Vedic society had some men and women slaves who acted as domestic servants, but they were not so considerable as to constitute the servile varṇa of the śūdras. The first and the only reference to the śūdras as a social class in the *Ṛg Veda* is to be found in the *Puruṣasūkta* passage already referred to, which recurs in the nineteenth book of the *Atharva Veda*.[5] In the same book there are two other

1. *AV*, *XIX*, 6.6.
2. Whitney, *HOS*, vii, p. CXLI; viii, 895-98.
3. *RV*, IX. 112.3.
4. Oldenberg, *ZDMG*, li, 286.
5. *AV*, XIX. 6.6.

passages, which also seem to refer to the existence of four varṇas. In one of them prayer is made to the *darbha* (grass) to make the worshipper dear to brāhmaṇa, kṣatriya, śūdra and ārya.[1] Here, ārya probably stands for vaiśya. In the second passage is expressed a desire to become dear to gods, to kings and to both śūdra and ārya.[2] It appears that here gods stand for brāhmaṇas and āryas for vaiśyas.[3] We have to bear in mind that all these passages occur in the nineteenth book, which, along with the twentieth, forms a supplement to the main collection of the *Atharva Veda*.[4] An earlier passage mentions a charm made by brāhmana, rājanya or śūdra and includes a spell that it may recoil on the maker.[5] This belongs to the second grand division (Book VIII-XII) of the *Atharva Veda*, which, according to Whitney, is 'palpably of hieratic origin.'[6] This suggests that the ideology of the varṇa system developed under priestly influence. The only other reference relevant to our purpose, which, on the basis of Whitney, can be assigned to the early period of the *Atharva Veda*, mentions brāhmaṇa, rājanya and vaiśya,[7] but leaves out the śūdra. It is evident then that the śūdras appear as a social class only towards the end of the period of the *Atharva Veda*, when the *Puruṣasūkta* version of their origin may have been inserted into the tenth book of the *Ṛg Veda*.

One would like to know why the fourth varṇa came to be called śūdras. It appears that just as the common European world 'slave' and the Sanskrit 'dāsa' were derived from the names of conquered peoples, so also the word śūdra was derived from a conquered tribe of that name. There is no doubt that Śudra existed as a tribe in the fourth century B.C., for Diodoros records the advance of Alexander against a tribe called Sodrai,[8]

1. *AV*, XIX. 32.8; *Paipp*., XII. 4.8.
2. *AV*, XIX. 62.1; *Paipp*., II. 32.5.
3. Whitney's note on the translation of *AV*, XIX. 62.1; *HOS*, viii, 1003.
4. Whitney quoted *supra*, p. 33.
5. *AV*., X. 1.3.
6. *HOS*, vii, p. CLV.
7. *AV*, V. 17.9; *Paipp*., IX. 16.7.
8. McCrindle, *Invasion of India*, p. 293. Arrian mentions Sogdoi (*Ibid*., p. 157), which may be wrong. Sydroi are again clearly mentioned by Ptolemy (VI. 20.3) as inhabiting the central portion of Archosia, whcih

who occupied portions of modern Sind. The existence of some of the tribes mentioned by the Greek writers can be traced back to a much earlier period. For instance, the Abastanoi of Arrian (called Sambastai by Diodoros) may be identified with the Ambaṣṭhas of the *Aitareya Brāhmaṇa*,[1] which mentions an Ambaṣṭha king.[2] The same case may apply to the Śūdra tribe, and thus it may be possible to trace the śūdra varṇa of *circa* 10th-8th century B.C. from the Śūdra tribe of the 4th century B.C.

Three references to śūdra in the earliest portion of the *Atharva Veda* can be interpreted in this light. They belong, according to Whiteny, to the first grand division of the *Atharva Veda* (Book I-VII) which is 'in very large measure of popular origin' and is by all odds 'the most characteristic part' of that collection.[3] In two of them the worshipper desires to see everybody whether Ārya or Śūdra with the help of a herb, in order to detect a sorcerer.[4] There is no mention of brāhmaṇa or rājanya in this connection. The question is whether the Ārya and Śūdra represent here two social classes (varṇas) or two tribal groups. The latter supposition seems to be plausible. The earlier opposition between Ārya and Dāsa or Dasyu is replaced by one between Ārya and Śūdra. It is worth stressing that these references do not give any idea of the social distance or disabilities, which are implicit in the conception of varṇa. They may be compared with another passage from the same collection which speaks of Ārya and Dāsa, and in which it is claimed by the priest or Varuṇa that no Dāsa or Ārya can damage the course he maintains.[5] Mention has been made of similar passages in the *Ṛg Veda* in which the worshipper desires to overcome his enemies, both Āryans and Dāsas or Dasyus. The one obstacle in the way of the correct interpretation by brāhmaṇical commentators of such Vedic texts as have direct bearing on

covered a considerable portion of eastern Afghanistan and the eastern frontier of which was skirted by the Indus. (McCrindle, *Ancient India as described by Ptolemy* p. 317).

1. *PHAI*, p. 255.
2. *Ait. Br.*, VII. 21.
3. *HOS*, vii, pp. CXLVIII and CLV.
4. *táyāhám sárvaṃ paśyāmi yáśca śūdrá utárvaḥ.* *AV*, IV. 20.4, 8; *Paipp.*, VIII, 6.8.
5. *AV*, V. 11.3.

social relations has been the tendency to look ahead to later developments. An example is the meaning of the words *ārya* and *dāsa* in the *Ṛg Veda*. Sāyaṇa takes *ārya* as a member of the first three varṇas, and *dāsa* as a *śūdra*;[1] this is obviously based on the later division of society into four varṇas, which Śāyaṇa's interpretation is meant to justify. Likewise in the Atharva Vedic reference under discussion Sāyaṇa explains *ārya* as a member of the three varṇas,[2] which naturally makes *śūdra* the representative of the fourth. But it becomes very hard to interpret earlier texts, if they are approached with the later conception of ārya and śūdra as developed in the Dharmaśāstras.

That the Śūdras appear as a tribe in the earliest part of the *Atharva Veda* can also be inferred from the third reference, in which the fever *takman* is asked to attack a wanton śūdra woman along with the Mujavants, Balhikas and Mahāvṛṣaṣ.[3] All these peoples seem to have been inhabitants of north-western India,[4] where, in the *Mahābhārata*, the Śūdra tribe is described as living along with the Ābhīras.[5] Another verse also repeats the desire that the fever should go to the foreign people.[6] All this would suggest that the context in which the Śūdra woman is mentioned relates to the attitude of hostility of the Āryans of the period of the *Atharva Veda* towards the foreign tribes inhabiting north-western India. And hence the word *śūdrā* here probably means a woman of the Śūdra tribe. In the parallel passage from the *Paippalāda* recension *śūdrā* is replaced by *dāsi*,[7] which shows that in the author's view the terms were interchangeable. Therefore, the occurence of the term *śūdra* in what is regarded as the earliest and the most characteristic part of the *Atharva Veda* should be understood not in the sense of varṇa, but in that of a tribe which suits the context better.

Coupled with the Ābhīras the Śūdras are repeatedly mentioned as a tribe in the *Mahābhārata*, which contains traditions that

1. Comm. to *RV*, II. 12.4.
2. Comm. to *AV*, IV. 20.4.
3. *AV*, V. 22.7 and 8.
4. Cf. *VA*, pp. 258-9.
5. *śūdrābhīrātha daradāḥ kāśmīrāḥ paśubhiḥ saha*. *Mbh*, VI. 10.66, 46 where *aparandhrāḥ* in the Cr. Edn. is a mistake for *aparāntāḥ*.
6. *AV*, V. 22. 12, 14.
7. *Paipp*., XIII. 1.9.

may look back to the 10th century B.C. This epic makes a clear distinction between the śūdra *kula* which is mentioned along with the *kulas* of kṣatriya and vaiśya,[1] and the śūdra tribe, which is mentioned with the Ābhīras, Daradas Tukhāras, Pahlavas etc.[2] As a tribe the Śūdras find place in the list of peoples conquered by Nakula in the course of his all round victorious march (*dig-vijaya*),[3] and in that of those sending presents to Yudhiṣṭhira on the occasion of his great coronation sacrifice (*rājasūya*)[4] They are bracketted with the Ābhīras in many references, and both of them seem to have existed in India earlier than the Śakas, Tukhāras, Pahlavas, Romakas, Chīnas and Hūṇas, whose names were later[5] interpolated into the list of the peoples mentioned in the *Sabhā Parvas*. Non-Indian sources of the first few centuries preceding or succeeding the Christian era give no indication of the foreign connections of the Śūdras and Ābhīras. There is hardly anything to support the view that the Ābhīras came to India in the early centuries of the Christian era. It appears that they existed as a tribe at the time of the Bhārata war[6] and in the period of chaos, which followed the aftermath of the great war, they spread themselves over the Panjāb.[7] The repeated mention of the Śūdras along with the Ābhīras would suggest that they were an old tribe flourishing at the time of the war. This fits in well with the interpretation of the term śūdra in the sense of tribe in the earliest part of the *Atharva Veda*.

The next question is whether the Śūdras were an Āryan or pre-Āryan tribe, and if Āryan, when did they come to India ? Contradictory views have been expressed on the ethnological classification of the Śūdra tribe. Formerly it was maintained that the Śūdras were an earlier wave of Āryans;[8] later it came

1. *Ibid.*, II. 29. 8-9. Pahlavas and Barbaras are also mentioned. *Ibid.*, II. 29-15.
2. *Mbh.*, VI. 10.65.
3. *Ibid.*, VI. 10.66.
4. *Ibid.*, II. 47-7.
5. *Ibid.*, II. 47.7 ff.
6. P. Banerjee, *JBRS*, xli, 160-1.
7. Budha Prakash, *JBRS*, xl, 255, 260-3.
8. Weber, *ZDMG*, iv, 301, fn. 2, cf. Roth, *ZDMG*, i, 84.

to be held that they were a stem of the pre-Āryan peoples.[1] No evidence has been adduced in support of either view, but in the light of the available data one may be inclined to think that the Śūdra tribe had some affinity with the Āryans. It is interesting to note that they are always bracketted with the Ābhīras,[2] who spoke an Āryan dialect called Ābhīrī.[3] The fact that the people of the śūdra class could understand the Āryan speech in the period of the Brāhmaṇas also may suggest, though remotely, that the Śūdra tribe was acquainted with the Āryan language. Further, the Śūdras are never mentioned in lists of the pre-Āryan peoples, such as Draviḍas, Pulindas, Śabaras etc. They are always located in the north-west,[4] which, in later times, was an area mainly occupied by the Āryans.[5] The Ābhīras and the Śūdras were settled near the Sarasvatī.[6] It is stated that, because of her hostility towards them, the Sarasvati vanished into the desert.[7] These references are significant, for along with the Dṛṣadvatī the Sarasvatī marked one of the boundaries of the region known as Ārya-deśa.

1. Fick, *SONI*, p. 315, Keith, *CHI*, i, 86; Lassen, *Ind. Alt.*, ii, 174. cf. Weber, *Indische Studien*, xviii, 85-86 and 255. Zimmer identifies the Sudroi of Ptolemy with Brāhūi (*Alt. Leb.*, p. 435), but there seems to be no basis for such a supposition. cf. Hopkins, *Religions of India*, p. 548, fn. 3. Pargiter thinks that Śūdras and Ābhīras were considerably intermixed and closely connected aboriginal races (*Mārk. P.*, Tr., pp. 313-14, fn.).

2. *Mbh.* VI. 10.45 and 46; 65 and 66; in the critical edition of the *Mbh.*, VII. 19.7, *śūrābhīra* seems to be a wrong reading. It should be *śūdrābhīrāḥ* as found in other Mss. (fn. on VII. 19.7). Śūdras and Ābhīras are again mentioned together in the *Mahābhāṣya* of Patañjali (Pat. on *Pa.*, I. 2.72.6).

3. The earliest specimens of *Ābhīrokti* are found in the *Nāṭyaśāstra* of Bharata, a work of the second or third century A.D. (P. D. Gune, Introduction to *Bhavisayattakahā*, pp. 50-51). These are clearly very much allied to Sanskrit.

4. The *Mbh.* list in practically the same form occurs in the Purāṇas, in which the Śūdras are mentioned as a people along with the Ābhiras, Kālatoyakas, Aparāntas, Pahlavas (wrongly mentioned as Pallavas in the Cr. Edn. VI. 10.66) and others. *Mārk. P.*, ch. 57. 35-36 and *Matsya P.*, ch. 113. 40. In the Gupta period the Śūdra tribe seems to have held a definite territory, which is listed in the *Viṣṇu Purāṇa* (IV. 24.18) along with the territories Saurāṣṭra, Avanti and Arbuda. There is no justification for Diksitar's reading *śūra* (*Gupta Polity*, pp. 3-4), for the text clearly mentions *śūdra* territory.

5. Muir, *Original Sanskrit Texts*, ii, 355-357.

6. *śūdrābhīragaṇāścaiva ye cāśritya sarasvatīm. Mbh.*, II. 29.9.

7. *śūdrābhīrān prati dveṣād yatra naṣṭā sarasvatī. Mbh.* (Cal.), IX. 37.1.

Reference has already been made to the *Dahae*, the Iranian parallel to Indian *Dāsa*, but it is difficult to establish such an equation in the case of Śūdra. It has been doubtfully suggested that Śūdra may be equated with the Greek word *kūdros*,[1] which is used by Homer (*circa* 10th cen.-9th. cen. B.C.) in the sense of great, and is applied as an epithet generally to divine beings and rarely to mortals.[2] In later times in India śūdra was a term of opprobrium applied to people disliked by the brāhmaṇas; on the contrary it was a term of approbation in Homeric Greece. This may be explained very tentatively by suggesting that members of a hypothetical Indo-European Kudra tribe became important among the leaders of the tribes which later invaded Greece, while those of this tribe who entered India were subjected by their fellow invaders. That the same term carries inverted meanings in different contexts is clear from the example of *asura*. While Asura was associated with evil in India, his prototype Ahura was a god in Iran. The analogy may apply to the use of the term śūdra in India and Greece but cannot be regarded as definitive unless it is proved that the *kūdroi* were a tribe in Greece. Nevertheless, on the basis of all that has been said above, it is probable that the Śūdras, like the Dāsas, were a people allied to the indo-Āryan stock.

If they were allied to the Indo-Āryans, when did they come to India? It has been suggested that they were an earlier wave of Āryan immigrants.[3] But since they are not mentioned in the *Ṛg Veda*, it is likely that they represent a later thrust of foreign tribes into north-western India towards the close of the Ṛg Vedic period. On the basis of archaeological evidence it is possible that the movement of peoples into India was a continuous process lasting for nearly a millenium after 2000 B.C.,[4] a hypothesis, which is also supported by linguistic evidence.[5] It is, therefore, probable that the Śūdras came to India towards the

1. Wackernagel, "Indoiranisches", *Sitzungsberichte der Koniglich Preussischen Akademie der Wissenschaften*, 1918, 410-411.

2. *s.v.* kūdròs, Liddell and Scott, *A Greek-English Lexicon*, i.

3. Weber, *ZDMG*, iv, 301, fn. 2; cf. Roth, *ZDMG*, i, 84.

4. Stuart Piggott, *Antiquity*, iv, *No.* 96, 218.

5. T. Burrow, *The Sanskrit Language*, p. 31.

end of the second millenium B.C., when they were defeated by the Vedic Āryans and were gradually absorbed into the later Vedic society as the fourth varṇa. Interestingly enough the area covered by the Sarasvatī, with which the Śūdra people are associated, is full of Painted Grey Ware sites which began around 1000 B.C.

It has been asserted that the kṣatriyas were reduced to the position of śūdras as a result of their long struggle with the brāhmaṇas, who ultimately deprived their adversaries of the right to the *upanayana* (investiture with sacred thread).[1] On the basis of a solitary tradition occurring in the *Śānti Parvan* of the *Mahābhārata*, that Paijavana was a śūdra king, it is claimed that śūdras were kṣatriyas in the beginning.[2] Such a view seems to be without any foundation in facts. First, kṣatriyas as a well-defined varṇa with their rights and duties did not exist in the Ṛg Vedic period. Fighting and management of the common affairs were the concern of the whole tribe and at best of the clan chiefs but not confined to a class of chosen warriors. From the very beginning the slowly emerging groups of warriors and priests co-operated in leading the *viś* in their fight against the Āryan as well as non-Āryan peoples. In times of peace the two groups together tried to collect tributes from the *viś*, and hence the king was called *viśamattā*. As time passed, the warriors bestowed on the priests generous gifts, and the religious rituals were much elaborated, so that the power of the priests who performed them and of the warriors who patronized them was much strengthened as against that of the common people. Secondly, in spite of the echoes of the struggle between priests and warriors during the later Vedic period, as reflected in the stories of Paraśurāma and Viśvāmitra, there is nothing to show that the *upanayana* formed the issue, and that it was decided against the kṣatriyas. Perhaps the struggle centred round the question of sharing the surplus in the form of gifts and tributes collected occasionally from the tribal peasantry called the *viś* and of enjoying social

1. Ambedkar, *op. cit.*, p. 239.

2. *Ibid.*, pp. 139-42. It was Lassen who drew attention to the fact that the ancient king Sudās was called śūdra in the *Mbh. Ind. Alt.*, i. 969.

supremacy, which determined the nature of the privileges to be enjoyed by them. There was some dispute regarding the brāhmaṇical monopoly of knowledge, which was successfully challenged by the kṣatriyas. It seems that Aśvapati Kaikeya and Pravāhaṇa Jaivali were not improbably teachers of the brāhmaṇas.[1] Kṣatriya princes such as Janaka of Mithilā contributed to the growth of the Upaniṣadic thought, and the kṣatriya ruler Viśvāmitra climbed to priesthood. In eastern Uttar Pradesh and Bihar the kṣatriya revolt reached its climax with the preachings of Gautama Buddha and Vardhamāna Mahāvīra, who claimed social primacy for the kṣatriyas and gave the next place to the brāhmaṇas. The real issue was, who would get the first place in society, brāhmaṇa or kṣatriya? But this was closely linked to the sharing of gifts tributes and labour power. Neither in post-Vedic nor in pre-Mauryan literature is there anything to show that the brāhmaṇas intended to reduce the kṣatriyas to the third or fourth varṇa, or that the kṣatriyas wanted to do the same to the brāhmaṇas.

Thirdly, it is wrong to think that in the beginning the loss of the *upanayana* was the decisive test of being a śūdra. In this case modern court decisions[2] cannot serve as a guide for conditions at the time when the śūdra class came into being. Loss of the *upanayana* in the case of the śūdra, as will be shown later, is to be found only from the end of the later Vedic period, and even so, it was not the only disability imposed on him as a mark of his servility but one of several. As will be noticed later, the loss of the *upanayana* was not the cause of the conversion of Āryans into śūdras but the consequence of their having sunk to the lower orders as a result of the rise of economic and social inequalities.

Fourthly, it is difficult to vouch for the authenticity of the tradition in the *Śānti Parvan* that Paijavana was a śūdra. He has been identified with Sudās, the head of the Bhārata tribe, and it is argued that this famous hero of the Battle of Ten Kings was a śūdra.[3] There is nothing in the Vedic literature to support

1. Kosambi, *JBBRAS*, NS, xxiii, 45.
2. Ambedkar, *op. cit.*, pp. 185-90.
3. *Ibid.*, p. 139.

this view, and the *Śānti Parvan* tradition is not corroborated by any other source, epic or Purāṇic. The tradition says that the śūdra Paijavana performed sacrifices, and occurs in a very late portion of the *Mahābhārata* where it is stated that the śūdras can perform five great sacrifices and make gifts.[1] It is difficult to judge whether the tradition was true or false, but clearly it was meant to serve as a precedent for śūdras making gifts and sacrifices, which, as will be shown later, was in keeping with the liberal attitude of the *Śānti Parvan*. It may be also pointed out that in later times the term śūdra or vṛṣala was applied indiscriminately by the brāhmaṇas to anybody who went against them. We do not know whether this was the case with the śūdra Paijavana. In many cases such statement do not mean that kṣatriyas and brāhmaṇas were reduced to the status of śūdras, but they merely suggest the śūdra origin of these personages, especially on the side of their mother.[2]

Evidently the Śūdra tribe performed military functions, as was the case with the Āryan tribes and their tribal institutions.[3] In the *Mahābhārata* the army of the Śūdra people is mentioned along with that of the Ambaṣṭhas, Śibis, Sūrasenas etc.[4] But this could not convert the whole tribe of the Śūdras into a kṣatriya varṇa, as we know it, with well defined functions and privileges. Therefore the theory that the kṣatriyas were reduced to the position of śūdras has hardly anything to commend itself.

The attempts at an etymological derivation of the term *śūdra* reflect the position of the fourth varṇa at the time they were made, and hardly help to elucidate the problem of the origin of the varṇa. The earliest attempt is to be found in the *Vedānta-sūtra* of Bādarāyaṇa, where the word is divided into two parts *śuk* 'grief' and *dra* from root *dru* 'to rush'.[5] While

1. *Mbh.*, XII. 60.38-40.

2. A number of ṛṣis, whose mother belonged to one or the other section of what was regarded as the śūdra varṇa, are enumerated in the *Bhaviṣya P.*, I.42.22-26. The list occurs in several other Purāṇas and the *Mbh.* Infra, p. 70.

3. R.S. Sharma, *JBRS*, xxxviii, 435-7; xxxix, 416-7.

4. *Mbh.*, VII. 6.6; cf. 19.7.

5. *śugasya tadanādaraśravaṇāt tadādravaṇatasūcyate. Ved. S.*, 1.3.34.

commenting on this passage Śaṅkara gives three alternative explanations why Jānaśruti[1] was called a śūdra; *viz*: (i) 'he rushed into grief' (*śucam abhidudrāva*), (ii) 'grief rushed on him' (*śucā vā abhidudruve*), and (iii) 'he in his grief rushed to Raikva' (*śucā vā raikvam abhidudrāva*).[2] Śaṅkara concludes that the word *śūdra* can be understood only by explaining the meaning of its components and not otherwise.[3] Bādarāyaṇa's derivation of *śūdra* and Śaṅkara's gloss thereon have rightly been regarded as unsatisafactory.[4] The Jānaśruti referred to by Śaṅkara is said to have ruled among the Mahāvṛṣas, a people who are mentioned in the *Atharva Veda* as living in north-western India. It is doubtful whether he belonged to the śūdra varṇa. Either he belonged to the Śūdra tribe, or to some other north-western people who were dubbed as śūdras by brāhmaṇical writers.

A very similar derivation of the term is given by the author of the *Uṇādi-sūtras* in the grammar of Pāṇini, where the term śūdra is resolved into two components, i.e. root *śuc* or *śuk+ra*.[5] It is difficult to account for the suffix *ra*, and in this case also the derivation seems to be fanciful and far-fetched.[6]

Brāhmaṇical traditions in the Purāṇas also connect the term *śūdra* with the root *śuc*, to be grieved. It is said that "those who grieved and ran, and were addicted to manual tasks, and were inglorious and feeble, were made śūdras."[7] But such explanations of the term śūdra rather reflect the position of the varṇa in later times than account for its etymological derivations. In this respect the Buddhist explanation of the term seems to be as fanciful as the brāhmaṇical. According to the Buddha, those who were of dreadful and mean conduct (*luddācārā khuddācārā ti*) came to be known as suddas, and thus the word *sudda* came into

1. Mentioned as a king in *Chā. Up.*, IV. 2.3.
2. Śaṅkara's comm. to *Ved. S.*, I. 3.34.
3. *śūdra avayavārtha sambhavāt rūḍhārthasya cāsambhavāt. Ibid.*
4. *IA*, li, 137-8.
5. *śucer daśca*. II. 19.
6. *IA*, li, 137-8.
7. *śocantaśca dravantaśca paricaryāsu ye ratāḥ; nistejaso alpavīryāśca śūdrās tānabravīttu saḥ. Vāyu P.*, i. VIII. 158. *The Bhaviṣya P.*, I.44. 23ff. adds that the śūdras were so called because they received droppings of the Vedic knowledge; *ye te śruterddrutiṃ prāptāḥ śūdrāsteneha kīrtitāḥ.*

existence.[1] In the Buddhist lexicon of early medieval times *śūdra* became a synonym of *kṣudra*,[2] and on this basis it is suggested that *śūdra* is derived from *kṣudra*.[3] Both derivations are philologically unsatisfactory, but are important as illustrating the ideas associated with the concept of the śūdra varṇa in ancient times. While the brāhmaṇical derivation betrays the miserable condition of the śūdra, the Buddhist tradition refers to his mean and inferior status in society. The derivations merely show how even etymological and linguistic explanations are influenced by prevailing social conditions. A recent writer derives the term *śūdra* from the root *śvi* 'swell'+the root *drā* 'run' and suggests that this term means 'one who runs after gross life'; therefore according to him the śūdra is 'an unintelligent fellow meant for manual labour.'[4] It is extraordinary that he should have derived the term *śūdra* from two roots, and that too hardly without any old etymological basis. The meaning which he labours to ascribe to this term only betrays the traditional attitude towards the śūdra, but does not throw any light on his origin.

The miserable or negligible status of the śūdra varṇa at the time of its origin is hardly borne out by the picture of society in the *Ṛg Veda* and the *Atharva Veda*. Nowhere in the collections is there any evidence of restrictions regarding food and marriage either between the Dāsa and the Āryan, or between the śūdra and the higher varṇas.[5] The only early reference, which implies such social distance between the varṇas, is to be found in the *Atharva Veda*, where it is claimed that the brāhmaṇa enjoys the right to become the first husband of a woman as against the rājanya and vaiśya.[6] The śūdra does not come in for notice, probably because his varṇa did not exist at that stage. There is nothing to show that dāsas or śūdras were

1. *suddā tveva akkharaṁ upanibbattam. Dīgha Nikāya*, iii. 95.
2. *s.v.* śūdra, *Mahāvyutpatti*.
3. *IA*, .i, 138-9.
4. Surya Kanta, "Kikaṭa, Phaligā, and Paṇi," *S. K. Belvalkar Commemoration Volume*, p. 44.
5. It is wrongly stated by N.N. Ghosh that such restrictions between the Āryan and the Dāsa are vouchsafed by the *Ṛg Veda*, *IC*, xii, 179.
6. *AV*, V. 17.8-9.

considered impure, or that their touch imparted pollution to the food or the body of the members of the higher varṇas.[1]

This discussion on the origin of the śūdra varṇa may be summed up by stating that large sections of people, Āryans and pre-Āryans, were reduced to that position, partly through external and partly through internal conflicts.[2] Since the conflicts centred mainly round the possession of cattle, and perhaps latterly of land and its produce, those who were dispossessed of these and impoverished came to be reckoned as the fourth class in the new society. The view that the śūdra varṇa was made up of the pre-Āryans seems to be as one-sided and exaggerated as the view that they mainly consisted of the Āryan peoples.[3] The sociological theory that a division into classes is always originally connected with ethnical dissimilarities[4] only partly explains the origin of the śūdras and dāsas (slaves). It is more than likely that dāsas and śūdras were respectively named after tribes of these names having affinities with the Indo-Āryans, but in course of time they came to include large groups of the pre-Āryan and degraded Āryan populations, who had ethnic connections neither with the Dāsa nor with the Śūdra tribe. It seems fairly clear that the Ṛg Vedic society had no recognisable śūdra order. Since it was predominantly a tribal and pastoral society, its military chiefs and their priestly supporters could not exact so much surplus produce and labour from their tribal kinsmen and others so as to alter their status into that of a servile order. Whatever was exacted as tributes from tribesmen or collected as spoils of war was redistributed among the kinsmen in the tribal assemblies. The possession of horses, chariots and slaves by the chiefs emphasised their ranks rather than their social class. The process of the formation of a servile class was carried forward only in later Vedic times when pastoralism gave way to agriculture and seminomadism to large-scale settlements, as can be inferred from both Painted Grey Ware sites and later Vedic texts.

1. Cf. Dutt, *Origin and Growth of the Caste System*, pp. 20 and 62.
2. G. J. Held, *Ethnology of the Mahābhārata*, pp. 89-95; B. N. Dutt, *Studies in Indian Social Polity*, pp. 28-30; Ambedkar, *Who were the Śūdras*, p. 239.
3. Cf. *VI*, ii. 265.
4. Landtman, *op. cit.*, p. 38.

CHAPTER III

TRIBE VERSUS VARṆA

(c. 1000-c. 500 B.C.)

The later Vedic literature, which is almost the only source for the study of the position of the śūdras during that period, mainly deals with rituals, pervading all aspects of the life of the people. Every important public or individual act is accompanied by an appropriate ritual, which not seldom takes into account the fact that society was divided into four varṇas.

Information gleaned from the rituals mainly relates to the land of the Kuru-Pañcālas, where the major part of the later Vedic literature was composed.[1] This literature roughly covers the period from *circa* 1000 to *circa* 500 B.C., and presupposes various phases of social development, differing according to the times to which a particular text can be assigned. Thus the collections (Saṃhitās) of the Black school of the *Yajus* are earlier than those of the White school.[2] Of the Brāhmaṇas the *Śatapatha* and the *Aitareya*, which make important statements on the inter-relation between the varṇas, are 'comparatively modern, while the *Pañcaviṃśa* and *Taittirīya* are the most ancient.[3] Even later than the *Śatapatha Brāhmaṇa* and the *Aitareya Brāhmaṇa* is the *Jaiminīya Brāhmaṇa*,[4] and so is the *Kauṣitaki* or *Śāṅkhāyana Brāhmaṇa*.[5] In some cases it is difficult to draw a line between the Śrautasūtras and the Brāhmaṇas; thus the *Baudhāyana Śrautasūtra* may be regarded as a late Brāhmaṇa.[6] The

1. Winternitz, *HIL*, i, 195-6. Keith says that the home of the *Taittirīya* school was the middle country, as was the home of the *Kāṭhaka*, the *Maitrāyaṇi*, and even the *Vājasaneyi* and the *Śatapatha*. *HOS*, xviii, p. XCIII.

2. Weber. *Ind. Lit.*, p. 86.

3. Wackernagel, *Altind. Grammatik*, i, pp. XXX-XXXI; Keith, *HOS*, xxv, 44.

4. Keith, *HOS*, xxv, 46.

5. Winternitz, *HIL*, i, 191.

6. B. K. Ghosh in *VA*, p. 235.

Āpastamba Śrautasūtra seems to be similarly old.[1] In addition to these, the dates of other principal Śrautasūtras (viz. *Āśvalāyana*, *Kātyāyana*, *Śāṅkhāyana* *Lāṭyāyana*, *Drāhyāyaṇa* and *Satyāṣāḍha*) have been fixed between 800 and 400 B.C.[2] Some authorities assign these texts to 400-200 B.C.,[3] but since they explain many rituals mentioned in the Saṃhitās and Brāhmaṇas we have preferred to use them mainly for the study of later Vedic society. However the fact of their overlapping with the Gṛhyasūtras, which we have used for post-Vedic times, cannot be overlooked. At present the number of the Upaniṣads exceeds even two hundred, but only six of them can be ascribed to the pre-Buddhist period.[4] In examining the material from the different strata of later Vedic literature regard has to be paid also to the relative dating of the various parts of individual texts.[5] Moreover, in the later Saṃhitās, and especially in the Brāhmaṇas, we find far more frequent use of optatives than in the *Ṛg Veda* and the *Atharva Veda*.[6] Hence many statements in the later Vedic literature are not in the form of the record of facts that actually occurred, but are to be interpreted as advice and instructions. But occasional evidence for things which may have happened can be culled from the main narrative portion of the *Mahābhārata*, which possibly reflects happenings in the later Vedic period.[7] A good portion of the *Jaya Saṃhitā* or the original epic, consisting of nearly 8000 verses, sounds archaic and can be used for supplementing information obtained from later Vedic texts.[8]

The material background to social developments in later Vedic times is formed by the Painted Grey Ware archaeology.

1. Keith, *HOS*, xviii, p. XI.I.
2. *VA*, p. 476.
3. Louis Ronou & J. Filliozat, *L'Inde classique*, i+ii, quoted in J. Gonda, *The Ritual Sūtras*, pp. 476-77, footnotes.
4. *VA*., p. 467.
5. Here it is not possible to do more than refer to the opinions of generally accepted authorities.
6. Macdonell, *A Vedic Grammar for Students*, p. 118.
7. Cf. *PHAI*, pp. 7-8.
8. The text *Ur-Mahābhārata* or *Jaya Saṃhitā* has been reconstructed by K. K. Shastree by selecting about 8,800 verses out of 78,000 verses found in the Critical Edition.

Both the PGW and the later Vedic texts belong to the same area and period. Hence the PGW evidence can be used for a study of the later Vedic period. 315 PGW sites were reported by 1975,[1] but by now in Haryana alone nearly 300 sites have been noticed.[2] Therefore the total number may have exceeded 500. Consistent carbon 14 dates for several excavated sites suggest that the PGW period roughly covered the period *circa* 1000-500 B.C.[3] They indicate the transformation of the Vedic people from a pastoral and semi-nomadic community into a sedentary and agricultural community. But by and large structures are poor and do not suggest social differentiation. However the use of fine PGW and a few glass objects might indicate the emergence of an upper crust in society. Iron objects appear in the upper Gaṅgā basin for the first time, but they were used mainly for war and did not contribute significantly to crafts and cereal cultivation. We therefore cannot expect much social surplus which would make possible the existence of too many professional priests, warriors, etc., living on the surplus produce and labour of peasants and various types of labourers. The material culture created conditions for the beginnings of social inequality,[4] which became prominent only in post-Vedic times.

Since the śūdras appear in post-Vedic times mainly as the serving class, we will begin the study of their position in the later Vedic period with an inquiry into their economic conditions. In an early reference they are described as being in possession of cattle, which could be taken away by the people of the higher varṇas for sacrifice.[5] This is corroborated by another reference in an early Brāhmaṇa, in which the śūdra is represented as being born without god and sacrifice, but owning

1. Vibha Tripathi, *The Painted Grey Ware*, Appendix I.

2. Based on information about explorations carried out by Dr. Suraj Bhan and his colleagues.

3. B.B. Lal, "Did the Painted Grey Ware continue up to the Mauryan Times ?" (Cyclostyled copy).

4. R.S. Sharma, "The Later Vedic Phase and the Painted Grey Ware Culture." *History and Society : Essays in Honour of Professor Niharranjan Ray,*" pp. 133-41; ibid., "Class Formation and its Material Basis in the Upper Gangetic Basin (*c.* 1000-500 B.C.," *The Indian Historical Review,* ii, 1-13.

5. *MS*, IV.2.7 and 10.

many cattle (*bahupaśuḥ*).[1] It is obvious that such śūdras, as held independent property in cattle, which seem still to have been the chief form of wealth, may not have been under the necessity to serve others.

Nevertheless, there are some references to the functions of the śūdras as a serving class. It is stated in the *Jaiminīya Brāhmaṇa* that the śūdra is created from the feet of Prajāpati without any god, and therefore the lords of the house are his gods and he is to earn his living by washing feet.[2] In other words, according to a later source he has to live by serving people of higher varṇas.[3] The former source further informs us that as a result of the Horse Sacrifice (*aśvamedha*) the nourisher vaiśya becomes wealthy, and the rising śūdra becomes an expert worker.[4] It is not known whether the term *karmakartā* is used here in the sense of hired labourer, a meaning always attached to a similar term *karmakara* in post-Vedic literature.[5] In an early Upaniṣad, however, the śūdra is called Pūṣan or the nourisher,[6] a title (*poṣayiṣṇuḥ*) applied to the vaiśya in the *Jaiminīya Brāhmaṇa*.[7] This would, then, suggest that he was the tiller of the soil,[8] engaged in sustaining and producing activities for the nourishment of society. Probably in the earlier part of this period, like the vaiśyas, he paid part of his produce as tribute, an obligation from which he was freed in post-Vedic times.

But the impression that the śūdras constituted the labouring class is gained from several other references. In the *puruṣamedha* (human sacrifice) a brāhmaṇa is to be sacrificed to the priesthood, a rājanya to the nobility, a vaiśya to the Maruts (the

1. *Pañc. Br.*, VI.1.11.

2. *śūdro' anuṣṭupchandā veśmapatidevas; tasmād u pādāvanejyenaiva jijīviṣati. Jai. Br.*, I. 68-69.

3. *suśrūṣā śūdrasyetareṣām varṇānām. Satyāṣāḍha Śr. Su.*, XXVI. 1-7, but this is not to be found in any other early *Śr. S.*

4. *utthātā śudro dakṣaḥ karmakartā. Jai. Br.*, II, 266. Perhaps there is no parallel for this passage in other Brāhmaṇas.

5. *Karmakara* occurs in *Tai. Br.* III, 11. 10. 3, in the sense of a ṛtvik priest and not as a hired labourer. There seems to be no mention of *karmakara* in other Brāhmaṇas.

6. *Bṛ. Up.*, I. 4.13.

7. II. 266.

8. Mookerji, *AIE*, p. 158.

class of peasants), and a śūdra to toil (*tapase*).[1] It was thought that the śūdra symbolised hard work. In the list of sacrificial victims, members of four varṇas are followed by those of various occupations such as chariot-maker, carpenter, potter, smith, jeweller, herdsman, shepherd, farmer, brewer, fisherman and hunter, in addition to certain peoples such as Niṣāda, Kirāta, Parṇaka, Paulkasa and Bainda,[2] who presumably were included in the broad term of the śūdra.[3] The list, therefore, shows that although the crafts had increased in number, they were no longer practised by the members of the viś. The idea was gaining ground that śūdras included artisans and workers of various kinds.

What was the nature of relations between the śūdra workers and their employers? The authors of the *Vedic Index* say that slaves were certainly included in the term śūdra.[4] But the number of slaves seems to have been very small. We learn of ten thousands of women slaves, captured from various countries and given away by Aṅga to his brāhmaṇa priest Ātreya.[5] The number is obviously exaggerated and conventional. Āruṇi, the father of Śvetaketu, boasts that he possesses gold, cattle, horses, maid-servants (*dāsis*), retinue and dress, but does not speak of men slaves.[6] Tradition has it that the brāhmaṇas received women slaves at the time of the great coronation sacrifice of Yudhiṣṭhira,[7] which may be ascribed to the later Vedic period. Clearly, then, during this period women slaves were owned on a considerable scale by the ruling chiefs and priests, but the same cannot be said of men slaves. The term *dāsa* is mentioned in the *Aitareya* and *Gopatha Brāhmaṇas*[8] but not in the sense of a slave. It is

1. *VS*, XXX. 5; *Śat. Br.*, XIII. 6.2.10; *Tai. Br.*, III. 4.1.1.
2. *VS*, XXX. 6-21; *Tai. Br.*, III. 4. 2.17.
3. *VI*, ii, 267.
4. *Ibid.*
5. *deśād-deśāt samoḷhānāṃ sarvāsām ādhyaduhitṛṇām; daśādadāt sahasrāṇi ātreyo niṣkakaṇṭhyaḥ. Ait. Br.*, VIII. 22. The chapter is a part of the later portion of this work.
6. *Bṛ. Up.*, VI. 2.7. There is no mention of land either.
7. *Mbh.* (Cal.). II. 33.52. Karṇa, the sūta king of Aṅga, is found offering a hundred Māgadhī slave-girls decked and trained in music and similar accomplishments. *Mbh.* (Cal.), VIII. 38.7.18.
8. *Ait. Br.*, VI. 18-19; *Gopatha Br.*, II. 4.2., 6.1.

remarkable that, in the list of words for servants (*paricaraṇakarmāṇaḥ*) given in the *Nighaṇṭu*,[1] there is no mention of *dāsa*, although there occur ten synonyms for servants. Perhaps the number of men slaves was so negligible as not to attract any notice. This would naturally rule out the possibility of male śūdras being employed as slaves on any considerable scale. Therefore Keith's statement, that in the period of the Brāhmaṇas the peasant working in his own fields was being substituted for the landowner cultivating his estate by means of slave labour,[2] may not represent the true state of affairs.

Slaves working on land are first heard of in the Śrautaśūtras, which were composed towards the end of the Vedic period and later. One of them informs us that two slaves are to be given away along with grain, plough and cattle,[3] suggesting thereby that slaves were employed in ploughing and could be freely disposed of by their masters. But in several passages the practice of making gifts of land and of the people working on it is looked upon with disfavour. Thus it is stated that at the *aśvamedha* sacrifice the sacrificial fee could not include land and men working on it (*bhūmipuruṣavarjam*).[4] Again, in connection with the gifts in the one-day (*ekāha*) sacrifice, it is laid down that land and śūdras could not be given away (*bhūmiśūdravarjam*).[5] There is, however, the alternative that sometimes the śūdras could be also given away,[6] but the commentary adds that this can be done only in the case of those who are born slaves.[7] There are two similar references from the *Śāṅkhāyana Śrautasūtra*. One of them says that in the *puruṣamedha* sacrifice land with men is given away as sacrificial fee.[8] One other is not clear, and perhaps suggests that in the sacrifice of all (*sarvamedha*) land is given 'along with' the people.[9] These references indicate a new social development

1. III. 5.
2. *CHI*, i, 128. Cf. Ghoshal, *Historiography and other Essays*, p. 87, fn. 9.
3. ...*dāsamithunau dhānyapālyaṃ sīraṃ dhenuriti*. *Lāṭyā. Śr. S.*, VIII. 4.14.
4. *Āśva Śr. S.*, X. 10.10.
5. *Kā. Śr. S.*, XXII. 10.
6. *śūdradānaṃ vā darśanāvirodhābhyām*. *Ibid.*, XXII. 11.
7. *na ca virodha garbhadāṣasya*. Çomm. to *Kā. Śr. S.*, XXII. 11.
8. *sahapuruṣaṃ ca dīyate*. *Śāṅkh. Śr. S.*, XVI. 14.18.
9. *sahabhūmi ca dīyate*. The comm. adds *sapuruṣaṃ ca*. *Ibid.*, XVI. 15.20.

possibly after the close of the Vedic period. Śūdras were employed as slaves working on lands owned by individuals (mostly ruling chiefs), and they could be given away as gifts along with the land itself, although this did not go without challenge from the authors of the *Āśvalāyana* and *Kātyāyana Śrautasūtras*.

It is held that śūdras were serfs in the Vedic period.[1] The term serf denotes one who is attached to the soil of his master. He owns a patch of land for which he pays taxes to his master and works on his fields, but can be transferred along with the land to other owners. He is allowed to keep his small plot and cultivate it only so long as he works on the much larger plot of his landlord with the result that small plots are attached economically and juridically to larger stretches of land under serfdom. But such a system did not prevail even towards the end of the Vedic period, and hence the interpretation of the word śūdra as serf does not quite suit the relevant references. First, individual ownership of land in the Vedic period was of a very limited nature. Ownership implies free disposal of property, but there are no examples of land grants in the Saṃhitās. There is one such example, however, in the *Chāndogya Upaniṣad*, in which a whole village is granted by the king Jānaśruti to Raikva.[2] Another instance is to be found in two later Brāhmaṇas. They inform us that land could be given away only with the consent of the clan,[3] and even there the earth refused to be transferred.[4] In the earlier period there is no example of śūdras being given away with the land. The development is to be found in some of the Śrautasūtras, but according to a commentary such śūdras appear to be born slaves (*garbhadāsa*)[5] and not serfs attached to the soil. This seems to be confirmed by the fact that in post-Vedic times the śūdras do not appear as peasants paying taxes. In the *vājapeya* ('the drink of strength') sacrifice peasants (viś or vaiśyas) are described as food for the

1. *VI*, ii, 389.
2. IV. 2. 4-5.
3. *Ait. Br.*, VIII. 21; *Śat. Br.*, XIII. 7.1.15.
4. *Ibid.*
5. Comm. to *Kā. Śr. S.*, XXII. 11.

nobility.[1] It is perhaps because of this that the vaiśya is to be afflicted with misery and sin.[2] In the *Aitareya Brāhmaṇa*[3] the vaiśya is described as one paying taxes (*balihṛt*) and oppressed at will (*ajayeyyam*). All this would indicate that the vaiśya had to pay part of their products to the rulers who lived on them. Absence of such a role prescribed for the śūdras shows that they were not supposed to possess any taxable property. In an Upaniṣad Soma is described as eating the kṣatriyas and vaiśyas respectively with his two mouths, the brāhmaṇa and the rājanya.[4] Here the rājanya is represented as paying tributes to the brāhmaṇa, and the vaiśya to the rājanya. As usual the śūdra is left out on the ground of his inability to pay.

It is difficult to define the position of the śūdras in the Vedic period in terms of slavery or serfdom. Although the references found in very late Vedic texts give the impression of their being the labouring masses, generally they do not seem to have been slaves or serfs owned by individuals. Apparently just as the community exercised some sort of general control over land, so also it exercised similar control over the labouring population. And, in this sense, the śūdras may be very roughly compared to the helots of Sparta, with the difference that they were not treated with the same amount of coercion and contempt.

Although in the later Vedic period artisan sections of the viś were reduced to the position of śūdras, there is nothing to show that crafts or agricultural operations in which they were employed were looked upon with contempt. So far as agriculture is concerned, there was a positive attitude of aiding, encouraging and honouring it by applying charms and performing a number of domestic rites.[5] As to the crafts, there is no evidence of contempt even for leather-work.[6] This would

1. *vaiśyo' dyamāno na kṣīyate...brāhmaṇasya ca rājanasya cādyo' dharohi sṛṣṭaḥ. Pañc. Br.*, VI. 1.10; *Śat. Br.*, V. 2.1.17; VIII. 7.1.2, 2.2.
2. *Śat. Br.*, V. 1. 5. 28.
3. VII. 29.
4. *Kauṣītaki Up.*, II. 8-9.
5. *AV*, III. 24, VI. 142; *VS*, IV. 10; *Śat. Br.*, I. 6.1. 1-8.
6. S.K. Das has collected the relevant references. *The Eco. History of Ancient India*, pp. 139-40.

suggest that impurity did not arise from the nature of the task, which remained unchanged even in subsequent times. Significantly enough in the Śrautasūtra a ceremonial act was called *śilpa*,[1] a word which also means craft. The absence of contempt for manual labour during the later Vedic period may be likened to a parallel development in Greece, where during the period from Hesiod to Socrates (*cir*. 800-*cir*. 400 B.C.) public conscience was favourably disposed towards it.[2] Respect for manual labour in the later Vedic period probably lingered from the old simple society in which even the king lent his hand to ploughing. The epic instances of prince Janaka actually ploughing the sacrificial ground and prince Duryodhana being asked to do it may reflect the archaic Vedic society, which still retained much of tribal equality. A survival of princes taking to ploughing is found in the Buddhist ceremony of *vappa-mangala*.[3] Interestingly enough in the ancient society of the Jews the rabbis supported themselves by manual labour and taught that god had commanded mankind not only to rest on the sabbath but also to work on the other six days of the week.[4]

The śūdras seem to have played a correspondingly important part in the political life of the period. In the formative stage of the Indo-Āryan polity they enjoyed a considerable share in the functions of the state. It is striking that they found place in the exalted body of about a dozen 'high functionaries of the state'[5] called *ratnins* (jewel-holders), which may be compared to the council of twelve, an institution of great antiquity among several Indo-European peoples such as the Old Saxons, Frisians, Celts etc.[6] The *ratnins* were so important that on the occasion of the *rājasūya* sacrifice the king had to repair to their houses to perform the ceremonies of offering jewels to various gods.

1. *Āśva. Śr. S.*, VIII. 4.5-8; IX. 10.11, 11.2.
2. *Past and Present*, No. 6, p. 1.
3. *s. v. vappa-maṅgala*, Rhys Davids and Stede, *Pali-English Dictionary*. Even now the ploughing ceremony is annually performed by the Buddhist king of Thailand.
4. Lynn White, Jr., *Medieval Religion and Technology*, p. 319.
5. Jayaswal, *Hindu Polity*, ii, 20.
6. Chadwick, *The Heroic Age*, p. 370.

The list of *ratnins* shows that they included the representatives of all the varṇas.[1] Thus two of the *ratnins*, the *rathakāra* and the *takṣan*, who are mentioned in several texts,[2] belonged to the artisan section of the śūdra varṇa. The fact that all kinds of metals are prescribed as the sacrificial fee[3] in the ceremonies at their homes shows that they owed their importance to their association with metal-working. It has been shown earlier how the king in the *Atharva Veda* tries to secure the aid of the *karmāra* and the *rathakāra*. But in several later texts the place of the *karmāra* is taken by the *takṣan*, who, along with the *rathakāra*, may have been in charge of all the activities connected with metal-working and cart-making, without which the Āryan expansion and settlements farther east and south could not have made any headway. These two *ratnins* are not, however, mentioned in the *Śatapatha Brāhmaṇa*, where their place is taken by the *govikartana* (huntsman) and *pālāgala* (messenger).[4] There are reasons to think that these two were non-āryanised aborigines who were admitted to the śūdra varṇa through rituals. The ceremony of offering jewels is followed by an act of expiation on the part of the king, who is considered guilty of having brought the non-sacrificing śūdras into contact with the sacrifice.[5] Sāyaṇa goes too far when he includes even the *senāni* (commander) among the śūdra *ratnins*.[6] In all likelihood the reference to non-sacrificing śūdras applies only to the

1. Ghoshal, *Historiography and other Essays*, p. 253.
2. ..*takṣarathakārayorgṛhe*. *MS*. II. 6.5; *Āp. Śr. S.*, XVIII. 10.17; *Satyā. Śr. S.*, XIII. 4.8. It is to be noticed that *takṣa* and *rathakāra* are not mentioned in a similar description of *ratnins* in *TS*, I. 8.9. 1-2 and *KS*, XV. 4.
3. *sarvāyasāni dakṣiṇā*. *Ibid.*
4. *Śat. Br.*, V. 3.1. 10-11.
5. *eṣa'etattamaḥ ppraviśattyetaṃ vvā tamaḥ praviśati yadayajñiyāniyojñena pprasajattyayajñiyānnvā' etadyajñena prasajati śūdrānstvadyāṃstu*. *Śat. Br.*, V. 3.2.2-4. The provision for expiation by means of offerings to Soma and Rudra, and Mitra and Bṛhaspati, looks like an attempt to reconcile two opposite views, one earlier and the other later, about the participation of the śūdra in the sacrifice. The king could enter into sacral relations with the śūdra, but the sin arising out of it had to be removed by another rite. It is to be noted that this does not occur in the Black *Yajus* texts or in the other texts of the White *Yajus* (Ghoshal, *Hin. P. L.*, i, 133.)
6. *śūdrān senānyādin*...Comm. to *Śat. Br.*, V. 3.2.2.

pālāgala and the *govikartana*. That the *pālāgala* was a śūdra can be inferred from the fact that the *pālāgalī* is addressed as a śūdra.[1] At another place the term *pālāgala* is defined as false envoy (*anṛtadūta*);[2] the quality here ascribed to the *pālāgala* is always in later times associated with the śūdra.[3] The *govikartana*, who is mentioned as a *ratnin* in several other lists besides that of the *Śatapatha*,[4] is specified as 'of low caste' (*hīnajāti*) by Sāyaṇa.[5] Presumably he was the keeper of game and forests and may have been a śūdra. Keith takes *kṣattṛ*, one of the *ratnins*, in the sense of a carver,[6] which would mean that he also was a śūdra. But this rendering seems to be doubtful, for in the epic *kṣattṛ* means a chamberlain,[7] and there is no special reason for believing that the word was used with a different meaning in the Brāhmaṇas. Among the *ratnins* it is *takṣan* who can be better rendered as a carver. Thus it would appear that in some cases artisans, and in other cases herdsmen and messengers, from the śūdra varṇa were considered important enough to be approached by the king on the occasion of his great coronation sacrifice.

But the position of the śūdra *ratnins* needs further clarification. First, they are not specified by their varṇa name, as is to be found in the case of the brāhmaṇa, the rājanya and the vaiśya *ratnins*.[8] Secondly, in respect of powers, functions and representation the scales may have weighed heavily against the śūdra *ratnins*, whose appearance in political rituals in course of time may have been reduced to a matter of form. The number of the śūdra *ratnins* in individual lists varies from two to three.[9]

1. *Śāṅkh. Śr. S.*, XVI. 4.4; cf. *Śat. Br.*, XIII. 5.2.8.
2. *Āp. Śr. S.* (Garbe's edn.), XVIII.10.26.
3. *Ibid.*, VI. 3.12.
4. *MS*, II. 6.5; *Āp. Śr. S.* (Garbe's edn.), XVIII. 10.20; *Satyā. Śr. S.*, XIII. 4.8.
5. Comm. to *Śat. Br.*, V. 3.2. 2-4.
6. He derives it from *kṣad* to carve. *HOS*, xviii, 120.
7. *s. v.* kṣattṛ, Monier-Williams, *Sansk.-Eng. Dict.* Acc. to Sāyaṇa he is the son of a kṣatriya woman by a śūdra.
8. The list of the *ratnins* in the Saṃhitās and Brāhmaṇas has been compiled by Ghoshal on the page facing p. 249 in *Historiography and other Essays*.
9. In one list (*MS.* II. 6.5; IV. 3.8) their number is three, and in two lists it is two (*KS*, XV 4; *Śat. Br.*, V. 3. 1ff.). It is strange that they are not mentioned in the texts of the Black School of the *Yajus* (*TS*, I.8.9. 1ff; *Tai. Br.*, I. 7.3).

There is nothing to indicate that their presence secured the representation of the whole śūdra varṇa, but certainly some sections of that community could find a place in the polity.

Jayaswal views the ceremony of the offerings of jewels (*ratnahavīṃṣi*) as a great constitutional change inasmuch as the śūdra, "the conquered helot, is now worshipped by the man who is going to become king".[1] This implies that the conquered pre-Āryan masses were deliberately given a high status in the Āryan polity. But it is clear that at least the two artisan *ratnins*, the *rathakāra* and the *takṣan*, owed their positions not to any deliberate policy of exalting the conquered in the Āryan political organization but to their original membership of the Āryan tribes which had now disintegrated into varṇas; for in the *Atharva Veda* the *rathakāra* and *karmāra* (whose place is now taken by the *takṣan*) are clearly described as part of the viś (folk) round the king.[2] Their indispensability as skilled workers in metals and chariot-making may have also contributed to their importance in early society. Nevertheless, it is not unlikely that in the sequel the existence of these śūdra *ratnins* gave some reflected importance to the other sections of the śūdra varṇa.

The śūdra's participation in the political life of the period is further evident from the ritual of the game of dice, which is prescribed as a rite in the *rājasūya* sacrifice and presented to us in two versions. In the earlier version, which occurs in the Black *Yajus* texts, the brāhmaṇa, the rājanya, the vaiśya and the śūdra participate in a game of dice for the sake of cow, which is won by the king.[3] In the later version, which occurs in the White *Yajus* texts, the vaiśya and śūdra are eliminated as candidates in competition for the cow, which is staked by the kinsman (*sajāta*) of the king and won for him by the officiating priest (*adhvaryu*).[4] It appears that this contest for the cow was originally a tribal custom to test the wit and sagacity of the leader. It is, therefore, the old

1. *Hindu Polity*, ii, 21.
2. *AV*, III. 5.6.
3. *tatra paṣṭhauhīṃ vidīvyante brāhmaṇo rājanyo vaiśyaḥ śūdraḥ*. *Vārāha Śr. S.*, III. 3.3.24; *MS.* IV. 4.6; *Āp. Sr. S.* (Garbe's edn.), XVIII. 19. 2-3; *Satyā. Śr. S.*, XIII. 6. 29-30.
4. *VS*, X. 29; *Śat. Br.*, V. 4.4.19-23; *Kā, Śr. S.*, XV. 7.7.11-20.

tradition of tribal solidarity and homogeneity which accounts for the participation of all the varṇas in the game of the dice. But with the passage of time the character of the ritual changed; the vaiśya and the śūdra were excluded from the game. Nevertheless, it is significant that in the earlier period even a śūdra could join as a competitor in a game, which formed one of the preliminaries to the formal consecration of the king.

Again, the śūdra appears in another ceremony of the *rājasūya* sacrifice, in which the sacrificer gives first gold to the brāhmaṇa and purchases splendour with it; then a bow with three arrows to the rājanya and purchases lustre with it; next a goad to the vaiśya with which he purchases nourishment; and finally a pot of beans to the śūdra with which he purchases longevity.[1] Although varṇa distinctions are maintained and śūdras are probably represented as labourers engaged in agriculture, none the less they are brought into contact with the king and are considered capable of conferring longevity on him.

The śūdra is possibly connected with another ceremony of the *rājasūya* sacrifice, in which the newly consecrated king is called on to ascend the four quarters of the sky, when brahma in the east, kṣatra in the south, viś in the west and *phala*, *varcas* and *puṣṭam* in the north are asked to protect him.[2] Jayaswal says that *phala* is evidently a substitute for śūdra.[3] This is not accepted by Ghoshal who takes the ceremony as symbolising the influence of the three higher castes in the Vedic polity.[4] It has been also suggested that *phala* denotes industrial classes.[5] In our opinion the term *phala*, which is used in Vedic literature[6] in its literal sense as meaning 'fruit' and not in its later secondary

1. *KS*, XXXVIII. 1. This passage has no parallel in *VS*, *Kap. S*, *TS* and *MS*, but it occurs in a modified form in *Tai. Br.*, II. 7.9.1. & 2, which mentions the gifts and results but does not bring in the four varṇas. In place of *ojas* it gives *vīryam*. Cf. *Sātyā. Śr. S.*, XXIII. 4.21, in which the passage occurs in connection with the *odanasava* oblation.

2. *phala* and *varcas* in *VS*, X. 10-13; *bala* and *varcas* in *TS*, I. 8.13; *puṣṭam* and *phalam in MS*, II. 6.10; *puṣṭam* and *varcas* in *KS*, XV. 7.

3. *Op. cit.*, ii, 29, fn. 2.

4. *Hist. and Essays*, p. 264.

5. S.V. Venkateswara, *Indian Culture Through the Ages*, pt. I, p. 11.

6. *VI*, ii. 57.

sense as 'result,' may not be unconnected with the producing activities of the śūdra, but the same cannot be said of the term *varcas* which means lustre. As to the word *puṣṭam* (nourishment), it is generally associated with the vaiśyas, but in one passage the śūdra is also called *pūṣan* (nourisher).[1] It may, therefore, be tentatively suggested that the terms *phalam* and *puṣṭam* reflect the producing activities of the śūdra, who is thus indirectly called upon to protect the king in the north.

The *Sabhā Parvan*, which is regarded as one of the earliest portions of the Mahābhārata, tells us that respectable śūdras were invited to the great coronation sacrifice (*rājasūya*) of Yudhiṣṭhira.[2] The contradictory statement that no non-sacrificing śūdra was present on the occasion[3] probably reflects a later attempt to exclude śūdras from political power. At any rate it seems clear that at least some sections of the śūdras participated in the coronations of kings.

According to a passage of the *Yajus* collections of both the schools,[4] on the occasion of the *rājasūya* sacrifice the king established among the viś (people)[5] prays to Sūrya for the expiation of the sin committed against the arya and the śūdra. Relying on Pāṇini[6] the commentators Uvaṭa and Mahīdhara take the word *arya* in the sense of vaiśya.[7] This shows that not even the king was free to oppress the members of the two lower varṇas, a situation entirely different from the one in the *Aitareya Brāhmaṇa*[8] where the vaiśya appears as one to be oppressed, and the śūdra as one to be beaten at the pleasure of the king.

In the *aśvamedha* sacrifice, which was supposed to confer universal sovereignty upon its performer, the śūdras appear as

1. *Br. Up.*, I. 4.13.
2. *viśaśca mānyāñśūdrāṃśca sarvānānayateti ca. Mbh.* II. 30.41.
3. *na tasyāṃ saṃnidhau śūdraḥ kaścidāsanna cāvrataḥ. Mbh.*, II. 33.9.
4. *yadcchūdre yadarye yadenaścakṛmā vayaṃ yadekasyā dhi dharmaṇi tasyāvayajanamasi. VS.* XX. 17 (on the occasion of the *sautrāmaṇi* sacrifice); *TS*, I. 8.3. 1; *KS.* XXXVIII. 5; cf. *Śat. Br.*, XII. 9.2.3.
5. *VS*, XX. 9.
6. *aryaḥ svāmivaiśyayoḥ. Pā.*, III. 1.103.
7. Comm. to *VS*, XX. 17. The *VI* takes it in the sense of *ārya*.
8. VII. 29.

the armed guards of the horse which is sent out on an expedition of world-wide conquest.[1]

That the śūdra could use weapons can also be inferred from an early passage, which states that with the king as helper they slay a king, with the vaiśya a vaiśya, and with the śūdra a śūdra.[2] The traditional account in the *Mahābhārata* refers to a king called Dambhodbhava who used every day to challenge armed soldiers of the kṣatriya, vaiśya and śūdra classes to prove themselves his equal in fighting.[3] While enumerating different leaders and peoples participating in battle, the epic refers to the case of all the four varṇas taking part and thereby gaining righteousness, heaven and glory.[4] Thus the fact that śūdras also acted as soldiers again betrays the influence of the old tribal polity, in which every member could take up arms.

It is to be further noted that the *āyogava*, who is defined by the commentator as a son of a vaiśya woman by a śūdra, is to act as a vigilant dog in the horse sacrifice.[5] Perhaps this refers to the practice of enlisting the aboriginals as watchmen. The *Śatapatha Brāhmaṇa* furnishes the unique case of an *āyogava* king Marutta Āvikṣita performing the *aśvamedha* sacrifice, in which the Maruts act as his body-guards, Agni as his chamberlain, and the All-Gods (Viśvedevas) as his courtiers (*sabhāsadas*).[6] This does not seem to be a case of a śūdra king but probably is an example of a non-brāhmaṇical ruler being assimilated to the brāhmaṇical polity. The definition of *āyogava* does not appear until the Dharmasūtras, and we cannot be sure that Marutta Āvikṣita was a low caste king.

1. *śataṃ śūdrā varūthinaḥ*. *Āp. Śr. S.* (Garbe's edn.), XX. 5.13; cf. *Kā. Śr. S.*, XX. 50. It seems that moved by later bias the *Satyāṣāḍha Śr. S.*, which is a popular version of the *Āp. Śr. S.*, leaves out the *śūdra varūthinaḥ*. *Satyā. Śr. S.*, XIV. 1.46.

2. *tasmād rājñā rājānam aśabhuvā ghnanti vaiśyena vaiśyaṃ śūdreṇa śūdram*. *TS*, VI. 4.8.

3. *asti kaścidviśiṣṭo vā madvidho vā bhavedyudhi; śūdro vaiśyaḥ kṣatriyo vā brāhmano vāpi śastrabhṛt*. *Mbh.*, V. 94.7.

4. *teṣāmantakaraṃ yuddhaṃ dehapāpapraṇāśanaṃ; śūdraviṭkṣatraviprāṇāṃ dharmyaṃ svargyaṃ yaśaskaram*. *Mbh.*, VIII, 32.18. The Cr. Edn. reads *vīrāṇām* in place of *viprāṇām*, but the latter occurs in *MS* T1. 3G and seems to be more suitable.

5. *Kā. Śr. S.*, XX. 37.

6. *Śat. Br.*, XIII. 5.4.6.

It was provided in the *aśvamedha* sacrifice that the house of the *rathakāra* should serve as the resting place for the horse and its guardians.[1] This shows that the *rathakāra* continued to hold his political position in the later ritual of the *aśvamedha* as well.

The *aśvamedha* sacrifice was performed with the object of conquering all the four varṇas, which shows that the ruler felt the necessity of securing the allegiance of all sections of society.[2] The same impression is acquired from another passage, in which on the occasion of the *rājasūya* sacrifice, the priest makes the king successful in gaining splendour, strength, offspring and firm footing, which qualities are respectively associated with the brāhmaṇa, the kṣatriya, the vaiśya and the śūdra.[3] A passage of similar import is to be found in the *Taittirīya Saṃhitā*.[4] According to it the rājanya has to repeat the kindling verses thrice, because in addition to the allegiance of the warrior, he has to secure the obedience of the three other classes of people, namely the brāhmaṇa, the vaiśya and the śūdra. All this shows that the obedience of the śūdra was not taken for granted as in some later sources. That it was found essential for the king to win his support also is evident from a passage of the *Jaiminīya Brāhmaṇa*. It informs us that the Pañcāla prince Darbha Śātānīki was honoured among the brāhmaṇas, the kṣatriyas, the vaiśyas and the śūdras successively through the use of the *gāyatri*, the *triṣṭubh*, the *jagati* and the *anuṣṭubh* metres.[5]

A remarkable passage occurring in all the collections of the *Yajus* contains a prayer to Agni to confer brilliance on 'our' priests, warriors, vaiśyas and śūdras.[6] The context, in which

1. *Śat. Br.*, XIII. 4.2.17; *Āp. Śr. S.* (Garbe's edn.), XX. 5.18; *Kā. Śr. S.*, XX. 55; *Satyā Śr. S.*, XIII. 1.47.

2. *Jai. Br.*, II. 266-67.

3. *Ait. Br.*, VIII. 4.

4. *TS*, III. 5.10. No parallel in other collections of the *Yajus*.

5. *Jai. Br.*, II. 102. The same idea is conveyed by the *Śāṅkh. Śr. S.*, XIV. 33.18-19 in a slightly different form.

6. *rucaṃ viśyeṣu śūdreṣu mayi dhehi rucā rucam.* *TS*, V. 7.6. 4; *VS*, XVIII. 48; *KS*, XL. 13; *MS*, III. 4.8; *TS*, *V*. 7.6. The *Śat. Br.*, IX. 4.2.14 has "*rucaṃ no dhehi brāhmaṇeṣvi' ti*". J. Eggeling thinks that the other three varṇas are understood, and, therefore, in translating the passage notes them in the brackets (*SBE*, xliii, 238). But the text probably furnishes a typical example of brāhmaṇical juggling with the old ritual in the interests of their priestly pretensions.

this passage occurs in the *Vājasaneyi Saṃhitā*, deals with formulas for the performance of the *vasordhārā*, a sort of consecration service of Agni as king. On this occasion the officiating priest (*adhvaryu*) recites formulas meant to bestow all temporal and spiritual blessings on the sacrificer. It is not clear, but may not be improbable, that the ritual is prescribed for the king, who prays to Agni to place lustre in all the varṇas of his subjects including the śudras.

There was no uniformity in the nature and extent of the śūdra's participation in what may be described as rituals of a political character. In some cases the minutiae of ceremonies varied according to varṇa, and naturally the śūdra was given the lowest place; in other cases all the varṇas, including the śūdra, participated in the ceremony in the same manner, and could expect similar blessings. At any rate, compared to rules in the Dharmaśāstras, it is worth notice that in the later Vedic period the śūdras could have some share in political power along with the members of the three higher varṇas.

But there is also the other side of the picture. Already during this period, particularly towards its end, a clear tendency had begun to exclude the śūdra from participating in the communal life. Thus the śūdra could not take part in the sprinkling ceremony on the occasion of the *rājasūya* sacrifices, unlike the members of the three higher varṇas.[1] It has been contended by Jayaswal that the *janya* or the *janya-mitra*, who appears in the texts as the fourth person to sprinkle water on the king, is a śūdra in the sense of a man of hostile tribe.[2] Such an interpretation seems to be without any authority. In our opinion like the *vrātya*, who was not a member of the *vrāta* or the tribal unit, the *janya* was also not a member of the *jana* or the tribal community concerned with the performance of the *rājasūya* or similar sacrifices but the member of an alien tribe who was assimilated into the growing brāhmaṇised society

1. *Śat. Br.*, V. 3.5. 11-14; *Tai. Br.* I. 7.8.7; *Vārāha Śr. S.*, III. 3.2.48.
2. *Hindu Polity*, ii, 25. What Jayaswal further says implies that in later times the śūdra always appears as a participant in the *abhiṣecana* ceremony, but there is nothing to prove this until we come to the coronation rites of the *Agni Purāṇa* (ch. 218. 18-20), a work of early mediaeval period.

through rituals. Whatever be the correct meaning of this term;[1] it is clear that it has nothing to do with the śūdra at any place in literature. It is also stated that on the occasion of the *rājasūya* sacrifice the three higher varṇas could request the king to grant a place for the worship of gods.[2] Although the exclusion of the śūdra would naturally follow from the theory that he was born without gods, it can be also taken to indicate his declining importance in political life.

The *Śatapatha Brāhmaṇa* explains certain rites as establishing the control of the kṣatra (ruling chiefs) over the viś (tribal community).[3] These rites probably suggest the process by which the cultivating kinsmen were compelled to convert their occasional gifts and tributes made over to their chiefs into regular taxes. The śūdra is left out, presumably because the king's control over him is taken for granted and because he is not considered capable of offering any strong resistance. Another passage, which speaks of the brahma and the kṣatra being established among the viś[4] but leaves out the śūdra, conveys a similar idea.

The śūdra was not admitted to the *vājapeya* (drink of strength) sacrifice, which was supposed to increase the strength of the king. According to one text it was open to the brāhmaṇa, kṣatriya and vaiśya,[5] but in other texts even the vaiśya came to be excluded.[6]

There is an indication of the lack of civic status of the śudra in a minor ceremony described in the *Taittirīya Brāhmaṇa*. In explaining a rite of new and full-moon day ceremonies (*darśapūrṇamāsa*) it is argued that the śūdras who are in front of their masters seek their favour, and those who are not capable of making contradictions are to be treated in the same manner

1. For various interpretations see Ghoshal, *Hist.* & *Essays*, pp. 265-66 and S.V. Venkateswara, *op. cit.*, pt. I, 11.

2. *Ait. Br.*, VII. 20.

3. *Śat. Br.*, I. 3.4.15; II. 5.2.6; II. 5.2.27; cf. XII. 7.3.15.

4. *Ibid.*, XI. 2. 7. 16.

5. *Śāṅkh. Śr. S.*, XVI. 17.4 quoted in *VI*, ii, 256.

6. *Vārāha Śr. S.*, III. 1.1.1; Ghoshal, *Hist.* & *Essays*, p. 283. The vaiśya was, however, associated with some of the minor ceremonies of the *vājapeya* sacrifice along with the kṣatriya (*Kāt. Śr.*, *S.*, XIV. 75).

as the śūdras.[1] This would suggest that the śūdras were not expected to speak against their master, and were thought to be completely servile.

An important development in later Vedic polity is the tendency to claim a special position for the brāhmaṇa and the kṣatriya, distinguishing them from the vaiśya and the śūdra. Ghoshal cites a number of examples to show the importance of the brahma and the kṣatra as two dominant forces in society, their mutual antagonism and their close political alliance.[2] Prayers for the protection of the two upper classes are to be found in the Saṃhitās[3] as well as in the Brāhmaṇas.[4] If such references are closely analysed, they seem to yield two results. First, most of them occur in later literature, especially in the *Śatapatha Brāhmaṇa*. Secondly, the earlier references generally point to the combination between the two upper varṇas, but the later do it to the specific exclusion of the vaiśya and the śūdra. Thus the *Śatapatha Brāhmaṇa* clearly states that the brāhmaṇa and the kṣatriya enclose the vaiśya and the śūdra.[5] The same text also states that those who are neither kṣatriya nor purohita (priest) are incomplete.[6] Attention has already been drawn to the exclusion of the vaiśya and the śūdra from the game of dice in the later version of this *rājasūya* rite.[7] In connection with the same coronation sacrifice the *Aitareya Brāhmaṇa* states that the brāhmaṇa precedes the kṣatra but the vaiśyas and the śūdras follow him.[8] Therefore it would appear that the tendency to equate the vaiśya with the śūdra and exclude them from public life is implicit in earlier texts, but becomes explicit and pronounced in later literature.

This review of the role of the śūdra in the public life of the later Vedic period may be closed with an examination of the

1. *Tai. Br.*, III. 3.11.2. with Bhaṭṭabhāskara's comm.
2. *Hin. P.L.*, i, 73-80.
3. *TS*, XVIII. 38-44; *Kāṇva S.*, XX. 2.
4. *Śat. Br.*, III. 5.2.11; III. 6.1.17-18; IX. 4.1.7-8.
5. *Ibid.*, VI. 4.4.12-13.
6. *Ibid.*, VI. 6.3.12-13.
7. *Supra*, p. 57.
8. *viśaṃ caivāsmai tacchaudraṃ ca varṇaṃ anuvartmānau kurvanti. Ait. Br.*, VIII. 4.

Aitareya Brāhmaṇa passage[1], which has been interpreted as indicating an absolutely servile position of the śūdra in the Vedic polity. Such a view is not justified by a close scrutiny of the context and meaning of the crucial passage. It is said that a king named Viśvantara Sauṣadmana performed a sacrifice without the priestly clan of the Śyāparṇas, who were removed from the altar. Their case was taken up by their learned leader Rāma Mārgaveya, who protested against the dismissal of the priests, on the ground that he possessed the knowledge of the food to be taken by the king in lieu of soma on the occasion of the *rājasūya* sacrifice.[2] The passage in question describes in his words the possible results of the various kinds of food to be taken by the king, and in doing so indicates the kind of relation which subsists between the ruling varṇa of the warrior and the three other varṇas. It is said that if the king takes soma, the food of the brāhmaṇa, his progeny will be a brāhmaṇa with all his characteristics. He will be an acceptor of gifts, a drinker of soma, a seeker of livelihood and one to be removed at will (*yathākāmaprayāpyaḥ*).[3] If the king takes curd, the food of the vaiśya, his progeny will be a vaiśya, and will have all the vaiśya's characteristics. He will be tributary to another, eaten by another, and oppressed at will. But we are more concerned with the epithets which describe the position of the śūdra. It is stated that if the king takes water, the food of the śūdra, he will favour the śūdras and his progeny will have all their characteristics.[4] He will be (i) *anyasyapreṣyaḥ*, (ii) *kāmotthāpyaḥ* and (iii) *yathākāmavadhyaḥ*. Keith correctly renders the first epithet as 'the servant of another', although in place of 'servant' 'messenger' would be a more precise rendering. But we cannot accept Keith's translation of the other two epithets. The second epithet *kāmotthāpyaḥ* is rendered by him as one 'to be removed at will[5]

1. VII. 29.
2. *Ait. Br.*, VII. 27-8.
3. Muir, Haug and Weber take the word as active in sense, 'moving at will'. But the verb is clearly used in the passive causative sense (*VI*, ii, 255), which Sāyaṇa recognises.
4. '*atha yadi ataḥ, śūdrāṇāṃ sa bhakṣah; śūdrāvistena bhakṣeṇa jimisyasi, śūdrakalpa te prajāyāmājaniṣyate*. *Ait. Br.*, VIII. 29.
5. *HOS*, xxv, 315.

and by Haug as one 'to be expelled'[1] at the pleasure of the master. On this basis it is said that the śūdra was a tenant-at-will who could be thrown out of his holding at any time.[2] But Sāyaṇa's comment to this term states that the śūdra could be made to work at any time of the day or night whenever the master desired.[3] His interpretation seems to be quite feasible because the plain meaning of the *utthāpana* is the act of causing to get up to rise. In early Sanskrit the sense of expulsion is conveyed by other words such as *nirvāsana*[4] or *niṣkāsana*. The third epithet *yathākāmavadhyaḥ* has been rendered by Keith as 'to be slain at will.'[5] but Sāyaṇa interprets the phrase as meaning that the śūdra could be beaten by the angry master if he went against his will.[6] Sāyaṇa's interpretation is supported by the *Nirukta*, in which, as against three places where *vadha* means to kill,[7] at five places it means to hurt or wound.[8] Haug is, therefore, right when he renders the third epithet 'as to be beaten at pleasure'.[9]

The ready and uncritical acceptance of the false view that according to the *Aitareya Brāhmaṇa* the śūdra could be slain at the plesure of the master[10] led to the natural corollary that in the Vedic period he had no wergeld, which he came to have in the period of the Dharmasūtras, when the relation of simple slavery was being abolished.[11] It is evident that such a view rests on a dubious interpretation of the term *yathākāmavadhyaḥ*. Moreover, although the wergeld (called *vaira* or *vairadeya*) was probably fixed at a hundred cows,[12] there is neither any reference to the variation of this amount according to the varṇa nor

1. *Tr. of Ait. Br.*, p. 485.
2. Ghoshal, *op. cit.*, i, 158.
3. *madhyarātrādau yadākadāciddina icchā bhavati tadānīm ayam uthāpyate.*
4. *Pā.*, II. 4.10.
5. *HOS*, XXV, 315.
6. *vadhyaḥ=kupitena svāminā tāḍyo bhavati icchāmanatikramya.*
7. III, 11; V. 16 and X. 11.
8. III. 9; IX. 15, 16, 18; X. 29.
9. *Tr. of the Ait. Br.*, p. 485.
10. *VI*, ii, 256.
11. Keith, *CHI*, i, 128-9; Dutt. *op. cit.*, p. 166; cf. Ghoshal, *Hin. P. L.*, i, 167.
12. *VI*, ii, 331.

to the denial of this right to any varṇa. There seems also to have been provision of penance for the expiation of the sin of manslaughter (*vairahatyā*) through sacrifice,[1] but this is also kept free from considerations of varṇa. Therefore it would appear that in later Vedic society varṇa distinctions were not so sharp and wide as to degenerate into the acute civic discriminations of the Dharmasūtras, in which the śūdra was entitled to the lowest wergeld of ten cows.

Reverting to the *Aitareya Brāhmaṇa* passage, the meanings which have been suggested for the two epithets applied to the śūdra seem to be plausible. In the whole of Vedic literature there is no parallel passage, which describes the śūdra as one to be expelled and slain at the will of the master.

Whether the alternative meanings suggested above represent the true state of affairs is difficult to determine. This is because Book VII of the *Aitareya Brāhmaṇa*, in which the passage in question occurs, is a later part.[2] It would not be surprising if some of the epithets here applied to the various varṇas were used by a discarded priest to ingratiate himself into the favour of his patron king. It is not without significance that even a brāhmaṇa is described as one to be removed at will. In such a case the position of other varṇas can be well imagined.

All these considerations, however, in no way disprove the low status of the śūdra in later Vedic polity. Our object is to define it as precisely as we can. And it is abundantly clear that while the śūdra was associated with several ceremonies of the two important sacrifices of political nature, the *aśvamedha* and the *rājasūya*, there had already begun, possibly towards the end of the Vedic period, a definite tendency to exclude him from rituals connected with political life. In some cases the vaiśya was also condemned to the position of the śūdra and deprived of his old rights. But if we rely on the *Aitareya Brāhmaṇa* passage and place it around the middle of the first millennium B.C., it would appear that by that time society in the upper

1. *Tai. Br.*, I. 5.9.5-6; cf. III. 4.1.7.
2. Keith, *HOS*, XXV, 29; cf. *VI*, ii, 256.

Gaṅgā basin had become class-divided, and although the vaiśyas and śūdras formed the two lower orders, their respective positions were sharply defined. The vaiśyas represented the peasants, for PGW sites producing rice and other cereals, suggest numerous rural settlements. They were expected to pay regular tithes, and hence are described as those who were meant to be eaten and extorted for the collection of tribute by the kṣatra; on the other hand the śūdras had emerged as a class of domestics for serving the upper and controlling classes.

Ritual literature can be also made to yield some information on the social conditions of the śūdra. A passage of the *Yajus* collections states that the vaiśyās and the śūdras were created together.[1] This runs counter to the *Puruṣasūkta* version, in which the vaiśya precedes the śūdra in the order of creation, with the result that the latter is assigned the lowest place in society. But the tendency to put the vaiśya and the śūdra in the same social category is noticeable in some rites, which show that a vaiśya can be the husband of a śūdra woman and *vice versa.*[2] It is ironically stated that the *arya* husband of a śūdra woman does not seek prosperity, the idea being that such a marriage condemns him to a life of prolonged penury.[3] The commentators take the term *arya* (with short initial vowel) in the sense of vaiśya,[4] which provides evidence of marriage between the vaiśya and tne śūdra woman; but the authors of the *Vedic Index* regard these references as instances of illicit union between the ārya and the śūdra[5]. In most cases the reading is *arya,* and therefore the interpretation of the commentators seems to be right. The reading *arya* is also accepted by J. Eggeling in his translation of the *Śatapatha Brāhmaṇa,*[6] where he rightly renders it as vaiśya. But it is not beyond all possibility that the texts may have been tampered with to suit new situations, when

1. *VS,* XIV. 30; *MS,* II. 8.6; *KS,* XVII. 5; *Kaṭ. S.,* XXVI. 24; *TS,* IV. 3.10.2.
2. *Śat. Br.,* XIII. 2.9.8; *Tai. Br.,* III. 9.7.3; *VS,* XXIII. 30-31.
3. *śūdrā yadaryajārā na poṣāya dhanāyati. VS,* XXIII. 30; *MS.* III. 13·1 *TS,* VII. 4-19. 13; *KS* (Aśvamedha), V. 4.8; *Śāṅkh Śr. S.,* XVI. 4.4-6.
4. Comms. of Mahīdhara and Uvaṭa to *VS,* XXIII. 30.
5. *VI,* ii, 391.
6. *SBE,* xliv, 326.

marriage between the members of the higher varṇas and the śūdra was looked upon with disfavour. On the basis of such an assumption it is possible to think of free marital relations between the Āryan and the Śūdra tribes or the people who came to be included in the śūdra varṇa. Later such relations came to be confined to the two lower varṇas.

In the Brāhmaṇas priests and nobles seem to have been free to intermarry with the lower classes, including the śūdra, as the cases of Vatsa and Kavaṣa indicate.[1] Vatsa was called a *śūdra-putra* by his brother Medhātithi, which shows that this was probably not used as a term of abuse.[2] It is said that Vatsa proved his brāhmaṇahood by walking through the fire unscathed and thus wiped out this reproach. This case shows that the social rank of a person was not determined by his birth but by his worth.[3] The case of Kavaṣa Ailūṣa being born of a dāsī seems to be doubtful. The epithet *dāsyāḥ putraḥ* applied to him is regarded by Sāyaṇa as a term of abuse.[4] The *Pañcaviṃśa Brāhmaṇa*[5] provides an instance of the legal marriage of the slave girl Uśij, the mother of ṛsi Dīrghatamas, if we may adopt her description given in the *Bṛhaddevatā*.[6] The Purāṇic traditions inform us that Kakṣīvat, a *brahmavādin*, was the son of Dīrghatamas by a śūdra maid-servant of King Bali,[7] and in the epic he is mentioned as being of śūdra birth (*śūdra-yoni*).[8] It has been pointed out that Mahīdāsa, the author of the *Aitareya Brāhmaṇa*, was a śūdra.[9] There is nothing to support this view unless his surname *Aitareya* be interpreted as his being the son of *Itarā*[10], which means vile, low or rejected, but this seems to be too far-fetched. In a late Brāhmaṇa Sudākṣiṇa Kṣaimi, a seer and priest, is addressed as a śūdra,[11] but there are no

1. Keith, *CHI*, i, 126.
2. *Pañc. Br.*, XIV, 6.6.
3. *Ibid.*
4. *Ait. Br.*, VII. 19 with Sāyaṇa's comm.
5. *Pañc. Br.*, XIV. 11.17.
6. *VI*, ii, 259; *Bṛhaddevatā*, IV. 24-25.
7. *Vāyu P.*, ii, 37.67-94.
8. *Ādi Parvan*, 98.25.
9. Mookerji, *Ancient Indian Education*, p. 52.
10. According to Sāyaṇa, *VI*, i, 121-122.
11. *Jai. Up. Br.*, II. 2.5-6.

particulars about his parentage, except that he was a descendant of Kṣema, and possibly in his case this epithet is used as a term of abuse. About a dozen ṛṣis, whose mothers belonged to what may be regarded as the one or the other section of the śūdrā varṇa, are enumerated in the *Bhaviṣya Purāṇa*.[1] With minor modifications the list recurs in several other Purāṇas and the *Mahābhārata*.[2] It informs us that Vyāsa was born of a fisherwoman, Parāśara of a śvapāka woman. Kapiñjalāda of a caṇḍāla woman, Vasiṣṭha of a prostitute (*gaṇikā*), and the best of sages (*muniśreṣṭha*) Madanapāla was the child of a boatwoman. As a justification for this kind of list, it is said at the end that the origins of the ṛṣis, rivers, pious people, great souls and of the bad character of woman cannot be discovered.[3] Nothing definite can be said about the chronological position of these ṛṣis or of their actual existence, but such a list testifies to the practice of priests and ṛṣis marrying śūdra or slave women probably during the later Vedic period. It seems that kings and chiefs too married śūdra women. The *pālāgali*, who was the fourth and the least respected wife of the king, was a śūdra.[4]

The above mentioned examples show that marriage between people of higher varṇas and śūdra women was not discountenanced.[5] Probably in the beginning the Vedic Indians and the aborigines married within their respective tribes.[6] Even when tribes disintegrated, and their members were divided among the four varṇas, the old practice may have continued for a time. But already during the later Vedic period varṇa distinctions had become so strong as not to permit marriage between the male members of the lower classes and the females of higher classes. There had begun also the tendency to look upon the śūdra woman as an object of pleasure for men of the higher varṇas. Thus in a comparatively

1. *I.* 42. 22-26.
2. *Anuśāsana P.* (Kumb. edn.), 53.13-19.
3. *Ibid.*, 53.38.
4. *Śāṅkh. Śr. S.*, XVI. 4.4.
5. Cf. Ghurye, *op. cit.*, p. 51.
6. *CHI*, i, 129.

later Brāhmaṇa the *anuṣṭubh* metre is compared to a śūdra harlot fit for being approached.[1]

During this period we also find traces of contempt for the caṇḍāla. It is stated that those who are of good conduct will attain good rebirth as a brāhmaṇa, a kṣatriya or a vaiśya; but those who are of bad conduct will enter the stinking womb of a dog, swine or caṇḍāla.[2] It is to be noted that, unlike the case of the caṇḍāla, birth in the śūdra varṇa is not described as impure (*kapūyām*), though it seems to have been looked upon as undesirable. It further appears that the caṇḍālas, who were an aboriginal tribe,[3] were coming to be regarded as of reprehensible conduct. But in the early texts of this period the caṇḍāla appears as a victim in the *puruṣamedha* sacrifice,[4] which gives no indication of his being untouchable. The Paulkasa, however, was associated with loathsomeness.[5]

In the social ethics of the period under review certain bad qualities had come to be associated with the śūdra. We find Śunaḥśepa of the Āṅgiras clan condemning his father Ajīgarta as a śūdra, because he had sold him for three hundred cows as an object of sacrifice to Varuṇa.[6] Though the son was released by the god and the father gave him a hundred cows to blot out his stain, Śunaḥśepa rebuked him in harsh words. As he said, "...thou art still not free from the brutality of a śūdra, for thou hast committed a crime for which no reconciliation exists".[7] This would suggest that, like Ajīgarta, in time of hunger the śūdras were prepared to part with their children. It was thought that for the sake of material gains they could be brutal and callous towards their near and dear ones.

It is interesting to note further that when Śunaḥśepa was adopted as a son by Viśvāmitra and given the first rank among

1. *Sāṅkh. Br.* XXVII. 1. This Brāhmaṇa is considered to be of later origin than the *Śatapatha* and *Aitareya Brāhmaṇas*.

2. *Chā. Up.*, VI. 10.7.

3. It seems that Triśaṅka, who is described as dark in complexion, was probably the leader of the Caṇḍāla tribe. *Rāmāyaṇa*, I. 58. 10-11.

4. *VS*, XXX. 21; *Tai. Br.*, III. 4.1-17.

5. *VS*, XXX. 17; *Tai Br.*, III. 4-1.14.

6. *Ait. Br.*, VII, 15-17; *Śāṅkh. Śr. S.*, XV, 24.

7. *nāpāgaḥ śaudrān nyāyād asaṃdheyaṃ tvayā kṛtaṃ Ait. Br.*, VII. 17.

his hundred sons, with the right of primogeniture, the fifty older sons refused to accept this position. This infuriated the father, who cursed them to have descendants of lower castes, such as those of the Andhras, Puṇḍras, Śabaras, Pulindas, Mutibas, Dasyus and *antas* (outcastes).[1] While this account provides an early example of the priestly ingenuity in the invention of genealogies for non-Āryan peoples in order to assimilate them to the lower ranks of brāhmaṇical society, it also shows that recalcitrant and disobedient sons were regarded as Dasyus and *antas*. In his commentary to this passage Sāyaṇa also includes caṇḍālas and other low castes, but they are not mentioned in the text.[2]

In one of the supplementary formulae of the *Vājasaneyi Saṃhitā*, to be used in connection with various seasonal and domestic sacrifices, a desire is expressed for talking *kalyāṇivak* to the member of all the varṇas.[3] It is contended that this refers to the equal right of all classes to the study of the Veda.[4] But the term *kālyāṇivāk* does not stand for the Veda. The commentators are right when they take it in the sense of kind and courteous speech.[5] It would imply that nice words were to be used in talking to the members of all the varṇas. A distinction, however, appears in the *Śatapatha Brāhmaṇa*, where, in the instructions for the performance of a certain ceremony, modes of address vary according to the varṇas. Thus the terms 'come hither' (*ehi*), 'approach' (*āgahi*), 'hasten hither' (*adrava*) and 'run hither' (*ādhāva*) are respectively used in calling the preparer of the offerings (*haviṣkṛt*) from the brāhmaṇa, the rājanyabandhu, the vaiśya and the śūdra varṇas.[6] Such discriminations are frequently noticed in the social intercourse of post-Vedic times.

Of the four stages of life (*āśramas*), which appear at the end of the Vedic period, only the life of the householder is prescribed for the śūdra in later times, but there is no reference to such

1. *Ait. Br.*, VII. 18.
2. *caṇḍālādir ūpānnīcajātiviśeṣān*. Comm. to *Ait. Br.*, VII. 18.
3. *yathemāṃ vācaṃ kalyāṇīmāvadāni janebhyaḥ; brahma rājanyābhyāṃ śūdrāya cāryāya ca svāya cāraṇāya ca. VS*, XXVI. 2.
4. Mookerji, *AIE*, p. 53.
5. Uvaṭa and Mahīdhara's comm. to *VS*, XXVI. 2.
6. *Śat. Br.*, I. 1.4.12.

a distinction during this period. Although the four *āśramas* are mentioned in the *Chāndogya Upaniṣad*, there is no reference to their connection with the varṇas.[1] This brings us to the question of the education of the śūdra, for, according to later texts, he cannot be admitted to the stage of studentship (*brahmacarya āśrama*), which begins with the ceremony of the *upanayana*. The earliest mention of the *upanayana* is to be found in the *Atharva Veda*, where the youth is initiated (*upa-ni*) into a new life by the teacher, for he is supposed to be born from his belly.[2] The initiate becomes a *brahmacārin*, but there is nothing to indicate his varṇa. On the basis of Āruṇi's exhortation to his son Śvetaketu that he ought to pass through the *brahmacarya* it has been held that for a long time the *upanayana* was confined only to priestly or literary families, from whom it was extended to the whole brāhmaṇa class and then finally to all the Āryans.[3] This may be true if the *upanayana* be taken as the starting point of literate learning, since in ancient societies education was generally in the hands of the priests. The fact that the *brahmacārin* was normally a brāhmaṇa is known for several sources.[4] But this does not seem to be true of the *upanayana* and the *brahmacarya* if they are taken as signifying the beginning of a new life by a person on his formal admission as a full-fledged adult member of the tribe. Such an interpretation can be put on the tradition that gods, men and demons spent their *brahmacarya* period under the guidance of their father Prajāpati, who was their teacher.[5] This cannot be taken to mean that literate learning was widespread among the early peoples, but can only suggest that some form of initiation into the life of the community was a universal practice among the Vedic Indians or their ancestors — a fact which is supported by the prevalence of similar practices among primitive peoples. The rite of

1. *Chā. Up.*, II. 23 1-2. A recent writer argues that the theory of the four *āśramas* was not pre-Buddhistic. G. C. Pande, *The Origins of Buddhism*, pp. 322-23.
2. *AV*, XI. 5.3.
3. Altekar, *Education in Ancient India*, p. 10.
4. *TS*, VI. 3.10; *Gopatha Br.*, I 2.2 and 4; *Śat. Br.*, XI. 54.12.
5. *Bṛ. Up.*, V. 2.1.

initiation was also extended to the Vrātyas, who were admitted into Āryan society through the acquisition of *brahmacarya.*[1]

It is significant that a practice of initiation similar to the *upanayana* also prevailed among the early Iranians. Speaking of the practice of the initation of the male and female Iranians by means of the investiture with a sacred thread at the age of fifteen, which marked their admission into the community of the followers of Ahura Mazda,[2] Geiger says that it was an ancient custom which was modified and developed in later times.[3] That the institution of initiation prevailed among the Spartans is also well known.[4] Hence we may suppose that initiation was practised among the Vedic Indians as well. As such in the beginning the śūdra members of the disintegrated Āryan tribes may have continued to perform the initiation rites of the *upanayana* and the *brahmacarya* in the same manner as they performed several other rituals. The Saṃhitās and Brāhmaṇas do not refer to the śūdra's exclusion from the rite of the *upanayana.*

The *Chāngdoya Upaniṣad* informs us that Jānaśruti, who was instructed in the knowledge of life (*prāṇa*) and air (*vāyu*) by Raikva, was a śūdra.[5] But elsewhere he appears as the chief of a people called Mahāvṛṣas,[6] who lived in the north-west. He was dubbed a śūdra either because of his association with the people of the śūdra tribe who also lived in the same region, or because of the defamatory use of this term[7] for those who lay outside the pale of brāhmaṇical society.

Jānaśruti may not have been a śūdra, but there are other indications to show that the śūdra was not completely debarred from acquiring certain kinds of knowledge. Thus it is stated in

1. *AV*, XI.5, XV; *Pañc. Br.*, XVII. 1.2. Bloomfield thinks that the converted Vrātya is exalted as a type of the perfect *brahmacārin. The Atharvaveda*, p. 94.

2. *Vendīdād*, XVIII, 9 and 54.9; Spiegel, *Altiranischeskunde*, iii, 700. cf. 548-9.

3. *Civilization of the Eastern Iraniams in Ancient Times*, i, 58-9.

4. Thomson, *Studies in Ancient Greek Society*, i, 272.

5. *Chā. Up.*, IV. 1.1-8, 3.1-4.

6. *Jai. Br.*, III, 7.3.2. Also called *Nagarin Jānaśruteyaḥ* in *Jai. Up. Br.*, III. 7.3.2. Aupavi Jānaśruteya performed the *vājapeya* ceremony (*Śat. Br.* V. 1.1.5 and 7.

7. Winternitz, *HIL*, i, 229, fn. 3.

the *Taittirīya Brāhmaṇa* that the vaiśya was born of the *Ṛg Veda*, the kṣatriya of the *Yajur Veda*, and the brāhmaṇa of the *Sāma Veda.*[1] This obviously implies that the *Atharva Veda* was meant for the śūdra — a provision which is later vaguely repeated in the *Āpastamba Dharmasūtra*. It means that the śūdra was excluded from the acquisition of the orthodox Vedic knowledge but not of the other forms of knowledge. This impression is also acquired from several passages of the *Śatapatha Brāhmaṇa*. They inform us that the priest could instruct snake-charmers, usurers, fishermen, bird-catchers, Selagas, Niṣādas, Asuras and Gandharvas, many of whom seem to have belonged to the śūdra varṇa.[2] The subjects taught are the *Itihāsa*, the *Atharva Veda*, the art of snake-charming (*sarpavidyā*) and demonology (*devajana-vidyā*).[3] The list of students and subjects suggest that during the early period the priests did not keep themselves aloof from the practice of arts and crafts, which came to be included within the scope of activities assigned to the śūdra varṇa. But it is not clear whether such instruction was accompanied by the imparting of literate learning to the śūdras.

Towards the end of Vedic period we notice the tendency to exclude the śūdra from the *upanayana* and consequently from education. Such an idea is possibly conveyed by a passage of the *Chāndogya Upaniṣad*, where a famous student claims to have been the glory of the brāhmaṇa, the rājan, and the vaiśya.[4] But at another place the learner wishes to be popular with every section of the people including the śūdra.[5] The first clear exclusion of the śūdra is found in a late Śrautasūtra, which lays down seasons for the *upanayana* of the three higher varṇas.[6] It clearly states that the *upanayana*, the study of the Veda and the establishment of fire can bear fruit only in the case of those who are not śūdras and do not indulge in wicked activities.[7] Another text provides that the initiated student (*upanita*) should not talk to

1. *Tai. Br.*, III. 12.9.2.
2. *Śat. Br.*, XIII. 4.3.7-13.
3. *Ibid.*, cf. *Chā. Up.*, VII. 1.1.
4. *Chā. Up.*, VIII. 14.1.
5. *Satyā Śr. S.*, XIX. 3.26.
6. *Ibid.*, XIX, 1.4; XXVI. 1.20.
7. *Ibid.*, XXVI. 1.6.

a śūdra.[1] It is further prescribed that the śūdra should wash the feet of the student who has completed his course (*snātaka*) in a ceremony known as the offering of honey (*madhuparka*).[2] It is difficult to say whether these references from the two Śrautasūtras indicate conditions in the later Vedic period. They may be assigned to the very end of that period, and perhaps even to post-Vedic times, for one of the earliest Gṛhyasūtras, contemporaneous with the early Śrautasūtras, makes it clear that the *rathakāra* was entitled to the *upanayana.*[3]

It seems, then, that in the beginning the *upanayana* was an affair of the whole tribe and its every member had to undergo initiation; but as the tribe disintegrated into classes, it became a prerogative, a honorofic distinction to be attained by means of wealth and high social position, which gave the initiated access to more or less exclusive, often secret societies[4]. Just as in Iran it was denied to the Hūiti class,[5] so also in India it was denied to the śūdra varṇa. Following Senart's view that clan exogamy and tribe endogamy later developed into the features of the caste system, it may well be argued that tribal initiation was transformed into the *upanayana* of the three higher varṇas, with the result that it helped to bring about the social degradation of the śūdra.

Although the loss of the *upanayana* led to the denial of education to the śūdra, perhaps it did not matter much in the period which we consider. We are still in doubt as to the precise nature of education during the later Vedic period, and there is no direct proof that writing prevailed at that stage.[6] It is likely that even the kṣatriya and the vaiśya "performed their duties towards the Veda in a very perfunctory way, if at all".[7] A later text shows that ordinarily the student made only a token

1. *Drāhā. Śr. S.*, VII. 3.14.
2. *Satyā. Śr. S.*, XIX. 4.13.
3. *Bau. Gṛ. S.*, II. 5.6.
4. Gheld, *Ethnology of the Mahābhārata*, pp. 241-42.
5. Senart, *Caste in India*, p. 118.
6. In recent excavations at Hastināpura several needle-like pointed tools have been discovered in the phase of occupation ascribed to 1100-800 B.C., but it is not certain that they were used for writing. *AI, No.* 10-11, 14.
7. Hopkins quoted in Mookerji, *AIE*, pp. 339-40.

performance of his Vedic studies,[1] and education may have been primarily the concern of the brāhmaṇa. But the *upanayana* indicated something more than a right to education. It came to signify the higher social status of those who were entitled to this ritual.

Tho śūdra was not admitted to the *upanayana*, on the ground that it was a Vedic ritual. But the religious life of Vedic times shows that certain sections of the śūdras were not always excluded from Vedic rituals. Many texts provide for the establishment of fire for sacrifice by the *rathakāra*,[2] who could perform it in the rainy season.[3] He occupies the fourth place in the list after the brāhmaṇa, the kṣatriya and the vaiśya. In the *Āśvalāyana Śrautasūtra* the place of the *rathakāra* is taken by the *upakruṣṭa*. This term literally means a person scolded at or chid, but, according to the commentator, it stands for a carpenter (*takṣaka*).[4] This would suggest that although the carpenters were reviled, they continued to perform the sacrifice. Another person, who enjoyed the right to the Vedic sacrifice, was the chief of the Niṣādas (*niṣāda-sthapati*).[5] But his sacrifice was meant for the pacification of animals through the worship of Rudra-Paśupati.[6] In a similar reference at another place only the Niṣāda is mentioned.[7] But the commentator says that it refers to the Niṣāda chief (*sthapati*), and adds that in the *Āpastamba Śrautasūtra* he is a *traivarṇika* (of the first three varṇas).[8] In the *Mahābhārata* also the head of the

1. *Śāṅkh. Gṛ. S.*, II. 7.21.25.

2. *Tai. Br.*, I. 1.4.8; *Āp. Śr. S.* (Garbe's edn.), V. 11.7; *Kā. Śr. S.*, I. 9; *Satyā. Śr. S.*, III. 1; *Vārāha Śr. S.*, I. 1.1.4.

3. *Āp. Śr. S.* (Caland's and Garbe's edn.), V. 3.19; *Kā. Śr. S.*, IV. 179-81; *Satyā. Śr. S.*, III. 2; *Vārāha Śr. S.*, I 4.1.1; *Vaikhā. Śr. S.*, I. 1; cf. *Āśva. Śr. S.*, II. 1.13.

4. *takṣakakarmopajīvyupakruṣṭa ityucyate. Āśva. Śr. S.*, II. 1.13. with the comm. of Nārāyaṇa.

5. *Āp. Śr. S.* (Garbe's edn.), IX. 14.12; *Satyā. Śr. S.*, XV. 4.20; *Vārāha. Śr. S.*, I. 1.1.5; cf. *Kā. Śr. S.*, I. 12.

6. *Āp. Śr. S.* (Garbe's edn.), IX. 14.11; *Satyā. Śr. S.*, XV. 4-19; *Vārāha Śr. S.*, I. 1.1.5.

7. *Satyā. Śr. S.*, III. 1.

8. Comm. to *Satyā. Śr. S.*, III. 1.

Niṣādas (*niṣādādhipati*) is said to have performed sacrifices.[1] A passage of the *Rg Veda* refers to the participation of 'five peoples' (*pañcajanāḥ*) in the sacrifice.[2] The *Nirukta* explains the term *pañcajanāḥ* as meaning the four varṇas and the *Niṣādas*.[3] This cannot be taken as applying to the period of the *Ṛg Veda*, as is sometimes done.[4] Neither does the word *niṣāda* occur in the *Ṛg Veda* nor is the existence of the four varṇas a well-established fact there. Obviously the term *pañcajanāḥ* refers to the *Ṛg Veda* tribes, whose members offered sacrifices without any distinction. Yāska's interpretation, however, shows that in his time the śūdras as well as the Niṣādas, who came to be specified in the Dharmasūtras as a mixed caste born of a brāhmaṇa and a śūdra woman, could take part in the sacrifice. Thus the references prove that occasionally the Niṣāda people and generally the Niṣāda chief enjoyed the right to the Vedic sacrifice. It was laid down that in the *viśvajit* sacrifice the sacrificer would have to stay for three nights with the Nisāda as well as with a vaiśya and rajanya.[5] This shows that the Niṣāda people were indirectly associated with this sacrifice.

Of the two categories of people enjoying the right to sacrifice, it is clear that the *rathakāra* or the *takṣaka* was a member of the Āryan community, but the Niṣādas seem to have been a non-Āryan people living in their own villages.[6] There are several references to the black colour of the Niṣāda people in the *Mahābhārata* and the *Viṣṇu Purāṇa*.[7] Probably as a step in their brāhmaṇisation, the Niṣādas as a tribe were allowed to carry on their own sacrifice in the Vedic way, which privilege later came to be confined only to their chief. Thus it is evident that right up to the end of the Vedic

1. *MBh.*, I. 61.48.
2. *RV*, X. 53-4.
3. *Nir.*, III. 8. Aupamanyava takes the term *niṣāda* as *niṣāda-sthapati*. Skandasvāmī and Maheśvara on *Nir.*, III. 8.
4. Mookerji, *AIE*, pp. 52-53.
5. ...*niṣādeṣu haiva tā vased*...*vaiśye vā ha tā bhrātṛyvye vā vased*...*rājoni haiva tā vased*. *Jai. Br.*, II. 184; *Pañc. Br.*, XVI. 6.7; *Kauṣitakī Br.*, XXV. 15; *Āp. Śr. S.* (Garbe's edn.), XVII. 26. 18; *Lāṭyā. Śr., S.*, VIII.2.8.
6. There is a reference to the Niṣāda-grāma is the comm. to the *Lāṭyā. Śr. S.*, VIII. 2.8.
7. Quoted in Shafer, *Ethnography of Ancient India*, p. 10.

period the right of sacrifice was enjoyed by the *rathakāra* and the Niṣādas, who fell under the category of śūdras. What is more important, Yāska's interpretation of the term *pañcajanāḥ* would show that in his opinion the whole śūdra varṇa enjoyed this right.

There is specific mention of the participation of the śūdra in several religious rites. He could take part in the preparation of the offerings (*haviṣ*) for the god along with the members of the three varṇas, although the mode of address employed for him reflects his lowest place in that rite.[1] Similarly along with the members of other varṇas he could drink soma, and had to undergo atonement in case of vomiting.[2] Referring to the case of the *dāsi-putra* Kavaṣa Ailūṣa Hopkins points out that the śūdrā's son shares the sacrifice and the śūdra drinks soma in one of the half-brāhmaṇical, half-popular festivals.[3] It is curious to note that a passage from the *Kāṭhaka Saṃhitā* does not permit śūdras and women to drink soma.[4] This is, however, not found in other collections of the *Yajus*, and hence seems to be either an interpolation or at best the view of the Kāṭhaka school.

The śūdra also participated in two other minor rites. He could take part in the rite of offering prepared food (*odanasava*) like the members of the other three varṇas, the condition being that food varied according to the varṇa.[5] Similarly the rite of offering first fruits could be performed by the members of all the varṇas.[6]

The śūdra's part in the solstice ritual known as the *Mahāvrata* furnishes important evidence of his participation in the religious life of the period. According to it the śūdra stays outside the *vedi* and the ārya stays inside. They fight over the

1. *Śat. Br.*, I. 1.4.11-12; *Āp. Śr. S.* (Caland's edn.), I. 19.9.

2. *cattvaro vai varṇāh. brāhmaṇo rājanyo vaiśyaḥ śūdro na haiteṣāmekaśccana bhavati yaḥ somaṃ vamati, sa yat haiteṣāmekaśccittsyāttsyāddhaiva prāyaścittiḥ. Śat. Br.*, V. 5.4.9.

3. *Ait. Br.*, II. 19; Hopkins, *Religions of India* p. 477.

4. *KS*, XI. 10.

5. *ājyamanthaṃ brāhmaṇaḥ payomanthaṃ rājanyo dadhimanthaṃ vaiśya udmanthaṃ śūdraḥ. Satyā. Śr. S.*, XXIII. 4-17. The passage suggests the comparative poverty of the śūdras.

6. *Āśva. Śr. S.*, II. 9.7.

possession of hide, and the victory goes to the ārya.[1] In some texts the śūdra varṇa and the ārya varṇa are distinctly mentioned.[2] Where the reading is *arya*, it means vaiśya;[3] on the other hand where it is *ārya* it means a member of the first three varṇas. In some text the place of the ārya is taken by the brāhmaṇa,[4] who appears as the opponent of the śūdra, a feature which becomes common in post-Vedic times. Another Vedic passage, in which the two come in for special notice, states that neither a brāhmana nor a śūdra can be offered as sacrifice to Prajāpati.[5] The passage which occurs in the later portion of the *Vājasaneyi Saṃhitā*, probably indicates that while the brāhṃaṇa is too high for the purpose, the śūdras is too low.

As to the significance of the *Mahāvrata* ceremony, it possibly preserves the memory of fights for cattle both among the Āryans themselves and between Āryans and non-Aryans, who were reduced to the position of śūdras. The *Śāṅkhāyana Śrautasūtra* states that this antiquated and obsolete custom ought not to be performed.[6] This would show that the śūdra could enter into sacral relations with members of the higher varṇas in an old ritual such as the *mahāvrata*, but ceased to do so when such rituals went out of vogue.

The śūdra also had his place in the funeral rituals of the later Vedic period. It was laid down that the śūdra could have his sepulchral mound, though it would be only as high as the knee, the height varying according to the varṇa[7]

The śūdras are described as having and worshipping gods like any other class of the community. In the *Bṛhadāraṇyaka Upaniṣad* the śūdra is called Pūṣan, which suggests that this god is assigned to him.[8] Similarly in the mythology of the *Mahābhārata* the

1. *śūdrāryaur carmmaṇi parimaṇḍale vyāyacchete. jayatyāryaḥ. Kā. Śr. S.*, XIII. 40-41; *Pañc. Br.*, V. 5.14; *Satyā. Śr. S.*, XVI. 6.28.
2. *Jai. Br.*, II. 404-5. The term *ārya varṇa* occurs in *KS.*, XXXIV. 5, but there is no mention of śūdra varṇa.
3. *Śāṅkh. Śr. S.*, XVII. 6. 1-2; *Lātyā. Śr. S.*, IV. 3.9.5.6.
4. *Tai. Br.*, I. 2.6.7.
5. *aśūdrā abrāhmāṇāste prājāpatyāḥ. VS*, XXX. 22.
6. XVII. 6.1-2.
7. *Śat. Br.*, XIII. 8. 3.11. It is interesting to note that the tomb of the kṣatriya is to be the greatest in height and that of the brāhmaṇa to be the next.
8. *Br. Up.*, I. 4.11-13.

twin Aśvins, physicians of the gods, are regarded as śūdras.[1] It is significant that in the *ratnahaviṃṣi* ceremony the Aśvins are associated with the *saṃgrahitṛ*[2] and Pūṣan along with the *bhāgadugha.*[3] But in the *Taittirīya Brāhmaṇa* Pūṣan, along with the Viśvedevas (All-Gods) and the Maruts (peasant-gods), is associated with the vaiśyas.[4] In a way the Viśvedevas are indirectly assigned to the śūdras as well. The *anuṣṭubh*, which is a later and popular metre ascribed to the śūdra,[5] is also assigned to the Viśvedevas.[6] It is stated that through the recitation of this metre Prajāpati[7] and Indra were honoured among the Viśvedevas, and the Pañcāla prince Darbha Śātānīki among the śūdras.[8] Therefore in this case the Viśvedevas of divine society correspond to the śūdras of human society.

Of the gods associated with the śūdras, Pūṣan seems to have been a shepherd god[9] and, as such probably represents the cattle-rearing and nourishing activities of the Āryan viś. The Aśvins, who are described in the later portion of the *Ṛg Veda* as sowing the grain with the plough and milking food for man,[10] may be associated with the agricultural activities of the viś. The Viśvedevas are assigned to the viś because of their being large in number. The fact that precisely the same three gods who were associated with the Āryan viś later came to be directly or indirectly ascribed to the śūdra would suggest that even when sections of the viś were reduced to the position of śūdras they continued to retain their old Vedic gods.

There is also evidence to show that considerable sectors of the lower orders, Āryan and non-Āryan, worshipped Rudra-Paśupati, who seems to have been a pre-Āryan deity. In the *śatarudrīya* litany, accompanying the offerings appropriate to

1. Hopkins, *Epic Mythology*, p. 168.
2. *Śat. Br.*, V. 3.1.8.
3. *Ibid.*, V. 3.1.9.
4. *Tai. Br.*, II. 7.2.1 and 2.
5. *TS*, VII. 1.1.4-5; *Pañc. Br.*, VI. 1.6-11.
6. *Jai. Br.*, II. 101; *Śāṅkh. Śr. S.*, XV. 10.1-4.
7. Prajāpati is not mentioned in the *Śāṅkhāyana Śrautasūtra*.
8. *Jai. Br.*, III. 101.
9. Dutt, *A History of Civ. in Anc. India*, i, 60-61.
10. *yávaṃ vṛ́keṇāsninā vápantéṣaṃ duhántā mánuṣāya dasrā...RV.* I. 117.21.

various forms of Rudra, reverence is shown to all sections of society headed by the brāhmaṇa and followed by the rājanya, the sūta and the vaiśya together with the different kinds of artisans and aboriginal peoples. But the first three varṇas are mentioned in only one collection of the *Yajus*.[1] While the śūdra as such is not mentioned in any of them, all the *Yajus* lists speak of reverence being shown to the *rathakāras* (cartwrights), the *kulālas* (potters), *karmāras* (smiths), the Niṣādas, the Puñjiṣṭhas (aboriginal people working as fishermen or catchers of birds), the *śvanis* (dog-feeders or dog-keepers) and the *mṛgayas* (hunters),[2] who may well be put in the fourth varṇa. Besides, the *Taittirīya Saṃhitā* mentions makers of bows and arrows (*dhanukāra* and *iṣukāra*),[3] who may also fall under this category.

These artisans and tribal peoples worshipped Rudra as their patron god.[4] According to Weber the "Rudra book dates from the time of these secret feuds on the part of the conquered aborigines as well as of the Vrātyas or unbrāhmaṇised Āryans, after their open resistance had been more or less crushed."[5] He further points out that various mixed castes were not established without vigorous opposition from those thrust down into the lower castes.[6] This would imply, then, that in the process of struggle against the growing privileges of the higher varṇas there went on considerable intermingling between the discomfited sections of the Āryan tribes and the masses of the conquered aborigines, with the inevitable result that some Āryans, such as the *rathakāra* and the *karmāra*, rallied under the banner of a non-Āryan god Rudra. It is worth notice that in the *ratnahaviṃṣi* ceremony Rudra is described as the god of the *govikartana*,[7] who is specified by Sāyaṇa as 'of whatever low caste'. It has been shown earlier that Rudra-Paśupati was the god of the Niṣāda

1. *MS*, II. 9.5.
2. *VS*, XVI. 27; *KS*, XVII. 13; *Kap. S.*, XXVIII. 3; *MS*, II. 9.5; *TS*, IV. 5.4.2; *Kāṇva S.*, XVII. 4.
3. *TS*, IV. 5.4.2.
4. *Cf. VI.* ii, 249-50.
5. *Ind. Lit.*, pp. 110-111.
6. *Ibid.*
7. *Śat. Br.*, V. 3.1.10.

chief. Thus it is beyond all doubt that the śūdras also had their gods, some Āryan others non-Āryan. Therefore the brāhmaṇical statement in the stories of creation that the śūdra did not have any gods[1] does not represent the correct position. One creation legend at least implies that Day and Night were the gods of the śūdras.[2] Clearly the brāhmaṇical legends show a deliberate attempt to deprive the śūdra of the right to worship and sacrifice, which he formerly shared with his Āryan fellowmen, or enjoyed independently as a member of the aboriginal tribes:

The mass of evidence in favour of the śūdra's participation in the Vedic sacrifice is more than counterbalanced by the evidence against it. It is repeatedly stated that the śūdra has no right to sacrifice[3] on account of his low birth, and that he is incapable of making sacrificial offerings.[4] A rite connected with the building of the fire altar (*agnicayana*), without which there can be no Vedic sacrifice, is explained as removing Agni from the śūdra varṇa.[5] But the fact that such direct statements about the exclusion of the śūdra from the Vedic sacrifice are not found in the Saṃhitās may suggest their later origin. None the less, even in those texts there are numerous references, which have this implication. The instructions for the ceremony of the establishment of fire sacrifice speak of only the first three varṇas.[6] whose seasons for this purpose are mentioned in the Brāhmaṇas. Even the *rathakāra* is left out. In this connection it is stated that the fire coincides with the universe, which consists of the brāhmaṇa, the kṣatriya and the viś.[7] It is also said that the rājanya and the viś are born of sacrifice and hence of the brāhmaṇa.[8]

1. *TS*, VIII. 1.1; *Pañc. Br.*, VI. 1.6-11.
2. *VS*, XIV. 30; *Śat. Br.*, VIII. 4.3.12.
3. *Tai. Br.*, III. 2.3.9; *Kāt. Śr. S.*, I. 5; cf. *Śāṅkh. Śr. S.*, I. 1. 1-3; *Āśva. Śr. S.*, I.3.3.
4. *Tai. Br.*, III. 2.3.9.
5. *Śat. Br.* VI. 4.4.9.
6. *MS*, III. 1-5; III. 2.2. Only the brāhmaṇa and rājanya are mentioned in *TS*, V. 1.4.5; *KS*, XIX. 4. and *Kap. S.*, XXX, 2. Even the vaiśya is excluded.
7. *Śat. Br.*, II. 5.2.36.
8. *Ibid.*, III. 2.1.40.

Again the assertion that only members of the first three varṇas are able to sacrifice and hence a śūdra cannot enter the sacrificial ground[1] is in accord with the above statements.

In addition to the śūdra's exclusion from the general Vedic sacrifice, there are instances of his dissociation from certain specific Vedic rituals. For instance, the Soma sacrifice (*soma-yāga*) is prescribed for the brāhmaṇa, the vaiśya and the rājanya.[2] The *agnihotra* (an oblation to Agni) is to be performed by an ārya, who according to the commentator, is a member of the three higher varṇas.[3] The śūdra is expressly prohibited from milking the cow for the milk required at the *agnihotra*,[4] because he is supposed to be born of untruth.[5] Accordingly the earthen pot for milking (*sthāli*) is to be prepared by an Āryan.[6] But such a prohibition does not occur in the *Vājasaneyi* and the *Taittiriya* collections of the *Yajus*; it occurs only in the supplementary portions of the *Maitrāyaṇi* and *Kapiṣṭhala* collections. The corresponding passage in the *Kāṭhaka Saṃhitā* is without accent, which suggests its later insertion. Furthermore, the *Āpastamba Śrautasūtra*, which is considered as the oldest of its kind,[7] gives the alternative provision that the śūdra can milk the cow.[8] The commentator tries to circumvent this meaning by pointing out that he can do it when allowed.[9] All this would show that the ban on the śūdra's milking of the cow at the *agnihotra* may not belong to the genuine portions of the Saṃhitās. It may be ascribed to the time of the *Taittiriya Brāhmaṇa*.[10]

Harsh provisions, which even forbid bodily contact with and sight of the śūdra on certain ceremonial occasions, began

1. *VI*, ii. 390.
2. *Kā. Śr. S.*, VII. 105.
3. *Āp. Śr. S.* (Garbe's edn.), VI. 3.7 with the comm. of Rudradatta.
4. *Tai. Br.*, III. 2.3.9.10; *Kap. S.*, XLVII. 2; *MS*, IV. 1.3; *Āp. Śr. S.* (Garbe's edn.), VI 3.11; *Baudhā. Śr. S.*, XXIV. 31; *Śāṅkh. Śr. S.*, II. 8.3; *Satyā. Śr.*, III. 7.
5. *asato vā eṣa saṃbhūto yacchūdraḥ. Āp. Śr. S.* (Garbe's edn.), VI. 3.12.
6. *MS*, I. 8.3.
7. Garbe, *Āp. Śr. S.*, ii, Preface, p. XII.
8. *duhyād vā. Āp. Śr. S.* (Garbe's edn.), VI. 3.13.
9. Rudradatta's comm. to *Āp. Śr. S.*, VI. 3.13.
10. *Tai. Br.*, III. 2.3.9-10.

to appear towards the end of the Vedic period. A person consecrated for the sacrifice is asked not to speak to the śūdra,[1] and the same condition is imposed on a person who has been initiated (*upānīta*).[2] The *Śatapatha Brāhmaṇa* lays down that at the *pravargya* ceremony (an introductory Soma rite) the performer should shun contact with a woman and a śūdra because they are untruth.[3] Except one such reference in the *Kāṭhaka Saṃhitā*, this is the earliest example of bracketting the woman with the śūdras — a practice which is frequently found in later literature.[4] It is also provided that a woman performing a rite for the sake of a son should not be touched by a vṛṣala, male or female,[5] who in later times is identified with the śūdra and depicted as anti-brāhmaṇical. In the *Śatapatha Brāhmaṇa* even a carpenter's touch is regarded as imparting ceremonial impurity to the sacrificial vessels.[6] But at another place, if the reading in the *Mādhyandina* recension of that text is correct, the *takṣan* appears as reciting the *mantra* for Āruṇi.[7] It has to be remarked that all such references about avoiding contact with the śūdra occur either in the *Śatapatha Brāhmaṇa* or the *Śrautasūtras*, which indicates that the idea of the ceremonial impurity of the śūdra involving prohibition of physical and visual contact with him appeared towards the close of the Vedic period and even later.

A review of the position of the śūdra in the religious life of the later Vedic period shows that, in addition to the *rathakāra* and the *niṣāda*, who could take part in the Vedic sacrifice, the śūdra varṇa as such had its gods and could participate in several Vedic rites. It is true that in most cases the mode of participation was meant to indicate the śūdra's low position in society,

1. *Śat. Br.*, III. 1.1.10; *na śudreṇa saṃbhāṣeran. Drā. Śr. S.*, VIII. 3.14; *Lāṭyā. Śr. S.*, III. 3. 15-16, applies this condition to the performer of the *sattra* sacrifice. *Satyā. Śr. S.*, X. 2.

2. *Drā. Śr. S.*, VIII. 3.14; *Satyā. Śr. S.*, XXIV. 8.16 also adds woman to whom a brahmacārin should not talk after initiation.

3. *Śat. Br.*, XIV. 1.1.31; also in *Satyā. Śr. S.*, XXIV. 1.13.

4. *R. S. Sharma, JBRS*, xxxvi, 183-191.

5. *Śat. Br.*, XIV. 9.4.12.

6. *aśuddhastakṣā. Śat. Br.*, I. 1.3.12. Brough suggests that this may be due to an earlier idea of offence to the wood-land-spirits in the desecration of the tree. Banerjea, *Studies in the Brāhmaṇas*, p. 127, fn. 2.

7. *Śat. Br.* II. 3.1.31. In the Kāṇva recension it is Dakṣa.

but on that account this privilege was not completely denied to him. The process of his exclusion, which is already in evidence in some of the earlier texts, became stronger towards the very close of the Vedic period. It seems that the growth of economic and social differentiation gradually changed the character of the tribal sacrifice, which tended to become individual and involved more and more gifts to the priests. In course of time the sacrifice came to be the prerogative of the higher varṇas, who could afford the means to pay for it. This can be inferred from the commentary of Śaṅkara to a passage of the *Bṛhadāraṇyaka Upaniṣad*,[1] where he says that God created the vaiśyas to acquire wealth, which is the means of performing rites. Similarly in the *Mahābhārata* Yudhiṣṭhira is represented as stating that sacrifices cannot be performed by people who are poor, for they require a large store of diverse kinds of articles. He further says that merit attaching to sacrifices can be acquired only by kings and princes, and not by those who are destitute of wealth and helpless.[2] This would imply that generally the śūdra, who could ill afford to make gifts on the occasion of the sacrifice, was unable to perform it. In the case of a rich śūdra association with sacrifice was not considered undesirable, for it was laid down that fire could be accepted from his house.[3]

It is argued that "a sense of danger with which the purity of the Brāhmaṇical faith was threatened from the idolatrous practices of the aboriginal subjects" first suggested to the brāhmaṇas the necessity of raising an insurmountable barrier between the Āryan freeman and the men of the servile class".[4] This seems to be a

1. I. 4.12.

2. *na te śakyā daridreṇa yajñāḥ prāptuṃ pitāmaha*; *bahūpakaraṇā yajñā nānā saṃbhāravistarāḥ. pārthivai rājaputrair vā śakyāḥ prāptuṃ pitāmaha*; *nārthanyūnairavaguṇairekātmabhirsaṃhataiḥ. Mbh.* (Kumb.), XIII. 164-2-3; - (Cal.) XII. 107-2-3. This passage seems to have been the product of a much later period, but it may be taken as reflecting conditions in the later Vedic period.

3. *yo brāhmaṇo rājanyo vaiśyaśūdro vā'sura iva bahupuṣṭassyāttasya gṛhādāhṛtyādadhyāt puṣṭikāmasya. Āp. Śr. S.* (Garbe's edn.), V. 14.1. Of course the adjective *bahupuṣṭah* is applied to the brāhmaṇa, the rājanya and the vaiśya as well but seems to be of special significance in the case of the śūdra, who is described as being removed from the fire.

4. Eggeling, *SBE*, xii, Introd., p. XIII. Pollution is considered by some sociologists and Sanskritists to be a crucial factor in caste formation, but really it was a consequence of socio-economic developments and not their cause.

rather naive explanation. It is obviously based on the assumption that the śūdras were made up only of the conquered peoples, which is incorrect. Even so the *Ṛg Veda*, the *Atharva Veda* and many earlier references in later Vedic literature do not show any indications of protecting the purity of the brāhmaṇical faith by raising strong barriers against the śūdras. Possibly the śūdras who were recruited from the conquered aboriginals were excluded from the Vedic sacrifice because of their different religious practices, but this cannot be regarded as the only cause of such a development. We have already pointed to the process of social and economic differentiation which led to the śūdra's exclusion.

The position of the śūdra, which emerges from an analysis of the Vedic rituals, does not seem to be consistent. Economically on the one hand, there is mention of his owning cattle and probably functioning as an independent peasant; on the other hand the śūdras appear in some texts as domestic servants, agricultural labourers and in some cases slaves. Politically, we hear of śūdra *ratnins*, but there is also mention of the śūdras and the vaiśyas being enclosed by the brāhmaṇa and the kṣatriya. Socially, it is inaccurate to think that the śūdras were saddled with restrictions regarding food and marriage;[1] there is, however, some evidence of contempt for birth in a caṇḍāla family and for the ascription of certain bad qualities to the śūdra, but much of this appears to be post-Vedic. Religiously, the śūdra was permitted to take part in certain rites, and yet excluded from several specific rituals as well as from the Vedic sacrifice in general. In other words, Keith is right when he says that in the Saṃhitās and Brāhmaṇas the position of the śūdra is ambiguous.[2]

The contradiction in the position of the śūdra during the later Vedic period may be partly explained by the chronological position of the references. Generally the non-admission of the śūdra to rituals, which permeated all spheres of life, is to be found almost exclusively in later texts. But we also find rights and disabilities existing side by side. This may be accounted for by the existence of decaying tribal features alongside growing varṇa distinctions. As a member of the Āryan tribes the śūdra

1. *IC*, xii, 183.
2. *CHI*, i, 129.

retained some of the tribal rights of taking part in various rituals, even when he was being thrown into the ranks of the serving order.

A striking feature of the śūdra's position during this period is the special status accorded to the artisan sections of that varṇa, such as the *rathakāra* and the *takṣan*. This was possibly owing to their great value as workers in wood and metal, without whom the Āryans could not expand and flourish. It has been shown earlier that the *takṣan* seems to have been a smith. His high status in Vedic society is in keeping with his honourable position in primitive agricultural communities, in which he serves even as a councillor of kings.[1]

We also detect a close connection between material culture and social organisation. The type of material life provided by PGW archaeology suggests possibilities of social differentiation, but it also indicates constraints on the production of social surplus. We have very little evidence regarding the use of iron tools for craft and agriculture, for the supply of iron to the upper Gaṅgā basin seems to have been limited and the technology of hardening iron tools through carburisation unknown. The later Vedic society seems to have been a small-scale non-monetary peasant society, strongly supplemented by cattle-rearing. Because of the difficulties of clearance in the upper Gangetic basin large agricultural fields may not have existed. The economy therefore generally did not need slaves and hired labourers for agricultural operations; every family looked after the land under its cultivation. The economy certainly needed artisans and herdsmen, but they still seem to have maintained ties of kinship with the princes and priests. Literary evidence suggests that tribal elements were considerably strong. The formation of a serving order had started, but its crystallisation into a class required certain conditions which appeared only in post-Vedic times. Wooden ploughshare based cultivation in later Vedic times allowed only marginal surplus for the support of priests and warriors although the latter could benefit from the use of iron weapons.[2]

1. R.G. Forbes, *Metallurgy in Antiquity*, p. 79.
2. For a discussion of this problem see R. S. Sharma, "Class Formation and its Material Basis in the Upper Gangetic Basin (*c.* 1000-500 B.C.)" *The Indian Historical Review*, ii, 1-13.

It is not possible to accept the thesis propounded in the *Vedic Index* and accepted by several writers[1] that the śūdra was a serf in the beginning, that his life was insecure and then gradually his old disabilities began to be removed. Such a view does not hold good of those Āryans who were degraded to the position of śūdras. Of course the non-Āryans were subjected to a policy of extermination in course of early wars, but there is nothing to show that at that time those who were conquered were encumbered with disabilities. On the contrary, the process seems to have been just the reverse. While the earlier references point to the participation of the śūdra in the communal life, the later references point to his exclusion, with the result that towards the close of the Vedic period disabilities overwhelmed the old tribal rights. They become so marked and perhaps so oppressive as to evoke protests from the *Upaniṣads*. It is stated in the *Bṛhadāraṇyaka Upaniṣad*[2] that even the caṇḍālas and paulkasas cease to be as such in the world of the soul, where all distinctions disappear. The *Chāndogya Upaniṣad*[3] states that even a caṇḍāla is entitled to the leavings of the *agnihotra* sacrifice, round which hungry children sit just as they sit round a mother. We do not know how far such protests in favour of the lower order were derived from the old ideal of tribal equality, but the possibility cannot be entirely ruled out. This tendency was carried forward by the reformation movements of post-Vedic times, while the opposite tendency, which sought to impose increasing disabilities on the śūdra varṇa, was continued by the compilers of the Gṛhyasūtras and Dharmasūtras.

1. *VI*, ii, 390 : Dutt, *Origin and Growth of Caste*, pp. 101-5; Valavalkar, *Hindu Social Institutions*, p. 288.
2. IV. 3.22.
3. V. 24.4.

CHAPTER IV

SERVILITY AND DISABILITIES

(c. 600 — c. 300 B.C.)

For the study of the position of the śūdras in post-Vedic times, the brāhmaṇical sources, which mainly comprise the Dharmasūtras (law-books), the Gṛhyasūtras (books dealing with domestic rites) and the grammar of Pāṇini, can be supplemented by the early Buddhist and Jain texts. The chronological position of these sources can be fixed only roughly. In the scholarly study of the subject made by Kane the principal Dharmasūtras have been assigned to the period 600-300 B.C.[1] The sūtras show a grammatical freedom which is hardly conceivable after the period of the full influence of Pāṇini,[2] whose grammar has been assigned to the middle of the 5th century B.C.[3] The law-book of Gautama, which contains most information relating to the śūdras, is believed to be the oldest of the Dharmasūtras.[4] But its mention of Yavanas as born of śūdra women and kṣatriya men,[5] more examples of the joint notices of the vaiśya and the śūdra[6] as found in the later Dharmaśāstras, the attempt to introduce uniform laws for the whole of India,[7] the provision of punishment for cow-killing,[8] the enumeration of nearly twenty mixed castes[9] — all these features show that its contents underwent great

1. *Hist. Dh. S.*, ii, pt. I, p. XI. Meyer (*Altin. Rechtsschriften*, p. VII) regards the *Bau.* and the *Āp. Dh. Ss.* as pre-Buddhist, and ascribes the *Vas. Dh. S.* to the fourth century B. C. Cf. Hopkins, *CHI*, i, 249.
2. Keith, *CHI*, i, 113.
3. Agarwala, *India as known to Pāṇini*, p. 475.
4. Bühler, *SBE*, ii, p. XLV; Kane., *Hist. Dh. S.*, i, 13.
5. *Gaut. Dh. S.*, IV. 21. Hopkins thinks that this refers to Bactrian and other Asiatic Greeks. *CHI*, i, 240. fn. 1.
6. *Gaut. Dh. S.*, V. 41-42, 45.
7. Bühler, *SBE*, ii, p. XLIX.
8. *Gaut. Dh., S.*, XXII. 18.
9. *Ibid.*, IV. 16-21.

revision in later times.[1] Therefore all its laws relating to society may not reflect conditions in the pre-Mauryan period.

The land of the Āryans (Āryāvarta), to which the Dharmasūtras were to apply, embraced the region between the Punjab and Bihar, and between the Himalayas and the hills of Malwa,[2] but the lawgiver Baudhāyana belonged to the south though the same cannot be said with certainty about Āpastamba, who refers to a peculiar *śrāddha* usage of the northerners (*udicyas*).[3] The school of Vasiṣṭha probably flourished in the regions of the north-west.[4]

To the period 600-300 B.C. may be also assigned the principal Gṛhyasūtras,[5] which have been characterised as 'the most reliable reports' on the daily life of the ancient Indians.[6]

Of the Buddhist sources the four collections of the *suttas* (dialogues), i.e., the *Dīgha*, the *Majjhima*, the *Saṃyutta* and the *Aṅguttara*[7] together with the *Vinaya Piṭaka*,[8] may be roughly ascribed to the pre-Mauryan period, though much of the *Vinaya* is considered to be Mauryan. It is more difficult to fix the date of the Jātakas,[9] in which the *gāthās* (verses), being the canonical texts, constitute the oldest stratum. The stories of the past, which are in the form of commentary in prose, are put in the pre-Mauryan period; nevertheless the present stories occasionally seem to reflect conditions in the Mauryan period, and are clearly later additions.[10] Curiously the scene of the stories of the past lies in the western or central part of India, but the scene of the majority of the stories of

1. Cf. B. K. Ghosh, *IHQ*, iii, 6.7-11.
2. *CHI*. i, 242.
3. *Bau. Dh. S.*, II. 7.17.17; cf. Kane, *Hist. Dh. S.* i, 44.
4. *CHI*, i, 249-50.
5. Kane, *Hist. Dh. S.*, ii, pt. I. p. XI.
6. Winternitz, *HIL*, i, 274.
7. Law, *HPL*, i, 30-33.
8. *Ibid.*, 15.
9. For early date of the Jātakas see T. W. Rhys Davids, *Buddhist India*, p. 207.
10. Cf. Law, *HPL*, i, 30; Hopkins, *CHI*, i, 260. fn 1. The most recent discussion of the question is to be found in the article of O. Fiśer, *AO*, xxii, 238-39.

the present is in Sāvatthi or Rājagaha.[1] Further, the third, fourth and fifth volumes of the Jātakas can be generally considered as parts that have assumed their present shape in a period posterior to the majority of the simple stories of the first and second volumes.[2]

It has been suggested that the Jātakas represent a state of society which provided suitable conditions for trade, perhaps during the Sātavāhana period.[3] But the finds of punch-marked silver and copper coins coupled with a large number of iron objects, assigned to the period of the North Black Polished Ware (*circa* 600-250 B.C.), clearly point to the definite beginnings of urban life[4] and the rise of trade and commerce.[5] Besides, Kauṭilya's regulations regarding industry and commerce, if true of Mauryan times, do presuppose some progress in such economic activities in the earlier period. Again, the Jātakas hardly refer to the trade and commerce of southern India, with which the Romans were in active intercourse under the Sātavāhanas. Nor do the Jātakas allude to so many guilds and occupations as we find in the Sātavāhana period.[6] Moreover, since the Buddhist birth stories are represented in the reliefs and sculptures of Sānchī and Bhārhut in the second century B.C., they can be taken back at least two centuries earlier, especially in a country where old religious traditions continued to provide the motif for works of art till mediaeval times. Thus although the *gāthās* and past stories may be regarded as reflecting the state of affairs existing in the two or three centuries preceding the establishment of the Mauryan empire, for the purpose of our study those parts of the Jātakas

1. *AO*, xii, 238-9.
2. *Ibid.*, xxii, 249; Rhys Davids, *op. cit.*, p. 208.
3. D. D. Kosambi, *An Introduction to the Study of Indian History*, pp. 259-60. cf. Daniel H. H. Ingalls, *JAOS*, lxxvii, 223-24.
4. Rude beginnings of urban life, as will appear from excavations at Hastinapura and Katra in Mathura, may be traced earlier than 600 B.C.
5. This line of study has to be pursued further; a comparison between the archaeological remains of the NBP period and the contents of the early Pāli texts will not only help to establish the date of these literary sources on a firm footing but will add to our knowledge and understanding of the material life in pre-Mauryan times.
6. *Infra.*, Ch. VI.

which deal with the caṇḍālas may be regarded as later additions because the Jātaka references to these despised people are not corroborated fully by the brāhmaṇical texts of the pre-Mauryan period. We may also note that the long list of mixed castes given by Manu does not find its counterpart in the Jātakas.

There are greater chronological uncertainties in the case of the Jain sources, which have not been edited and studied as well as the Buddhist texts. It is held that the canonical works were first compiled somewhere towards the end of the fourth or the beginning of the third century B.C.[1] But, dealing as they do with the life of Mahāvīra, they may be utilised for the pre-Mauryan period, from which they were not far removed in point of time.

Diverse opinions have been expressed on the authenticity of these literary sources, which are difficult to interpret in the absence of historical works or epigraphic records. There is a tendency to discard the brāhmaṇical works in favour of the Buddhist texts.[2] It is said that the attempt of the Dharmaśāstras to fit the varṇas into fixed patterns seems to be artificial and speculative.[3] Against this it is urged that what is common to a number of Dharmasūtras must have some basis in fact.[4] It is argued that such a charge used to be made against the scholastic writers of mediaeval Europe and has been rebutted by modern scholars.[5] It will not be proper, however, to place absolute reliance upon either brāhmaṇical or non-brāhmaṇical sources. A correct picture of the social conditions of the pre-Mauryan period can be based only on a co-ordinated study of all kinds of texts.[6] Unfortunately this is to be found neither in the *Cambridge*

1. Jacobi, *SBE*, xxii, Introd., p. XLIII. *The Age of Imperial Unity*, p. 423. Charpentier (*Uttarā.*, Introd, pp. 32 & 48) ascribes them to the period between 300 B.C. and the beginning of the Christian era.
2. T. W. Rhys Davids, *Dialogues of the Buddha*, i, 286.
3. Senart, *Caste in India*, p. 101. Author's note, p. x; Author of the *Census Report of India*, 1901, p. 546 quoted in Baines, *Ethnography*, p. 11.
4. K. V. Rangaswami Aiyangar, *Aspects of the Social and Pol. System of Manu*, p. 56; cf. Hopkins, *CHI*, i, 293-4.
5. K. V. Rangaswami Aiyangar, *Indian Cameralism*, p. 48.
6. So far these sources have been studied only piecemeal. Jolly's *Hindu Law and Custom* and the encyclopaedic work of Kane on the *History of the Dharmaśāstra* do not treat the contents of the law-books chronologically.

History of India Vol. I.[1] nor in *The Age of Imperial Unity*, which tries to put together materials available in literary sources bearing on the period from 600 B.C. to A.D. 300, but leaves out of consideration the *Dharmasūtras* and the *Gṛhyasūtras*.[2]

There can be no difficulty in accepting facts attested by all these sources; where such concord is wanting, materials furnished by Buddhist and Jain sources may be taken as reflecting more of actual conditions than the rules laid down in the Dharmasūtras. None of our sources, however, represent the view point of the śūdras and other submerged sections of society. While the Dharmasūtras emphasise the supremacy of the brāhmaṇas, the Buddhist and Jain sources emphasise the primacy of the kṣatriyas, only occasionally showing some lurking sympathy for the lower orders. Moreover the information gleaned from the former is generally limited to Northern India, but that from the latter to north-eastern India.

There is some direct information about the śūdras in the Dharmasūtras, a little in the early Pāli texts and still less in the Jain texts. Perhaps on account of the scantiness of such information it has been argued by Fick that except for the theoretical discussions nothing points to the real existence of the fourth caste, the śūdras, in the early Pāli texts.[3] This view has been rightly questioned by Oldenberg.[4] We can quote instances to show that a person was to be known and his status defined by the name of his caste. Thus the identity of an archer is enquired in terms of his being a kṣatriya, a brāhmaṇa, a vaiśya or a śūdra.[5] A common illustration provided by the Buddha in the course of his discourses is that a wise man is expected to know

Excellent monographs based on the Pāli sources by Fick, Rhys Davids, R. Mehta and A. N. Bose suffer from the same defect. J. C. Jain's *Life in Ancient India as Depicted in the Jain Canons* lumps together all material without any regard to time and place. In spite of chronological treatment in some cases works on the Indian caste system hardly take into account non-brāhmaṇical sources.

1. Separate chapters (VIII-IX) are devoted to social conditions as known from early Buddhist literature and the Dharmasūtras respectively.
2. Ch. XXI.
3. *SONI*, p. 314; Dutt, *Origin and the Growth of Caste*, pp. 268-69.
4. *ZDMG*, li, 286.
5. *Majj. N.*, i, 429.

whether his lady-love is of the kṣatriya, brāhmaṇa, vaiśya or śūdra class.[1] Even T.W. Rhys Davids, who is inclined to reject the priestly evidence in toto, points out that in a general way the fourfold varṇa system in the Buddhist texts corresponds to the actual facts of life.[2] All this establishes beyond doubt that the śūdras exist as a social class in the Buddhist texts, although their position and functions are not so sharply defined as in the brāhmaṇical laws.

The nature of social inequality in the age of the Buddha cannot be understood without a reference to its material background, which is provided by the Northern Black Polished (NBP) Ware archaeology. The NBP period lasted roughly for more than three centuries from around 600 B.C. In its pre-300 B.C. phase the NBP culture was almost confined to eastern U.P. and Bihar, i.e., lands of Kosala and Magadha, but its post-300 B.C. phase obtained in almost the whole of north India and in a good portion of Madhya Pradesh. NBP sherds are found even in the Deccan. Even its initial phase was marked by a greater use of iron for agricultural tools, large-scale settlements in the thickly forested and heavy-soil areas after clearance, beginnings of town life and use of metallic money in the form of the punch-marked coins made of silver and copper. Once one of the most fertile lands in the country were opened to cultivation through the use of the iron ploughshare,[3] the near subsistence economy of western U.P. was turned into the surplus-producing economy of the middle Gaṅgā basin. For clearing and cultivating large stretches of land a good many peasants and labourers were required. Probably the method of paddy transplantation leading to wet paddy production were learnt in this period.[4] The paddy surplus produced by the peasants and labourers made possible not

1. *Dīgha N.* i, 193; *Majj. N.*, ii, 33 and 40.

2. *Buddhist India*, p. 54.

3. So far no iron ploughshare belonging to the NBP phase has been discovered, but the term *ayo-nāṅgala* is used in the Pāli texts.

4. R. S. Sharma, "Development of Productive Forces and its Social Implications in India in the first Millennium B.C. with Special Reference to the Age of the Buddha". Paper presented to International Conference on Development of Productive Techniques and their Consequences for Social Formation held in Berlin, GDR, in November, 1978.

only the rise of sixteen great kingdoms with their towns but also the support of professional types of religious, political administrative, and military functionaries who tended to close their folds. On account of the new methods of production it was possible to have a full-fledged class society in which taxes, tributes, tithes and gifts in cash and kind were available for collection by the religious and administrative segments of the ruling class. For the first time we encounter a large number of monks and nuns living on charities. Similarly interests could be collected by moneylenders and profits could be made by traders, and thus the market exchange could intensify social stratification. Because of the use of money, it was possible to accumulate wealth and create wide chasms between those who produced and those who were engaged in the distribution and appropriation of the social surplus. The brāhmaṇical ideologues devised and elaborated a social mechanism through which the fruits of economic expansion in the age of the Buddha could be cornered by priests and warriors to the exclusion of peasants and labourers. The Buddhist ideologues helped to stabilise the new material culture and social set-up by laying emphasis on non-killing of animals and shutting the doors of the Saṃgha to slaves and debtors; at the same time it tried to soften its rigours by giving ordination to women and śūdras and stressing kindness towards slaves and servants.

We may indicate some steps by which land and labour came to be appropriated in the age of the Buddha. The well-known story of Videgha Māthava, the existence of northern brāhmaṇas and close affinities of the NBP with the PGW and black slipped ware suggests that the middle Gaṅgā settlements were pioneered by people from the upper Gaṅgā basin. The colonisers may have encountered a few pockets inhabited by the chalcolithic people in the middle Gaṅgā basin and the lands of the original settlers may have been seized by the newcomers. The chiefs of the advancing colonisers may have appropriated village lands to the exclusion of those who did not belong to the clan or those clansmen who had been impoverished or dispossessed. As reward for the initiative, enterprise and fighting qualities of their chiefs the kinsmen may have presented to them the best piece of land or a good portion af land. In later Vedic times such leading princes as Janaka and Duryodhana[1] were supposed to lend their hands to the plough, and till the end of the period the clan was considered to be the owner of the land. Even in post-Vedic times the king performed the ploughing ceremony called *vappa-maṅgala*[2] in Pāli, which is still observed by the Buddhist king of Thailand. But it is clear that during this period some princes, priests and seṭṭhis/gahapatis came to occupy large stretches of land, although the process of this appropriation can be guessed only by extrapolating anthropological evidence.

We have no clear idea of land rights even in post-Vedic times. The law-books provide for the partition of property, but they never introduce land in this context. Gautama asserts that what is considered to be livelihood (*yogakṣema*) cannot be divided.[3] This obviously includes land. The school of Gautama exercised some influence in later times; several smṛtis stress that land and water belonging to brāhmaṇas having common ancestor (*sagotra*) are indivisible up to the thousandth generation.[4] What applied to brāhmaṇa families in ancient times may have been a mere survival of what applied to ancient society in general. In pre-Maurya times the idea of communal rights in land is also emphasised by Jaimini, who states in his *Mimāṃsā Sūtra* that the earth is common to all and, therefore, cannot be an item of gift.[5] For practical purposes land may have been distributed periodically among the dominant clans as their size increased or as they proliferated into sub-clans. This possibly applied to families of brāhmaṇaṣ, kṣatriya or vaiśya, for significantly enough in the Pāli texts no śūdra with land rights is mentioned. On the other hand we hear of kṣatriyas enjoying revenues, and of brāhmaṇas and seṭṭhis and gahapatis possessing fields and villages. In all probability they possessed the land on behalf of the families over which they presided as head or patriarch. The patriarchal family consisted of about three to four generations, as can be inferred from laws regarding partition in the Dharmasūtras; and as such it was a very large family.

1. *Mbh.*, III. 241. 29-30.
2. *Jāt.*, i, 57 quoted in *Pali-English Dictionary.*
3. XXVIII. 46.
4. *Dharmakośa,* i, 1231.
5. VI. 7.3.

The idea of private or individual property in such a family would not be very strong. Just as the co-parceners held landed property and general village resources in common so also for the exploitation of these resources they came to hold the labour power in common. The labouring or servile population of every village was called śūdra, over whom the three upper varṇas exercised general social control. Thus we have the clear beginnings of a society based on śūdra labour.

That the śūdras constituted the serving class was only implied in the texts of the later Vedic period. But during this period the Dharmaśūtras made the explicit and emphatic statement that the duty of the śūdra was to serve the three higher varṇas, and thus to maintain his dependants.[1] He was expected to run his independent house, which he supported by agricultural and artisanal occupations. Gautama informs us that the śūdra could live by practising mechanical arts.[2] It seems that sections of the śūdra community worked as weavers, wood-workers, smiths, leather-dressers, potters, painters etc. Although these crafts are mentioned in the early Pāli texts,[3] there is no indication of the varṇa of their followers. The gahapati[4] (generally landed householder) who roughly corresponds to the vaiśya in the brāhmaṇical system, is described at one place as living by arts and crafts.[5] If a man of substance could become a gahapati, it is possible that some of the well-to-do śūdra artisans such as the smith Cunda, who served a sumptuous dinner to Gautama Buddha and his followers,[6] or the conspicuously rich potter Saddālaputta, who was in possession of five hundred potter's shops and a large number of potters working under him,[7] were gahapatis. This may be also true of the head of the village of a thousand smiths, who gave his daughter in marriage to the Bodhisatta.[8] Although the term gahapati is

1. *Āp. Dh. S.*, I. 1. 1-7 : *Gaut. Dh. S.*, X. 54-57.
2. *śilpavṛttiśca*. X. 60.
3. Mehta, *Pre-Buddhist India*, pp. 194-204.
4. Known as *gābhāvai* in the Jain texts.
5. *sippādhiṭṭhānā*. *Ang. N.*, iii, 363.
6. *Dīgha, N.*, ii, 126.
7. *Uvāsag.*, p. 184.
8. *Jāt.*, iii, 281.

now here applied to such artisans, it is possible that some of them rose to this position by virtue of their wealth.

We cannot go into the history of crafts and craftsmen, which might well form the subject of a separate monograph. But certain broad points may be noticed. The artisan members of the śūdra varṇa played an important role in the agrarian economy of the pre-Mauryan period. Workers in metal not only made axes, hammers, saws, chisels etc. meant for the carpenters and smiths,[1] but also supplied agriculture with ploughshares, spades and similar implements,[2] which enabled the farmers to provide surplus food for people living in the towns. The urban life[3] and the thriving trade and commerce, which appear for the first time in north-eastern India during this period, could not have been possible without considerable amount of commodity production by the artisans. In the principal towns the crafts were organised into guilds, the chiefs of which stood in a special relation to the king.[4] Certain artisans were attached to the household of the king and enjoyed his patronage. According to the gloss on Pāṇini's grammar these were known as royal artisans, of which the royal barber (*rāja-nāpita*) and the royal potter (*rāja-kulāla*) are especially mentioned.[5] This is also corroborated by a later Jātaka story, which speaks of the royal potter (*rāja-kumbhakāra*) and the royal garland-maker (*rāja-mālākāra*).[6] Some artisans were also attached to the seṭṭhis and gahapatis. We learn that a seṭṭhi had his own tailor (*tunnakāra*), who lived under his patronage and worked for his house.[7] Mention is also made of the weavers of the gahapati, who supplied yarn to him.[8] But the majority of the artisans were

1. *Jat.*, v, 45.
2. Mehta, *op. cit.*, pp. 198-99.
3. Big cities such as Sāvatthi were twenty in number, and six of them were considered important enough to be the scene of the Buddha's passing away (*Dīgha N*, ii, 147).
4. Mrs. Rhys Davids, *CHI*, i, 206.
5. *Vṛtti* to *Pā.*, VI. 2.63.
6. *Jāt.*, v. 290 and 292.
7. *Ibid.*, vi, 38.
8. *gahapatikassa tantūvāyehi*. *Jāt.*, iii, 258-9. Obviously such a gahapati probably employed them for commodity production for trade.

probably not attached to such masters; as instances of independent craftsmen we might cite the villages of the carpenters[1] and smiths,[2] or the artisans living in towns.[3] Possibly the king exercised some sort of loose control over the artisan villages through the patronage of their chief. Thus the *jeṭṭhaka* (head) of the village of a thousand smiths is called a favourite of the king (*rājavallabho*).[4] There was no such control over the scattered families of artisans, who lived in the villages catering to the needs of the agriculturists. They are mentioned as *grāmaśilpins* by Pāṇini.[5] Probably villages had their potters, carpenters, smiths, weavers and barbers, but they were not attached to their clients in the same manner as in the *jajmāni* system. According to Pāṇini there were two kinds of carpenters, the *grāmatakṣa* who worked for daily wages at the house of his clients in the village, and the *kauṭatakṣa* who worked at his own residence.[6] and was "an independent artisan, not particularly bound under engagement to any one."[7] A Jātaka *gāthā* refers to an itinerant smith, who carries his furnace wherever he is called to go.[8] The artisans owned their implements and in some cases had free access to materials. Thus we learn of a brāhmaṇa carpenter, who gained his livelihood by bringing wood from the forest and making carts.[9] This may have been the case with the potter, who could obtain a free supply of clay and fuel, but not with the weavers and workers in metal. Nevertheless, by and large, those who were served by the artisans were not their masters, as was the case in Greece and Rome, where slaves were employed in handicrafts,[10] but just their clients. The only control exercised

1. *Jāt.*, iv, 159.
2. *Ibid.*, 281.
3. *CHI*, i, 208.
4. *Jāt.*, iii, 281.
5. VI, 2.62.
6. *Pā.*, *V.* 4.95.
7. Gloss. on *Pā.*, *V.* 4.95.
8. *Jāt.*, vi, 189.
9. *Ibid.*, iv, 207.
10. There is a reference to the craft of the home born slave in *Dīgha N.*, i, 51, but this may indicate domestic service. Another reference speaks of slaves and servants being engaged by a brāhmaṇa in trade (*Jāt.*, iv, 16).

by the state over the artisans in general lay in the imposition of a kind of corvée. It was laid down that in lieu of taxes they would have to work for a day in a month for the king.[1] Otherwise the Dharmasūtra rules give the impression that those śūdras who worked as craftsmen and artisans were independent people, for these occupations are prescribed for them in case they fail to maintain themselves by service,[2] which would imply domestic or agricultural work.

How artisans were remunerated in pre-Maurya times is not quite clear. It seems that some artisans were attached to big households; this can be said of the royal barber and royal potter and also of a few craftsmen attached to big merchants. Other artisans such as smiths and carpenters lived in their own artisan villages, which were situated in the vicinity of towns. Obviously artisans living in suburban villages found their own raw material and produced their own commodities which they took to the town markets for the use of both the urban and rural folk. Five hundred potters' shops under Saddālaputta and a large number of potters working under him were clearly meant for supplying pots to both rural and urban people. People had certainly to pay for the *de lux* NBP ware and possibly for numerous inferior other kinds of pottery such as red ware produced in profuse quantities. We hear of a village trader depositing five hundred ploughs with a town merchant,[3] which shows that these ploughs were meant for sale to the peasants. In the layers belonging to the NBP phase in Kausambi 250 iron tools including axes, adzes, knives, razors, nails, sickles, etc., have been discovered.[4] Many of these may be assigned to the pre-300 B.C. phase, and were probably meant for the use of peasants who purchased them by paying in cash or kind. A third category of artisans lived in villages for catering to the needs of the peasants; they may have been paid by their clients in kind. But it is not clear whether the *jajmāni* system prevailed on any scale. Literary sources are not very helpful; possibly the progress of rural archaeology will throw

1. *śilpino māsi masyekaikaṃ karma kuryuḥ. Gaut. Dh. S.*, X. 31 ; *Vas. Dh. S.*, XIX. 28.
2. *Gaut. Dh. S.*, X. 53-55; cf. Ghoshal, *IC*, xiv, 26.
3. *Jat.*, ii. 181.
4. G.R. Sharma, *The Excavations at Kausambi*, 1957-59, pp. 45-46.

light on the pattern of settlements and the nature of rural economy. Meanwhile we may venture to suggest that in the age of the Buddha in the midst of clusters of rural settlements lay towns or artisan villages which met the artisanal needs of the peasants, for which payments were made in both cash and kind. The fact that artisans were required to work for kings in lieu of taxes suggests that they were able to earn their livelihood from independent sources but could not earn enough to be able to pay taxes.

The mass of śūdra population seems to have been employed in agricultural operations. The Dharmasūtras assign agriculture to the vaiśyas,[1] who were independent peasant proprietors paying a part of the produce as taxes to the state.[2] The vaiśyas, mainly as peasants and secondarily as traders, seem to have been the principal taxpayers in post-Vedic times. The fact that the śūdras had not to pay any land revenue shows that they were landless labourers. Āpastamba states that the śūdras, who live by washing the feet, are exempt from taxes.[3] This would imply that non-serving śūdras could become taxpayers. But in an older manuscript of this law-book the term *pādāvanektā* does not occur,[4] which suggests that it was inserted later to provide justification for the exemption of the śūdras. Generally, therefore, the śūdras possessed no taxable property in the form of land, and as such most of them had to work on the land of others. This is amply clear from a passage of the *Majjhima Nikāya*, which presents a classification of the earnings of the four varṇas. It informs us that the brāhmaṇa lives on gifts, the kṣatriya on the use of the bow and the arrow, the vaiśya on agriculture and tending of cattle, and the śūdra on the use of the sickle and the carriage of crops on the pole hung over his shoulder.[5]

1. *Gaut. Dh. S.*, X. 47; cf. *Āp. Dh. S.*, II. 11. 28. 1 with the comm. of Haradatta.
2. *Vas. Dh. S.*, I. 42.
3. *śūdrāśca pādāvanektā*. *Āp. Dh. S.*, II. 10.26.5.
4. *MS. G* according to Bühler's classification.
5. *suddassa sandhanam...asitabyabhaṅgim*. *Majj. N.*, ii, 180.

The character of slavery, which first appears in Vedic times, was modified in the post-Vedic period in several ways. Vedic slavery was mostly confined to women, who were employed in domestic work. In the age of the Buddha it also embraced men, for the term *dāsakaṁmakaraporisa* is frequently used. What is significant, these slaves were also employed in production. Possibly their number went up, and one of the main reasons was the new system of production based on iron technology agriculture, growth of crafts and commerce, rise of towns, and use of punch-marked silver and copper coins. The continuous wars waged by Magadha, the first large territorial state, and similar kingdoms may have added to their numbers. The use of coins from the fifth century B.C. created conditions for the accumulation of money leading to the impoverishment and indebtedness of certain sections of society. The earliest provisions regarding the rate of interest are found in the Dharmasūtras, which prescribe the highest rate for the śūdras. Even Buddhism offered no relief, for it shut the doors of the Saṃgha to debtors and insisted on the clearing of debts on their part. The Buddhist texts show that failure to pay debts led to the enslavement of the debtors. Money transactions not only produced debt slaves but also facilitated sale and purchase of slaves, especially in cities which developed in northern India in this period. Slaves for production, therefore, appeared in a period and situation which saw continuous wars, the widespread use of metallic money and some degree of market economy in India.

Many references in the early Pāli texts speak not of the śūdras as such, but of the dāsas (slaves) and kammakaras (hired labourers) as being employed in agricultural operations. There can be little doubt that the landless śūdras were employed as kammakaras. There is evidence to show that the dāsas also mostly belonged to the śūdra varṇa. This can be deduced from the phrase *suddo vā sudda-dāso vā*, which is used by the Buddha to define the position of the śūdra after his enumeration of the first three varṇas.[1] It would be wrong to translate the term *sudda-dāso vā* as the slave of a workman.[2] The crucial phrase is

1. *Dīgha N.*, i, 104.
2. *T. W.* Rhys Davids, *SBB*, ii, 128.

clearly an example of a case in apposition, and means the śūdra who is a slave. It is inconceivable that here the kṣatriyas, the brāhmaṇas, and the seṭṭhis, who are elsewhere represented as owning slaves, should be left out and the śūdra should be singled out as owning slaves. Therefore Oldenberg is right in inferring that the statement in question does not make any distinction between the śūdra and the dāsa.[1] It is significant that the earliest identification of the śūdra with the slave is found in an early Pāli text and not in the Dharmasūtras, from which this position can be inferred only indirectly. It is only in the post-Mauryan period that Manu states this position in clear and strong words.

Slavery was not exclusively confined to the members of the śūdra varṇa. Even *gāmabhojakas* (village headmen),[2] ministers,[3] brāhmaṇas, kṣatriyas and men of high birth might be reduced to slavery,[4] but the nature of their subjection may have been different. In any case the number of such people cannot have been considerable, the mass of the slave labour being supplied by the śūdra varṇa.[5] Slavery arising out of debt, purchase, free will and fear[6] can be rather expected in the case of the people of the lower orders than in that of the members of the higher varṇas. For example, Isidāsī, the daughter of a cart-driver was carried off as a slave by a merchant on account of her father's failure to pay his bebts.[7] But it is indicative of the limited number of slaves during this period that in the Jātakas there is no mention of slaves captured in war.[8]

While some of the slaves, especially women, were employed in domestic service,[9] others were engaged in agriculture. The slaves

1. *ZDMG*, li, 286. N. K. Dutt writes that in the Buddhist literature the slaves are nowhere called by the name of śūdra (*op. cit.*, p. 272). This case provides a clear implication to the contrary.
2. *Jāt.*, i, 200.
3. *Ibid.*, vi, 389.
4. Bandyopadhyaya, "Slavery in Ancient India", *Calcutta Review* (1930) No. 8, p. 254.
5. Bose, *Social and Rural Economy of N. India*, ii, 423.
6. *Jāt.*, vi, 285 (*gāthā*); *Vin.*, iv, 224.
7. *s. v.* Isidāsī Therī, *Pāli Dict. of Proper Names*, i, 323.
8. Fick, *op. cit.*, p. 308.
9. *dāsī-bhāraḥ*. Pā., VI, 1.42; *Sūyagaḍam*, I. 1.4.8; *Jāt.*, iii, 59, 98-99.

and hired labourers worked even on smaller holdings,[1] but more often on larger plots. In the early Pāli texts there are at least two examples of big farms in Magadha, each of a thousand karīsas (8000 acres according to Childers,)[2] and of another field in Kāsī being ploughed with five hundred ploughs,[3] all owned by the brāhmaṇas. Five hundred or a thousand may be conventional numbers, but they provide an indication of the tendency towards consolidation of holdings, which reached its climax with the state control of agriculture in the Mauryan period. It is obvious that larger holdings could not have been worked without a considerable number of dāsas and kammakaras.

We have hardly any idea about the numerical strength of slaves and hired labourers in relation to their employers. Even in the case of Attica, where statistics are available, it is very difficult to reach agreement on the proportion of the free to slave population.[4] It is likely that Magadha's wars, particularly against the comparatively non-brāhmaṇical zones of Āṅga and Avanti, added to the number of slaves. But the paucity of data in the case of India makes it much more difficult to obtain any definite information on this point. A *sutta* states that few are those who abstain from accepting men and women slaves.[5] The brāhmaṇical theory that the śūdras are meant for the service of the three higher varṇas is broadly reflected in the employment of slaves and labourers by the brāhmaṇas,[6] the kṣatriyas,[7] and seṭṭhis and the gahapatis.[8] According to the Dharmasūtras the brāhmaṇas could exchange slaves for slaves but could not sell them.[9] All this would suggest that slavery prevailed on a considerable scale, but in any case it cannot be compared to the

1. *CHI*, i, 207; *Vin.*, I. 240. cf. *Sūya.*, II. 1.13 which refers to both large and small fields. The dāsas and kammakaras of the Śākyas and Koliyas were employed in irrigating their fields (*Jāt.*, v, 413).
2. *Jāt.*, iii, 293; iv, 276.
3. *Sut. Nipā.*, I. 4.
4. Westermann, *The Slave Systems of Greek and Roman Antiquity*, pp. 8-9.
5. *Sut. Nipā.*, V. 472.
6. *Jāt.*, iv, 15; *Majj. N.*, ii. 186.
7. *Jāt.*, v, 413.
8. *Vin.*, i, 243, 272; ii, 154.
9. *Āp. Dh. S.*, I. 7.20.15; *Vas. Dh. S.*, II. 39; *Gaut. Dh. S.*, VII. 16.

position in Attica where in the 5th century B.C. slaves comprised about a third of the total population.[1]

The Dharmasūtras throw some light on the living conditions of the members of the śūdra varṇa. Gautama provides that the śūdra servant should use the shoes, umbrellas, garments and mats, thrown away by the people of the higher varṇas.[2] The same picture is obtained fröm a Jātaka story, which informs us that clothes gnawed by rats were intended for the use of the dāsas and the kammakaras.[3] Gautama further adds that the remnants of food are meant for the śūdra servant.[4] The *Āpastamba Dharmasūtra* instructs the pupil to put down the remains of food left in his dish either near an uninitiated ārya or near a śūdra slave belonging to his teacher,[5] which clearly implies that the remains of food were to be eaten by the śūdra servant This is also attested by the *Hiraṇyakeśin Gṛhyasūtra*, which lays down that, in a three-day vow undertaken after the completion of his studies, a student should not give the leavings of his food to a śūdra.[6] Paṇini refers to special terms applied to food leavings, which were presumably given to domestic servants.[7] We learn from a passage of the *Vinaya Piṭaka* that the sick wife of a merchant preserved the ghee which she had vomited, for the use of the dāsas or the kammakaras who might apply it to their feet or burn it in a lamp.[8] It is also recorded that five hundred people accompanied the Order of the monks led by the Buddha in the hope of eating the remnants of their food.[9] All this would show that there was nothing unusual about the śūdra servants eating the remnants of the food of their masters.

1. Westermann, *op. cit.*, p. 9.
2. *jirṇānyupānacchatravāsaḥ kūrcāni.* X. 58.
3. *Jāt.*, i, 372. (present story).
4. X. 59.
5. *antardhine vā śūdrāya. Āp. Dh. S.*, I. 1.3.40. with the comm. of the *Ujjvalā*.
6. I. 2.8.1-2. (*SBE* tr.).
7. Agrawala, *op. cit.*, p. 114.
8. *varam etaṃ sappi dāsānaṃ vā kammakarānaṃ vā pādabhañjanaṃ vā pādipakaraṇe vā āsittam. Vin.*, *iv*, 272.
9. *Vin.*, i, 220.

Āpastamba expresses the noble statement that a person should stint himself, his wife and children but neither his slave nor his hired labourer who works for him,[1] but we can hardly believe that this maxim was taken very seriously, though it shows that in the better households slaves were well fed and kindly treated. The slaves and hired labourers may have not been starved, but in general the food served to them was definitely inferior to that of their masters. Thus a brāhmaṇa monk boasts that even his slaves and servants eat rice and meat, and use clothes and ointment made in Kāsī,[2] which shows that ordinarily such people were given inferior food and dress. A similar claim is made by the Buddha, who says that while in the houses of others the dāsas and kammakaras are fed on rice, with sour gruel, in the house of his father they receive rice, meat and milk.[3] That the slave received a fixed type of food is clear from the repeated use of the abusive phrase *dāsa-paribhoga*.[4] Sour gruel was the food of a poor man working for wages.[5] A Jātaka story refers to a potter's hireling, who after a full day's work with the clay and the wheel "sat all clay-besmeared on a bundle of straw eating balls of barley groat dipped in a little soup."[6]

The phrase that a person lived a hard life on a workman's wages commonly occurs in the Jātakas.[7] At one place, the workman, who is the Boddhisatta, bewails his lot in these words: "I get a *māsaka* or a half-*māsaka* for my wages and can hardly support my mother."[8] The daily earning of a grass-cutter is mentioned as two *māsakas*, which he gets in the market in return for the grass mown.[9] The *māsaka* of this period was probably a punch-marked copper coin. According to the commentaries of

1. *kāmamātmānaṃ bhāryāṃ putraṃ voparundhyānna tveva dāsakarmakaram. Āp. Dh. S.*, II. 4.9.11.

2. *dāsakammakarāpi no sālimaṃsodanaṃ bhuñjanti, kāsikavaṭṭhaṃ nivāsenti. Jāt.*, i. 355 (present story).

3. *kaṇajakaṃ bhojanaṃ diyyati. Aṅg. N.*, i, 145.

4. *Ibid.*, i, 451, 459.

5. *Ibid.*, iii, 406-7.

6. *Ibid.*, vi, 372.

7. *paresaṃ bhatiṃ katvā kicchena jīvati. Jāt.*, i, 475; ii, 139 : iii, 325, 406, 444.

8. *Jāt.*, iii, 326.

9. *nagaradvāre vikiṇitvā māsake gahetvā. Jāt.* iii, 130.

the early Pāli texts this coin occupied such a low position in the scale of currency that it was considered next to nothing.[1] The *māsaka* of the later period was one-sixteenth in value of the silver paṇa,[2] but we are not certain whether this represents its relation to the silver paṇa in pre-Mauryan times. During this period the *māsaka* counted in value only when it amounted to five in number,[3] but even this paltry sum was not given to a wage-earner. Therefore it is not possible to make much of the story in the *Gaṅgamāla Jātaka*,[4] in which a water-carrier proposes to enjoy a city festival along with his wife with the meagre savings of one *māsaka*, each contributing half of it. It is characteristic of the didactic nature of the story that the water-carrier refuses to part with his petty sum of a half-*māsaka* even when he is offered unlimited wealth by the Bodhisatta king Udaya. Ultimately he gets half the kingdom, but realises the evils of desire and becomes an ascetic to achieve its final extinction. The evident moral is that a person could remain satisfied even with half a *māsaka*, although it would be ideal to do even without that. As the *gāthā* says: "Little desire is not enough, and much but brings pain".[5] On the whole the estimate of Fick that wages of the day-labourers in the Jātakas were hardly sufficient to enable them to eke out their livelihood seem to be fair. This may well apply to large sections of the śūdras, who worked as hired labourers.

There does not seem to be much difference between the various sub-sections of the serving population. A Jaịn text places slaves, servants (pessas) and beasts of burden in the same category.[6] The Pāli texts make frequent mention of the dāsas, pessas and kammakaras.[7] The pessas were messengers or servants, who were sent on minor errands. As noticed earlier, there was no difference either in the nature of work[8] assigned to the dāsas and the

1. *s.v.* māsaka, *Pāli-Eng. Dic.*
2. S. K. Chakravorty, *Ancient Indian Numismatics*, pp. 56.
3. *The Book of the Discipline*, i, Tr. I. B. Horner in *SBB*, x, pp. 71-72.
4. Bose, *op. cit.*, ii, 428.
5. *appāpi kāmā na alaṃ, bahūhi pi na tappati. Jāt.*, iii, 446-50.
6. *Sūya.*, I, 4.2.18.
7. *Dīgha N.*, i, 141; *Aṅg. N.* ii, 207-8; iii, 37; iv, 266, 393.
8. *Gaut. Dh. S.*, XX. 4.

kammakaras or in the type of food given to them.[1] It will be shown later that if they committed offences they were subjected to the same punishments. There is nothing to show that socially the hired labourer was classed beneath the domestic slave.[2] Perhaps the difference between the dāsas and the kammakaras lay in the nature of their relation with their masters. In contrast to the kammakara, the slave was regarded as the property of the master[3] and could be inherited and shared.[4] The absolutely servile status of the slave was indicated by his distinguishing mark, which seems to have been a shaved head with a topknot.[5] At one place, however, along with the dāsas the kammakaras also are reckoned among the property of the seṭṭhi.[6] This indicates the tendency to reduce the hired labourer to the status of a slave. A Jātaka story shows that while the slaves lived in the house of their masters, the kammakaras went to their lodgings in the evening.[7] But we do not know how far this was a general practice. Obviously the life of the hireling was sometimes harder than that of the slave.[8] He could not enjoy that security of livelihood which was assured to the slave or the permanent domestic servant. Gautama lays down that the *ārya*, under whose protection the śūdra places himself, should support him if he becomes unable to work.[9] But the practice did not conform to this precept, for a *gāthā* states that people throw away the outworn servant like a she-elephant.[10]

There seems to be some difference between the kammakara and the *bhaṭaka* (wage earner).[11] In the *Vinaya Piṭaka* the kammakara is defined as a bhaṭaka who is *āhataka.* The authors of the *Pāli-English Dictionary* interpret the term *āhataka* as 'beaten'

1. *Jāt.*, iii, 300.
2. References quoted in *CHI*, i, 203, fn. 8 do not support this view.
3. *Sutta-nipāta*, 769; *Ovaiya*, verse 6; *Uttara.*, III. 17; *Sūyagoḍam*, II. 7.1.
4. *Gaut. Dh. S.*, XXVIII. 13.
5. *Jāt.*, vi, 135.
6. *Ibid.*, iii, 129.
7. ..*attano vasanaṭṭhānaṃ gantvā. Jāt.*, iii, 445.
8. *CHI*, i, 205.
9. *Gaut. Dh. S.*, X. 61.
10. *yāvatāsiṃsatī poso tāvad eva pavīṇati; aṭṭhāpāye jahanti. Jāt.*, iii, 387.
11. Also written as *bhataka.*

This would mean that the kammakara is a worker who can be beaten — a definition which sounds curious and is not given even in the case of a dāsa. Perhaps the term *āhataka* is not cognated with the Sanskrit word *āhata*,[1] but with the term *āhṛta*, which means taken, seized or brought.[2] This would suggest that the kammakaras were attached to their master in a special way. They were probably brought under his control either on account of their failure to pay debts or owing to having their habitations on his land. They seem to have been in the position of semi-slaves, who could be sometimes treated even as an item of property. Thus there is little evidence for the view that in the pre-Mauryan period the kammakaras were free labourers who entered into contracts as to their work and wages and that in the case of disputes wages were settled by experts.[3] This view better represents the position of the *bhṛtakas*, whose relation with their employers was comparatively free from elements of subjection. The bhṛtaka lived on wages, i.e. *bhṛti*, which is mentioned by Pāṇini either in the sense of service for hire or simply as wages.[4] It seems that the bhṛtaka was hired for a particular period.[5] According to an early Jain text there were four kinds of bhṛtakas: (i) the *divasabhayaga* who worked on daily wages, (ii) the *jattabhayaga* who was engaged for the duration of a journey, (iii) the *uccattabhayaga* who was employed on contract to complete the work in an agreed time, (iv) the *kabbālabhayaga* (such as an earth digger) who was paid according to the amount of work done.[6] As workers on contract some artisans may have been also employed as bhṛtakas. A later Jātaka distinguishes between the bondsmen (*attano purisā*) who are asked to keep watch over the various portions of their master's rice fields, and a *bhataka* who gets a salary (*bhati*) for the same work and is liable to pay compensation in the case of any damage to the crops.[7] A

1. This derivation is adopted in *s.v. āhataka*, *Pāli-Eng. Dic.*
2. An alternative derivation from the term *āhitaka* (i.e. pledged) is not favoured by grammatical rules.
3. Bandyopadhyaya, *Eco. Life and Progress in Anc. India*, p. 94.
4. *Pā.*, I. 3.36; III. 2.22.
5. *Ibid.*, V. 1.80.
6. *Thaṇāṅga*, IV. 271 with the comm. of Abhayadevasūri.
7. *Jāt.*, iv, 276-8.

gāthā states that the *purisa* should always work for the interest of the person in whose house he is fed.[1] The use of the phrase *dāsakammakaraporisa* shows that the bondsman served either as a slave or a hired labourer[2] and that there was not much distinction between these different types of workers.

Hiring people for wages appears as a widespread phenomenon in the age of the Buddha. We come across several terms such as *pessa*, *bhataka*, *purisa* and *kammakara*, for wage earners. But the term *kammakara* is repeatedly mentioned in Pāli texts along with the term *dāsa*. The practice is also found in Āpastamba[3] and continued in Kauṭilya's *Arthaśāstra* and some other Sanskrit texts which use the word *karmakara*. All this suggests that the *dāsa* and *karmakara* belong to the same social category. Economically however wage earning appear only at an advanced stage of social development, for it presupposes considerable rational judgement and deliberate decision making. Indo-European languages have no common term for wage or wage earner. In Sanskrit terms for wage appeared in post-Vedic times. Later Vedic society did neither develop much private property nor produce much surplus. Only when these limitations were overcome, did the wage system appear. Although wages could be paid in kind, the wage system came into general vogue in India only with the increasing use of money and coming of some degree of marketisation which made it possible to purchase labour. As has been pointed out, the process involves several abstract ideas such as (1) purchase of labour power, (2) use of labour time according to the wishes of the purchaser, (3) calculation of the wages according to the labour time spent and the nature/kind of work performed, (4) some kind of contract regarding wages based on such a measurement and (5) separation of product from the producer and its consumption in a household to which he does not belong.[4] The conditions for hiring labour were created in the post-Vedic society of the middle Gaṅgā basin because of the emergence of propertied households which needed to hire labour in order to exploit the resources which were

1. *yasseva ghare bhuñjeyya bhogaṃ tasseva atthaṃ puriso careyya. Jāt.*, vi, 426.
2. *Jāt.*,-iv; *Aṅg. N.*, i, 206; *Vin.*, i, 240.
3. *Āp. Dh. S.* II. 4.9.11.
4. M.I. Finlay, *The Ancient Economy*, pp. 65-66.

beyond the capacity of the family labour. This factor was coupled with the availability of impoverished people, who either on account of war or on account of social subjection, found themselves unable to eke out a living out of their own family resources. Constant wars waged by Magadha from about 550 B.C. may have been a great source of slavery and dependent labour. Once slaves and hired labourers were made available in good numbers, rules and regulations had to be formed not only for governing wage labour but also for creating, identifying and maintaining a social order which could ensure its supply. Those who worked as slaves and hired labourers came to be known as śūdras.

We can have some idea of the economic position of the śūdras from some rules governing the relations between the employers and the employees. It is characteristic of the predominantly agrarian and pastoral economy of the pre-Mauryan period that the rules of this kind refer to the relations between the master on the one hand and his agricultural labourers and herdsmen on the other. It is laid down by Āpastamba that, if the servant in tillage gives up his work, he shall be given physical punishment.[1] The same provision applies to the herdsman who abandons tending the cattle;[2] it is further provided that in such a case the cattle shall be entrusted to some other herdsman.[3] If the loss of the cattle is due to the negligence of the herdsman, he is held responsible for it.[4] Gautama does not refer to these provisions, but he ordains that the master of the cattle or his herdsman, as the case might be, shall be called to account for any damage caused to anyone by the cattle in his charge.[5] None of these lawgivers state the obligations of the master towards his herdsman or agricultural labourers. Thus, compared to their masters, these wage-earners were placed in a disadvantageous position.

The economic disabilities imposed on the śūdras by the Dharmasūtras shed further light on their material condition. Reference has been made to the imposition of compulsory service

1. II. 11. 28. 2.
2. *Ibid.*, 3.
3. *Ibid.*, 4.
4. *Ibid.*, 6.
5. XII. 16-7.

on the artisans for a day in a month by the king. Gautama lays down that in order to defray the expenses of the wedding of a girl, and when engaged in a rite enjoined by the sacred law, a person could take money by fraud or force from a śūdra.[1] Members of the vaiśya, the kṣatriya and perhaps of the brāhmaṇa varṇas, who did not observe the rites and duties of their class, could also be subjected to this procedure in the order of their social status but only when the śūdra was not available.[2] This law, which provides a license for the extortions from the śūdra community by the members of the upper varṇas, is not to be found in any other Dharmasūtra, although it has its parallel in the *Manu Smṛti.*[3] It may be a later insertion which reflects the tendency of a brāhmaṇical school to exploit the śūdra to the full.

The law of inheritance contains discriminatory provisions relating to the share of the son of a śūdra wife. According to Baudhāyana in the case of issues from the wives of different varṇas, four shares would go to the brāhmaṇa, three to the kṣatriya, two to the vaiśya and one to the śūdra son.[4] In such a case Vasiṣṭha provides for the shares of the sons of only the three higher varṇas, leaving out the śūdra son.[5] He quotes the opinion of others as stating that the śūdra son may be regarded as a member of the family but not an heir,[6] a provision which is confined by Baudhāyana[7] to the case of the niṣāda son of a brāhmaṇa father and śūdra mother.[8] Gautama provides for the disinheritance of the śūdra son of a brāhmaṇa in very clear and emphatic terms. According to him if the brāhmaṇa died without male issue, though his son by the śūdra wife might be obedient like a pupil, yet he could receive only a provision for

1. *dravyādānaṃ vivāhasiddhyarthaṃ dharmatantrasaṃyoge ca śūdrāt. Gaut. Dh. S.*, XXVII. 24 with Haradatta's comm.

2. *anyatrāpi śūdrād bahupaśorhīnakarmaṇaḥ. Ibid.*, XXVIII. 25 with Haradatta's comm.

3. *Manu*, XI. 13.

4. *Bau. Dh. S.*, II. 2.3.10.

5. *Vas. Dh. S.*, XVIII. 47-50.

6. *śūdrāputra eva ṣaṣṭho bhavatītyāhuirtyete dāyādabāndhavāḥ. Vas. Dh. S.*, XVII. 38.

7. *Bau. Dh. S.*, II. 2.3.32.

8. *Ibid.*, II. 2.3.10.

maintenance out of the estate of his deceased father.[1] Thus it would appear that of the authors of the Dharmasūtras only Baudhāyana provides for the share of the śūdra son of a brāhmaṇa, Vasiṣṭha and Gautama being opposed to this. Possibly the liberalism of Baudhāyana was due to his connections with the south, where brāhmaṇism had not penetrated deeply. Further, the provisions show that they related only to the śūdra son of a brāhmaṇa. It is not clear whether such rules of inheritance applied to the śūdra sons of the kṣatriya and the vaiśya, although this is very probable. There is no corroborative evidence in the light of which the actual operation of these rules can be known. At any rate these could affect only a fringe of the śūdra population, for the regular marriage of śūdra women with persons of higher varṇas was not a widespread practice.

In an appraisal of the general economic position of the śūdra during the pre-Mauryan period, a special note has to be taken of their characterization as the serving class, which was first clearly started during this time. It was this function of service which imparted homogeneity to the otherwise heterogeneous elements of that varṇa. As members of the serving class, along with the vaiśya peasants,[2] the śūdras performed the role of the primary producers, and thus provided the material foundations for the growth of society. As agricultural labourers they helped to open to cultivation the thickly wooded areas of Kosala and Magadha, which in the texts[3] are referred to as being divided into large and small holdings worked by slaves and hired labourers. As will be noticed later, Kauṭilya advocated the policy of employing śūdra labour for the breaking of virgin soil in the new settlements. Further, as artisans the śūdras contributed to technological development and produced marketable commodities, which led to the rise of numerous towns with their thriving trade and commerce.

1. *Śūdrāputro'pyanapatyasya śuśrūṣuścellabhet vṛttimūlamantavāsividhinā. Gaut. Dh. S.*, XXVIII. 37.

2. It was laid down by Gautama that the vaiśya and the śūdra should make their gains by labour. *nirviṣṭaṃ vaiśyaśūdrayoḥ. Gaut. Dh. S.*, X. 42.

3. Cf. Kosambi, "Ancient Kosala and Magadha", *JBBRAS*, xxvii, 195-201.

But the śūdras did not enjoy the same standards of living as did members of the higher varṇas, who employed them. Repeatedly in the Pāli texts the khattiya, the brāhmaṇa and the gahapati are called *mahāsāla* (opulent),[1] implying thereby that the dāsas, pessas, kammakaras, purisas and bhatakas were not in that fortunate position. Some of the rich śūdra artisans might be prosperous gahapatis, but in a predominantly agrarian economy, and being mostly in the hands of the brāhmaṇas, the kṣatriyas[2] and the seṭṭhis,[3] most of the śūdras had to live on wages in the fixation of which they had no voice. It is said that 'the great mass of the people were well-to-do peasantry or handicraftsmen, mostly with land of their own'.[4] This may apply to the vaiśya or the gahapati class but not to the śūdras, who had to live by working on the land of others. They were condemned to this position not simply because of their birth, but because of their birth in poor families. This point is clearly underlined in the course of a Buddhist argument to disprove the brāhmaṇa's claim to supremacy. It is said that, if the śūdra grew wealthy, he could engage not only another śūdra as his servant, but also another kṣatriya, brāhmaṇa or vaiśya.[5] Normally in such cases, which would be few, the contradiction between the low social status and the high economic position of a person could be resolved by raising him in the social scale. In later times such a policy was practised by the brāhmaṇas in assimilating the foreign ruling chiefs to the kṣatriya fold. It is possible, therefore, that those śūdras who were favoured by fortune could rise to a high social status.

As producing masses the śūdras correspond to the slaves and helots in contemporary Greek city states. Theoretically just as

1. *Aṅg. N.*, iv, 239; *Jāt.*, i, 49. Literally the term means 'having great halls'. Phrases of similar import for indicating rich people are even now used in popular parlance in Bihar.

2. Fick, *op. cit.*, p. 119. According to Gautama (X. 5-6) agriculture, trade and usury are lawful for a brāhmaṇa provided he does not carry on the work himself.

3. For instance see Fiśer, "The Problem of the Seṭṭhi in Buddhist Jātakas", *AO*, xxii, 238-265.

4. Rhys Davids, *Buddhist India*, p. 102.

5. *Majj. N.*, ii, 84-85.

the Greek citizens could claim the service of their unfree men, so also the Indian dvijas (twice-born) and āryas could claim the labour power of the śūdras. But in several respects the economic position of the śūdra was different. Neither the śūdra agricultural labourers nor the śūdra artisans, especially the latter, were so completely at the mercy of their employers as the slaves of Greece and Rome. In contrast to the slave in Greece,[1] the śūdra held property, not sufficient enough to be taxable, but subject to some other liabilities. Thus the law imposed on him the obligation to maintain his master of a higher varṇa by drawing upon his savings, if the latter fell on evil days.[2] It was further laid down that the vaiśya and the śūdra should overcome their misfortunes by means of their property.[3] The use of the phrase *dāsa-bhoga* shows that even the slave held property,[4] though to hold it may have required the consent of his master. Perhaps on account of these differences the varṇa system, which mainly rested on the śūdra class as its chief source of labour power, proved to be a more effective organization of production than slavery. Though fuctioning in an evidently larger area and population than those of Greece, it never felt the necessity of making the śūdras work under the same conditions as the slaves and helots.

The politico-legal status of the śūdras during this period seems to be a counterpart of their economic position. In contrast to their importance in later Vedic polity they lost their place in the political organization of the period. According to Āpastamba the king could appoint only the āryas, i.e. the members of the first three varṇas as officials in charge of the villages and towns.[5] Lesser officers serving under them were also required to fulfil the same qualifications.[6]

1. An exception is to be made in the case of the Cretan agricultural slave who could own property, in which the dowry rights of the female slave were protected. Westermann, *op. cit.*, p. 16.

2. *Gaut. Dh. S.*, X. 62-3.

3. *kṣatriyo bāhuvīryeṇa taredāpadamātmanaḥ dhanena vaiśyaśūdrau. Vas. Dh. S.* XXVI. 16.

4. *Vin.*, iii, 136.

5. *grāmeṣu nagareṣu ca āryāñcchucīn satyaśīlān prajāguptaye nidadhyāt. Āp. Dh. S.*, II. 10.26.4.

6. *Ibid.*, II. 10.26.5.

Āpastamba also lays down that the king's court should be adorned by pure and truthful āryas, who were to act as the councillors and judges of the king.[1] In these references the term *ārya* is rightly interpreted as the member of the first three varṇas.[2] No śūdra was ever regarded as an ārya, any more than he could be 'reborn'.[3] But it is wrong to think that even during this period the use of the term *ārya* indicates racial distinction.[4] Thus the term *ārya-kṛta* in Pāṇini[5] evidently means one who is made free.[6] It is stated in a Buddhist text that among the Kāmbojas and Yavanas the āryas become dāsas and the dāsas become āryas,[7] which clearly shows that the āryas were free, in contrast to the dāsas who were unfree. Therefore the political distinction between the ārya and the śūdra seems to have been of the same type as that between the citizen and the non-citizen in Greece and Rome. Since the śūdra was considered unfree, it was not thought proper to associate him with the work of administration. It would thus appear that the lower classes had no influence in the affairs of the states of the time. Thus a Jain source mentions various categories of kṣatriyas and brāhmaṇas attending the assembly of the king, but does not speak of the gahapatis (i.e. vaiśyas) or the śūdras.[8] It seems that normally even the vaiśyas could not be appointed as councillors, although according to the Pāli texts the seṭṭhis, who received the *seṭṭhichatta* (the canopy of a seṭṭhi) from the king,[9] may have been given some administrative functions. A Jātaka informs us that a tailor's son was made treasurer (*bhāṇḍāgārika*),[10] but such instances are rare.

It is said that one of the most powerful dynasties of this period was of śūdra extraction and that the śūdras acquired

1. *Ibid.*, II. 10.25.12-13.
2. Haradatta's comm. to *Āp. Dh. S.*, II. 10.25.13.
3. Hopkins, *CHI*, i, 240.
4. *Ibid.*
5. *Pā.*, IV. 1.30.
6. Agrawala, *op. cit.*, p. 79.
7. *Dīgha N.*, ii, 149.
8. *Sūyagaḍam*, III.1.9.
9. Fišer, *AO*, xii, 261.
10. *Jāt.*, iv, 43.

supreme power in the lower Gaṅgā valley.[1] These statements can be considered true only in so far as they indicate the low birth of the Nanda rulers. They should not be taken to mean that political power passed into the hands of the śūdra community; for there is nothing to show that the rise of the Nandas put an end to the political disabilities of the śūdra.

As to their role in the republican governments of this period, it has been rightly said that the "ruling assembly in the *Saṃgha-Gaṇa* consisted of a kṣatriya aristocracy ranking higher in the social scale than the brāhmaṇas and the gahapatis, not to speak of inferior classes."[2] On the basis of a passage from the *Gautama Dharmasūtra* Jayaswal says that the śūdra could be a member of the *paura* (relating to the town or capital) body which was consulted by the king.[3] Assuming that the *paura* was a corporate body, Jayaswal's interpretation in the case of the śūdra is not borne out by the commentary of Maskarin, who explains the term *paura* as *samānasthānavāsi*, i.e. an inhabitant of the same place.[4]

As regards the right to appear as witness in the law-courts, Baudhāyana extends this privilege to the members of all the varṇas with certain exceptions.[5] He does not debar the śūdra from acting as a witness in the cases of the higher varṇas, — a provision which is also noticeable in the law-book of Vasiṣṭha.[6] According to Gautama the śūdras could be summoned as witnesses, but in the opinion of his commentators this eventuality could occur only when the twice-born with the requisite qualifications were not available.[7] It is not clear whether this relates to their presence as witnesses in the cases of the twice-born or in their own cases. Probably it refers to the former situation. Vasiṣṭha, however, clearly states that a twice-born of the same varṇa can appear as a witness for men of his own class, good

1. Raychaudhuri, *An Advanced History of India*, p. 71.
2. Ghoshal, "The Constitutional Significance of Saṃgha-Gaṇa in the post-Vedic Period." *IC*, xii, 62.
3. *Hindu Polity*, ii, 69-70.
4. Comm. to *Gaut. Dh. S.*, VI. 10.
5. *catvāro varṇāḥ putriṇaḥ sākṣiṇah syuḥ. Bau. Dh. S.*, I. 10. 19.13.
6. *sarveṣu sarva eva vā. Vas. Dh. S.*, XVI. 29.
7. Maskarin and Haradatta on *api śūdraḥ. Gaut. Dh. S.*, XI II. 3.

śūdras for good śūdras, and men of low birth for similar people.[1] Good śūdras were evidently those who strictly followed the brāhmaṇical precepts regarding their duties. This would suggest that bad śūdras were not to be entertained as witnesses in the suits of good śūdras. Thus the later authors of the Dharmasūtras, Gautama and Vasiṣṭha, exhibit the tendency to exclude the śūdra witnesses from the cases of the higher varṇas. We have no means of finding out whether this discrimination was observed, but it is in keeping with the spirit of the varṇa legislation which pervaded the Dharmasūtras. It may be noted, however, that in the taking of testimony in Greece during this period the slave might be subjected to interrogation under the use of the bastinado or the rack,[2] but such cruel measures for extracting confessions are not prescribed in the Dharmasūtras.

Gautama lays down that members of the various castes, and guilds of cultivators, traders, herdsmen, moneylenders and artisans could administer their affairs according to their respective customs, provided they did not override the dharma law.[3] In other words those sections of the śūdras who were organised into guilds of artisans or castes could follow their own rules in the administration of their internal affairs. But if they were involved in civil or criminal suits with the members of the other varṇas, they might be subjected to legal discriminations. As noticed earlier, in civil law the śūdra son of a brāhmaṇa father could only claim either the smallest share in inheritance or no share at all.[4]

In criminal cases also the Dharmasūtras provide no equality before the law. According to the law of Gautama if a brāhmaṇa abused a kṣatriya or a vaiśya, he would have to pay a fine, but if he abused a śūdra, he would go scot-free.[5] Further, if the śūdra intentionally reviled the twice-born man by criminal abuse, or criminally assaulted him with blows, he was liable to be deprived of the limb with which he offended.[6] Āpastamba bluntly states that,

1. ...*śūdrāṇāṃ santaḥ śūdrāścāntyānāmantyayonayaḥ. Vas. Dh. S.*, XVI.30.
2. Westermann, *op. cit.*, p. 17.
3. *Gaut. Dh. S.*, XI. 20-21.
4. *Supra*, pp. 113-14.
5. *brāhmaṇastu kṣatriye pañcāśat, tadardhaṃ vaiśye, na śūdre kiñcit. Gaut. Dh. S.*, XII. 11-13.
6. *śūdro dvijātīnatisandhāyābhihatya vāgdaṇḍapāruṣyābhyāmaṅgam mocyo yenopahanyāt, Gaut. Dh. S.*, XII. 1.

if the śūdra abuses a law-abiding ārya, his tongue shall be perforated.[1] Penances provided for the expiation of the sins of abusing respectable persons and speaking minor untruths also discriminate against the śūdra, who was ordered to fast for seven days in such cases;[2] on the other hand a member of the first three varṇas had merely to abstain from milk, pungent condiments and salt for three days only.[3] And finally Āpastamba and Gautama lay down that, if in conversation, sitting, lying down or on the road, the śūdra assumed a position equal to that of the twice-born man, he should be flogged.[4]

Laws relating to adultery provide the most severe punishment for the śūdra. Āpastamba lays down that, if a śūdra commits adultery with an āryā, i.e. a female member of the first three varṇas, he should be put to death,[5] while the woman might be purified by a penance if no child was born from their adulterous intercourse.[6] But, according to the same authority, if an ārya commits the same offence with the śūdra woman, he should be banished.[7] In the case of theft, the law, as laid down by Gautama, imposes the smallest fine upon the śūdra, which increases if the offender belongs to a higher varṇa. Thus, if the śūdra is required to pay eight times the value of the stolen property, the brāhmaṇa has to pay sixty-four times.[8] While it may indicate the former's inability to pay higher fines, the law presupposes a higher standard of conduct on the part of the members of the higher varṇas, who were little expected to commit thefts. This is in keeping with the provision that only members of the first three varṇas should be appointed officials, one of whose chief functions was to protect the people against thieves.[9]

1. *jihvācchedanaṃ śūdrasya āryaṃ dhārmikam ākrośataḥ.* *Āp. Dh. S.*, II. 10.27.14.
2. This is also prescribed for women. *Āp. Dh. S.*, I. 9.26.4.
3. *Ibid.*, I.9.26.3.
4. *vāci pathi śayyāyāmāsana iti samībhavato daṇḍatāḍanam.* *Āp. Dh. S.*, II. 10.27.15; *Gaut. Dh. S.*, XII. 7.
5. *vadhyaḥ śūdra āryāyām.* *Āp. Dh. S.*, II. 10.27-9.
6. *Ibid.*, II. 10.27. 10.
7. *nāśya āryaḥ śūdrāyām.* *Āp. Dh. S.*, II. 10.27-8.
8. *aṣṭapādhyaṃ steyakiviṣaṃ śūdrasya; dviguṇottarāṇītareṣāṃ prativarṇam. Gaut. Dh. S.*, XII. 15-16.
9. *Āp. Dh. S.*, II. 10. 26. 6-8.

So far as the operation of these criminal laws is concerned, a passage from the *Majjhima Nikāya* shows that in cases of adultery and theft the same punishment applied to the offender, irrespective of his varṇa.[1] Therefore the discriminatory laws of the Dharmasūtras in this regard need not be taken so seriously. But the non-brāhmaṇical sources show that the offending dāsas, kammakaras and other classes of workers were subjected to corporal punishments by their masters. Thus we can cite two instances of beating, in which the victims are women slaves.[2] In one case the offence is the neglect of work[3] and in another the failure to bring her wages back to her master.[4] Although there is mention of a slave who was patted and permitted to learn writing and handicrafts, he lived under the perpetual fear of getting 'beaten, imprisoned, branded and fed on slave's fare'[5] at the slightest fault.

Corporal punishment was, however, not only confined to the dāsas, who were not *sui juris*. Along with them the pessas and the kammakaras are frequently described in the Buddhist dialogues as working under the king harried by stripes and fear, weeping with tears on their faces.[6] A simile from a Jain text informs us that the preṣyas (messengers or servants) are made to work by being beaten with sticks.[7] Such being the treatment of workers who seem to have committed no fault, the fate of the guilty can hardly be expected to be better. That the smallest offence of the wageearners was visited with the most severe punishments forms the subject of the following passage from the *Sūyagaḍam*: "A man will (occasionally) severely punish even the smallest offence of his domestics, viz., a slave or messenger or hired servant or vassal (*bhāgilla-bhāgika*)[8] or parasite ; e.g.

1. *evaṃ sante ime cattāro vaṇṇā samasamā honti.* ii, 88.
2. *CHI*, i, 205.
3. *Ibid.*
4. *Jāt.*, i. 492.
5. *Ibid.*, i, 451.
6. *daṇḍa-tajjitā bhaya-tajjitā assumukhā rudamānā parikammāni karonti.* *Majj. N.*, i, 344; *Saṃy. N.*, i, 76; *Aṅg. N.*, ii, 207-8; iii, 172; cf. *Dīgha N.*, i, 141.
7. *Sūyagaḍaṃ*, I. 5.2.5.
8. One who gets the sixth part of the products (e.g. of agriculture) of the work for which he is hired. *SBE*, xlv. 374. fn. 9.

punish him, pull out his hair, beat him, put him in irons, in fetters, in stocks, into prison, screw up in a pair of shackles (his hands and feet) and break them, cut off his hands or feet or ears or nose or lips or head or face (?),[1] pierce his feet, tear out his eyes, teeth, tongue, hang him, brush him, whirl him round, impale him, lacerate him, pour acids (in his wounds), belabour him with cutting-grass, bind him to a lion's tail (!), or a bull's tail, burn him in a wood on fire, let him be devoured by crows and vultures, stop his food and drink, keep him a prisoner for life, let him die any of these horrid deaths."[2]

The above passage describes the conduct of the unrighteous people, who were evidently outside the fold of Jainism, and therefore may not be free from an element of exaggeration. But it undoubtedly shows that the master inflicted different kinds of cruel punishments not only on his slaves but on various other categories of workers employed by him. All this would suggest that corporal punishment for the offending members of the serving class was not uncommon though the artisan members of the śūdra varṇa were perhaps free from this humiliation. In Greece also the slave might pay for minor misdeeds with corporal punishment, but the free man was exempt from this indignity.[3]

For the first time the Dharmasūtra law introduces different rates of wergeld for the members of the different varṇas, there

1. Jacobi finds it difficult to translate the two words *vegacchahiya* and *aṅgacchahiya*. *Ibid.*, 375. fn. 1.

2. *jā vi ya se bāhiriyā parisā bhavai, taṃ jahādāse ivā pese i vā bhayae ivā bhāille i vā kammakarae i vā bhogapurise i vā tesiṃ pi ya ṇaṃ annayaṃrasi ahālahugaṃsi avarāhaṃsi sayameva gaṇuyaṃ daṇḍaṃ nivattei, taṃ jahāimaṃ daṇḍehe, imaṃ muṇḍeha; imaṃ tañjeha, imaṃ tāleha, imaṃ aduyabandhanaṃ kareha, imaṃ niyalabandhanaṃ, kareha, imaṃ haḍḍibandhanaṃ kareha, imaṃ cāragabandhanaṃ kareha, imaṃ niyalaju-yala saṃkodhiyamaḍiyaṃ kareha, imaṃ hathacchinnavaṃ kareha, imaṃ pāyacchinnaṃ kareha, imaṃ kaṇṇachinnahaṃ kareha, imaṃ nakkaoṭṭhasīsamuhachinnayaṃ kareha, veyagacchahiyaṃ aṅgacchahiyaṃ pakkhāphoḍiyaṃ kareha, imaṃ nayaṇuppāḍiyaṃ kareha, imaṃ daṃsaṇuppāḍiyaṃ vasaṇuppāḍiyaṃ jībbhuppāḍiyaṃ olambiyaṃ kareha, ghasiyaṃ kareha, gholiyaṃ kareha, sūlāiyaṃ kareha, sūlabhinnayaṃ kareha, khāravattiyaṃ kareha, vañjhavattiyaṃ kareha, sīhapucchiyagaṃ kareha, vasabhapucchiyagaṃ kareha, davaggi-daḍḍhayaṅgaṃ kāgaṇimaṃsakhāviyaṅgaṃ bhattapāṇanirudvagaṃ imaṃ javañjīvaṃ vahabandhanaṃ kareha, imaṃ annayarena asubheṇaṃ kumāreṇaṃ māreha. Sūyagaḍam,* II. 2.20. Jacobi's tr., *Sūya.*, II. 2.63, *SBE*, xvi, 374-5.

3. Westermann, *op. cit.*, p. 17.

being no such distinction in Vedic times. Three of them lay down that for slaying a kṣatriya the offender shall give one thousand cows, for slaying a vaiśya one hundred cows and for slaying a śūdra ten cows, with a bull in every case.[1] Baudhāyana says that the amount should go to the king,[2] but Āpastamba seems to favour the brāhmaṇa in his place.[3] In any case the amount is not to be paid to the relations of the murdered man. The nature of penances provided for the expiation of the sin of murder also varies according to the varṇa of the murdered person. According to Gautama, for killing a kṣatriya the guilty man should maintain the normal vow of continence for six years, for killing a vaiśya for three years and for killing a śūdra for one year.[4] Vasiṣṭha, however, increases the term of the penance by three years in the case of a vaiśya, and by two years in the cases of a kṣatriya or a śūdra.[5] But the *Sāmavidhāna Brāhmaṇa*, which is regarded by Burnell a work of this period,[6] provides the same penance for the expiation of the sin of killing the members of the first three varṇas, prescribing a different penance for the sin of killing a śūdra.[7] This may suggest that the first distinction in respect of the wergeld was made between the śūdra and the *traivarṇika*. Later this was pushed to extremes by prescribing different rates of fine for the murder of the members of the different varṇas. There must be some basis for the law of the wergeld, which is found in most of the Dharmasūtras. Different rates of wergeld varying according to class are found only in those societies which have ceased to be tribal. But how far and in what ways such a law was observed in the case of the śūdra cannot be determined in the absence of the court decisions on this point.

What is most shocking to the modern democratic mind is the fact that Āpastamba and Baudhāyana provide the same

1. *Bau. Dh. S.*, I. 10. 19. 1 and 2; *Āp. Dh. S.*, I. 9.24. 1-4; *Gaurt. Dh. S.*, XXII. 14-16.
2. I. 10.19.1
3. I.9.24.1 with Haradatta's comm.
4. XXII. 14-16.
5. XX. 31-33.
6. *Sām. Br.*, Introd., p. X.
7. *Sam. Br.*, I. 7.5-6.

penance for killing a śūdra as for killing a flamingo, a *bhāsa*, a peacock, a brāhmaṇī duck, a *pracalāka*, a crow, an owl, a frog, a muskrat, a dog etc.[1] This extreme view, which attaches the same importance to the life of a śūdra as to that of an animal or a bird, may not have found universal acceptance,[2] for the same lawgivers prescribe a wergled of ten cows and a bull for killing a śūdra.[3] But there is no doubt that the early brāhmaṇical law attached very little importance to the life of a śūdra.

Thus, with the general substitution of society based on varṇa for tribal society during post-Vedic times, the members of the śūdra varṇa ceased to have any place in the work of administration. They were probably excluded from all administrative appointments and subjected to corporal punishments for minor offences. In a way this was natural, for they could not generally afford to pay fines. The penalties laid down by the rules of penances and criminal law in respect of the śūdras are indeed proportionately much higher than those prescribed for offences committed by the higher varṇas. But they at least imply that the śūdra was invested with rights of person and property.[4] He could not be killed with such impunity as a slave in Greece.

In the pre-Mauryan period the social position of the śūdra also underwent a change for the worse. The lawgivers emphasised the old fiction that the śūdra was born from the feet of the god,[5] and apparently on this basis imposed on him numerous social disabilities in matters of company, food, marriage and education, amounting in several cases to his social boycott by the members of the higher varṇas in general and the brāhmaṇas in particular. It was laid down by Baudhāyana that a *snātaka* should not go on a journey with outcastes, a woman or with a śūdra.[6] Haradatta's comment on a passage of Gautama states that the term *snātaka* here means a brāhmaṇa or a kṣatriya,[7]

1. *Āp. Dh. S.*, I.9.25.13; *Bau. Dh. S.*, I. 10.19.6.
2. It is interesting to note that the *Sām. Br.*, 1.7.7, prescribes almost the same penance for killing a śūdra as for killing a cow.
3. *Supra.* p. 123.
4. Ghoshal, *IC*, xiv, 27.
5. *Vas. Dh. S.*, IV. 2. *Bau. Dh. S.*, I. 10. 19. 5-6.
6. II. 3.6.22.
7. Comm. to IX. 1, *SBE*, ii, 216.

which implies that the rule did not apply to the vaiśya. Again, one of the rites essential for securing success was that the student desiring it should not talk to women and śūdras.[1] All association with the outcaste (*patita*), who is defined as the son begotten by a śūdra on a female of an unequal caste (evidently higher),[2] was considered undesirable. These were obviously meant to reduce opportunities of social contact between the śūdra and the higher varṇas. In this respect the Dharmasūtras exhibit a clear tendency to widen the social distance between the brāhmaṇa and the śūdra. Āpastamba and Baudhāyana hold that, if a śūdra comes as a guest to a brāhmaṇa, he should be given some work to do and may be fed after the work had been performed.[3] He should not be fed and received by the brāhmaṇa, but by his slaves, who should fetch rice from the royal stores for this purpose.[4] According to Gautama a non-brāhmaṇa should not be the guest of a brāhmaṇa, except on the occasion of a sacrifice,[5] when the vaiśyas and the śūdras should be fed with his servants for mercy's sake.[6] On the occasion of the *vaiśvadeva* ceremony, however, even the caṇḍālas, dogs and crows should be given a portion, if they came at the end of the rite.[7] It seems that this sacrifice, in which a number of deities were invited to partake of the offerings, retained some of the communal and tribal characteristics, which transcended the new class distinctions.

Gautama lays down that the śūdra should be shown consideration by a young person if he was eighty years old and lived in the same town.[8] Weight age given to age was a tribal practice which continued even in class societies. However it was obligatory on a śūdra to honour an ārya, although

1. *Bau. Dh. S.*, IV. 5.4., cf. *Bhār. Gṛ. S.*, III. 6; *Kauśika Sūtra*, III.4.24.
2. *asamānāyām ca śūdrāt patitavṛttiḥ. Gau. Dh. S.*, IV 27.
3. *śūdramabhyāgataṃ śūdrocedāgatastaṃ karmaṇi niyuñjyāt. Āp. Dh. S.*, II 2.4.19; *Bau. Dh. S.*, II. 3.5.14.
4. *Āp. Dh. S.*, II 2.4.20. These stores were to be maintained by the king for the brāhmaṇas.
5. V. 43.
6. *anyānbhṛtyaiḥ sahānṛśaṃsārtham.* V. 45.
7. *Āp. Dh. S.*, II. 4.9.5; *Bau. Dh. S.*, 3.5.11; *Vas. Dh. S.*, XI.9.
8. VI.10.

the latter might be younger in age.[1] Forms of salutation and greeting, which are regulated in the Dharmasūtras according to varṇa, reflect the servile position of the śūdra in society. It is laid down by Āpastamba that a brāhmaṇa should salute by stretching forward his right arm on a level with his ear, a kṣatriya holding it on a level with his breast, a vaiśya holding it on a level with his waist, and a śūdra holding it on a level with his feet.[2] Different terms are prescribed for making inquiries about the welfare and health of the members of the different varṇas. Thus the term used for the health of a kṣatriya is '*anāmaya*' and for that of a śūdra is '*ārogya*'.[3] It is further provided that in greeting a kṣatriya or a vaiśya a person should use pronouns and not their names,[4] which implies that only the śūdra could be addressed by his name, the position of the twice-born classes being too high for such familiarity. In the early Pālī texts a kṣatriya is never addressed by his name or in the second person by any person belonging to the lower classes.[5] The mother of king Udaya, whom the barber Gaṅgamāla calls by his family name, shouts angrily; "This filthy son of a barber, of low origin, forgets himself so much that he calls my son, lord of earth, who is a khattiya by caste, Brāhmaṇa."[6]

The idea that the food touched by the śūdra is defiled and cannot be taken by a brāhmaṇa is first expressed in the Dharmasūtras. According to Āpastamba the food touched by an impure brāhmaṇa or a higher caste person becomes impure, but is not unfit for eating.[7] But if it is brought by an impure śūdra, it cannot be taken.[8] The same is the case with the food which is looked at by a dog or an *apapātra*, to whose class belong the *patita* (outcaste) and caṇḍāla.[9] Another rule states that if a śūdra touches a brāhmaṇa while the latter is eating,

1. *avaropyārya śūdreṇa. Ibid.*, VI. 11.
2. I.2.5.16.
3. *Āp. Dh. S.*, I. 4.14.26-29; *Gaut. Dh. S.*, V. 41-42.
4. *sarvanāmnā striyo rājanyavaiśyau ca na nāmnā. Āp. Dh. S.*, I.4.14.23.
5. Fick, *op. cit.*, p. 83.
6. *Jāt.*, iii, 452.
7. I. 5.16.21.
8. *Ibid.*, I.5.16.22.
9. *Āp. Dh. S.*, I.5.16.30 with Haradatta's comm.

he should leave off eating, because the śūdra's touch defiles him.[1] Āpastamba appears to be more conservative when he says that it is not permissible to take the food offered by a śūdra even if he follows the prescribed laws.[2] But the word *śūdravarjam*, which is taken as prohibiting receiving the food of a śūdra, does not occur in an older manuscript of Āpastamba.[3] This shows that such a view did not prevail in the earlier stage, when only the food of an impure śūdra was to be avoided. Nevertheless, the Dharmasūtras unanimously enjoin the brāhmaṇa to shun the food given by a śūdra.[4] A passage of the *Āpastamba Dharmasūtra*[5] read with the commentary of Haradatta allows him to accept the food of a śūdra in times of distress, provided it is purified by contact with gold and fire and abandoned as soon as the brāhmaṇa gets an alternative source of livelihood.[6] No such condition is attached by Gautama, who, while permitting a brāhmaṇa to accept a śūdra's food in the case of his loss of livelihood,[7] allows him to accept food from a herdsman, a labourer in tillage, an acquaintance of the family, and a servant.[8] But Gautama does not permit him to support himself by following the occupations of a śūdra.[9] Moreover, he is alone in laying down the rule that a snātaka (i.e. a brāhmaṇa or a kṣatriya according to Haradatta) should not sip the water of a śūdra.[10] In some cases the rules regarding the brāhmaṇa's boycott of the śūdra's food were sought to be enforced by various threats and penances. According to Vasiṣṭha, the most deserving brāhmaṇa was one whose stomach did not contain the food of a śūdra.[11] Such a rule would

1. *Ibid.*, I. 5.17.1.
2. *sarvavarṇānāṃ svadharme vartamānānāṃ bhoktavyaṃ śūdravarjamityeke. Ibid.*, I. 6.18.13.
3. Ms. G U. according to Bühler's classification, *Āp. Dh. S.*, Introd., P. III.
4. *Āp. Dh. S.*, II. 8. 18.2; *Bau. Dh. S.*, II. 2.3.1; *Vas. Dh. S.*, XIV. 2-4.
5. *tasyāpi dharmopanatasya.* I. 6.18.14.
6. *Āp. Dh. S.*, I. 6. 18.15.
7. *vṛttiścennāntareṇa śūdrāt.* XVII. 5.
8. *paśupālakṣetrakarṣakakulasaṃgatakārayitṛparicārakā bhojyānnāḥ.* XVII. 6.
9. VII. 22.
10. IX. 11.
11. VI. 26.

naturally deprive the guilty brāhmaṇa of the sacrificial gifts, which constituted the main source of his income. It was further declared by the same authority that, if a brāhmaṇa died with the food of a śūdra in his stomach, he would be born either as a village pig or in the family of that śūdra.[1] Further, a brāhmaṇa whose body is nourished by the essence of a śūdra's food may daily recite the Veda, may offer prayers, but cannot find the path that leads upwards. Again, if, after eating the food of a śūdra, he has conjugal intercourse, even his sons would belong to the śūdra caste and he would not ascend to heaven.[2] Baudhāyana lays down that, if a person commits the offence of eating the food of a śūdra or of cohabiting with a śūdra woman, his sin can be expiated by performing seven *prāṇāyāmas* (suppressions of breath) daily for a week.[3] For the same purpose he also provides the penance of performing the ceremony of taking boiled barley grain.[4] These penances, however, should not be taken as representing the state of affairs in this period. The first occurs in the fourth praśna, which according to one view is as late as the 10th century A.D.,[5] and the second occurs in the third praśna, which according to Bühler, is a later addition to the original work.[6]

The Dharmasūtras give the impression that generally the ideal brāhmaṇa avoided the food of a śūdra,[7] especially if he was impure. But the penance and threats for enforcing this ban seem to be of later origin and were probably not effective during this period. It is clear that no such ban was imposed on the kṣatriya and the vaiśya. Thus at the *vaiśvadeva* ceremony the śūdra could be engaged in the preparation of the food under the superintendence of the men of the first three varṇas.[8] While

1. VI. 27-29.
2. *Ibid.*
3. IV.1.5.
4. *Bau. Dh. S.*, III.6.5.
5. Hultzsch, *The Baudhāyanadharmaśāstra*, Introd., p. IX.
6. *Ibid.*
7. The contrast between the brāhmaṇa and the vṛṣala is emphasised in the *Nirukta*, III. 16.
8. ...*āryādhiṣṭhitā vā śūdrāḥ saṁskartāraḥ syuḥ. Āp. Dh. S.*, II. 2.3.1-4. The passage does not occur in a later ms. (G according to Bühler's classification). Obviously it was removed in later times to exclude the śūdras completely from preparing food.

cooking he should remain absolutely neat and clean so that the food might not be contaminated. For this purpose he should cause the hair of his head, his beard, the hair on his body and his nails to be cut, preferably on the eighth day of each half of the month or on the days of full and the new moon. Besides he should take his bath with his clothes on.[1] Ordinarily it was provided that the śūdras living in the service of the āryas should trim their hair and nails every month; their mode of sipping water, according to Baudhāyana, being the same as that of the āryas.[2] The fact that a śūdra could be permitted to prepare food even at a religious ceremony, in which the greatest degree of purity was expected, shows that ordinarily his food was accepted by the members of the higher varṇas, perhaps excluding the brāhmaṇa in some cases. Even in a later Jātaka the occupation of a cook is described as one to be practised by slaves or hired labourers.[3] In one case, however, the kṣatriya father avoids eating with his daughter by a slave wife. But this passage occurs in the present story of a later Jātaka,[4] and hence may not apply to this period. Prescriptions which forbade contact with food touched by the impure, and especially with the leavings of their table, and punished transgressions of the rules, are found in the early Pāli texts,[5] but there is nothing to show that they were particularly directed against the śūdras. This was probably due to the fact that the old Indo-European practice, according to which all the members of the clan could partake of the common meals provided on special occasions,[6] continued to exercise influence for some time even when tribes and clans had broken up into varṇas. The practice of pollution became important only when the upper classes used it as an instrument to strengthen and perpetuate their socio-economic and other privileges.

1. *Ibid.*, II. 2.3.6-8.
2. I.5.10.20; this passage is not to be found in the ms. Ct (according to Hultzsch's classification), one of the southern group of the mss. derived from a more original form of the text than the northern. (The *Baudhāyanadharmaśāstra*. Introd., p. VIII).
3. *Jāt*, v., 293.
4. *Ibid.*, iv, 145-6.
5. Fick, *SONI*, p. 47.
6. Senart, *Caste in India*, pp. 182-3.

The marriage rules of the Dharmasūtras were dictated by considerations of varṇa. Of the eight forms of marriage, which first appear during this period, the *gāndharva* (love marriage) and the *paiśāca* (marriage by seduction which implied some sort of consent) were considered lawful for the vaiśyas and the śūdras. According to Baudhāyana the first was meant for the vaiśyas and the second for the śūdras.[1] In justification of this view he states that because of their preoccupation with agriculture and service the wives of the vaiśyas and the śūdras cannot be kept under control.[2] This suggests that the employment of the womenfolk of the lower orders for earning their livelihood rendered them comparatively independent of their husbands; the inability of the women of the higher varṇas to earn their living made them more dependent but more respectable in society.

The stability of marriage relations was considered in terms of varṇa. In the opinion of Vasiṣṭha, the higher the varṇa the more stable would be the marriage. Thus it was laid down that, if the husband leaves his home, a wife of the brāhmaṇa or the kṣatriya varṇa, who has issue, shall wait for five years, a wife of the vaiśya varṇa for four years, and one of the śūdra varṇa for three years. If she has no issue, the waiting period will be cut down by one year in the case of the brāhmaṇa, and by two years each in the cases of the kṣatriya, the vaiśya and the śūdra,[3] with the result that in such a case a wife of the śūdra varṇa will have to wait for only one year. Such a rule again implies the comparative independence of the women of the lower orders, among whom marriage ties were easily dissoluble.

But the śūdra women were not treated on a footing of equality by their husbands from the higher varṇas. It is stated by Vasiṣṭha that a śūdra wife, who belongs to the black race, can be espoused as concubine for the sake of pleasure,[4] but cannot be accepted

1. I.11.20.13.

2. *ayantritakalatrā hi vaiśyaśūdrā bhavanti, karṣaṇaśuśrūṣādhikṛtvāt. Bau. Dh. S.*, I. 11. 20. 14-15. Bühler's translation that the vaiśyas and śūdras are not particular about their wives does not convey the meaning of the passage accurately (*SBE*, xiv, 207).

3. *Vas. Dh. S.*, XVII. 78.

4. *kṛṣṇavarṇā yā rāmā ramaṇāyaiva na dharmāya. Vas. Dh. S.*, XVIII. 18.

in a regular marriage.[1] A passage from the same source allows an ārya to marry wives from the śūdra caste, if the wedding is not accompanied by the recitation of the proper Vedic texts, but Vasiṣṭha himself does not consider it desirable.[2] For such a marriage causes the degradation of the family and the loss of heaven after death.[3] In the opinion of Āpastamba it is not desirable that a brāhmaṇa should cohabit with a śūdra woman or serve a person of the black race.[4] Both Āpastamba and Baudhāyana provide for purificatory rites for those who have connections with a woman of the śūdra varṇa.[5] But the two passages occurring in the *Baudhāyana Dharmasūtra* are found in the fourth praśna, which, as shown earlier, is a later addition. Therefore such penances need not be seriously taken as applying to this period. The view that the śūdra wife should be avoided comes into conflict with an earlier rule of Vasiṣṭha, which says that a brāhmaṇa can take three wives, a kṣatriya two, and a vaiśya and a śūdra one each, in the order of their varṇas.[6] This clearly allows the members of the first two varṇas to enter into regular marriage relations with śūdra women, and hence the idea that the śūdra wife should be accepted only for the sake of pleasure may have been of later origin. Further, it is obvious that a large number of wives could be maintained only by well-to-do people. Thus while the rule of polygamy for the members of the higher varṇas seems to be in line with their better economic status, the monogamy of the śūdra[7] is in keeping with his unhappy economic situation.

Although marriage with women of lower castes was permissible the Dharmasūtras show great aversion for connections of the

1. *Ibid.*, cf. Ghoshal, *IC*, xiv, 22.
2. *śūdrāmapyeke mantravarjam tadvat, tathā na kuryāt. Vas. Dh. S.*, I. 25-26.
3. *ato hi dhruvaḥ kulāpakarṣaḥ pretya cāsvargaḥ. Vas. Dh. S.*, 1.27. Among the ancient Teutons a free man who wedded a slave was himself reduced to slavery. Landtman, *The Origin of the Inequality of the Social Classes*, p. 282.
4. 1.9.27.10-11.
5. *Āp. Dh. S.*, I. 9.26. 7; 27.11; *Bau. Dh. S.*, IV. 2.13, 6.5-6.
6. *Vas. Dh. S.*, I. 24. Baudhāyana (I.8.16. 1-4) allows four wives to the brāhmaṇa, three to the kṣatriya, two to the vaiśya and one to the śūdra.
7. Both Vasiṣṭha and Baudhāyana prescribe only one wife for the śūdra, although the former prescribes this for the vaiśya also.

reverse type.[1] According to Gautama a son begotten by a śūdra on a woman of unequal caste was regarded as a *patita*.[2] It is mostly to such marriages and connections that the early law-books trace the origin of about a dozen mixed (*varṇasaṃkara*) castes. Thus the issue begotten by a śūdra on a woman of the kṣatriya varṇa is known as a kṣattṛ, and the one begotten on a female of the vaiśya caste as a māgadha.[3] The son of a śūdra by a brāhmaṇa woman is branded as a caṇḍāla.[4] According to Gautama people begotten by the brāhmaṇa, the kṣatriya, the vaiśya and the śūdra on a woman of the śūdra caste are respectively known as pāraśavas, yavanas, karaṇas and śūdras.[5] The son of a brāhmaṇa by a śūdra woman is called a niṣāda.[6] His issue by a woman of the śūdra caste is known as the pulkasa, and the son begotten by a śūdra on a woman of the niṣāda caste is known as a kukkuṭaka.[7] The issue of the union of a kṣatriya and a śūdra woman is known as an ugra,[8] while that of a vaiśya and a śūdra is to be regarded as a rathakāra.[9] The above list of castes would show that in the opinion of the Dharmasūtras *anuloma* (in regular order) and *pratiloma* (inverted order) connections between the śūdra and members of the higher varṇas were regarded as the most plentiful source of the origin of the mixed castes, many of whom were relegated to the position of untouchables. But most of these mixed castes were nothing more than backward tribes, who were annexed to the four original and recognised varṇas by giving them a wholly arbitrary genesis.[10] Nevertheless, in course of time such explanations may have influenced new formations of castes, for these have been taken place even in recent times.[11]

1. Generally the jātis of this age were endogamous, Fick, *SONI*, p. 51.
2. IV. 27.
3. *Bau. Dh. S.*, I. 9. 17.7.
4. *Ibid.*, *Vas. Dh. S.*, XVIII. 1.
5. IV. 21; cf. *Bau. Dh. S.*, II. 2.3.30.
6. *Bau. Dh. S.*, II. 2.3.29; *Gaut. Dh. S.*, IV. 16; *Vas. Dh. S.*, XVIII. 8.
7. *Bau. Dh. S.*, I. 9.17. 13-14.
8. *Ibid.*, I. 9.17.5.
9. *Ibid.*, I. 9.17.6.
10. Fick, *SONI*, p. 9.
11. There are several tribes of this type in Chotānāgpur, and some castes of this type in eastern Nepāl.

Although the early Gṛhyasūtras nowhere clearly refer to the exclusion of the śūdra from the rite of initiation, the *Āpastamba Dharmasūtra* states that he cannot be admitted to the *upanayana* and the study of the Veda.[1] The presence of a śūdra, and particularly that of a caṇḍāla, is considered a sufficient ground for stopping the recitation of the Veda.[2] Under such conditions Baudhāyana and Gautama prefer the interruption of all studies.[3] The latter further adds that the study should not be always carried on in the same town.[4] This has been interpreted by Maskarin to mean a town which is inhabited mainly by the śūdras.[5] Gautama alone states that, if a śūdra recites the Vedic texts, his tongue should be cut out; and if he rem embers them, his body should be split in twain.[6] This terrible measure seems to reflect the extremist attitude of Manu,[7] and hence may be treated as an interpolation in the law-book of Gautama. Nevertheless, it is evident that even during this period the idea of imparting Vedic education to a śūdra was vehemently opposed.

A passage from Āpastamba, however, favours the education of the śūdra in Vedic literature. While stating that a student should pay the fee to the teacher for the teaching of the Veda, he declares that the latter can accept it either from an ugra or a śūdra, under all circumstances.[8] This may indicate an earlier state of things, when the śūdra was admitted to Vedic education. But later this was denied to him, not only by Gautama and Vasiṣṭha but also by Āpastamba himself. The Veda being the source of the law (dharma), as a natural corollary Vasiṣṭha declares that a śūdra is neither worthy of receiving any advice nor the contents of law.[9] Apparently such a dictum was meant to

1. *aśūdrāṇām aduṣṭakarmaṇāmupāyanaṃ vedādhyayanamagnyādheyaṃ phalavanti ca karmāṇi.* I.1.1.6.

2. *Ibid.*, I. 3.9.9; *Śāṅkh. Gṛ. S.*, IV. 7.33.

3. *Bau. Dh. S.*, I. 11.21.15; *Gaut. Dh. S.*, XVI. 19.

4. *Gaut. Dh. S.*, XVI. 46.

5. *tatra śūdrādibhūyiṣṭhe anadhyāyaḥ.*

6. *udāharṇe jihvācceddaḥ, dhāraṇe śarīrabhedaḥ.* XII 4-6.

7. VIII. 270-272.

8. *...sarvadā śūdrata ugrato vācāryārthasyāharaṇaṃ dhārmyamityeke. Āp. Dh. S.*, I. 2.7.19-21.

9. *na śūdrāya matiṃ dadyāt...na cāsyopadiśeddharmam. Vas. Dh. S.*, XVIII.14.

keep the śūdras in complete ignorance of the law by which they were governed.

Āpastamba provides that women and śūdras may learn a supplement to the *Atharva Veda.*[1] It is suggested that this comprises dancing, music, and other branches of everyday art and learning.[2] In commenting on a passage of Gautama Maskarin refers to a similar type of education. He quotes the Smṛtis as stating that a niṣāda should be initiated and educated in the art of elephant training.[3] All this may imply that the śūdras could receive training in arts and crafts but were debarred from receiving Vedic education, which was more or less identical with literate learning. Thus the Dharmasūtras sought to establish a divorce between literate education, which was confined to the members of the twice-born varṇas, and technical training, which lay in the sphere of the śūdras. It was also stated that Vedic study impedes pursuit of agriculture and *vice versa.*[4] Such a rule would naturally affect not only the śūdras but also those vaiśyas who carried on agriculture themselves. We do not know how far this policy worked in practice. A later Jātaka informs us that two caṇḍāla boys went in disguise to receive education at Taxila, but, when they were detected through the inadvertant use of their own dialect, they were expelled from the institution.[5] Nevertheless, other Jātaka stories show that the schools had on their rolls sons of merchants and tailors,[6] and even fishermen.[7] Thus in practice even during this period the śūdras were not completely excluded from receiving education.

The Dharmasūtra's exclusion of the śūdra from Vedic education naturally led to his exclusion from sacrifices and sacraments, which could be performed only with the Vedic mantras. A rule of the *Āśvalāyana Gṛhyasūtra*[8] is interpreted as suggesting that the śūdra could hear the Vedic mantras to be recited on the occasion

1. *Āp. Dh. S.*, II. 11.29.11-12 with the comm. of Haradatta.
2. *SBE*, ii. 169.
3. *Gaut. Dh. S.*, IV. 26.
4. *vedaḥ kṛṣivināśāya kṛṣi vedavināśinī. Bau. Dh. S.*, I. 5.10.30.
5. *Jāt.* iv, 391-2.
6. *Ibid.*, iv, 38.
7. *Ibid.*, iii, 171.
8. I. 21.12. (Trivandrum edn.); I. 24.12-15 (*SBE tr.*).

of the *madhuparka* ceremony.[1] Similarly Jaiminī quotes an old teacher Bādari as stating that the Vedic sacrifice can be performed by members of all the four varṇas.[2] But he does not approve of this idea,[3] and thus seems to represent the dominant view of his age. The śūdra could not lay the sacred fire for the Vedic sacrifice.[4] He could not perform any sacrament.[5] He came to be excluded from the Vedic sacrifice to such an extent that in the performance of certain rites even his presence and sight were to be avoided.[6] Ordinarily a śūdra could not use even the current exclamation *namaḥ*;[7] he could do this only if he was especially permitted to do so.[8] Gautama, however, quotes certain athorities who allow a śūdra to perform a select list of small Vedic sacrifices known as the *pāka-yajñas* (simple domestic rites).[9] Baudhāyana quotes others as stating that submersion in water and bathing are prescribed for all the varṇas, but sprinkling water over the body along with the recitation of the mantras is the particular duty of the twice-born.[10]

It is argued that the non-performance of various ceremonies and sacrifices were an advantage to the śūdra, who was free from the obligation of observing them.[11] But what was an advantage to him from the modern point of view was a disadvantage according to the dominant social outlook of those times, which condemned those who did not perform sacrifice to a low social status.[12]

Gautama lays down that a śūdra shall live with his wife.[13] Haradatta quotes another commentator as interpreting this to the effect that a śūdra can only lead the life of a householder

1. Hopkins. *Mutual Relations of the Four Castes*, p. 86, fn.1.
2. *Jai. Mī. S.*, VI. 1.25-27.
3. *Ibid.*, VI. 1.33f.
4. *Āp. Dh. S.*, I. 1.1.6.
5. *śūdramityasaṃskāryo vijñāyate. Vas. Dh. S*, IV. 3.
6. *Pāraskara Gṛ. S.*, II. 8.3.
7. *Gaut. Dh. S.*, X. 64.
8. *Ibid.*
9. X. 65.
10. II. 4.7.3.
11. Dutt, *op. cit.*, p. 175.
12. Dutt implicitly recognises this fact on pp. 177-78 of his book.
13. X. 55.

and not that of a student, a hermit or an ascetic.[1] It seems that in later times a brāhmaṇa, as a rule, passed through four, a nobleman through three, a citizen through two, and a śūdra through one of the āśramas.[2] This may not have always been the case, but the discrimination against the śūdra is consistent with his function of service to the members of the upper varṇas, a task which he could only perform as a householder.

The śūdra was, however, permitted to offer funeral oblations.[3] But Gautama and Vasiṣṭha provide that the impurity caused to him by birth or death of a kinsman (*sapiṇḍa*) shall last for a month.[4] According to Vasiṣṭha this period lasts for ten, fifteen and twenty days respectively in the case of a brāhmaṇa, a rājanya and a vaiśya.[5] Gautama, however, cuts down the period by four days in the case of a kṣatriya and eight days in that of a vaiśya.[6] The longest period of impurity in the case of a śūdra, if observed, must have caused great hardship to him. Unable to earn his living, he would be compelled to throw himself at the mercy of a creditor or his master. Even in recent times, in the period of impurity caused by death, poor śūdras have been seen begging from door to door. But in one respect the śūdra's position was better. He was not considered so impure as to be forbidden to touch the corpse of the higher varṇas. He could carry the corpse even of a brāhmaṇa[7] to the cremation ground, where he could touch the funeral pyre.[8]

Of the three higher varṇas, the brāhmaṇa was expected to carry out his religious duties most scrupulously. Thus Baudhāyana lays down that a brāhmaṇa who does not perform the *saṃdhyā* morning and evening should be made by the king to do the work of a śūdra.[9] The brāhmaṇa also fell from status if he

1. *nā'śramāntarā prāptiriti.*" Comm. to *Gaut. Dh. S.*, X. 55.
2. Max Müller, *The Hibbert Lectures.* p. 343.
3. *Gaut. Dh. S.*, X. 53.
4. *Ibid.*, XIV, 2-4; *Vas. Dh. S.*, IV. 30.
5. *Vas. Dh. S.*, IV. 27-29.
6. XIV. 2-4. According to others the period of impurity in the case of a vaiśya may last for half a month (*Ibid.*).
7. R. L. Mitra, *Indo-Aryans.* ii, 131-2.
8. *Āśva. Gṛ. S.* (*SBE* tr.), IV. 2. 19-21. The word used here is '*vṛṣala*'.
9. *Bau. Dh. S.*, II. 4.7.15.

took to manual occupations. Baudhāyana states that the brāhmaṇas who tend cattle, live by trade, work as artisans, actors, servants or usurers should be treated like śūdras.[1] Gautama goes a step further and states that, if an ārya adopts the occupations of a non-ārya, (i.e. a śūdra), he is reduced to his status.[2] Commenting on this passage, Haradatta thinks that even a brāhmaṇa who performs the occupation of a non-ārya need not be served by a śūdra. He curiously adds that a śūdra who does the work of an ārya must not be despised by others following non-āryan occupations. Evidently there seems to be no point in such a contempt, for the āryas were higher in status. Such rules suggest that the members of the higher varṇas, especially the brāhmaṇas, felt contempt for manual occupations, which reduced them to the position of śūdras when they were forced to earn their living with their hands.[3] In the *Vinaya Piṭaka* agriculture, trade and tending of cattle are regarded as a high type of work.[4] This obviously refers to the functions of the vaiśya. On the other hand the work of a carpenter and a sweeper is regarded as of low type.[5] The same text enumerates five low occupations (*hīnasippāni*) of the nalakāra (bamboo worker). the kumbhakāra (potter), the pesakāra (weaver), the chammakāra (leather worker) and the nahāpita (barber).[6] At one place, however, the occupations of the weaver, the bamboo worker, the potter and the barber are put in the list of ordinary crafts,[7] which shows that generally the fifth craft, that of the leather worker, was universally looked upon with contempt.

Taking the social status of these crafts separately, the potter does not generally appear in dark colours.[8] But at one place

1. *Ibid.*, I. 5.10.24; cf. *Vas. Dh. S.*, II. 27.
2. *āryānāryayorvyatikṣepe karmaṇaḥ sāmyaṃ*. X. 67.
3. In the Jātakas there are instances of brāhmaṇas living by manual occupations.
4. *Vin.*, iv, 6.
5. *Ibid.* The term *koṭṭhakakammam* is explained as *tacchakamma* in the *Vin. A.*, p. 439; but Horner translates it as work of a store-(room) keeper. *SBE*, xi, 175.
6. *Vin.*, iv, 7.
7. *Dīgha. N.*, i, 51.
8. Bose, *op. cit.*, ii, 460.

the work of the weaver (tantavāya) is described as of inferior type.[1] The barber also seems to have been an object of derision.[2] Thus although the barber Upāli became a monk, he was reviled by the nuns as one of low birth whose occupations are shampooing and cleaning of dirt.[3] All this indicates a tendency to hold some crafts in low esteem. Since these crafts were practised by various sections of the śūdras in course of time the occupations of the śūdra varṇas as a whole came to be stigmatized. This is evident from a passage of the *Dīgha Nikāya*, which uses the phrase "*luddācāra khuddācāra ti*"[4] in defining the functions of the śūdras. This means that the śūdras are those who live on hunting and other humble pursuits. In a Jain text also the terms *vṛṣala*, *gṛhadāsa* (born slave) and 'low born wretch' are used as terms of contempt like dog, thief, robber, cheat, liar etc.[5]

The early Pāli texts often mention the five despised castes of the caṇḍāla, the niṣāda, the veṇa, the rathakāra and the pukkusa.[6] They are described as having low families (*nīca kula*)[7] or inferior births (*hīnajāti*).[8] The enumeration of low trades, crafts and castes seems to be broadly true of pre-Mauryan times, for the Buddha argues at length with the monks that they should not create such distinctions in the order by insulting speech referring to the former *jāti*, the *sippa*, the *kamma* etc. of the monks.[9]

Several despised *jātis* of the Buddhist texts roughly correspond to the untouchable sections of brāhmaṇical society. According to the Buddhist and Jain texts the caṇḍālas and the pukkusas were not included in the śūdra varṇa.[10] But the Dharmasūtras incorporate them in the list of the mixed castes, who are supposed to have śūdra blood. According to Patañjali Pāṇini seems

1. *lāmaka-kamma*. *Jāt.*, i. 356.
2. *Jāt.* iii, 452-3.
3. *kasavato malamajjano nihīnajacco*. *Vin.*, iv, 308.
4. *Dīgha N.*, iii, 95.
5. *Āyār.*, II. 4.1.8; cf. *Dīgha N.*, i. 92-3.
6. *Majj. N.*, iii, 169-78; ii, 152, 183-4.
7. *Ibid.*
8. *Vin.*, ii, 6; cf. *Aṅg. N.*, ii, 85; *Saṃy. N.*, i, 93.
9. *Vin.*, iv, 4-11.
10. *Saṃy. N.* i, 102, 166; *Sūya.*, 1.9.2-3; Fick, *op. cit.*, pp. 20-30.

to have included the caṇḍāla and the mṛtapa (a person who watches dead bodies) in the list of those śūdras who lived outside towns and villages, and whose contact permanently defiled the bronze vases of the brāhmaṇas.[1]

Oringinally the caṇḍālas seem to have been an aboriginal tribe. This is clear from their use of their own dialect.[2] In a Jain text they are mentioned along with the other tribes such as the Śabaras, the Draviḍas, the Kaliṅgas, the Gauḍas and the Gāndhāras.[3] But gradually the caṇḍālas came to be looked upon as untouchables. Āpastamba holds that to touch and see a caṇḍāla is sinful.[4] This passage, however, is not to be found in the two earlier manuscripts of his Dharmasūtra,[5] which shows that untouchability appeared probably towards the end of the pre-Mauryan period. A similar provision occurs in the later work of Gautama, who provides that, if a caṇḍāla defiles the body, it can be purified by bathing dressed in clothes.[6]

In the Pāli texts the caṇḍālas are clearly depicted as untouchables. A later Jātaka describes the caṇḍālas as the meanest men on earth.[7] Contact with the air that touched a caṇḍāla's body was regarded as pollution.[8] The very sight of a caṇḍāla foreboded evil.[9] Thus the daughter of a seṭṭhi of Banaras, seeing a caṇḍāla, washes her eyes, that have been contaminated by a mere glance at that despised person.[10] Food and drink, if seen by him, were not to be taken.[11] Partaking of his food, even without knowledge, led to social ostracism. It is said that sixteen thousand brāhmaṇas lost their caste because they unknowingly took food which had been polluted by contact with the leavings

1. *śūdraṇāmanirvasitānām*. *Pā.*, II. 4-10; *Mahābhāṣya*, i, 475.
2. *Jāt.*, iv, 391-2.
3. *Sūyagaḍam* (*SBE* tr.), II. 2.27.
4. *Āp. Dh. S.*, II. 1.2.8.
5. MSS. Gu 2, 3 according to Bühler's classification (*op. cit.*, Introd., p. III.)
6. XIV. 30.
7. *Jāt.* iv, 397.
8. *Ibid.*, iii, 233.
9. *Ibid.*, iv, 376, 391.
10. *Ibid.*
11. *Ibid.*, iv, 390.

of a caṇḍāla's meal.[1] There is also the case of a brāhmaṇa, who ate the table leavings of a caṇḍāla from hunger, and committed suicide in order to avoid the contempt of his former caste people.[2] In a Jātaka story when a caṇḍāla enters a town, the people beat him and render him senseless.[3] A similar story recurs in a Jain text of later times. It is said that when two sons of a mātaṅga leader of Banaras led a singing and dancing party during the festival of a god of love, the high caste people belaboured them with kicks and blows and turned them out of the town.[4] By and large, the Jātaka references suggest that although the caṇḍālas were despised as untouchables by the members of the higher varṇas, they were especially hated by the brāhmaṇas.

When the caṇḍālas were absorbed in brāhmaṇical society, this assimilation did not mark a complete break with their former style of life. Probably on account of their being hunters and fowlers, they were assigned the task of removing dead bodies of animals and human beings. They always appear to be associated with the removal and cremation[5] of corpses.[6] This work was also done by the paṇas, who were known as caṇḍālas.[7] The caṇḍālas were also sometimes engaged for street sweeping.[8] The caṇḍāla does not appear as an executioner of criminals in the Dharmasūtras. In the Jātaka he is employed in whipping and cutting off the limbs of the criminal.[9] It has been suggested that the *coraghātaka* (executioner of a thief) of the Jātaka may have been a caṇḍāla.[10] Some of the caṇḍālas earned their living by the occupations of jugglers and acrobats,[11] — a practice which is still followed by the backward

1. *Ibid.*, iv, 387.
2. *Ibid.*, ii, 82-84.
3. *Ibid.*, iv, 376, 391.
4. *Uttarā. Ṭīkā*, 13, p. 185a quoted in Jain, *op. cit.*, p. 144.
5. *Rm.*, I. 58.10.
6. *chavachaḍḍaka-caṇḍāḷā*. Comm. to *Jāt.*, iii, 195.
7. *Antaga.*, 65.
8. *Jāt.*, iv, 390.
9. *Ibid.*, iii, 41, 179.
10. Bose, *op. cit.*, ii, 438.
11. *Ibid.*, 439-440.

nomadic people wandering from place to place in Northern India.

The caṇḍāla led a life of misery and squalor. A simile from a Pāli text informs us that a caṇḍāla boy or girl, clad in rags, with begging tray in hand, on entering village or town assumes a humble mein and then goes on.[1] We learn from a later Jātaka that the caṇḍāla possessed a pair of coloured garments (in order to distinguish him from the rest of the population), a girdle, a ragged robe and an earthen bowl.[2]

In popular parlance the term caṇḍāla signified a person who was without any virtues, a person without faith and morals.[3] Fick rightly says that in their depiction of the caṇḍāla the Jātakas show that the reality was not far different from the priestly theory.[4] But it is important to note that most of the references relating to the caṇḍālas are found in the later Jātakas, especially in the fourth volume, and hence may apply to the end of the pre-Mauryan period or even to later times.

The pulkasas or the pukkusas seem to have been an aboriginal tribe that lived by hunting,[5] but they were gradually absorbed in brāhmaṇical society for certain tasks such as removing flowers from the temple and the palace.[6] The fact that they could approach the temple premises to remove flowers shows that they were not regarded as being quite as degraded as the caṇḍāla.

The veṇas were another aboriginal tribe, who lived by hunting and working in bamboo.[7] A later Jātaka mentions a veṇukāra or velukāra who goes into the forest with his knife to collect a bundle of bamboos for his trade.[8] The Dharmasūtras invent an origin for the veṇas as well. According to Baudhāyana

1. *...kalopihattho nantikavāsī gāmaṃ vā nigamaṃ vā pavisanto nīcacittaṃ yava utaṭṭhapetvā pavisati. Aṅg. N.*, iv, 376.

2. *Jāt.*, iv. 379.

3. *Aṅg. N.*, iii, 206.

4. Fick, *op. cit.*, p. 318.

5. There is no indication of this in the Pāli texts, but Manu (X. 49) and Viṣṇu (XVI. 9) prescribe hunting as their occupation.

6. *Jāt.*, iii, 195; cf. Fick, *op. cit.*, p. 321.

7. Bose *op. cit.*, ii, 454-55.

8. *Jāt.*, iv, 251.

a vaiṇa is the offspring of a vaidehaka father (born of a vaiśya father and a kṣatriya mother) and an ambaṣṭha mother (born of a brāhmaṇa and a vaiśya mother).[1] Thus, unlike the caṇḍāla and the pulkasa, the vaiṇa was not supposed to have śūdra blood. Although in a later Jātaka verse the term *veṇi* is bracketted with the caṇḍāla as a term of rebuke,[2] there is nothing to show that the veṇas were regarded as untouchables like the caṇḍālas. The commentary to the *Vinaya Piṭaka* clearly states that birth as a veṇa means birth as a carpenter (tacchaka).[3] The veṇa and the takṣaka being identical, it appears strange that the latter, who enjoyed a high status in later Vedic society, was relegated to the position of a despised caste in the Buddhist texts.

The rathakāra is also regarded as a despised caste in the Buddhist texts, but in the brāhmaṇical texts he continues to enjoy a high social standing. The Gṛhyasūtras provide for his *upanayana*.[4] Rhys Davids suggests that the rathakāras were an aboriginal tribe.[5] But this does not seem to be correct, because they formed part of the āryan viś in Vedic times. It is likely, however, that in later times some of the aborigines were assimilated to the ranks of the rathakāras. On the basis of a passage from a later Jātaka[6] it is suggested that the rathakāra fell in status because of his having taken to leather work.[7] But the rathakāra also continued to be employed to make the wheels of the chariot, which was used by the kings.[8] Further, although the craft of the leather worker (*cammakāra*) is regarded as low, he himself is not put in the list of the despised castes. Perhaps one of the reasons why the rathakāra is treated as a condemned caste in the Buddhist texts is the Buddhist aversion to war, for which the rathakāra prepared chariots. In any case it is clear

1. *Bau. Dh. S.*, 1.9.17.12.
2. *Jāt*, v, 306.
3. *veṇajāti ti tacchakajāti. SBB*, xi, 173; cf. *Jāt.*, v, 306.
4. *vasante brāhmaṇamupanīta...varṣāṃ rathakāraṃ śiśire vā. Bhāradvāja Gṛ. S.*, I. 1; *Bau. Gṛ. S.*, II. 5-6. cf. II. 8.5; cf. *Jai. Mī. S.*, VI. 1.50.
5. *Dialogues of the Buddha*, i, 100.
6. *Jāt.*, vi, 51; cf. *Peta VA*, III. 1.13.
7. Bose, *op. cit.*, ii, 456.
8. *Aṅg. N.*, i, 111-113.

that they were not degraded to the same level as the caṇḍāla and the pukkusa.

It is not so difficult to explain the inclusion of the neṣādas in the Buddhist list of despised castes. This agrees with their low position in the Dharmasūtras. They were a pre-āryan tribal people, who are described as short-limbed, of the complexion of charred wood, with blood-red eyes,[1] high cheekbones, low-topped nose, and copper-coloured hair.[2] The tradition of their curious origin from the body of Veṇa,[3] the king who proved tyrannical to the priestly class, may indicate the resistance they offered to the process of brāhmaṇization Even when adopted into brāhmaṇical society, the niṣādas continued mainly as hunters,[4] who lived in their own villages.[5] Possibly some of the niṣādas found their way into the priestly class. The niṣāda gotra reported by the *gaṇapāṭha* of Pāṇini,[6] though not mentioned in any of the standard gotra lists, would not be possible unless some brāhmaṇas had been adopted from aboriginal priests or had served the aborigines as priests.[7] All the same, it is clear that during this period the niṣādas definitely fell from the status which they enjoyed in later Vedic society.

At least some of the despised castes of the Pāli texts, particularly the niṣādas and the caṇḍālas, were treated as untouchables. Collectively the untouchables were known as the *antyas* or the *bāhyas*, i.e. people living outside villages and towns. Gautama condemns an *antya* as the vilest person[8] (*pāpiṣṭhaḥ*). Vasiṣṭha distinguishes between the good śūdras and the *antyayonis*, who can appear as witness only in their own cases.[9] In the *Āpastamba*

1. *Mbh.*, XII. 59. 102-3.
2. Dutt, *op. cit.*, p. 107.
3. *Mbh.*, XII. 59.99-101. B. C. Law argues that these were Niṣadhas, and not Niṣādas (*Tribes in Ancient India*, p. 100), but the Cr. Edn. of the *Mbh.* clearly mentions Nisādas.
4. *Jāt.*, ii, 200; vi, 71 f., 170.
5. *Ibid.*, vi, 71f.
6. IV. 1.100.
7. Kosambi, *JAOS*, lxxv, 44. This depends on the assumption that the niṣāda gotra was a brāhmaṇical gotra, which is doubtful.
8. IV. 28. At another place Gautama states that the *antyas* should be given impure garments (XIV. 42).
9. XVI. 30.

Dharmasūtra the word *antaḥ* is used in relation to the caṇḍālas and shows that he lived at the end of the village.[1] In the same text the *bāhyas*, among whom the recitation of the Veda is forbidden, are explained by Haradatta as the ugras and the niṣādas.[2] The *antāvasāyins* are described by Vasiṣṭha as a caste begotten by a śūdra on a vaiśya woman.[3] It is said that a brāhmaṇa father who dwells with the *antāvasāyins* or cohabits with one of their women should be rejected.[4] Generally the untouchables lived at the end of villages or towns or in their own settlements. Their segregation was not the result of any deliberate policy of expulsion from old āryan settlements. It seems rather that the whole population of tribal villages were condemned to the position of untouchables by the brāhmaṇas.

It is not possible to accept the explanation of the origin of untouchability given in the Dharmasūtras, which attribute it to the intermixture of castes. It has been suggested that in the majority of instances the origin of untouchables took place as a result of complete isolation and loss of tradition of the Buddhist communities.[5] But such a view is untenable, for this social phenomenon appears in the pre-Mauryan period, which witnessed the rise and growth of Buddhism. It has been contended that those who continued beef-eating were condemned as untouchables.[6] This may have swelled the ranks of the untouchables in later times, but cannot be taken as an explanation of their origin, for except for a late reference in the *Gautama Dharmasūtra*,[7] there is nothing which may imply that beef-eating was prohibited in brāhmaṇical society during this period. It is also argued that the spirit of contempt leading to untouchability "was evidently not a part of the original Indo-Aryan institutions, but was a thing borrowed from the Dravidians, among

1. I. 3.9.15.
2. I. 3.9.18.
3. XVIII. 3.
4. *Gaut. Dh. S.*, XX. 1; cf. XXIII, 32.
5. *MR* (Dec. 1923), 712-13. This view has been further developed by Ambedkar. *The Untouchables*, Ch. IX.
6. Ambedkar, *The Untouchables*, Ch. X.
7. XXII. 13 declares cow-killing as a minor sin which has to be expiated by a penance.

whom in the south even in modern times untouchability plays such a prominent part."[1] But there is no evidence that untouchability prevailed in the south among the Dravidians before their brāhmaṇization. On the contrary, Baudhāyana, a lawgiver from the south, and Āpastamba, who is also sometimes associated with that region, maintain a less conservative attitude towards the śūdras in matters of food and company than the two other authors of the Dharmasūtras from the north. Besides, it has been shown earlier how certain crafts and occupations were held in ill repute by the members of the upper varṇas, who claimed to be āryas. Finally, the idea of untouchability has been traced to the theoretical impurity of certain occupations.[2] But the vital question is why certain occupations should be regarded as impure.

One of the reasons for the origin of untouchability was the cultural lag of the aboriginal tribes, who were mainly hunters and fowlers, in contrast to the members of brāhmaṇical society, who possessed the knowledge of metals and agriculture,[3] and were developing urban life. The low material culture and the consequent wretched condition of these tribes is described in the Buddhist texts in these words : "A fool, should he become a human being after the lapse of a very long time, comes into one of the low stocks—caṇḍālas, nesādas, veṇas, rathakāras and pukkusas, he is reborn to a life of vagrancy, want and penury, scarcely getting food and drink for his stomach or clothes to his back. ..."[4] This would suggest that these despised castes had a very precarious living, and were in far worse conditions than those śūdras who were employed as dāsas and kammakaras, and as such enjoyed some security of livelihood. This contrast in material life was accentuated by the spirit of contempt growing in brāhmanical society itself. As in the case of contemporary Greek society,[5] there had appeared in post-Vedic society a

1. Dutt, *op. cit.*, pp. 106-7; cf. p. 31.
2. Ghurye, *Caste and Class*, p. 159.
3. Fick, *op. cit.*, p. 324.
4. *...na lābhī annassa pānassa vatthassa yānassa..Majj. N.*, iii, 169-70; Aṅg., ii. 85.
5. *Past and Present.* No. 6,

spirit of contempt for manual works and occupations. Gradually as the upper varṇas, especially of the brāhmaṇas and the kṣatriyas, withdrew more and more from the work of primary production and tended to be hereditary in their positions and functions, they not only developed a contempt for manual work but also extended it to the hands that practised it.

Against the background of a very low material culture of the aborigines, the increasing contempt for manual work, combined with primitive ideas of taboo and impurity associated with certain materials, produced the unique social phenomenon of untouchability. This was particularly true of the work of the caṇḍālas who dealt with corpses, with which were linked primitive ideas of impurity and horror. Consequently it was felt necessary to avoid contact with such persons. In later times the idea of untouchability was extended not only to the niṣādas and pukkusas but also to craftsmen such as the leather workers and the weavers. For during this period although the crafts of the cammakāras and pesakāras were considered contemptible, they themselves were not regarded as untouchables.

We may finally consider how far the religious reforming movements of this period affected the position of the śūdras. So far as religious emancipation is concerned, Buddhism opened its door not only to the members of the four varṇas, who could be admitted to the Saṃgha and become ascetics,[1] but even to the caṇḍālas and the pukkusas, who could attain the bliss of the *nirvāṇa*.[2] When the robber Aṅgulimāla is admitted to the Buddhist Order, he exclaims : "Verily I have obtained an āryan birth".[3] This would show that the Buddhist admission of the śūdras to their church was as good as restoring to them the old tribal right of initiation, of which they were dispossessed by brāhmaṇical society. But while the tribal initiation prepared the people for the practical life of this world, this prepared them for the spiritual emancipation from the miseries of life.[4]

1. *Majj. N.*, i, 211; ii, 182-84; *Saṃy. N.*, i, 99; *Vin.*, ii, 239; *Aṅg. N.*, iv, 202; cf. *Majj. N.*, iii, 60; i, 384; *Dīgha. N.*, iii, 80-98.
2. *Jāt.*, iii, 194; iv, 303.
3. *ariyāya jātiyā jāto. Majj. N.*, ii, 103.
4. Cf. Thomson, *Studies in Ancient Greek Society*, ii, 238.

Buddhism made no distinction in the imparting of knowledge. The Buddha argues that just as the king or the owner of the royal domain should not appropriate all revenues to himself, so also a brāhmaṇa or a śramaṇa should not monopolise all knowledge to himself.[1] In the Buddhist view anybody could be a teacher irrespective of his caste. It is said that a teacher is always to be respected, be he a sudda, a caṇḍāla or a pukkusa.[2] It is typical of the Buddhist attitude that in a Jātaka story a brāhmaṇa loses the charm learnt from a caṇḍāla because of denying his teacher out of shame.[3] In another case the caṇḍāla, who is the Buddhisatta, kicks a fellow brāhmaṇa pupil, who is defeated in an academic dispute, but the action is condemned by the teacher.[4]

Early Jainism also admitted to its monastic order members of all the varṇas, and tried to uplift the caṇḍālas. Thus a later Jain source refers to the case of a king who occupied a lower seat in learning spells from a mātaṅga.[5] The *Uttarādhyayoana* informs us that Harisena, a sovāga (i.e. caṇḍāla) by birth, visited the sacrificial enclosure of a brāhmaṇa teacher and lectured to him on the value of penance, good life, right exertion, self-control, tranquility and celibacy.[6]

Unlike the brāhmaṇas, the early Jain monks did not refuse food from lower class families including those of the weavers.[7] Similarly a Buddhist monk or nun could approach families of all the four varṇas for a meal, or could eat at their houses when invited by them.[8] But we do not know whether the lay devotees of these religions followed their teachers in this respect.

That the members of the lower orders actually got into the Buddhist church is suggested by a number of instances. Mātaṅga, the son of a caṇḍāla, is said to have attained infinite bliss, which

1. *Dīgha N.*, i, 226-30.
2. *Jāt.*, iv, 200ff.
3. *Ibid.*
4. *Jāt.*, iii, 233.
5. *Dasa. Cu.*, p. 45. quoted in Jain, *op. cit.*, p. 229.
6. *Uttarā.*, XII ff.
7. *Āyār.*, II. 1.2.2.
8. *Vin.*, iii, 184-5; iv, 80, 177.

many kṣatriyas and brāhmaṇas could not attain;[1] a monk is described as a former vulture-trainer,[2] and caṇḍālas appear as adopting the homeless state although Fick thinks that "the acutal existence of such holy men is extremely doubtful".[3] He gives no good reason however for his lack of faith in the statement of the Pāli canon on this point. In the list of the authors of the *Thera*— and *Therigāthās*, at least ten among 259 theras[4] and eight out of about fifty-nine therīs[5] belonged to sections of society which may be regarded as śūdras. They included an actor, a caṇḍāla, a basketmaker, a trapper, a prostitute and a woman slave.[6] We have no similar information to throw light on the proportion of the members of the lower orders in the Jain chruch. But it is significant that the first woman disciple of Mahāvīra is said to have been a captured slave.[7] It is suggested that the homeless condition was often a reaction to surfeit of wealth and power which the people of the lower orders were totally denied.[8] But this is hardly borne out by evidence either in the case of the Buddhist or the Jain church. According to a Jain canon some of the causes of the renunciation of the world were poverty, sickness, sudden anger and insult.[9] There might be some truth in the following abuse hurled by the householders at the monks : "those who become śramaṇas are the meanest workmen, men unable to support their families, low-caste men, wretches, idlers."[10] In order to discourage the influx of such people, it was said that a miserable man who becomes a monk in order to get food from others will be reborn as a boar greedy of wild rice.[11] A Buddhist text informs us that in the realm of Bimbisāra the Saṃgha enjoyed special protection from the king,

1. *Sut. Nipā.*, 137 and 138.
2. *Dictionary of Pāli Proper Names*, i, 174.
3. Fick, *op. cit.*, pp. 77-78.
4. Bose, *op. cit.*, ii, 285 fn. 1.
5. Calculated on the basis of the list given in Law, *HPL*, ii, 503-16.
6. *Ibid*, ii, 501-508; 508-516.
7. Jain, *Life in Ancient India as Depicted in the Jain Canons*, p. 107.
8. Bose, *op. cit.* ii, 485.
9. *parijunā, rogiṇītā, rosā* and *aṇāḍhitā pavvjjā*. *Thāṇānga*, X. 712.
10. *Sūyagaḍam*, II. 2.54.
11. *Ibid.*. I. 7.25.

on account of which at times prisoners, thieves, persons condemned to the punishment of whipping, debtors and runaway slaves took refuge in the Buddhist Order and got themselves ordained.[1] When these cases were brought to the notice of the Buddha, he laid down that such people should not be admitted into the Order. A passage of the *Digha Nikāya* also makes it clear that members of the lower orders sought an end of their misery by becoming Buddhist monks. In the *Sāmaññaphala Sutta* Ajātaśatru of Magadha, after pointing out the advantages derived by mahouts, horsemen, home-born slaves, cooks, barbers, bath attendants, confectioners, garland-makers, washermen, weavers, basket-makers and potters from their occupations,[2] enquires of the Buddha whether the members of the Order, who have given up the world, derive any corresponding advantages visible in this life from their own profession. In his reply the Buddha lays bare the contrast between the luxurious and full life of the king, who is in possession of the five pleasures of sense, and the life of a slave-servant who rises up earlier, goes to bed later, is always keen to carry out the master's orders and anxious to make himself agreeable to his master in everything.[3] The Buddha further adds that the slave wants to live like a king and in order to earn merits for that purpose becomes a recluse. And he poses the counter-question : "The very man whom, under ordinary circumstances, you would treat as a slave-servant, — what treatment would you meet out to him after he had joined the Order ?" The king confesses that he would treat him as a person worthy of honour and respect, and would honour him with a seat, robes, a bowl, a lodging place and medicine.[4] The above discourse of the Buddha leaves no doubt that the life of a renouncer offered to the members of the lower orders not only prospects of immediate relief from poverty, but was also supposed to earn merit for a happier life in the next birth. In the same

1. ...*kārabhedako coro...coro...kasāhato katadaṇḍakammo...iṇāyiko...dāso*...In every case it is said : *palāyitvā bhikkhūsu pabbajjito hoti. Vin.*, i, 74-76.

2. ...*hatthārohā assārohā...dāsakaputtā āḷārikā kappakā nahāpakā sūdā mālākārā rajakā pesakārā...Dīgha. N.*, i. 51.

3. *dāso kammakaro pubbuṭṭhāyī pacchā-nipātī kiṃkarapaṭissāvī manāpa-cārī piya-vādī mukhullokako. Ibid.*, i, 60.

4. *Ibid.*, i, 60-61.

passage the Buddha contrasts the luxurious life of the king with the life of a tax-paying agriculturist householder, and states that he may also be actuated by similar motives for a happier life and decide to become a recluse.[1] It is significant that there is no mention of the brāhmaṇas and the kṣatriyas in this connection, which may suggest that in joining the Saṃgha the poorer sections of the vaiśyas, and the śūdras, were generally moved by materialistic interests. They envied the life of the monks, who 'having eaten good meals, lie down in beds sheltered from the wind.'[2]

But the rules of the Buddhist and Jain churches did not favour the release of considerable sections of the labouring masses from their worldly obligations. There was no permission either for a slave or a debtor to join the Buddhist church,[3] unless the former had been manumitted by his master and the latter had cleared his debts. But the Buddhist position with regard to the admission of the slave to the church seems to be contradictory. In the course of a discourse the Buddha pointedly asks Ajātaśatru if he would claim back the ex-slave, who is a member of the Order, and compel him to work again as slave. To this the king replies in a clear negative.[4] This may suggest the possibility of a *dāsa-kammakara* joining the Buddhist church without the permission of his master, but such cases were probably rare. In the Jain church also, among those who were excluded from entering the monastic order, were robbers, king's enemies, debtors, attendants, servants, and forcibly converted people.[5] Almost all these categories were barred from entering the Buddhist church also.

While stabilising the existing social and economic relations Buddhism and Jainism tried to improve the position of slaves in some other ways. Thus a Dharmasūtra forbids trade in human beings only for the brāhmaṇa,[6] who can, however,

1. *kassako gahapatiko kāra-kārako rāsi-vaḍḍhako. Dīgha N.*, i, 61.
2. *samaṇā sakyaputtiyā...subhojanāni bhuñjitvā nivātesu sayanesu sayanti. Vin.*, i, 77.
3. *Dīgha N.*, i, 5.
4. *Ibid.*, i. 60.
5. *Thāṇānga*, III. 202; Jain, *op. cit.*, p. 194.
6. *Āp. Dh. S.*, I. 7.20. 11-12.

exchange slaves for slaves.[1] But the Buddhist and Jain sources prohibit trade in human beings even for their lay devotees.[2] Nevertheless, a Buddhist text states that the āryan disciple grows in servitors and retinue,[3] which shows that the lay devotees could increase the number of their slaves by other methods. The monks did not keep slaves. A passage from a Jātaka story[4] has been represented as meaning that the slaves of the bhikkhus go to town to get dainty fare for their sick masters.[5] But this is based on an incorrect rendering of the passage,[6] which does not refer to slaves or servants but to other bhikkhus who attended on their sick brethren and who are addressed as *āvuso* — a term usually applied to the monks.[7]

Buddhism and Jainism tried to inculcate among their followers a spirit of generosity and kindness towards their employees. Thus a passage from the *Dīgha Nikāya* enjoins that employers should treat their slaves and workpeople decently. They should not be given tasks beyond their strength. They should receive food and wages, be cared for in times of sickness, and be given occasional holidays and shares in the unusual delicacies of the master. On the other hand the servants should be content with their wages, work satisfactorily and maintain the reputation of their master.[8] Similar instructions were issued by Aśoka to his subjects. In the Jātakas also, if the master is the Bodhisatta, the slave receives good treatment.[9] A Jain text states that wealth should be accumulated not only for the sake of kinsmen and kings, but also for the sake of dāsas, dāsīs, kammakaras and kammakarīs, suggesting thereby that these latter deserve to be well maintained by the employer.[10] Such an instruction was required for the consolidation of the new social formation marked by the

1. *manuṣyāṇāṃ ca manuṣyaiḥ. Ibid.*, I. 7.20.15; *Vas. Dh. S.*, II. 39.
2. *Aṅg. N.*, ii, 208; *kesāvāṇijje...Uvāsaga.*, p. 51.
3. *dāsakammakaraporisehi vaḍḍhati. Aṅg N.*, v. 137.
4. *Jāt.*, iii, 49.
5. Bose, *op. cit.*, ii, 414.
6. *Jāt.*, iii, tr., 33; text, 48.
7. *Ibid.*
8. *Dīgha N.*, iii, 191.
9. *Jāt.*, i. 451.
10. *Āyār*; I. 2.5.1.

appearance of the state and of clear-cut social classes, for in a tribal society wealth is primarily meant for distribution among kinsmen.

We have no precise idea about the extent of the lay following of the heretical sects among the people of the lower classes Buddhism counted some followers in the artisan community.[1] The Ājīvika sect was in some way especially connected with the potter caste, and made a special appeal to its members.[2] But in any case the reforming religions did not make any fundamental change in the position of the lower orders. The proportion as well as the importance of such people in the Buddhist church seems to have been negligible. In spite of its theory of equality a marked leaning to artistocracy (of all the three varieties, birth, brain and bullion) lingered in ancient Buddhism as an inheritance from the past.[3] It may be going too far to assert that the social organization in India was not in the least altered by Buddha's appearance.[4] But evidently the Buddhists rarely questioned the fundamentals of the varṇa system, which identified the śūdras with the serving class. Thus while refuting the brāhmaṇical claims to superiority over the three other varṇas, Gautama argues that as regards descent the kṣatriyas are higher and the brāhmaṇas are lower. But he does not question the superiority of either the brāhmaṇas or the kṣatriyas over the vaiśyas and the śūdras.[5] Buddhism, therefore, merely tries to show that caste is of no value in the search for emancipation.[6] Like Christianity, none of the religious reforming movements of this period ever attacked the basis of slavery; they never tried to abolish the economic and political disabilities of the śūdras.

Our study shows that the ambiguous position of the śūdras disappeared in post-Vedic times, when they were deprived of the remnants of their tribal rights and saddled with economic, political, social and religious disabilities. They were sharply

1. Case of the smith Cunda, *Dict. of Pāli Proper Names*, i, 876-77.
2. Basham. *History and Doctrines of the Ājīvikas*, p. 134.
3. Oldenberg, *Buddha*, pp. 155-59.
4. Fick, *SONI*, p. 32.
5. *Dīgha N.*, i, 91-98.
6. Fick, *SONI*, p. 31.

distinguished from the three upper varṇas, denied the right to Vedic sacrifice, initiation, education, and administrative appointments, and above all were specifically assigned the task of serving the twice-born as slaves, agricultural labourers and artisans. Although, like the vaiśyas, the śūdras were also engaged in production, they were not tax-paying peasants which was the case with most of the vaiśyas. The vaiśyas shared certain ritualistic rights with the two higher varṇas and therefore differed from the śūdras in this respect also. In fact the picture of the lower orders, as it appears in the early Buddhist and Jain works, is not essentially dissimilar. The Buddhist texts repeatedly describe the members of the first three varṇas as opulent,[1] but leave out the śūdras, the dāsas and the kammakaras. The Buddha is described as having visited the assemblies of the brāhmaṇa, the khattiya and gahapati devotees (upāsakas),[2] but the assembly of the śūdras is not mentioned.

It would be superficial to suggest that mere ideas of ceremonial purity and cleanliness led to the exclusion of the śūdras from the sacrificial rites and table of the people of the higher varṇas.[3] The fact has to be stressed that such ideas could develop only after a considerable section of society had been condemned to the position of a hereditary working class and consequently had come to be regarded as impure because of their manual work. This spirit of contempt for the physical labour of the lower orders ultimately degenerated into the practice of untouchability.

The Dharmasūtras, especially of Vasiṣṭha and Gautama, display a strong tendency to reduce the vaiśyas to the position of śūdras in matters of purity, food and marriage—a process which has its parallel in the Buddhist texts. The Buddha declares that in the way they are addressed, received, approached and treated, the kṣatriyas and the brāhmaṇas take precedence over the vaiśyas and the śūdras.[4] In a Buddhist text gotras are

1. *Aṅg. N.*, iv, 239; *Saṃy. N.*, iv, 239, *Jāt.*, i. 49.

2. *Aṅg. N.*, iii, 307 f.

3. Dutt, *Origin and Growth of Caste in India*, p. 133. Even during this period the śūdras prepared food for the higher varṇas on the occasion of the *vaiśvadeva* sacrifice.

4. *Majj. N.*, ii, 128; cf. ii, 147ff.

associated only with the kṣatriyas and the brāhmaṇas.[1] In an introductory passage of a Jātaka it is claimed that the Buddhas are never born in the vaiśya or the śūdra caste but they are born in the two other higher castes.[2] This passage, however, does not form part of the Jātaka proper, and may be ascribed to a later period. A similar idea is expressed with regard to the birth of the Jain teachers, who are supposed to be never born in low, mean, degraded, poor, indigent or brāhmaṇical families.[3] Apparently the brāhmaṇas are included in this list because of heretical hostility to them. But the remaining members of the list may be roughly assigned to the lower orders. The tendency to approximate the vaiśyas to the position of śūdras probably gained ground towards the end of our period. It may have swelled the numbers of the śūdras by throwing into their ranks impoverished sections of the vaiśyas, but this does not seem to have affected their status during this period. Similarly the reforming religions did not effect any significant change in the existing social system, and in the main the economic and politico-legal disabilities of the śūdras continued as ever.

There is very scantly information as to how the śūdras reacted to these disabilities. But even on this basis it is difficult to accept the view that "the bitter struggle for existence was wanting" and that the social order worked harmoniously.[4] A passage from Vasiṣṭha enumerates the following characteristics of the śūdras: backbiting, untruth, cruelty, fault-finding, condemnation of the brāhmaṇas and continued hostility.[5] This may give an indication of the hostile attitude of the śūdras to the existing order in general and to its ideological leaders, the brāhmaṇas, in particular. But, as shown earlier, the masters seem to have been more hostile and callous towards their slaves and

1. *Sut. Nipā.*, 314-15.

2. *Jāt.*, i, 49; cf. *Lalitavistara.* I.20.

3. *antakulesu vā panta...tuccha...daridda...kiviṇa...bhikkhāga..māhaṇa... Kalpasūtra,* II. 17, cf. 22.

4. Bandyopadhyaya, *Eco. Life and Progress in Ancient India*, p. 302, 309-10.

5. *dīrghavairamasūyā cāsatyaṃ brāhmaṇadūṣaṇaṃ; paiśunyaṃ nirdayatvaṃ ca jāniyāt śūdralakṣaṇaṃ. Vas. Dh. S., VI.* 24.

hired labourers[1] than the latter towards their masters. The solitary instance of the revolt of the dāsas, which is found in the *Vinaya Piṭaka*,[2] is of a mild nature. It is said that at one time the slaves of the Śākyas of Kapilavastu got out of hand, and robbed and violated some Śākyan women, who had gone off to a jungle for feeding some monks.[3]

The usual form of protest adopted by the members of the lower orders was to run away from their master's work. This happened not only in the case of the gahapatis oppressed with taxes[4] but also in that of the artisans and the slaves. A later Jātaka informs us that, failing to carry out the orders for which pre-payment had been made, a settlement of woodworkers were summoned to fulfil the contract. But instead of "abiding in their lot" with "oriental stoicism" they made a mighty boat secretly and emigrated with their families, slipping down to the Gaṅgā by night, and so out to sea till they reached a fertile island.[5] Escape from work seems to have been a common practice with the dāsas. Mrs. Rhys Davids wrongly states that there are no instances of runaway slaves.[6] In the Jātakas there are at least two instances of slaves gaining freedom by flight.[7] Runaway slaves are also mentioned as joining the Buddhist church.[8] In a later Jātaka, in order to save their lives, intended victims for sacrifice offer to work in chains as slaves of a tyrannical priest.[9] This may suggest that in some cases chains were used to prevent the escape of the slaves. The late Buddhist tradition about Makkhali Gosāla, the Ājīvika leader, being a runaway slave, even if not true,[10] presupposes the possibility of escape on the part of a slave. In one case the dāsas and the kammakaras, in the absence of any control from the master, run away with his

1. Supra, pp. 121-2.
2. iv, 181-2.
3. *sākiyadāsakā avaruddhā honti...sākiyaniyo acchindimisu ca...Vin.*, iv, 181-2.
4. *Jāt.*, v, 98-99.
5. *Jāt.*, iv, 159; *CHI*, i, 210.
6. *CHI*, i, 205.
7. *Jāt.*, i, 451-2, 458.
8. *Vin.*, i, 74-6.
9. *Jāt.*, vi. 138.
10. Basham, *History and Doctrines of the Ājīvikas*, p. 37.

possessions.[1] All these instances show that usually the members of the working class expressed their resentment against the existing order by fleeing from their work, slave revolts of the Greek or the Roman type being absent. The Dharmasūtras, however, state that in the case of an intermixture of the varṇas, even the brāhmaṇas and the vaiśyas can take up arms in self-defence, the kṣatriyas always enjoying this right.[2] The fact that in an emergency only the members of the three varṇas could bear arms[3] suggests that the lawgiver had in mind an eventuality when the śūdras might attempt to remove by force the frontiers of the varṇas. Although there is no examples of such an attempt, except the mild revolt of the slaves in Kāpilavastu, the provision laid down by Vasiṣṭha implies that, in view of the disabilities imposed on the śūdras, the members of the upper varṇas apprehended revolts on their part.

1. *Jāt.*, vi, 69 (present story).
2. *Bau. Dh. S.*, II. 2.4.18. *ātmatrāne varṇasaṃvarge*. . *Vas. Dh. S.* III. 24-25. The word *varṇasaṃvarge* occurs in MS. B, which is considered as the most important by Führer (*Vasiṣṭha Dharmaśāstra*, Introd, p. 5). Other MSS. use the terms *dharmasaṃbarge* and *varṇasaṃkare*.
3. Slaves were not used as combatants in war among the Greeks and Romans. Westermann, *The Slave Systems of Greek and Roman Antiquity*, p. 37.

CHAPTER V

STATE CONTROL AND THE SERVILE ORDER

(c. 300 B.C.—c. 200 B.C.)

Our chief source for the study of the position of the śūdras during the Mauryan period is the *Arthaśāstra* of Kauṭilya, which can be supplemented by the fragments from the account of Megasthenes, and the inscriptions of Aśoka. But perhaps no single question in ancient Indian history has been debated so much as the date and authenticity of the *Arthaśāstra*.[1] On the one hand it is passionately held that the work belongs to Kauṭilya, the minister of Candragupta; on the other this is vehemently denied and the work is ascribed to the first or the third century A.D. It is not possible to recapitulate the whole controversy, but certain observations seem to be necessary. The one great weakness of the arguments of the opposite school is their negative character. A verse at the end of the *Arthaśāstra* clearly attributes this work to one who destroyed the Nandas,[2] —a tradition which is recorded in later brāhmaṇical and Jain literature. This verse is particularly valuable in view of the fact that such biographical notices about the authors of the Dharmasūtras and the Smṛtis are conspicuously wanting in other cases. Further, no literary source gives any alternative information suggesting that Kauṭilya belonged to some other period.

Some new grounds have been adduced to show that the *Arthaśāstra* was a work of the period from the first to the third centuries A.D.[3] It is contended that in Kauṭilya's

1. A fairly exhaustive bibliograhy on the subject is to be found on pp. 285-86 of *The Age of Imperial Unity*. Kangle and Trautman give longer lists of publications.

2. *AŚ*, XV. 1.

3. V. Kalyanov, "Dating the Arthaśāstra", *Papers presented by the Soviet Delegation at the XXIII International Congress of Orientalists*, pp. 40-54.

classification of knowledge positive sciences had begun to be separated from philosophy, and that this process can be assigned to the early centuries of the Christian era.[1] But there is no doubt that the principal disciplines mentioned by Kauṭilya, i.e. *kalpa* (ritual), *vyākaraṇa* (grammar), and *nirukta* (etymology), existed as subjects of study in the pre-Mauryan period. It is to be further noted that the mention of the *lokāyata* (materialistic) system of philosophy in the *Arthaśāstra* does not imply any later date for that work.[2] The *lokāyata* system is perhaps pre-Buddhistic,[3] and definitely pre-Mauryan, for it is clearly mentioned in the early Buddhist texts.[4]

It is also argued that the compilation of the *Arthaśāstra* presupposes a long tradition in the field of political science which could only develop in the course of several hundred years.[5] This fact is acknowledged by Kauṭilya himself, who mentions as many as ten predecessors in his filed.[6] That there was a long tradition of this kind in the pre-Mauryan period is testified by the Dharmasūtras. According to one calculation the *artha* contents account for $\frac{1}{15}$ of the *Āpastamba Dharmasūtra*, $\frac{1}{12}$ of the *Baudhāyana Dharmasūtra*, $\frac{1}{8}$ of the *Gautama Dharmasūtra* and $\frac{1}{8}$ of the *Vasiṣṭha Dharmasūtra*.[7] This points to the growing importance of the subject of *artha*, ultimately leading to the creation of an independent work on the *Arthaśāstra* of Kauṭilya.

It is further maintained that the Arthaśāstra policy of avoiding extremes and following a middle path is found in the philosophical work *Madhyānta-vibhaṅga*,[8] which can be ascribed to the third century A.D. But the enunciation of the doctrine of the middle path known as the *majjhimā paṭipadā* is as old as the text of the *Vinaya Piṭaka*,[9] where in his very first sermon the Buddha

1. *Ibid.*, pp. 44-45.
2. *Ibid.*, p. 45.
3. R. Garbe, Hasting's *Encycl. of Religion and Ethics*, viii, 138; cf. Ruben, *Einfuhrung in die Indienkunde*, p. 126.
4. *Dīgha. N.*, i, 130; *Majj. N.*, ii, 165.
5. Kalyanov, *op. cit.*, p. 46.
6. *AŚ*, I. 2,8.
7. K. V. Rangaswami Aiyangar, *Indian Comeralism*, p. 50.
8. Kalyanov, *op. cit.*, p. 48.
9. *Vin.*, i, 10; *Saṃy. N.*, *v*, 421.

is represented as teaching his followers to abandon the two extremes of asceticism and luxury.

Finally, it is held that the kind of relations of production, the social system and political institutions described in the *Arthaśāstra* are in a much more advanced stage of development than those referred to in the reports of Megasthenes and in the inscriptions of Aśoka, and seem to be characteristic of the period between the first and the third centuries A.D.[1] But the evidence for such a view seems to be tenuous. The capital fact in the relations of production as known from the *Arthaśāstra* is a large measure of state control over all sectors of economy. The Kauṭilyan state does not only control trade, industry and mining, but the superintendents of agriculture, while working the state farms with the help of the dāsas and karmakaras, mobilise the services of the blacksmiths, the carpenters, the diggers etc. for the purpose.[2] This development is borne out by the fragments quoted by Strabo from Megasthenes. We learn that great officers of the state not only superintended the rivers and looked after irrigation, but also measured the land and supervised occupations connected with land such as those of woodcutters, carpenters, blacksmiths and miners.[3] Similarly the social system outlined in the *Arthaśāstra* is modelled after the brāhmaṇical pattern.

The distinctive feature of the *Arthaśāstra* polity is to exalt monarchical power (*rāja-śāsana*) over all the other sources of authority,[4] and to make it felt among the subjects through as many as nearly thirty departments. This general policy of the Mauryan empire is in the main borne out by the inscriptions of Aśoka, who acted as a promulgator of the dharma and who possessed a fairly well organised bureaucracy. Significantly enough the tendency towards the all-pervading power of the state as represented by the king also manifested itself in the empire of Alexander and was carried forward by the Hellenistic monarchies which arose on its ruins.[5] Thus Strabo, quoting from

1. Kalyanov, *op. cit.*, p. 52.
2. *AŚ*, II. 24.
3. McCrindle, *AIMA*, p. 86, Frag. 34.
4. *AŚ*, III. 1.
5. K. A. Nilakanta Sastri, "Royal Power in Ancient India", *The Proceeding of the IHC* (1944), p. 46.

Megasthenes, rightly compares the magistrates in India with similar officers in Hellenistic Egypt.[1] Kauṭilya claims to have studied the practices prevailing in the contemporary states,[2] and hence his exaltation of the monarchical power seems to reflect the spirit of the age.

But there is no denying the fact that, like so many other works, the *Arthaśāstra* may have been recast in later times. Therefore the problem is to find out the later accretions made to the primary kernel.[3] Books II and III of the *Arthaśāstra* seem to contain genuine Mauryan reminiscences, and are mainly used in the present chapter.

Although the Mauryan empire extended practically over the whole of India except the far south and although Kauṭilya shows a wide geographicel horizon, possibly the provisions laid down in the *Arthaśāstra* reflect conditions obtaining in Northern India. In so far as the *Arthaśāstra* measures were meant to serve the needs of the empire by overriding parochial and sectarian considerations, they may have been applied to the whole of it; but the detailed instructions regarding the control of economic activities or the policy of bringing virgin soil under the plough may have been limited to the areas near the heart of the empire, namely, to the middle Gangetic basin and its peripheries.

In defining the functions of the śūdra varṇa Kauṭilya uses the Dharmasūtra terminology. He states that the śūdra's means of livelihood is derived from his service of the twice-born.[4] But they can support themselves by the professions of artisans, dancers, actors etc.,[5] which are apparently independent occupations not implying the service of the twice-born.

The Dharmasūtra terminology used by Kauṭilya may suggest that the śūdras continued to be completely dependent for their livelihood on their masters of the upper varṇas. On the basis

1. McCrindle, *AICL*, p. 53, Frag. 50.
2. *AŚ*, II. 10.
3. Kalyanov, *op. cit.*, p. 54.
4. *AŚ* I. 3. In the phrase '*śūdrasya dvijātiśuśrūṣā vārtā*' the term '*vārtā* is not used in the sense of the three occupations of agriculture, tending of cattle and trade, as Shamasastry thinks (*Tr.*, p. 7), but in the sense of livelihood (*Jayamaṅgalā*) *JOR*, xx. 11.
5. *AŚ*, I. 3.

of a passage in Book II of the *Arthaśāstra* of Kauṭilya it is suggested that śūdras appeared as peasants and cultivators, but this interpretation of the passage seems to be doubtful. Kauṭilya lays down that in founding a rural settlement villages, consisting of a hundred to five hundred families each, should be set up at the interval of two or four miles and should be inhabited mainly by śūdra and *karṣaka* (cultivators).[1] In our opinion the terms[2] *śūdra* and *karṣaka* form a compound, and indicate that *śūdras* were not peasants. Several scholars treat śūdra as an adjective of *karṣaka*[3] and hold that śūdra peasants were requisitioned for founding settlements. The interpretation of the phrase *śūdrakarṣakaprāya* is rendered difficult by the fact that it does not occur anywhere else in the *Arthaśāstra.* In indicating the nature of settlements Chapter XXI of the *Ādi Purāṇa* uses the term *śūdrakarṣakabhūyiṣṭhāḥ*;[4] in our opinion in such cases *karṣaka* is a substitute for vaiśya. For the same chapter of the Purāṇa speaks of vaiśyas and śūdras as two separate categories. As usual the vaiśyas are described as those living on trade, agriculture and cattle rearing, and the śūdras as those who are meant for the service of the vaiśyas as artisans and non-artisans,[5] i.e. as domestic servants, agricultural labourers etc. Obviously the verses in the *Ādi Purāṇa* are based on Kauṭilya, for it also prescribes one hundred families as the minimum population for a village and five hundred as the maximum.[6] Therefore the interpretation of the *Arthaśāstra* passage by the Tamil-Malayalam commentary, which takes

1. *śūdrakarṣakaprāyaṃ kulaśatāvaraṃ pañcaśatakulaparaṃ grāmaṃ krośadvikrośasīmānamanyonyārakṣaṃ niveśayet.* AŚ, II. 1.

2. I. J. Sorabji, *Some Notes on the Adhyakṣapracāra* Bk. II *of the Kauṭilīyam Arthaśāstram, s.v., śūdrakarṣakaprāyam in AŚ*, II. 1; *J. J. Meyer, Das altindische Buch vom Welt und Staatleben*, tr. of *AŚ*, II. 1.

3. TGS, i, 109; SS tr. of AŚ, II. 1; Kangle's tr.

4. *śūdrakarṣakabhuyiṣṭhāḥ śārāmā sajalāśayā, Ādi Purāṇa*, XVI. 162-65.

5. *vaiśyāsca kṛsivāṇijyapaśupālyopajīvitāḥ, tesāṃ śuśrūṣaṇācchūdrāste dvidhā kārvakāravaḥ.* ibid., 184.

6. *śūdrakarṣakabhuyiṣṭhaḥ . . . grāmaḥ kulaśateneṣṭo nikṛṣṭaḥ samadhiṣṭhitaḥ, parastatpañcaśatyā syāt susanirddhakṛṣībalaḥ. Ibid.*, XVI. 164-65.

śūdra and *karṣaka* as two independent words, seems to be correct.[1] On the other hand the commentary of Yogghama which treats śūdra as an adjective of *karṣaka*[2] reflects the state of affairs in medieval times when śūdras were treated as peasants. Yogghama clearly states that vaiśya peasants are few in number.[3] This obviously applies to the medieval period when the vaiśya peasantry had become practically extinct;[4] in ancient times till the Gupta period the vaiśya peasants were the principal taxpayers. Kauṭilya's instruction therefore does not signify any fundamental change in the position of the śūdras. It merely focuses on the role of śūdras as slaves, artisans and agricultural labourers in opening virgin lands to cultivation and in founding new villages.

In the new settlements, besides agriculture, the services of the śūdra population could be utilised for other purposes. It is stated that a new stettlement, which is mainly inhabited by the śūdras (*avaravarṇaprāya*), is capable of yielding sure results and bearing all burdens imposed on them by the state.[5] According to the commentary *Nayacandrikā* the meaning of the term *bhoga* indicates that the śūdras were to be engaged not only in cultivation but also in carrying loads and building forts[6]. It is also said that a settlement inhabited by śūdras enjoys the advantage of numerical strength.[7] For the purpose of opening up new lands to cultivation or rehabilitating old sites the śūdras were to be drafted from the areas which were overpopulated or induced to migrate from foreign kingdoms.[8] It is stated that

1. Quoted in R. P. Kangle, *The Kouṭilīya Arthaśāstra*, pt. II, 62, fn. 2; also see pt. I, Preface, pp. 2, 5-6.

2. *A Fragment of the Kouṭalya's Arthaśāstra alias Rājasiddhānta with the fragment of the commentary named Nītinirṇīti of Āchārya Yogghama alias Mugdhavilāsa*, ed. Muni Jina Vijaya, p. 2.

3. *vaiśyakarṣakāḥ svalpāḥ, ibid.*

4. The process had started in the third-fourth centuries A.D.

5. *tasyāṃ cāturvarṇyābhiniveśaṃ sarvabhogasahatvādavaravarṇaprāyā śreyasī bāhulyāt dhruvatvācca..AŚ*, VII, 11. The *Nayacandrikā* (p. 33) explains the term *avaravarṇaprāya* as *śūdraprāya.*

6. *karṣaṇabhāravahanadurgakaraṇādiviniyogaḥ, tadyogyatvādityarthaḥ. Nayacandrikā*, p. 33.

7. *AŚ*, VII. 11.

8. *paradeśāpavāhanena svadeśābhiṣyandavamanena vā. AŚ*, II. 1.

the *janapada* should have a numerous populaticn of the lowest varṇas.[1] All this would suggest that the country had a considerable śūdra population, perhaps the majority belonging to this varṇa. And in other parts of the country, mainly inhabited by established vaiśya peasants, the śūdras may not have been principally liable for payment of the land revenue and other charges, as is suggested by Ghoshal.[2]

Probably the main body of the śūdra population continued to be employed as agricultural labourers and slaves. Slavery as known from the Dharmasūtras, was domestic in nature. Kauṭilya is the first and the only brāhmaṇical writer who furnishes evidence of dāsas being employed in agricultural production on a substantial scale.[3] In the early Pāli texts there are only three instances of big farms, but in the Mauryan period there seem to have existed numerous such farms, worked with slaves and hired labourers in the direct employ of the *sitādhyakṣa* (superintendent of agriculture). He supplied them with agricultural implements and other accessories, and requisitioned the services of carpenters, blacksmiths and other artisans for the purpose.[4] This fact is broadly attested by Megasthenes, who mentions the officers superintending occupations connected with land and also those of the artisans.[5] Arrian speaks of the superintendents of agriculture,[6] who probably performed the functions of the *sitādhyakṣa*. Strabo informs us that the third caste of shepherds and hunters led a nomadic life and were given an allowance of corn from the king for keeping out the wild beasts and birds from the land.[7] They seem to be similar to the nomadic aboriginals (*sarpagrāhādikāḥ*, i.e. people engaged in catching snakes and others),[8] who were pressed into the service of agriculture by the *sitadhyapṣa*.[9] The Mauryan state therefore

1. *avaravarṇaprāyaḥ*. *AŚ*, VI. 1.
2. *Hindu Revenue System*, p. 55.
3. *AŚ*, II. 24.
4. *Ibid.*
5. McCrindle, *AIMA*, p. 86, Frag. 34.
6. *Ibid.*, *AICL*, p. 53, fn. 4.
7. *Ibid.*, p. 48, Frag. 41.
8. According to Bhaṭṭasvāmin the *rajjuvartakas* were śvapākas and others, and the *sarpagrāhādik as* were śabaras and others. *JBORS*, xii, 143.
9. *AŚ*, II. 24.

was a great employer of dāsas and karmakaras, artisans and the aboriginal peoples, who apparently belonged to the śūdra class. And in this respect the organization of agricultural production in this period resembles to some extent that which prevailed in Greece and Rome.

Kauṭilya lays down that, if fields cannot be sown (apparently due to shortage of labour power), they can be leased to those who cultivate for half the share of the produce.[1] Those who live by bodily labour (i.e. karmakaras) and therefore do not possess seeds and oxen necessary for cultivation can cultivate such lands, but may retain only one fourth or one fifth of the produce; presumably their seed and oxen were provided by the state.[2] Kauṭilya enunciates the principle that the sharecroppers should pay to the kings as much as they can without entailing any hardship upon themselves, but he does not indicate the nature of such hardships.[3] It seems that the sharecroppers were also allotted some land with hard soil, for which they had not to pay anything to the state.[4] Evidently there were two kinds of sharecroppers — the one retaining half and the other retaining $\frac{1}{4}$th or $\frac{1}{5}$th of their crops; the former are described by the commentator Bhaṭṭasvāmin as *grāmyakuṭumbinaḥ*.[5] In the section on the *durganiveśa* (founding of the capital) Kauṭilya provides that the *kumṭumbins* should be settled on the boundary of the capital to meet the requirements of their field work and other occupation.[6] It is said that they shall work in flower gardens, forest gardens, vegetable gardens and paddy fields[7] and collect plenty of grain and merchandise as authorised. In this context the term *kuṭumbinaḥ* is explained by T. Gaṇapati Śāstrī as a person belonging to the lowest varṇa (*varṇāvarāṇām*),[8] and by Shamasastry as families of workmen.[9] Thus the *kuṭumbins* were

1. *AŚ*, II. 24.
2. *Ibid.*, II. 24. Commentary of Bhaṭṭasvāmin, *op. cit.*, 137.
3. *AŚ*. II. 24.
4. *anyatra kṛcchrebhyaḥ. Ibid.*
5. *JBORS*, xii, 137.
6. *karmāntakṣetravaśena vā kuṭumbinaṃ sīmānaṃ sthāpayet. AŚ*, II. 4.
7. In his translation SS says that these were *allotted* to them, but there is nothing in the text to support this.
8. i, 130.
9. *Tr.*, p. 54.

probably śūdra sharecroppers and agricultural labourers. This use of the term is rather unusual since in most sources *kuṭumbin* means simply the head of a family,[1] but the context indicates that here it has a specialised meaning.

Possibly in the old settlements a large number of śūdras, agricultural labourers, slaves and artisans was employed by proprietors of the higher varṇas. The gopa, who is in charge of the collection of taxes from the peasants, is required to register the total number of the inhabitants in each village and also of half a dozen producing sections of society—namely the karṣakas (cultivators), the gorakṣakas (herdsmen or owners of cattle), the vaidehakas (traders), the kārus (artisans), the karmakaras and the dāsas.[2] It seems that the list includes the members of the two lower varṇas, the first three groups belonging to the vaiśyas and the remaining three to the śūdras. Megasthenes does not enumerate the producing castes in this order. While the vaiśya agriculturists (karṣakas) of Kauṭilya roughly correspond to the caste of husbandmen mentioned by Megasthenes,[3] the vaiśya traders and śūdra artisans and labourers correspond to the third caste of Megasthenes the members of which work at trades, vend wares and are employed in bodily labour.[4] Megasthenes further adds that some of these pay taxes and render to the state certain prescribed services.[5] The first part of the statement probably refers to traders and the second part to artisans and labourers. In the *Arthaśāstra* the śūdras probably come under the category of the non-taxpayers, whose number also is to be recorded by the gopa.[6] In the taxpaying villages a list is to be maintained of those who supply free labour (*viṣṭi*) to the state.[7] Commenting on a passage of the *Arthaśāstra* Bhaṭṭasvāmin suggests that one type of villages was meant only for supply of free labour in lieu of taxes and

1. *Hindu Revenue System*, p. 200, fn. 2.
2. *AŚ*, II. 35.
3. McCrindle, *AIMA*, pp. 83-84, Frag. 33.
4. *Ibid. AICL*, p. 53. Strabo, Frag. 46.
5. *Ibid.*
6. *AŚ*, II. 35.
7. *Ibid.*

its inhabitants were employed in building fortresses etc.[1] T. Gaṇapati Śāstrī rightly says that this type of work was done by the karmakaras,[2] for along with some others the dāsas and karmakaras were regarded as always liable to forced labour, which meant that they were not adequately paid for their work.[3] All this would suggest that, excepting those who were sharecroppers working on the crown lands, the śūdras were mostly tax-free and were generally employed as agricultural labourers and slaves, who did not possess any independent means of livelihood.

Kauṭilya gives us some information about the working conditions of the herdsmen, who seem to have been employed in large numbers by the state, under the general control of the superintendent of cattle.[4] He fixes their wages at 1/10 of the butter clarified,[5] but is very particular about their functions. While emphasising the responsibilities of the herdsmen, Kauṭilya provides that, if the loss of the animal is on account of the fault of the herdsman, even capital punishment can be inflicted on him.[6] This extreme measure, which is not mentioned in the law-books of the pre-Mauryan period, was either inspired by the great economic importance attached to animal wealth, or by the teachings of Buddhism and Jainism, or by both the factors.

We may next examine the *Arthaśāstra* evidence regarding the employment, control and wages of the artisans in so far as they throw light on the general position of the śūdras. Reference has already been made to the artisans who were mobilised by the state to help agriculture. Many others seem to have been employed by the state in weaving,[7] mining,[8] storekeeping,[9] manufacture of arms,[10] metal work[11] etc. In the earlier period

1. *AŚ*, II. 15. *etāvanto viṣṭip atikarāḥ...durgādikarmopayogibhiḥ*. *JBORS*, xii, 198.
2. i, 344.
3. ..*dāsakarmakarvargaśca viṣṭiḥ*. *AŚ*, II. 15.
4. *AŚ*, II. 29.
5. *Ibid*., III. 13.
6. *svayaṃ hantā ghātayitā hartā hārayitā ca vadhyaḥ*. *Ibid*., II. 29.
7. *AŚ*. II. 23.
8. *Ibid*., II. 12.
9. *Ibid*., II. 15.
10. *Ibid*., II. 18.
11. *Ibid*., II. 17.

artisans such as weavers appear in the employment of the gahapati, but now they are employed in large numbers by the state.[1] The artisans probably owned their tools, but were supplied with raw materials by the state. There is no mention of slaves being engaged in any of these crafts. They also did not work in mining operations, which were conducted by the karmakaras.[2]

But the employment of artisans by the state seems to have been mainly limited to the capital and perhaps the important cities, which had a considerable artisan population. It is laid down that the artisans can reside to the north of the royal palace and the guilds of workmen and others should be allotted their residence in the several corners of the capital.[3] It is further stated that people of the śūdra caste and artisans manufacturing worsted threads, cotton threads, bamboo mats, skins, armour, weapons and scabbards should be allotted their dwellings to the west of the royal palace.[4] Probably some of these worked under the sūtrādhyakṣa or the superintendent of spinning,[5] while others worked under the superintendent of armoury.[6] Megasthenes informs us that the armour-makers and shipbuilders received wages and provisions from the kings and worked only for them.[7] Besides, in the city there was a committee of five to look after everything relating to industrial arts.[8] All this suggests that the state control and employment of artisans was mainly confined to the cities. But Megasthenes also states that great officers of the state supervised the occupations of woodcutters, carpenters, blacksmiths and miners,[9] which may indicate some sort of general control over the artisans living outside the city but working for the state.

1. *AŚ*, II. 23.
2. *Ibid.*, II. 12.
3. *Ibid.*, II. 4.
4. *tataḥ paramūrṇāsūtraveṇucarmavarmaśastrāvaraṇakāravaśśūdrāsca paścimāṃ diśamadhivaseyuḥ. AŚ.* II. 4.
5. *AŚ*, II. 23.
6. *Ibid.*, II. 18.
7. McCrindle, *AICL*, p. 53, Strabo, Frag. 46.
8. *Ibid.*, *AIMA*, p. 87, Frag. 34.
9. *Ibid.*, p. 86, Frag. 34.

The *Arthaśāstra* is the earliest Indian text which lays down general rules regarding the relation between the employers and the employees. Artisans are regarded as a source of trouble, against which several measures are provided in the section on the *kārukara-rakṣaṇam*. The artisans must fulfil their engagements as to time, place and form of work. Failure in this respect, except when due to "troubles and calamities", shall involve not only the forfeiture of a quarter of their wages, but also a fine twice the amount of wages and the payment of damages into the bargain.[1] The violation of instructions in the course of work shall be punished with the forfeiture of wages and a fine twice the amount.[2] A servant, who neglects his work, for which pre-payment has been made, shall be fined 12 paṇas and be made to work till his job is finished.[3] He will not be, however, subjected to such a fine if he is incapable of doing work due to reasons beyond his control.[4] On the other hand Kauṭilya also lays down certain regulations protecting the artisans. Thus those who seek to deprive the artisans of their just earnings, by minimising the quality of their work or obstructing the sale and purchase of gods, shall be fined a thousand paṇas.[5] An employer not taking work from his labourer shall be fined 12 paṇas,[6] and if he refuses to take work without any sufficient grounds, the work will be taken as done.[7] Kauṭilya concedes one privilege to the artisans who are organised into guilds. They can have a grace of seven nights over and above the period agreed upon for executing the contract.[8]

As regards the fixation of wages, Kauṭilya enunciates the general principle that wages should be fixed according to the time and quality of the work. This certainly indicates a high stage of social development in which the importance of time,

1. *AŚ*, IV. 1.
2. *Ibid.*
3. *AŚ*, III. 14.
4. *Ibid.*
5. *AŚ*, IV. 2.
6. *bharturkārayato bhṛtakasyākurvato vā dvādasapaṇo daṇḍaḥ*. *AŚ*, III. 15.
7. *Ibid.*
8. *AŚ*, III. 14.

skill and labour invested in a piece of work was very well recognised, Kauṭilya further states that artisans, musicians, physicians, cooks and other workmen shall obtain as much wages as similar persons employed elsewhere usually get, or as much as experts shall fix.[1] The servant shall get the promised wages; but if they are not settled first, a cultivator (i.e. an agricultural labourer) should get $\frac{1}{10}$ of the crops grown, a herdsman $\frac{1}{10}$ of the butter clarified and a trader $\frac{1}{10}$ of the sale proceeds.[2] Here a distinction has to be made between the share-cropping agricultural labourers who were entitled to receive $\frac{1}{4}$ or $\frac{1}{5}$ of the crops on the crown lands, and the general agricultural labourer who received only $\frac{1}{10}$ of the crops.

According to Kauṭilya disputes regarding wages are to be decided on the strength of evidence furnished by witnesses. If they are not available, the employer shall be examined.[3] The fact that the employer is not to be examined in this connection obviously makes it difficult to establish the guilt of the master. But if it is found that he has failed to pay wages, the master should be punished with a fine either ten times the amount of the wages or six paṇas. Besides, misappropriation of wages will mean a fine of twelve paṇas or of five times the amount of the wages.[4] On the basis of these rules we get two different rates of wages, namely $\frac{3}{5}$ paṇa or $2\frac{2}{5}$ paṇa. Thus it seems that the daily wage of a worker varied from $\frac{3}{5}$ paṇa to $2\frac{2}{5}$ paṇas. At one place Kauṭilya states that, in addition to the provisions, the agricultural workers should receive a monthly wage of $1\frac{1}{4}$ paṇas. The *Arthaśāstra* shows a wide gap between the pay of the higher officials, who, as will be shown, were recruited from the upper classes, and the artisans who belonged to the lower orders. The highest pay is provided for the priest (ṛtvij), the teacher, the minister, the purohita, the commander of the army etc., who get a (monthly) salary of 48,000 paṇas.[5] Lesser officials are

1. *kāruśilpikuśīlavacikitsakavāgjīvanaparicārakādirāśākārikavargastu yathā'nyastadvidhaḥ kuryāt, yathā vā kuśalāḥ kalpayeyuḥ, tathā vetanaṃ labhet*, *AŚ*, III. 13.
2. *AŚ*, III. 13.
3. *Ibid.*
4. *Ibid.*
5. *AŚ*. V. 3.

recommended a salary of 24,000, 12,000 or 8,000 paṇas,[1] but the artisans are recommended 120 paṇas.[2] It is important, however, to note that the *vardhaki*, who seems to have been the chief carpenter, is provided a salary of 2,000 paṇas like the physician and the charioteer.[3] Consideration is also shown to the *grāmabhṛtaka* (the village officer)[4] and the servant leading the spies, the first getting a salary of 500 paṇas and the second getting 200 paṇas.[5] The smallest salary of 60 paṇas is recommended for the servants who are in charge of quadrupeds and bipeds, workmen doing miscellaneous work, attendants upon the royal person, bodyguards and the procurer of free labour.[6] Presuming that this payment was made on a monthly basis, it works out at the rate of two paṇas a day for an ordinary labourer. But the rate of $\frac{3}{8}$ paṇa a day worked out earlier may suggest that private individual paid even less than 2 paṇas.

The artisans and wage earners were the worst paid members of society, but we can have no precise idea about their standard of living on account of the lack of information about the purchasing power of the paṇa. Kauṭilya, however, provides that the dāsas and karmakaras in the employ of the state should be given "particles of rice" for their support by the superintendent of the storehouse.[7] What remains after such disposal should be given to the cooks engaged in preparing cakes,[8] who may have been slaves, for these were engaged in cooking in the pre-Mauryan period. In connection with the disposal of bad liquor it is said that this should be given as wages to the dāsas and

1. *Ibid.*
2. *Ibid.*
3. *Ibid.*
4. The *gràmabhṛtaka* cannot be taken as an ordinary village servant, as SS thinks (Tr., 277); his salary of 500 paṇas shows that he was a village officer of some importance.
5. *AŚ*, V. 3.
6. *Ibid.*
7. *kaṇikāḥ dāsakarmakarasūpakāārṇāmato'nyad udanikāp ūpikebhyaḥ prayacchet.* *AŚ*, II. 15. The term *kaṇikā* here presumably means a broken part of a grain. The workmen were given the broken grain after threshing.
8. *Ibid.*

karmakaras because of the low type of their work.[1] Kauṭilya differentiates between the diet of an ordinary ārya and that of a śūdra. An ārya should get as his ration one prastha of pure and unsplit rice, $\frac{1}{64}$ prastha of salt, $\frac{1}{4}$ prastha of soup and $\frac{1}{64}$ prastha of butter or oil; while an avara should get the same quantity of rice and salt but $\frac{1}{6}$ prastha of soup and only half of oil recommended for an ārya,[2] butter being not provided in his case. In this context an avara means a person of the low caste (*nikṛṣṭānām*) and is a śūdra. But an ārya stands for an ordinary member of the higher varṇas,[3] for rations for the āryas of higher grades such as the king, queen and chiefs of army are provided in much greater quantities.[4] All this would show that the śūdras were fed on inferior food.

During the Mauryan period the economic position of the śudras seems to have undergone several changes. For the first time the śūdras came to be engaged as sharecroppers on the crown lands. But probably the śūdras were employed on a far larger scale as slaves and labourers in agricultural production by the state. The members of the lower order, who lived in village either working under the individual cultivators or independently, were subjected to corvée on a much larger scale than in the period of the Dharmasūtras, when it was mostly confined to the artisans.[5] The phenomenon had become now so widespread that a class of government servants known as the *viṣṭibandhakās* worked as procurers of forced labour.[6] Though as workers and artisans the śūdras were the worst paid people in society, fixation of wages may have helped to improve their position. Nevertheless, there seems to have been no

1. *dāsakarmakarebhyo vā vetanaṃ dadyāt*. *AŚ*, II. 25 with the comm. of TGS, i, 292.

2. *puṃsaḥ ṣadbhāgassūpaḥ ardhasnehamavarāṇām*. The term *prastha*, the alternative reading for *puṃsa*, mentioned by SS and accepted by TGS seems to be the correct reading. cf. Pran Nath, *Eco. Condition in Anc. India*, pp. 150-51.

3. He is described as a *madhyamapratipattika sādhupuruṣa by* Bhaṭṭasvāmin. *JBORS*, xi, 91.

4. *AŚ*, II. 15.

5. T. W. Rhys Davids, *Buddhist India*, p. 49.

6. *AŚ*, V. 3.

appreciable change in their standard of living, except perhaps in the case of the śūdra sharecroppers.

Unlike the Dharmasūtras, Kauṭilya does not make any explicit statement excluding the śūdras from high administrative posts. But his list of requisite qualifications for kingship and high governmental posts shows that these were looked upon as the special preserve of the members of the three higher varṇas. He states that, in preference to a strong and base-born king, people will naturally obey a king of noble birth, even if he be weak,[1] and therefore in his opinion the king should be born of a higher family.[2] He says that just as the reservoir of water belonging to the caṇḍālas serves only their purpose, so also the king of low birth confers patronage only on low-born people and not on the āryas. Incidentally Kauṭilya's dislike of a low-born king shows that he could not have agreed to serve under a king born of a śūdra mother. Hence it is not possible to make much of the śūdra origin of the Mauryas, as has been done in some cases.[3] It is practically certain that Candragupta belonged to the Moriya clan of the kṣatriya community.[4]

In the *Arthaśāstra* the amātyas constitute the highest cadre of officials from which the chief priest (purohita), the minister (mantrin), the collector (samāhartā), the treasurer (sannidhātā), officers in charge of the harem, ambassadors and the superintendents of more than two dozen departments are to be recruited.[5] But an item common to the qualifications of the amātyas laid down by Kauṭilya and other thinkers whom he quotes is noble birth. This is expressed variously as "father and grandfather being amātyas", *abhijana* and *jānapadobhijātaḥ*.[6] It is doubtful whether such a qualification could provide any scope for the śūdras. As Aristotle puts it, good birth is nothing but ancient wealth and virture combined,[7]—a thing which could

1. *AŚ*, VIII. 2.
2. *Ibid.*, VI. 1.
3. B. N. Duṭt, *Studies in Indian Social Polity*, pp. 185-7. Jayaswal, *Manu and Yājñavalkya*, p. 171.
4. *PHAI*, p. 267.
5. *AŚ*, I. 8 & 9.
6. *Ibid.*
7. *Politics*, p. 163.

hardly be found among the lower orders. Megasthenes mentions the professional class of councillors and assessors, who, though small in number, monopolised the highest posts of government, executive and judicial.[1] At another place he states that the noblest and the richest took part in the direction of the state affairs, administered justice and sat in council with the king.[2] That they formed an exclusive caste is obvious from the rules that they could not marry outside their own caste, exchange one profession or trade for another, or follow more than one business.[3] All this shows that the avenues to the higher bureaucracy were closed to the people of the lower orders.

The śūdras, however, were given a place in the espionage system, which constituted a vital part of the Mauryan administrative machinery. Kauṭilya provides that, amongst others, women of the śūdra caste can be employed as wandering spies.[4] It is further said that those who are employed as procurers of water for bathing, shampooers, bed makers, barbers, toilet makers, water servants, actors, dancers and singers, should keep an eye on the private character of the officers of the king.[5] Evidently most of these seem to have been śūdras. Working as domestic servants, and thus coming into contact with their masters every minute, they were thought to be the best persons to report correctly on their private character. Further, according to Kauṭilya, almost all sections of people, including cultivators, herdsmen and jungle tribes, should be recruited as spies to watch the movement of enemies,—a provision which covers śūdras as well.[6] Members of the lower orders also acted as messengers, for Kauṭilya states that messengers, though untouchables, do not deserve death.[7]

What is more important, the *Arthaśāstra* provides for the enrolment of śūdras in the army. The Dharmasūtras give the impression that normally only the kṣatriyas, and in emergency

1. McCrindle, *AIMA*, p. 85, Frag. 33.
2. *Ibid.*, p. 138, Frag. 56.
3. *Ibid.*, pp. 85-86, Frag. 33.
4. *AŚ*, I. 12.
5. *Ibid.*
6. *Ibid.*
7. ..*antāvasāyino'pyavadhyāḥ*. *AŚ*, I. 16.

only the brāhmaṇas and the vaiśyas, could take up arms. While defining the army as an indispensable element of the state, Kauṭilya also declares that the hereditary army purely composed of kṣatriya soldiers is the most splendid.[1] But he has no liking for the army of brāhmaṇas, who can be won over by salutations and supplications.[2] On the other hand he prefers an army composed of vaiśyas and śūdras on account of its numerical strength.[3] But it is doubtful whether the members of the two lower varṇas were actually recruited as soldiers during this period. Megasthenes clearly states that the husbandmen (roughly corresponding to the vaiśyas) were exempted from military service, and soldiers were meant to protect them.[4] Both Arrian and Strabo speak of the fighting men as forming the fifth caste of the Indian population and being maintained at the expense of the state.[5] That there was a class of soldiers can also be inferred from the use of the term *bhaṭamayeṣu* in the Aśokan inscriptions.[6] We learn from Megasthenes that one division of the army supplied servants, who performed miscellaneous tasks, such as acting as bandsmen, looking after the horses, and serving as mechanics and their assistants.[7] Arrian also refers to the servants who attend not only on the soldiers but also on their horses, elephants and chariots.[8] Possibly śūdras were recruited as menial servants and attendants in the standing army and not as full-fledged soldiers. Kautilya's rule, however, may suggest that vaiśyas and śūdras could be enlisted in the army in times of emergency. In the new settlements aboriginal tribes such as the vāgurikas, the śabaras, the pulindas and the caṇḍālas were entrusted with the work of internal defence.[9]

In the administration of law and justice Kauṭilya follows the principle of varṇa legislation. According to him, degraded

1. *Ibid.*
2. *AŚ*, IX. 2.
3. *bahulasāraṃ vā vaiśyaśūdrabalamiti. Ibid.*
4. McCrindle, *AIMA*, pp. 83-84, Frag. 33.
5. *Ibid.*, p. 217, Arrian, Frag. 12; *AICL*, p. 53, Strabo, Frag, 47.
6. *R. E.* 4 (Shāhbāzgarhī) I. 12.
7. McCrindle, *AIMA*, p. 88, Frag. 34.
8. *Ibid.*, p. 217, Frag. 12.
9. *AŚ*, II. 1.

people (*patita*), caṇḍālas and persons of mean avocations are among those who cannot act as witnesses in civil suits, except in the transactions of their respective communities.[1] He also lays down that the servant cannot give evidence against the master.[2] Similarly the pledged labourer and the slave cannot enter into agreements on behalf of their masters.[3] Kauṭilya provides for different kinds of warnings tendered by the court to the members of the different varṇas. The most severe warning is to be given to a śūdra who is reminded of terrible spiritual and worldly consequences which shall follow as a result of his false deposition.[4] In this connection only the śūdra is to be fined and bound down to service by the court, there being no mention of these things in the case of the three upper varṇas.[5] This provision is immediately followed by another, in which Kauṭilya prescribes a fine of 12 paṇas for witnesses giving false evidence.[6] This may suggest that the penal measure was probably meant for the śūdra witness. Megasthenes says that a person convicted of bearing false witness suffers the mutilation of his extremities.[7] This measure may have been confined either to the members of the lower orders or to a particular area.

In the award of punishments Kauṭilya upholds the varṇa distinctions of the Dharmaśūtras. Thus according to him, if among the members of the four varṇas and the antâvasāyins (untouchables), anyone of a lower caste speaks ill of a person of a higher caste, he shall have to pay a higher fine than in the case of a person of a higher caste defaming a person of a lower caste.[8] The *Arthaśāstra* has also the rule that the limb of a śūdra with which he strikes a brāhmaṇa should be amputated.[9] We are in doubt whether this passage is the work of Kauṭilya, for

1. *AŚ*, III. 1.
2. *Ibid.*
3. *AŚ*, III. 1.
4. *AŚ*, III. 11.
5. ... *anyathāvāde daṇḍaścānubandhaḥ. Ibid.* In his translation SS (p. 200) leaves out the word '*anubandhaḥ*'.
6. *AŚ*, III. 11.
7. McCrindle, *AIMA*, p. 70, Frag. 27.
8. *AŚ*, III. 18.
9. *AŚ*, III. 19.

it agrees rather with the extremist attitude of Manu. In another provision Kauṭilya states that, if a kṣatriya commits adultery with an unguarded brāhmaṇa woman, he shall be punished with the highest amercement, a vaiśya shall be deprived of his property, and a śūdra shall be burnt alive wound round in mats.[1] A śvapāka who commits adultery with an ārya woman shall be put to death, while the woman shall have her ears and nose cut off.[2] It is not surprising that these severe measures were applied against the śūdras and śvapākas, for even in the case of adultery against a woman of the śvapāka caste Kauṭilya provides for the branding and banishment of the guilty.[3]

Kauṭilya's law of prohibition of some kinds of food and drink does not apply in the same way to the members of all the varṇas. Thus a person who causes a brāhmaṇa to partake of prohibited food or drink shall de punished with the highest amercement; the same offence against a kṣatriya will be punished with the middle amercement, against a vaiśya with the first amercement and against a śudra with a fine of 54 paṇas.[4] In the case of embezzlement or misappropriation the most severe punishment is laid down for domestic servant. If an officer or a clerk is guilty of this offence, he shall be fined, but in such a case a servant shall be given capital punishment.[5]

In the law of inheritance Kauṭilya maintains the old distinction between the varṇas. Sons born out of the intermixture of castes such as the sūta, the māgadha, the vrātya and the rathakāra are entitled to their shares only in the case of abundance of paternal property.[6] Kauṭilya further provides that the sons who are inferior in birth to the above kinds of sons are entitled to no share but can depend for subsistence on the eldest son.[7]

1. *brāhmaṇyāmaguptāyāṃ kṣatriyasyottamaḥ, sarvasvaṃ vaiśyasya, śūdraḥ kaṭāgninā dahyeta*. *AŚ*, IV. 13.

2. TGS construes this passage differently from SS. While the former has *śvapākasyāryāgamane vadhaḥ* (ii, 181), the latter has *śūdraśvapākasya bhāryāgaman vadhaḥ*, (*AŚ*, IV. 13, p. 236). TGS, however, seems to be correct in using the word *āryā* which also occurs in the Munich manuscript (Tr., p. 264). Kangle (i, 149) follows TGS.

3. *AŚ*, IV. 13.

4. *Ibid.*

5. *AŚ*, II. 5.

6. *AŚ*, III. 6.

7. *Ibid.*

This naturally excludes the āyogava, the kṣattā, the niṣāda, the pulkasa and the caṇḍālas from shares. The position of the pāraśava (i.e. a son begotten by a brāhmaṇa on a śūdra woman), however, is better. It is said that, if a brāhmaṇa has no issue, the pāraśava son shall get one third share in paternal property;[1] the remaining two shares shall devolve either on his surviving sapiṇḍas, or, failing them, on his teacher or student.[2] This may suggest that, if the brāhmaṇa father had no issue, even the sons born from the śūdra wife were given considerable shares. In the case of a brāhmaṇa having sons from wives of all the four castes, Kauṭilya accepts the Dharmasūtra principle of division of shares.[3] He extends this even to the case of kṣatriya and vaiśya fathers begetting sons on the wives from three or two castes, in every case the śūdra son getting the smallest share.[4]

The question of the civic status of the śūdra *vis-a-vis* the position of slaves in the *Arthaśāstra* needs some consideration. Like the authors of the Dharmasūtras, Kauṭilya clearly recognises an ārya as a free man, and states that on no account can an ārya be subjected to slavery.[5] As a corollary to this he ordains that the selling or mortgaging by kinsmen of a śūdra who is not a born slave, has not attained majority, but is an *āryaprāṇa* (ārya in birth), shall be punished with a fine of 12 paṇas, and that everybody engaged in the transaction shall be severely penalised.[6] This implies that sons of the three higher varṇas begotten on a śūdra woman,[7] cannot be reduced to slavery through the process of purchases or pledging: perhaps they might be relegated to that position through other processes such as judicial punishment, capture in war, voluntary enslavement etc.[8] Thus Kauṭilya refers to the *āryaprāṇa* captured in war

1. *Ibid.*
2. *Ibid.*
3. *AŚ*, III. 6.
4. *Ibid.*
5. *AŚ*, III. 13.
6. *udaradāsavarjamāryaprāṇamaprāptavyavahāraṃ śūdraṃ vikrayādhānaṃ nayatasvajanasya dvādaśapaṇo daṇḍaḥ AŚ*, III 13.
7. Cf Jayaswal. *Manu and Yājñavalkya, p.* 242.
8. Altogether nine sources of slavery are specified in the *AŚ* (III. 3). Other varieties also may have existed.

being reduced to slavery.[1] Therefore his rule clearly shows that, with the exception of the minor śūdra sons of the members of the three varṇas, other members of the fourth varṇa could be made slaves. Even in the case of these specified śūdras, whose numbers must have been very small, the fine prescribed for making them slaves is the smallest, i.e. 12 paṇas, which gradually increases in the cases of the vaiśya, the kṣatriya and the brāhmaṇa.[2]

But under certain special circumstances such as domestic distress or inability to pay fines or debts even the life of an ārya could be mortgaged.[3] So far as these mortgaged people (*āhitakas*) are concerned, Kauṭilya lays down a number of liberal rules. It is provided that his kinsmen shall redeem the pledged person as soon as possible. He cannot be employed in impure work. If a pledged woman attends on her master while bathing naked, or if the master violates her chastity or abuses or hurts her, he shall not be entitled to the value of that woman, which will automatically secure her freedom. In the case of rape with a pledged young woman, the master shall not only forfeit the purchase value, but also pay a certain amount (śulka) to her and twice the amount (of the śulka) to the government. If the master has illicit connection with a pledged woman slave working as a nurse, he shall be punished with the first amercement. In the same context it is stated that use of violence towards a high born attendant shall entitle him to run away.[4] This shows that the *āhitakas* also probably hailed from the higher varṇa. Unfortunately in the translation of the above passage Shamasastry does not make any distinction between the *dāsa* and the *āhitaka*, and indiscriminately uses the word slave for both of them.[5] But that the *dāsas* and the *āhitakas* were two distinct categories of employees is clear from several statements of Kauṭilya. He prescribes that agreements entered into by the

1. *AŚ*, III. 13.
2. *Ibid.*
3. *atha vā'ryamādhāya kulabandhanāryāṇamāpadi niṣkrayaṃ cādhigamya bālaṃ sāhāyyadātāraṃ vā pūrvaṃ niṣkriṇīran*. *AŚ*, III. 13. Kangle has been followed.
4. *sidhamupacārakasyābhiprajātasya apakramaṇam*. *AŚ*, III. 13.
5. *Tr.*, p. 206.

dāsa and the *āhitaka* shall be declared void.[1] He also states that the king should see to it that people pay attention to the claims of their *dāsas* and *āhitakas*.[2] Kauṭilya further lays down that a woman who yields herself to a *dāsa*, a *paricāraka* (servant) or an *āhitaka* shall be put to death.[3] In all these cases Shamasastry recognises that the *āhitaka* is different from a *dāsa* and describes him as a pledged labourer or a hireling.[4] Since in the chapter on the *dāsakarmakarakalpa* the *āhitakas* are confounded with the *dāsas*, the liberal rules applying to the former have been taken as applying to the *dāsas* as well.[5] But the above analysis would show that these rules of Kauṭilya apply to the pledged labourers, mostly women and presumably belonging to the āryan varṇas. The rules referred to above also imply that the ordinary dāsas could be assaulted, abused and employed in impure work by the master.

Several provisions of Kauṭilya regarding the emancipation of slaves seem to apply exclusively to the āryas reduced to servile status. It is enacted that the child of one who sells himself should be considered as an ārya (free).[6] A person can earn without prejudicing the work of his master, inherit his ancestral property and thus regain his āryahood (*āryatvam*) by paying his purchase value.[7] An *āryaprāṇa* who has been captured in war can secure his emancipation through the payment of ransom.[8] Failure to recognise a dāsa as an ārya on the receipt of proper ransom shall be punished with a fine of 12 paṇas.[9] In all such instances the question of regaining āryahood can arise only in the case of those who had it before and not in the case of the śūdras. At best the above-mentioned provisions can apply to the sons of the three higher varṇas born from śūdra mothers.

Kauṭilya uses two terms to indicate the emancipation of servile

1. *AŚ* III. 1.
2. *Ibid.*, II. 1.
3. *Ibid.*, IV. 13.
4. Tr. of *AŚ*, III. 1 and II. 1.
5. Jayaswal, *Manu and Yājñavalkya*, p. 209.
6. *ātmavikrayiṇaḥ prajāmāryāṃ vidyāt*. *AŚ*, III.13.
7. *AŚ*, III. 13
8. *Ibid.*
9. *Ibid.*

people. In the case of the āryas the term *āryatvam* is used. But when the non-āryan slaves are to be freed, the term *adāsa* is used. For instance, it is laid down that, if the master begets a child on his woman slave, the mother along with the child should be regarded as free.[1] If, for the sake of supporting her family, the mother decides to continue as a slave, her mother, brother and sister shall be liberated (*adāsāḥ syuḥ*).[2] It seems that these dāsas ceased to be slaves, but they could not become āryas. We may note that in the early Pāli texts the term used for the manumission of the slaves is *bhujjissa*,[3] and it is expressly stated that only among the Yavanas can an ārya become a dāsa and *vice versa*.

It is difficult to say whether the rule providing for the emancipation through the payment of purchase value applied to the non-āryan slaves in the same way as it did to the āryan slaves. Perhaps even on payment the liberation of the śūdra slaves lay at the discretion of the master. But they were also sometimes emancipated, for it is laid down that selling or mortgaging the life of a man or woman slave once liberated shall be punished with a fine of 12 paṇas, with the exception of those who enslave themselves.[4] It appears that even an ordinary slave could keep property of which he could not be deprived by his master.[5] This could naturally help him in securing his liberation.

Kauṭilya lays down some rules to regulate the treatment of slaves, which may have applied to the śūdra slaves as well as to those of higher varṇas. He directs that a slave who is less than eight years old and without relatives cannot be employed in mean avocations against his will, and cannot be sold or mortgaged in a foreign land.[6] Similarly a pregnant slave cannot be sold or pledged without any provision for her confinement.[7] Again, the master cannot put his slave under confinement

1. *samātṛkam adāsaṃ vidyāt*. *AŚ*, III. 13.
2. *AŚ*, III. 13 after TGS.
3. *s. v.* bhujjissa, *Pali-Eng. Dict.*
4. *AŚ*, III. 13.
5. *Ibid.*
6. *Ibid.*
7. *Ibid.*

without any reason.[1] In the chapter on the *janapadaniveśa* it is enjoined that the king should compel the people to pay attention to the claims of their *dāsas* and *āhitakas*.[2] This sounds similar to the repeated instructions of Aśoka that slaves and servants should be treated kindly.[3]

But the liberal laws of Kauṭilya mostly cover the *āhitakas* and the ex-āryan slaves whose numbers must have been small; only a few of these laws apply to the greater number of ordinary slaves, who are evidently śūdras. Failure to see this point had led to the wrong inference that Kauṭilya's laws indirectly abolish slavery or that he introduced a policy of making his countrymen a nation of freemen.[4] His liberal laws mainly indicate his concern to protect the position of the ex-āryan slaves as distinguished from the non-āryen or śūdra slaves. This is natural, for Kauṭilya seems to draw a line between the śūdra and the members of the three upper varṇas in the laws relating to evidence, adultery and inheritance.[5] Although Kauṭilya does not explicitly distinguish between an ārya and a śūdra as the Dharmasūtras do, he makes an unambiguous distinction between an *ārya* and an *avara* in matters of providing rations.[6] And there is no doubt that the term *avara* stands for śūdra.

The comparatively detailed laws of Kauṭilya regarding slavery, not to be found in the Dharmasūtras, show that there was a considerable number of slaves in Mauryan India. Quoting from Megasthenes Arrian states that none of the Indians employ slaves.[7] But this version is substantially modified by the account of Onesikritos, whom Strabo considers more reliable, for Strabo places Megasthenes among a set of liars.[8] Onesikritos states that the custom of not keeping slaves was peculiar to the people in the country of Mousikanos,[9] which included a large

1. *Ibid.*
2. *AŚ*. II. 1.
3. R.E. 9 (*Girnār*), l. 4; P. E. II (Girnār), 1.2.
4. Jayaswal, *Manu aud Yājñavalkya*, p. 209. *B.N. Dutt*, *Studies in Indian Social Polity*, pp. 184-87.
5. Supra, *pp*. 175-77.
6. *AŚ*, II. 15. distinction between an *ārya* and a *nīca* in *AŚ*, 1. 14.
7. McCrindle, *AIMA* pp. 211-13, Frag. 10.
8. *Ibid.* pp. 18-19.
9. McCrindle, *AICL*, p. 58, Strabo, Frag. 54.

part of modern Sindh. According to him instead of slaves they employed young men in the flower of their age, as the Cretans employed the *aphamiotai*,[1] and the Lacedemonians the helots.[2] This suggests that even the Mousikanoi had a class of people who worked as the helots of society as a whole, not being owned individually. The practice bears out the brāhmaṇical theory that the śūdras are meant for serving the members of the three upper varṇas as slaves and hirelings.

That the Mauryan empire had a substantial number of slaves can be inferred from several circumstances. The continuous expansion of Magadha from Bimbisāra to Aśoka, for a period of about three centuries, must have brought in a large number of slaves from the tribal areas to work in the middle Gaṅgā basin. Aśoka captured 150,000 people in the Kaliṅga war,[3] but Candragupta, who had overrun the whole country with 600 000 men, may have acquired many more captives. *Dhvajāhṛt* or war captives being an important category of slaves in Kauṭilya[4] and other sources, it is fair to assume that every war meant acquisition of a large number of slaves. This is understandable because the existence of thick forests prevented any fruitful exploitation of the middle Gaṅgā alluvium before the NBP/iron phase; on the other hand at the initial stage of this phase the non-alluvial peripheral, hilly areas seem to have been more inhabited and hence better suited for the supply of agricultural labour. In the case of Magadha's conquest of Kosala and Vaiśāli fewer people, though materially advanced, may have been made slaves, but more slaves, mostly tribal and non-brāhmaṇised combatants, may have been obtained from the defeat of Aṅga, Kaliṅga, Aṭavi and Avanti. War was therefore possibly the single greatest factor that contributed to the growth of slavery. Secondly, in the Mauryan period because of standardisation the punch-marked coins seem to have become imperial and their issue seems to have reached its peak, leading to more and more money transactions. This factor may have added to the number of slaves through debt and sale.

1. Like helots they were attached to the soil.
2. McCrindle, *AICL*, p. 41. Strabo, Frag. 34.
3. XIII Rock Edict.
4. *AŚ*, III. 13.

It has been argued that classical Athens, Roman Italy, the West Indian Islands, Brazil and the southern states of the USA were "slave societies" because in each case slaves played an important part in production and formed over 20 per cent of the population.[1] Although we have no statistics for the Mauryan empire, the state sector of agricultural production was certainly run by slaves and agricultural labourers, and in this sense dependent labour formed the back of the Mauryan state. Most Pāli references to slaves and hired labourers working on farms belong to the Mauryan period, and if these are considered along with those found in Kauṭilya, we can legitimately assume that slavery played a very considerable role in agricultural production under the Mauryas. There may be a few doubts about the Mauryan society being considered a slave society, but it can undoubtedly be called a slave-owning society. Had the number of slaves been not substantial and the problem of controlling them insignificant, Aśoka would not have found it necessary to issue instructions for showing mercy and consideration to them; nor would have Kauṭilya given a full section to slavery and wage labour in his *Arthaśāstra*.[2]

On the whole there is no indication of any fundamental change in the civic and political status of the śūdras in the Mauryan period. The politico-legal disabilities imposed on them during the pre-Mauryan period continued in the main. In the fourth pillar Edict Aśoka enjoins the rājuka to introduce *vyavahāra-samatā* and *daṇḍa-samatā* among the people of the *janapada* placed under his charge.[3] These two terms have been rendered as "impartiality in judicial proceedings" and "impartiality in punishments".[4] But, in the context of the old legal discriminations based on varṇa, the above terms perhaps indicate an attempt on the part of an idealist ruler to do away with such distinctions. In what ways and how far this policy actually operated is not known. Possibly in the face of the long standing prejudices such a measure was doomed to failure. Besides, since it was issued towards the end of his reign in

1. Keith Hopkins, *Conquerors and Slaves*, pp. 99-100.
2. III. 13.
3. P. E.. 4 (Delhi—Topra Inscription), 1, 15.
4. *CII*, i, 225.

238 B.C.,[1] it may hardly have been long carried into effect before his death. Therefore this decree may have only served to arouse the brāhmaṇical hostility without achieving anything for the members of the lower orders.

As a work mainly concerned with the questions of economics and politics, the *Arthaśāstra* naturally does not supply as much information about the social conditions of the śūdras as the Dharmasūtras do. But it throws welcome light on the marriage practices of the śūdras and the position of their women. It informs us that, among the three higher varṇas, rejection of the bride before the rite of hand-taking (*pāṇigrahaṇa*) is valid, but among the śūdras this is valid before the time of cohabitation.[2] Again, it is said that divorce is not permissible in the case of the first four approved forms of marriage,[3] which implies that it is permissible in the case of the *gāndharva*, the *āsura* the *rākṣasa* and the *paiśāca* forms of marriage. It has been shown earlier that the *gāndharva* and *paiśāca* forms of marriage prevailed among the vaiśyas and śūdras,[4] which would suggest that dissolution of the marriage tie was considered easier among them. Kauṭilya also states that while the approved forms of marriage require the consent of the father, the unapproved forms require the consent of the mother as well.[5] This indirectly suggests that the continuity of matriarchal elements among the people of lower orders lent some importance to their women.

The above-mentioned provisions of Kauṭilya are not noticeable in the early Dharmasūtras. But Kauṭilya fixes practically the same waiting periods for the wives of the absent husbands of the different varṇas as is done by Vasiṣṭha, the shortest period being prescribed in the case of the wife of a śūdra.[6] All such

1. *Ibid.*, Introd., p. XXXVI.

2. *vivāhānantu trayāṇāṃ pūrveśāṁ varṇānāṃ pāṇigrahaṇātsiddhamupāvartanaṃ śūdrāṇāṃ ca prakarmaṇām.* *AŚ*, III. 15. *TSS* has *prakarmaṇaḥ* (II. p. 92). He explains this as *yonikṣatimavadhīkṛtya*, i.e. the loss of virginity of the girl. SS's translation of this term as 'nuptials' does not make sense. Meyer translates it as 'Beischlafung' (p. 296).

3. *AŚ*, III. 3.

4. Supra, *p.* 130.

5. *AŚ*, III. 2.

6. *Ibid.*, III. 4.

injunctions show that the marriage tie was not considered so strong in the case of the śūdras as in the case of the members of the higher varṇas, among whom women were much more dependent upon man.

It has been suggested that Kauṭilya's provision fixing the age of sixteen for the bridegroom and twelve for the bride[1] was meant for the non-brāhmaṇa castes, especially the working class who desired early progeny.[2] Such an assumption is not at all warranted by the context in which the above provision occurs. On the other hand, in the absence of any references to the application of this measure to the lower varṇas, this provision may be taken to set the standard of conduct for the four varṇas in the order of their superiority.

Kauṭilya informs us that actors, players, singers, fishermen, hunters, herdsmen, wine distillers and vendors, and similar persons usually travel with their women.[3] This was not the case with the women of the higher varṇas, whose activities were limited to the sphere of home. The outside life of the women of the śūdra varṇa was due to the necessity of working in the fields and pastures for the subsistence of their family. For Kauṭilya provides that wives of sharecroppers and herdsmen are responsible for the payment of debts incurred by their husbands.[4]

Normally the castes were endogamous during this period. Arrian informs us that the husbandman could not take a wife from the artisan class and *vice versa*.[5] But some marriages also took place between the members of the higher varṇas and the śūdras, as is evident from Kauṭilya's law of inheritance and his list of the mixed castes known as the *antarālas*. He repeats the brāhmaṇical theory of the origin of the niṣāda, the pāraśava, the caṇḍāla, the pulkasa, the śvapāka, the kṣattā, the āyogava, the kuṭaka (kukkuṭaka of the Dharmasūtras), the rathakāra,

1. *Ibid.*, III. 3.
2. K. V. Rangaswami Aiyangar, *Indian Comeralism*, p. 66, fn. 5.
3. *tāḷāpacāracāraṇamatsyabandhakalubdhakagopālakaśauṇḍikānāmanyeṣām ca prasṛṣṭāstrīkāṇāṃ pathyanusaraṇamadoṣaḥ*. *AŚ*, III. 4.
4. *strī vā pratiśrāviṇī patikṛtaṃ ṛṇaṃ anyatra gopālakārdhasītikebhyaḥ*. *AŚ* III. 11.
5. *IA*, v 92:

the vaiṇya etc.[1] Kauṭilya states that the function of the vaiṇya and the rathakāra are identical.[2] He further declares that members of these mixed castes should marry within their own castes.[3] The king should see to it that they follow their respective avocations.[4] He enjoins the king to recognise these orders and guide his subjects accordingly.[5] It is also laid down that among all the mixed castes there will be equal shares of inheritance.[6] According to him the mixed castes (*antarālas*), with the exception of the caṇḍālas, can live by the occupations of the śūdras.[7] Hence only the caṇḍālas are regarded as a despised caste, and the rathakāras, veṇas, pukkusas and nesādas of the Buddhist list are left out.

It has been shown earlier that Pāṇini seems to have included the caṇḍālas in the śūdra varṇa. But Kauṭilya does not consider them as śūdras.[8] They have no place in the fourfold varṇa system. Thus, according to Kauṭilya, damage done to the animals and birds of the caṇḍālas and forest tribes should be punished with half the fine of that done to the similar possessions of the members of the four varṇas.[9] In addition to the four varṇas Kauṭilya mentions the caste of the *antyāvasāyins*,[10] who seem to be identical with the caṇḍālas, for the latter lived outside villages near the burial grounds.[11] It is laid down that, if the caṇḍāla touches an ārya woman, a fine of a hundred paṇas shall be imposed on him.[12] This may imply that no such fine will be imposed if he

1. *AŚ*, III. 7. Kauṭilya introduces a new definition of the vrātyas, who, according to him, are sons begotten by impure men of any of the four varṇas on a woman of lower caste. *Ibid.*
2. *karmaṇā vaiṇyo rathakāraḥ. AŚ*, III. 7.
3. *Ibid.* This interpretation is on the basis of the construction of the passage according to TGS (ii, 44). SS gives a different construction, which suggests that marriage within the castes was confined only to the vaiṇyas.
4. *purvāparagāmitvaṃ vṛttānuvṛttaṃ ca svadharmān sthāpayet AŚ*, III. 7.
5. *AŚ*, III. 7.
6. *Ibid.*
7. *AŚ*, III. 7 after TGS, ii, 44.
8. *AŚ*, III. 7.
9. *caṇḍālāraṇyacarāṇāmardhadaṇḍāḥ. AŚ*, IV. 10.
10. *AŚ*, III. 18.
11. *AŚ*, II. 4.
12. *AŚ*, III. 20.

touches a śūdra woman. Similarly the tank of water used by the caṇḍālas could not be used by anybody else.[1] So there is no doubt that the caṇḍālas continued to be regarded as untouchables. But the same cannot be said of the other mixed castes such as the pāraśavas and the niṣādas. For Kauṭilya provides for the share of the pāraśava son in the case of the brāhmaṇa father having no other issue.[2] The *Arthaśāstra* introduces us to a new avocation of the caṇḍāla. He is to be engaged in whipping a transgressing woman in the centre of the village.[3] He may be also asked to drag with a rope, along the public road, the bodies of such men and women as commit suicide by various methods.[4]

Kauṭilya furnishes some information about the religious conditions of the śudras. He lays down that if a person entertains at a dinner dedicated to a god or ancestors such *vṛṣala* ascetics as the Buddhist and the Ājīvikas, a fine of hundred paṇas shall be imposed on him.[5] Shamasastry renders *vṛṣala* as śūdra, but the passage does not actuallty refer to the śūdra but to the ascetics, who were branded indiscriminately as śūdras by brāhmaṇas. Nevertheless, the ascetics were respected by Aśoka without any consideration of caste. It is said that on one occasion when Aśoka was criticised for this by his minister, he replied that considerations of caste prevail in marriage and invitations and not in the observance of the dhamma.[6]

A provision of Kauṭilya envisages the possibility of admitting some śūdras to religious and educational facilities. While prescribing certain methods to test the character of the amātyas, he recommends a particular measure through which their temptation to disobey his orders on account of religious conviction is put to trial. The king should dismiss a priest, who, when ordered, refuses to teach the Veda to an undeserving person or to officiate in a sacrificial performance undertaken by a person who does

1. *AŚ*, I. 14.
2. *AŚ*, III. 6.
3. *AŚ*, III. 3. The caṇḍālas may have been specially chosen for the purpose because of the ferocity associated with these aboriginal peoples.
4. Read *rajjunā*. *AŚ*, IV. 7. SS translates *ghātayetsvayamātmānam* as "cause others to commit suicide", which does not seem to be correct.
5. *AŚ*, III. 20.
6. Quoted in P. L., Narsu, *The Essence of Buddhism*, p. 137.

not enjoy the right to sacrifice (*ayājyāyajanādhyāpane*).[1] The dismissed priest should try to mobilise the amātyas for the overthrow of the king on the ground of his being irreligious. If the amātyas do not succumb to this religious temptation, they should be considered pure.[2] In this passage the *ayājya* is described by the *Jayamaṅgalā* as the son of a śūdra woman (*śūdrāputra*).[3] Therefore the rule suggests the possibility of the śūdra sons of the higher varṇas performing sacrifice and taking to study if the king so desires, thereby indicating the absolute power of the ruler during the Mauryan period. But perhaps the normal position in this respect is suggested by another statement of Kauṭilya, who declares that sacrificial virtues fall in value when performed in the company of the husband of a śūdra woman;[4] so he instructs that such a priest should not be entertained.[5]

During the Mauryan period śūdras were employed by the state largely as slaves, labourers and artisans in the middle Gangetic plains. In spite of the fixation of their wages the economic organization was showing signs of strain. Since sufficient dāsas and karmakaras were not forthcoming for agriculture carried on by the state, it was found necessary to adopt the practice of leasing royal lands to sharecroppers, who presumably belonged to the lower orders. Secondly, by drafting śūdras from overpopulated areas, the state seems to have adopted the policy of opening up new lands, but the landless śūdras seem to have been used as agricultural labourers. Politically and socially the śūdras continued to be subject to the old discriminations, although Kauṭilya seems to have made a number of concessions in the case of the śūdra sons of the people of the higher varṇas. They could not be reduced to slavery, could have share in the paternal property,[6] and under special circumstances could enjoy the right to Vedic sacrifice and education. But the larger body of the śūdras continued to suffer from the old disabilities.

1. *AŚ*, I. 10.
2. *Ibid.*
3. *JOR*, xxii, 32. TGS interprets *ayājya* as *vṛṣalīpati*, i.e., husband of a śūdra woman (i, 48).
4. *AŚ*, III. 14.
5. *adoṣaḥ tyaktumanyonyam. Ibid.*
6. This was limited to the rathakāra and the pāraśava.

The *Arthaśāstra* gives us some idea about the general conduct of the lower orders, which shows that they were not altogether happy about the conditions in which they lived. Kauṭilya's list of offenders and suspects includes many of those whose castes and avocations were held low in society (*hīnakarmajātim*). They were suspected of being murderers, robbers or people guilty of misappropriation of treasures and deposits.[1] Kauṭilya says that, in the case of thefts and burglaries, poor women and servants of condemnable nature should be also examined.[2] He further provides that, if the master is murdered, his servants should be examined as to whether they had received any violent and cruel treatment at his hands.[3] This shows that at times domestic servants might make fatal attempts at the life of their masters. Kauṭilya also ordains that when a śūdra calls himself a brāhmaṇa, steals the property of gods, or is hostile to the king, either his eyes shall be destroyed by the application of poisonous ointment or he shall have to pay a fine of 800 paṇas.[4] This indicates the hostility of some śūdras to the priestly and royal powers. There is also a reference to the seditious activities of the pāraśava. His anti-state activities are to be countered by the same measure as those used againt a seditious minister. It is provided that the king should employ his spies in fomenting quarrels in the family of the suspect, leading to his ultimate execution by the government.[5] The above-mentioned references show that members of the śūdra varṇa were not happily disposed towards their masters. Since there were no peaceful channels into which their reaction could canalise itself, it occasionally found expression through criminal activities such as robberies, burglaries, theft of temple property, murder of the master, attack on the pretensions of the

1. *AŚ*, IV. 6.
2. *Ibid.*
3. *dagdhasya hṛdayamadagdhaṃ dṛṣṭvā vā tasya paricārakajanaṃ vā daṇḍapāruṣyādatimārget. AŚ*, IV. 7.
4. *śūdrasya brāhmaṇavādino devadravyamavastṛṇato rājadviṣṭamādiśato dvinetrabhedinaśca yogāñjanenāndhatvamaṣṭaśato vā daṇḍaḥ. AŚ*, IV. 10. There does not seem to be any justification for regarding the *brāhmaṇavādī śūdra* as distinct from the person who steals the property of god or is hostile to the king, as SS has done in the translation of this passage (Tr., p. 255).
5. *AŚ*, V. I based on the commentary of TGS.

brāhmaṇas and seditions against the head of the state. These actions seem to be symptomic of the discontent that prevailed among them. But there is no evidence of any organised revolt on their part. In this respect conditions during the Mauryan period were probably somewhat better than they had been in the earlier period. The *Arthaśāstra* does not contain any special provision to meet organised revolts on the part of the śūdras, such as can be inferred from some passages of the Dharmaśūtras On the other hand Kauṭilya's readiness to enrol śūdras in the army, though perhaps not put into practice, indicates a sense of confidence which was born of his twofold policy of conciliation and ruthless control.

However the lower orders and the tribal people were a source of headache to Aśoka. His emphasis on showing consideration towards slaves and hired labourers indicates an atempt to pacify them. What is important, he made use of Buddhism to indoctrinate the frontier tribes and win them over to the existing social set-up. They were asked to observe dhamma, which would imply following the rules regarding patriarchal family, property and social orders. To those who defied and proved intrasigient Aśoka held out a veiled threat of punishment. In some cases Aśoka claims success in his efforts.

CHAPTER VI

CRISIS IN THE OLD ORDER

(*circa* 200 B.C.—*circa* A.D. 300)

Most of our direct information about the position of the śūdras during this period is derived from the law-book of Manu, which is ascribed to the period 200 B.C.—A.D. 300.[1] But its major portion probably belongs to the second century A.D. As has been shown later in Appendix I, Chapter X, which deals with the mixed castes, may have been included in the text in about the fifth century A.D. Manu looks upon Brahmāvarta (the country between the Sarasvatī and the Dṛṣadvatī[2] and Brahmarṣideśa (the plains of the Kurus, the Matsyas, the Pañcālas and the Śūrasenas) as sacred.[3] On this basis it has been suggested that the law-book arose, and was first considered authoritative within this comparatively narrow province.[4] Such a view, though possible, is by no means necessary, and the influence of the code of Manu may have extended over a much wider area.

The extreme form of brāhmaṇical fanaticism displayed by Manu makes it difficult to evaluate the evidence furnished by his work. But his passages bearing on the position of the śūdras can be scrutinised in the light of information gleaned from the *Mahābhāṣya* of Patañjali, the dramas of Bhāsa[5] and the Buddhist

1. Bühler, *SBE*, xxv, Introd., pp. CXIV-CXVIII; cf. Jayaswal, *Manu and Yājñavalkya*, pp. 25-32; Kane, *Hist. Dh. S.*, ii, p. XI. Ketkar's argument that the work belongs to A.D. 272-320 (*History of Caste*, p. 66) may apply to some portions of the text.

2. *Manu*, II. 17.

3. *Ibid.*, II. 19.

4. Johantgen quoted in Hopkins, *Mutual Relations of Four Castes*, pp. 4-5.

5. The extreme view assigning Bhāsa to the 5th or the 4th cen B.C. is not generally accepted. Bhāsa's date may be placed in the second or third cen. A.D. (*The Age of mperial Unity* p. 261.)

works such as the *Questions of Milinda*, the *Divyāvadāna*, the *Mahāvastu* and the *Saddharmapuṇḍarika*.[1] A Jain work known as the *Pannavaṇā*, which supplies valuable information about artisans, may be also ascribed to this period.[2] Memorial and votive inscriptions of this period also throw welcome sidelights on the position of the śūdra community.

The descriptions of the Kali age in several early Purāṇas perhaps allude to this age[3] when the varṇa divided society was marked by strong social conflicts and undermined by the activities of heretical sects and the incursions of the Bactrian Greeks, Śakas, Parthians and Kuṣāṇas. Partly as a reaction to the pro-Buddhist policy of Aśoka, and partly because of the advent of these new peoples, Manu desperately tries to preserve brāhmaṇical society, not only by ordaining rigorous measures against the śūdras, but also by inventing suitable genealogies for the incorporation of foreign elements into varṇa society. Moreover, his undue glorification of the power of the sword (daṇḍa)[4] is also meant to serve that end.

Manu reaffirms the old theory that the śūdra is ordained by God to serve the higher castes.[5] The king should order a vaiśya to trade, to lend money, to cultivate the land or to tend cattle, and a śūdra to serve the three upper varṇas.[6] But in the chapter on times of distress (*āpad-dharma*) Manu declares that a śūdra should serve the brāhmaṇa, which would secure him all his ends;[7] failing that he may serve a kṣatriya, or may maintain himself by attending even on a wealthy vaiśya.[8] In this

1. Since the earliest Chinese translation of the *Saddharmapuṇḍarīka* took place in the 3rd cen. A.D. (*SBE*, xxi, Introd., p. XXI), the original composition may be assigned to the 2nd or even the first cen. A.D. (N. Dutt, *Saddharmapuṇḍarīka*, Introd., p. XVII).

2. Jain, *Life in Ancient India as Depicted in the Jain Canons*, p. 38. The book mentions, Śakas, Yavanas, Muruṇḍas, Pahlavas etc. (i. 58), which seems to make it a work of the post-Mauryan period.

3. Hazra, *Studies in the Purāṇic Records on Hindu Rites and Customs*, pp. 208-10.

4. *Manu*, VII. 13-30.

5. *Ibid.*, I. 91.

6. *Ibid.*, VIII. 410.

7. *Ibid.*, X. 123; cf. IX. 334.

8. *dhaninaṃ vāpyupārādhya vaiśyaṃ śūdro jijīviṣet...Ibid.*, X. 121-2.

connection the phrase *api* (even) should be particularly noted, since it seems to imply that the vaiśya was seldom the master of the śūdra.[1] This further suggests that in times of distress the service of the śūdra was to be mainly reserved for the brāhmaṇas and kṣatriyas. At another place Manu ordains that the king should carefully compel the vaiśyas and the śūdras to perform the tasks assigned to them; since, if these two varṇas swerve from their duties, they will throw the whole world into confusion.[2] This passage is of particular importance, for it is not to be found in any earlier text. Such a measure seems to reflect a period of socio-economic crisis, which is also evident from the *Yuga Purāṇa*, which informs us that during this period even women took to ploughing.[3] That there seems to have been decaying farmers and traders, who were recruited as spies by the king, can be inferred from the comment of Kullūka to a passage of Manu.[4] Another rule of Manu that the śūdras distressed for subsistence may settle down in any part of the country[5] (i.e. even in the land of the Mlecchas) also points to some kind of crisis, which deeply affected the producing masses and encouraged migration. Hence Manu's measure for making the vaiśyas and śūdras work may have been necessitated by social convulsions made worse by foreign invasions. Perhaps, when the strong rule of the Mauryans broke down, it was found increasingly difficult to keep the vaiśyas and the śūdras within the bounds of their assigned duties.

The above-mentioned references also show that distinctions between the functions of the vaiśyas and the śūdras were being gradually obliterated. Manu lays down that, if in times of distress the vaiśya finds it difficult to support himself by his own occupations he should take to the occupations of the śūdras, i.e. live by

1. Hopkins, *op. cit.*, p. 83.
2. *Manu*, VIII. 418.
3. *Yuga Purāṇa*, 167.
4. Kullūka interprets the term *pañcavargam* in *Manu*, VII. 154 as five classes of spies, including *karṣakaḥ kṣīṇavṛttiḥ* and *vāṇijakaḥ kṣīṇavṛttiḥ*. Hopkins takes the word in the sense of minister, realm, city, wealth and army (*op. cit.*, p. 69). but there does not seems to be any justification for taking the *pañcavarga* in the sense of the five elements of the state, which are generally enumerated as seven.
5. II. 24.

serving the members of the twice-born caste.[1] This is also supported by a passage of the *Questions of Milinda*, where cultivation, trade and tending of cattle are described as the functions of the ordinary folk such as the vaiśyas and the śūdras,[2] there being no separate mention of the functions of these two classes.

In spite of the tendency to approximate the vaiśya to the śūdra there is no evidence of the existence of independent śūdra peasants. Generally they continued to be employed as hired labourers and slaves, for Manu repeats the old rule that, instead of paying taxes, artisans, mechanics and śūdras who subsist by manual labour should work for one day per month for the king.[3] He lays down a new provision that the vaiśyas should meet times of emergency by paying $\frac{1}{8}$ of their corn as tax and the śūdras by their manual labour.[4] In this connection Kullūka states emphatically that even in bad times taxes should not be imposed on the śūdras.[5] Manu's exemption of śūdras from taxes is corroborated by the *Milinda-pañha*. It informs us that every village had its slaves, men and women, wage earners (bhatakas) and hired labourers (karmakaras), who were exempted from taxes.[6] Therefore, unlike the vaiśyas, the śūdras do not appear as peasants paying taxes to the state. While enumerating the eightfold functions (*aṣṭavidhaṃ karma*) of the king Medhātithi mentions trade, agriculture, irrigation, digging mines, settling uninhabited districts, cutting forests, etc.[7] But there is no evidence of dāsas and karmakaras being employed in agriculture by the state, as we find in the Mauryan period. The *Mahāvastu* describes a village headman as hurrying out of the village to inspect the work in the fields, but we do not know whether he did this on

1. *Manu*, X. 98.
2. *avasesānaṃ puthuvessasuddānaṃ kasivaṇijjā gorakkhā karaṇīyā. Milinda*, p. 173.
3. *Manu*, VII. 138.
4. *Ibid.*, X. 120.
5. *na tu tebhya āpadyapikaro grāhyaḥ*. Comm. to *Manu*, X. 120.
6. *Milinda*, p. 147.
7. Comm. to *Manu*, VII. 154. Hopkins thinks that the *aṣṭavidhaṃ karma* reminds one of the seven elements of the state (*op. cit.*, pp. 70-71), but there is no similarity between the *aṣṭavidha karma* and the *saptāṅga*.

behalf of the king.[1] It seems that śūdras were mostly employed as agricultural workers by individual proprietors. Patañjali refers to the landowner sitting in a corner and supervising the ploughing done by five hired labourers.[2] Manu also speaks of the servants of the peasant proprietors.[3] According to him the cultivator should form an item in the additional portion to be given to the brāhmaṇa son in the partition of family property.[4] This obviously refers to the employment of agricultural labourers by the brāhmaṇas.

The position of śūdra artisans may be viewed better in the context of commerce and handicrafts in the post-Maurya period. Undoubtedly this period was the most flourishing era in ancient India's foreign trade. On account of the discovery of the monsoons in the first half and the opening of the Silk Roads in the second half of the first century A.D., the country carried on booming land trade with Central Asia and China and overseas trade with the Roman empire. The stability and protection afforded by the Han, Kuṣāṇa, Roman and Arcasid empires promoted international trade in the first two centuries A.D., and India exported precious woods, cotton textiles, silk, gems, iron objects, and above all long and black pepper.[5] Some raw materials such as crude glass, lead, tin, red coral and asbestos and finished products including wine and Roman storage and table ware were imported, but payment was made principally in Roman coin.[6] Numerous hoards of Roman gold coins have been discovered, south of the Vindhyas, especially in the cotton producing areas of Maharashtra. Probably the largest documented and apparently reliable business transaction for ancient times of free private trade without state control or subvention was the flow of imports to the value of 55 million sesterces

1. i, 301.
2. *Mahābhāṣya*, ii, 33.
3. *...bhṛtyānāmajñānātkṣetrikasya tu*. *Manu*, VIII. 243.
4. *Manu*, IX. 150.
5. Michael Loewe, "Aspects of World Trade in the First Seven centuries of the Christian Era", *JRAS*, no. 2 (1971), 176.
6. *Ibid.*

(16 million gold francs.) from India to Egypt in one year under Vespasian.[1]

Increasing internal trade is indicated by the use of coppers on a large scale. From the second century B.C. to the third century A.D., almost all kings from the Indo-Greek to the late Kuṣāṇa, and many 'tribes' and cities issued large numbers of copper coins, many of which contain considerable tin and can be called bronze coins. These coppers indicate increasing money transactions even among ordinary people. All this could not be possible without the progress of different crafts and trades.

The progress of crafts is attested by archaeological evidence regarding thriving urban life in the first three centuries of the Christian era. A dozen ports are mentioned in Greek and Latin accounts, and a few ports such as Tamluk, Arikamedu and Kaveripattanam have been excavated. In addition we know about numerous urban sites from excavations conducted since 1947. Towns existed in the middle Gaṅgā basin, and many were located on the *uttarāpatha* route following the course of the Jamna and then turning north-westward towards Taxila. Excavations show prosperous urban sites in western India under the Sātavāhanas. In eastern Andhra Pradesh and in the western Deccan they appeared first in the first century A.D. and continued for about three hundred years. The same holds good of Kuṣāṇa towns and structures in the provinces of Pakistan, and also in Afghanistan and Soviet Central Asia. All this means congenial conditions for the progress of crafts and commerce, which may have promoted considerable social and geographical mobility and added to the number of artisans in towns.

Archaeology gives us some idea about the crafts thriving in the centuries immediately preceding and following the beginning of the Christian era. Iron objects of various types recovered from the Sirkap city of Taxila,[2] and found at various places in Andhra Pradesh, suggest that the craft of ironsmith was

1. Max Weber, *The Agrarian Sociology of Ancient Civilizations* (London, 1976), p. 41.
2. Marshall, *Taxila*, ii, 533.

flourishing. This is attested by the export to the Roman empire of Indian steel, on the tempering of which a monograph was prepared in Greek.[1] An examination of some iron objects from Rajghat in Banaras shows that by the second century B.C. the art of making true steel was well known in the country. With the use of iron technology bronze objects including household goods and personal ornaments began to be prepared on a large scale. In addition to tin, lead, zinc and nickel were used in this period to make bronze, which made it more tough.

India did not have a proper bronze age, but from Taxila have been recovered numerous bronze objects,[2] which testify to the importance of the *kāṃsyakāra*. The use of brass objects also appears in this period,[3] and suggests the appearance of brassmakers. Reference has already been made to bronze coins.

A new category of craftsmen must have come into existence because of the glass manufacture on a large scale. Numerous glass objects, costly beads and bangles, have been recovered from Sirkap and Arikamedu.[4] The spurt in the craft was caused by the adoption of glass blowing by the Indian artisans some time before the beginning of the Christian era,[5] and there is nodoubt that the Indians had attained proficiency in glass technology.[6] It seems that crude glass was imported from the western world and China. In any case specimens of beads found throughout India indicate that in the early centuries of the Christian era they were in most prolific use.[7] M. G. Dikshit considers the post-Maurya period to A.D. 200 as that of affluence of glass in India;[8] this would not have been achieved without the skill of a good many glassmakers.

The presence of artisans working in ivory or *dantakāra* is attested by beautiful ivory objects of Indian make and origin

1. Marshall, ii, 534.
2. Adhya, *Early Indian Economics*, pp. 58-59.
3. *Ibid.*, pp. 56-57.
4. Adhya, *op. cit.*, pp. 76-80.
5. *Ibid.*, p. 80.
6. B. B. Lal, "Examination of Some Ancient Indian Glass Specimens," *AI*, viii, 26-27.
7. M. G. Dikshit, *History of Indian Glass*, p. 57.
8. *Ibid.*, chap. II.

found in Begram in Afghanistan.[1] A few objects have been also found in various parts of the country, and Banaras was an important centre of ivory-carving. As in the case of glass, the period is noted for the progress of ivory work. It is significant that for a few centuries after the third century A.D. both these crafts languished.

In addition to these the recovery of ornaments from Sirkap indicates the presence of jewellers. Although not much of gold and silver jewellery belonging to post-Maurya times has been recovered,[2] we have evidence of ten types of gems of semi-precious stones being used for jewellery at Sirkap. These include garnet, agate, jade, rock crystal, amethyst, lapis lazuli, turquoise, beryl, acquamarine and jasper.[3] For the first time we have a large number of gold coins in this period. It is therefore clear that the work of goldsmiths was supplemented by various types of jewellers and gem-cutters.

The pottery of the period, which is remarkable for the use of different types of Roman ware and their imitations, is found in plenty at Arikamedu and scattered in almost all parts of the peninsula. In addition to the Sātavāhana ware and the 'red' polished Kuṣāṇa ware we come across the remnants of the older pottery types and the emergence of local types. Although pottery did not form an article of export, we may presuppose the existence of a numerous class of potters to serve the cooking and storing needs of the growing town population. A good portion of the red ware was beautifully decorated, apparently for satisfying the sophisticated taste of the rich urban population. Urbanism provided an unprecedented market for terracottas which reached the peak point in numbers in the Kuṣāṇa-Sātavāhana phase.[4] Tiles for flooring and roofing appeared in this period, and ring-wells became far more numerous. All this naturally needed more and more potters.

1. These are now deposited in the Kabul Museum.
2. Adhya, *op. cit.*, pp. 66-67.
3. *Ibid.*
4. Devangana Desai, Terracottas and Urban Culture of Ancient India (*circa* 600 B.C.—A.D. 600). Cyclostyled copy of Paper presented to the "Art and Society" Symposium of the Indian History Congress. 37th Session, Calicut, 1976.

Finally building activities, as shown by structures of burnt bricks all over the country, attest the existence of a large number of bricklayers together with that of masons, builders and sculptors. This being the most flourishing period of town development, all these may have formed important artisan classes although some of them do not appear as functional groups in literary texts or as donors in inscriptions. In any case the nature of trade and archaeological evidence regarding towns and crafts would suggest the existence of a good number of potters, builders, bricklayers, gemcutters, jewellers, goldsmiths, ironsmiths, brass-smiths, bronzesmiths, sculptors, terracotta makers, glassmakers and ivoryworkers.

What is known indirectly about artisans from archaeological evidence is supported and supplemented by epigraphic and literary records. Manu's view that śūdras should take to the occupations of artisans only if they fail to secure livelihood through direct service of the upper varṇas[1] is traditional, for post-Maurya inscriptions suggest considerable increase in the number and variety of artisans and also some improvement in their conditions. We have a large number of recorded gifts of caves, pillars, tablets, cisterns etc. to the Buddhist monks by smiths, perfumers, weavers, goldsmiths and even leather workers in Gaya, Sanchi, Bharhut and the Nasik area.[2] Besides these, dyers, workers in metal and ivory, jewellers, sculptors and fishermen figure as donors in inscriptions.[3] Perfumers, and to a lesser degree, smiths are repeatedly mentioned as liberal votaries, and therefore seem to have formed the well-to-do and perhaps numerous sections of artisans. Although weavers do not appear as donors as often as perfumers, the evidence from Manu suggests that they were an important class of artisans; for it is laid down that they should pay 11 *palas*, and in the case of failure 12 *palas*.[4] These apparently were taxes in kind levied on

1. *Ibid.*, X. 99 and 100.

2. *Lüders' List*, Nos. 53, 54, 68, 76, 95, 331, 345, 381, 495, 857, 986, 1006, 1032, 1051, 1061, 1177, 1203-4, 1210, 1230, 1273, 1298; cf, *IC*, xii, 83-85.

3. *Ibid.*, Nos. 32, 53-54, 345, 857, 1005, 1092, 1129.

4. Quoted from *Vyākhyāsaṃgraha*, steyaprakaraṇa, pp. 1727-28 in *Dharmakośa*, i, pt. III, p. 1927.

the produce of the weavers, who probably owed their affluence to trade in textiles produced in Mathurā[1] and other cities. Most of the artisans known from inscriptions were confined to the Mathurā region, and to the western Deccan where their prosperity was stimulated by the growing trade with Rome.

The epigraphic evidence shows that the artisans were organised under their headmen, who probably enjoyed the favour of the king. Thus we hear of the gift of Ānanda who was the foreman of the artisans of Śrī Śātakarṇī.[2] But the literary evidence suggest that guilds of artisans flourished on a far larger scale during this period than in earlier times. At one place the *Mahāvastu* mentions eleven kinds of artisans such as garland makers, potters, carpenters, washermen, dyers, makers of bowls, goldsmiths, jewellers, workers in conch shell, armourers and cooks, all working under their respective heads.[3] The same source also refers to the eighteen guilds (*aṣṭādaśa śreṇis*) of Rājagaha including, goldsmiths, perfumers, gemcutters, oilmen, makers of flour, etc. The list also includess vendors of fruits, roots, flour, and sugar.[4] Goldsmiths and workers in gems are common to both the lists; yet there seem to have existed about two dozen guilds of artisans during this period.[5] It is to be also noted that the second list of guilds is quite different from that mentioned in the Jātakas.[6] Although artisans were employed by the king,[7] increase in the number of guilds may have weakened the direct control of the state over artisans. What is more significant, we do not come across so many kinds of artisans even in the *Arthaśāstra*, as we find during this period. The *Mahāvastu* gives a list of thirty-six kinds of workers living in the town of Rājagaha.[8] The list does not seem to be exhaustive, for it is said at the end of it that there are others besides those

1. *Mahābhāṣya*, i. 19.
2. *Lüders' List*, No. 346.
3. ii, 463-78.
4. *Mahāvastu*. iii, 442 ff.
5. Computed on the basis of *Mahāvastu*, ii, 463-78 and iii, 442ff. Many of these artisans were also small traders.
6. *IC*, xiv, 31-32.
7. Pat. on *Pā*., II. 1.1.
8. iii, 442-3.

mentioned.[1] A still longer list is to be found in the *Milinda-pañha*, which enumerates as many as seventy-five occupations, mostly of artisans.[2] Many artisans of the Buddhist lists also recur in a Jain work, which enumerates eighteen kinds of craftsmen and significantly describes even the tailors, weavers and silk weavers as āryans by craft,[3] showing thereby that these crafts were not held in low esteem by the Jains. It may be noted that in early medieval times weavers came to be considered untouchables.

An analysis of the lists of these artisans would show that there arose a number of new crafts during this period. As against about two dozen trades in the *Digha Nikāya*[4] we meet about five dozen trades in the *Milinda-pañha*. Of these eight crafts are associated with metal working,[5] which shows considerable advance in that field. Occupations connected with cloth making, silk weaving,[6] making of arms and luxury articles,[7] also seems to have made progress All this shows that artisans of this period made a significant contribution to technological and economic developments, although much of this may have been to the benefit of upper classes.

These artisans were not attached to their clients in the same way as the dāsas and the karmakaras were attached to their masters. Thus Patañjali informs us that the weaver was an independent worker.[8] While the dāsās and the karmakaras worked in the hope of getting clothes and food, the artisans worked in the hope of getting wages.[9]

Manu lays down a number of laws which affect the economic position of the śūdras adversely. Thus he introduces rates of

1. *Ibid.*
2. *Milinda*, p. 331.
3. *Pannavaṇā*, i, 61.
4. *Dīgha N.*, ii. 50.
5. *suvanna-, sajjha-, sīsa-, tipu-, loha-, vaṭṭa-, aya-, maṇi-kāra. Milinda*, p. 331.
6. *Pannavaṇā*, i, 61.
7. *Milinda*, p. 331.
8. Pat. on *Pā.*, I. 4.54.
9. *tathā yadetaddāsakarmakaraṃ nāmete'pi svabhūtyarthameva pravartante bhaktaṃ celaṃ ca lapsyāmahe.* Pat. on *Pā.*, III. 1.26.

interest differing according to varṇa.[1] The monthly interest charged should be two, three, four or five per cent according to the order of the varṇas.[2] But probably this law did not work in practice. According to a Nāsik Inscription when money was deposited with a weavers' guild, the rate of interest paid by them amounted to from 1 to $\frac{3}{4}$ per cent per month.[3] There is nothing to show that as śūdras they had to pay the highest rate of interest. A modern apologist has tried to justify this gradation of interest on the ground that it is in proportion to the social services of the borrowers,[4] which implies that the services rendered by the śūdras were negligible when in fact, along with the vaiśyas, they sustained the entire social fabric by their producing activities. Although Manu's law regarding interest may not have worked in practice, in charging interest probably the brāhmaṇas were shown some consideration while the śūdras were made to work off their debts. In any case such preferential treatment prevailed till recent times.

Manu lays down that a śūdra should not be permitted to accumulate wealth, for he gives pain to the brāhmaṇas.[5] It is suggested that this injunction is an exaggerated statement (*arthavāda*) addressed to the śūdra himself,[6] but the text does not provide any basis for such an interpretation. The injunction is also compared to an admonition in the English prayer-book advising a poor man "therewith to be contented".[7] Since the passage in question occurs in the chapter on times of distress, it may have been directed against the Buddhist monks or foreign rulers who were looked upon as no better than śūdras. At any rate it is evident from the law of inheritance that the

1. A similar rule occurring in *Vas. Dh. S.*, II. 48 seems to be an interpolation, for it is not found in the three other Dharmasūtras.

2. *Manu*, III. 142. According to Kṛṣṇapaṇḍita and the commentators on the parallel passage of *Viṣṇu* (VI. 2), *Manu* and other Smṛtis, this rule applies only to loans for which no security is given. *SBE*, xiv, 15.

3. *Lüders' List*, No. 1133.

4. K. V. Rangaswami Aiyangar, *Aspects of the Pol. and Soc. System of Manu*, p. 148.

5. *Manu*, X. 129.

6. K. V. Rangaswami Aiyangar, *Dharmaśāstra* p. 120.

7. Ketakar, *History of Caste*, p. 98.

śūdra owned property.[1] This can also be inferred from the old rule repeated by Manu that vaiśyas and śūdras should surmount their misfortunes through payment.[2]

According to Manu, one of the qualifications of the person with whom money should be deposited is that he should be an ārya.[3] This naturally excludes the śūdras. But in the second century A.D. in the Sātavāhana territory money was deposited with the potters, the oil millers[4] and even the weavers.[5] This practice prevailed among the lay devotees of Buddhism, who made such deposits for the purpose of providing robes and other necessities for the monks. But the orthodox also followed such practices, for we have a record which shows that during the reign of Huviṣka (*circa* A.D. 106-138) a sum of money was deposited by a chief with the guild of flour makers at Mathurā, out of the monthly interest of which a hundred brāhmaṇas were to be served daily.[6] These practices provide further evidence of the independent functioning of craftsmen organised in guilds. Evidently they could purchase their raw materials and implements with money deposited with them, and could pay interest on it out of the proceeds from the sale of their commodities.

Manu lays down that the brāhmaṇa can confidently seize the goods of his śūdra slave, for he is not allowed to own any property.[7] Jayaswal thinks that this probably legalises seizure of property of the Buddhist Saṃgha which had become enormously rich.[8] But perhaps the rule applies only to those śūdras who work as slaves. In Manu's opinion, even when starving, a kṣatriya can never seize the possessions of a virtuous brāhmaṇa, but he can appropriate the possessions of a dasyu or of one who neglects his sacred duties.[9] This suggests that the kṣatriyas and

1. *Manu*, IX. 157.
2. *Ibid.*, XI. 34.
3. *Ibid.*, VIII. 179.
4. *Lüders' List*, No. 1137.
5. *Ibid.*, No. 1133.
6. *EI*, xxi, Inscr. No. 10. The term used is *samitakaraśreṇī* (*Ibid.*, 1.12).
7. *Manu*, VIII. 417.
8. *Manu and Yājñavalkya*, p. 171.
9. *Manu*. XI. 18.

vaiśyas who neglected their essential rites could be subjected to such expropriation. In such a case the śūdras cannot be considered to be safe. For Manu provides that as the śūdra has nothing to do with the sacrifice, the sacrificer of the twice-born caste may take from him two or three articles required for it.[1] All these rules show a definite attempt on the part of Manu to keep down the śūdras economically.

We can obtain some idea about the wages of the workers and the general living conditions of the lower orders during the post-Mauryan period. In one respect, Manu followed the principle of Kauṭilya and states that a hired herdsman may milk with the consent of the owner the best cow out of ten.[2] In this case Manu seems to be more generous towards the hired labourer then Kauṭilya,[3] for he permits the labourer to milk the best cow. The responsibility of the herdsmen for the cattle under their charge is emphasised also by Manu, who enumerates their functions under various circumstances.[4] But in the case of loss of cattle he does not provide for the flogging of the herdsmen, as is done by Āpastamba, or for his death, as is done by Kauṭilya. Manu introduces a new provision, according to which an area of about 400 cubits in width round the villages, and thrice as much around the towns, are to be set apart as pasture ground. And if the cattle stray into the unfenced plots of anyone in this area and destroy his standing crops, the herdsman cannot be held answerable for this.[5] Thus to some extent this lawgiver safeguards the interests of the herdsmen.

While stating that the śūdras are meant for serving the brāhmaṇas he lays down that in fixing maintenance for them regard should be paid to their ability, work and the number of people they have to support.[6] He repeats the instruction of Gautama that these servants should be given leavings from the table, old clothes and beds, but adds that they should also be given the

1. *Ibid.*, XI. 13.
2. *Ibid.*, VIII. 231.
3. Kauṭilya only specifies 1/10 of milk as the share of a herdsman, but does not state that he should milk the best cow.
4. VIII. 229-44.
5. VIII. 237-8.
6. X. 124.

refuge of grain.[1] These rules obviously refer to the remuneration of those śūdras who served as domestic servants. Manu further states that the wages of those employed in the service of the king—maids and servants—should be fixed according to the consideration of time and place.[2] These workers, high (*utkṛṣṭa*) and low (*apakṛṣṭa*), should get the daily wages varying from one paṇa to six paṇas.[3] Besides, they should get provisions such as food, clothes etc. differing according to respective status.[4] It is not clear whether the terms *utkṛṣṭa* and *apakṛṣṭa* refer to high and low varṇas, as they are interpreted in another context.[5] But we learn from Patañjali that there was a wide difference between the wages of the karmakaras and the bhṛtakas on the one hand and those of the priests on the other. Thus, while the latter received cows as their wages, the former received only $\frac{1}{4}$ of a niṣka daily,[6] i.e. 7$\frac{1}{2}$ niṣkas per month. It is suggested that the niṣka is identical with the kārṣāpaṇa.[7] But if this proposition is accepted the daily wages of a worker will come to $\frac{1}{4}$ paṇa, while the nearly contemporary evidence of Manu indicates that the minimum wage of a labourer amounted to one paṇa, the maximum being six paṇas. In the *Arthaśāstra* the daily wage of a worker varies from $\frac{3}{5}$ paṇa to 2$\frac{2}{5}$ paṇa, i.e. one to four times,[8] but we have no means of estimating the relative purchasing power of the paṇa known from these sources.

Manu's provisions regulating the working conditions of the labourers are not so detailed as those of Kauṭilya. But, like Kauṭilya, he is severe towards a negligent workman. A hired workman who fails to perform his work according to the agreement out of pride, without being ill, shall be fined eight kṛṣṇalas, and no wages shall be paid to him.[9] Nevertheless, the worker who fails to do his work on account of illness but completes it on

1. X. 125.
2. VII. 125.
3. VII. 126.
4. *Ibid.*
5. Infra, p. 212.
6. Pat. on *Pā.*, I. 3.72.
7. V. S. Agrawala, *India as known to Pāṇini*, pp. 236-7.
8. Supra, p. 169.
9. *Manu*, VIII. 215.

his recovery shall be paid his wages for the long period of absence.[1] On the other hand, if he does not complete his work when he has recovered, he shall not be paid any wages even for the period he has worked.[2] This would suggest that workers were not penalised if they had to abandon work on account of illness, provided they undertook to finish the work on their recuperation or arranged to get it done by others. Manu does not make any further corresponding provision protecting the interests of the labourer as against the employer, such as we find in the *Arthaśāstra*. From a simile used by him it appears that the servant had to wait patiently for the payment of his wages.[3]

There seems to have been separate streets of the wage-earners in towns. A Buddhist source speaks of the *bhṛtakavīthi*, presumably in Rājagṛha, where the brāhmaṇas and householders (probably vaiśyas) went to hire labourers.[4] Another source draws a contrast between the street of the poor (*daridravīthi*) and the luxurious house of a rich man in a town.[5] Possibly this *daridravīthi* was identical with the *bhṛtakavīthi* and was inhabited by poor people who lived on wages. We also learn about three *bhṛtakas*, who cleared dirt near a rich man's house and lived in its vicinity in a hovel of straw.[6] Patañjali repeatedly states that the house of a vṛṣala, i.e. śūdra, is reduced merely to a wall (*kuḍya*).[7] This suggests that presumably it had an earthen or brick wall and the other three sides were enclosed by straw. It is also possible that the term *kuḍya*[8] here indicates a hut.

The *bhṛtaka* was distinguished by his lacerated body, dishevelled hair and dirty clothers,[9] for a well dressed person could

1. *Ibid.*, VIII. 216.
2. *Ibid.*, VIII. 217.
3. *Ibid.*, VI. 145.
4. *Divya.*, p. 304.
5. *Saddharmapuṇḍarīka*, Ch. IV, p. 76.
6. ...*kaṭapalikuñcikāyām*. *Ibid.*, IV. p. 78. *SBE* tr. of the phrase seems to be correct. It does not occur in Edgerton's *BHS Dictionary*.
7. *kuḍyībhūtaṃ vṛṣalakulamiti*. Pat. on *Pā.*, I. 2.47 & VI. 3.61.
8. *kuḍī* is a wrong reading for *kuṭi* (*s. v.* Monier-Williams, *Sansk-Eng. Dict.*), and *kuḍya* may be a form of *kuḍī*.
9. *sphaṭitapuruṣā rūkṣakeśā malinavastranivasanāḥ*. *Divya.*, p. 304. Edgerton doubts the correctness of *puruṣā* and suggests *paruṣā* (?) in its place (*s. v.* sphaṭita. *BHS Dict.*), but the existing reading gives a better sense.

not find employment in the *bhṛtakavithi*, although he waited there for the whole day.[1] Manu gives some idea of the food and dress of the śūdras who were employed as domestic servants. In this respect he merely repeats and to some extent elaborates the old provision of Gautama. A śūdra servant should be allotted by his master suitable maintenance commensurate with his ability, industry and the size of his family.[2] He should be given remnants of food, refuse of grain, worn out clothes and old beds[3] In the *Milinda-pañha* tender wives of kṣatriyas, brāhmaṇas and gahapatis are described as eating tasteful cakes and meat,[4] but there is no mention of the wives of śūdras in this connection.

Although the śūdras chiefly continued as agricultural workers employed by individual landowners, those who worked as artisans seem to have functioned more independently than in the earlier period. They increased not only in number and variety but also showed signs of prosperity. Manu's laws imposing new economic disabilities on the śūdras were probably ineffective. But there is no indication of any change in the living conditions of the main body of the śūdras.

Manu supplies considerable information about the position of the śūdras in post-Mauryan polity. He lays down that a snātaka should not dwell in the country of a śūdra ruler.[5] This apparently points to the existence of śūdra rulers during this period. But they do not seem to have arisen from the fourth varṇa, for contemporary political history does not know of such rulers. They probably refer to the Greek, Śaka, Parthian and Kuṣāṇa rulers, who were affiliated to Buddhism or Vaiṣṇavism, and whom Manu describes as degraded kṣatriyas reduced to śūdrahood on account of their failure to consult brāhmaṇas and to perform enjoined Vedic rites.[6] The Purāṇic descriptions of the Kali age speak of the śūdra kings performing the *aśvamedha*

1. *Divya.*, p. 304.
2. *Manu*, X. 124.
3. *Ibid.*, X. 125. Cf. V. 140.
4. *Milinda*, p. 68.
5. *na śūdrarājye nivaset. Manu*, IV. 61.
6. *vṛṣalatvaṃ gatā loke...Manu*, X. 43-44.

sacrifice[1] and employing brāhmaṇa priests.[2] While referring to the Kali rulers, the *Viṣṇu Purāṇa* states that the people of various countries will intermingle with them and follow their examples.[3] This seams to refer to the rulers of foreign extraction. They were the followers of heretical sects,[4] which further aroused Manu's hostility towards them. It is in order to prevent contact between brāhmaṇas and these rulers that Manu forbids the snātakas to dwell in their kingdoms. He further prescribes that brāhmaṇas should not accept presents from a king who is not descended from the kṣatriya race.[5] All these rules are obviously meant to prevent the recognition of foreign rulers by the brāhmaṇas. But gradually this open hostility gave way to tolerance and ultimate recognition of the alien rulers as ksatriyas, though of an inferior kind. During this period some Buddhists also did not favour rulers from low castes. The *Milinda-pañha* states that a person who is low born and base in lineage is not fit for kingship.[6]

Manu lays down that the king should appoint seven or eight ministers whose ancestors have been royal officers, who are skilled in the use of weapons, descended from noble families and are men of experience.[7] It is obvious that the śūdras could be hardly expected to fulfil these qualifications. Manu warns that the kingdom of that monarch who looks on, while a śūdra settles the law, will sink low like a cow in morass.[8] Such a rule perhaps again refers to the kingdoms of the barbarian rulers, who may have appointed some śūdras to carry on the administration of justice or to perform other administrative functions. But Manu emphatically states that

1. *Mat. P.*, 144. 43a; *Brahmāṇḍa, P.*, ii, 31. 67b; *Vā. P.*, 58.67a wrongly reads '*nāśvamedhena*' for '*cāśvamedhena*' of the *Brahmāṇḍa* (Hazra, *op. cit.*, p. 206, fn. 59).
2. *Kūrma P.*, Ch. 30, p. 304.
3. *Viṣṇu P.*, IV. 24.19.
4. *rājānaḥ śūdrabhūyiṣṭhāḥ pākhaṇḍānāṃ pravarttakāḥ*. *Brahmāṇḍa P.*, ii, 31.41.
5. *Manu*, V. 84.
6. *Milinda*, p. 358.
7. *Manu*, VII. 54.
8. *Ibid.*, VII. 21.

even a brāhmaṇa who subsists mainly by the name of his caste (i.e. merely by calling himself a brāhmaṇa) can interpret the law, but a śūdra can never be appointed a judge (*dharma-pravaktā*).[1] The commentators add that kṣatriyas might be employed in cases of necessity,[2] but they do not mention vaiśyas. This fits in with the scheme of Manu, in which kṣatriyas cannot prosper without brāhmaṇas and *vice-versa*, but closely united they prosper in this world and in the next.[3] Probably in brāhmaṇical kingdoms the first two varṇas monopolised all administrative and judicial posts.

Manu repeats the old principle that members of the four varṇas and the untouchables can act as witnesses in the transactions of their respective communities.[4] But he adds that kṣatriyas, vaiśyas or śūdras, provided they are householders, have sons and are indigenous, are competent to give evidence when called by a suitor.[5] In the opinion of Kullūka this applies to debts and similar civil cases, which means that the śūdras were not considered reliable in criminal cases.[6] However, the provision of Manu makes a definite advance on the provisions of earlier times which do not permit the śūdras to appear as witnesses in the cases involving members of the higher varṇas. As to cases such as defamation, assault, adultery and theft, anybody can be called as a witness irrespective of the qualifications required in civil cases.[7] If qualified witnesses are not available, Manu permits even slaves and servants to act as witness.[8] Manu does not introduce any varṇa distinctions in boundary disputes between villages; witnesses are to be examined in the presence of the crowd of villagers.[9] Amongst those whom Manu does not permit to appear as witnesses (evidently in civil cases) are artisans, actors and

1. *Ibid.*, VIII. 20.
2. Kullūka, Rāghavānanda and Nandana on *Manu*, VIII. 20.
3. *Manu*, IX. 322.
4. *Ibid.*, VIII. 68.
5. *Manu*, VIII. 62.
6. Kull. on *Mauu*, VIII. 62.
7. *Manu*, VIII. 62 and 69 with the comm. of Kull.
8. *Ibid.*, VIII. 70.
9. *Ibid.*, VIII. 254.

dancers.[1] Kullūka justifies this on the ground that these people are always occupied with their work and that they can be won over by bribery.[2] Born slaves are also not permitted to act as witnesses.[3]

Manu repeats the old rule of giving warning to the members of the various varṇas before making deposition.[4] If a śūdra gives false evidence, he is held guitly of all sins,[5] and is threatened with the most terrible spiritual consequences.[6] But he adds that a judge should cause a brāhmaṇa to swear by his veracity, a kṣatriya by his chariot or the animal he rides on, a vaiśya by his kine, grain and gold, and a śūdra by imprecating on his head the guilt of all grievous sins.[7] Significantly, however, Manu does not ordain any special royal punishment for the śūdra witness. He states the general principle that, in the case of giving false evidence, the king should fine and banish men of the three lower castes, but should only banish a brāhmaṇa.[8] Similarly, according to Manu, brāhmaṇas are not liable to corporal punishments, which can be inflicted only on the members of the three lower varṇas.[9] Therefore in these respects the śūdra is placed on a footing of equality with the kṣatriya and the vaiśya.

It is laid down that the king should take up the cases of the litigants in the order of their varṇas.[10] In settling the law he should take into account the customs of every caste.[11] Conduct of good people is regarded as a source of law by Manu,[12] and

1. *Ibid.*, VIII. 65.
2. Kull. *Manu*, VIII. 65.
3. *Manu*, VIII. 66 with the comm. of Kull; *adhyadhīna* is explained as a *garbhadāsa* (*Ibid.*).
4. *Ibid.*, VIII. 88.
5. *Ibid.*
6. Possibly a whole series of exhortations made by the judge in *Manu*, VIII. 89-101 are addressed to the śūdra witness.
7. *Manu*, VIII. 113.
8. *Ibid.*, VIII. 123.
9. *Ibid.*, VIII. 124-25.
10. *Ibid.*, VIII. 24.
11. *Ibid.*, VIII. 41.
12. *Ibid.*, II. 6.

according to a commentator of the 17th cen. A.D., this includes the practice of the good śūdras as well.[1]

Like the early lawgivers, Manu is guided by considerations of varṇa in the administration of justice, which affects the position of the śūdras adversely. If a kṣatriya defames a brāhmaṇa, he shall be fined a hundred paṇas, a vaiśya 150 or 200 paṇas, but a śūdra shall suffer corporal punishment.[2] If a brāhmaṇa defames a kṣatriya, a vaiśya or a śūdra, he shall be fined respectively 50, 25 or 12 paṇas.[3] The fact that a fine of 12 paṇas is prescribed in the case of a brāhmaṇa abusing a śūdra is significant, for in the *Gautama Dharmasūtra* no fine is provided in such a case.[4]

Generally Manu lays down very severe punishments for śūdras offending against the members of the superior varṇas. Thus if a śūdra insults a twice-born with gross invective, he shall have his tongue cut out.[5] The term twice-born (*dvijāti*) indicates only the brāhmaṇa and the kṣatriya, for this punishment is expressly forbidden in the case of a śūdra reviling a vaiśya.[6] Manu further provides that, if a śūdra mentions the names and castes of the twice-born (*dvijāti*) with contumely, an iron nail, ten fingers long, shall be thrust red-hot into his mouth.[7] If he arrogantly teaches brāhmaṇas their duties, the king shall cause hot oil to be put into his mouth and into his ears.[8] Jayaswal suggests that these provisions are directed against the 'dharma'-preaching learned śūdras, i.e. the Buddhist or Jain śūdras and śūdras who claim equality with the higher classes.[9] Apparently these provisions are laws against the author's political opponents, who flout the established order.[10]

1. Quoted in K. V. Rangaswami Aiyangar, *Rājadharma*, pp. 155-56.
2. *Manu*, VIII. 267.
3. *Ibid.*, VIII. 268.
4. XII. 13.
5. *Manu*, VIII. 270.
6. *Manu*, VIII. 277.
7. *Ibid.*. VIII. 271. The term *dvijāti* is explained by Kull, as 'brāhmaṇas and others', but probably it refers to brāhmaṇas alone.
8. *Manu*, VIII. 272.
9. *Manu and Yājñavalkya*, p. 150.
10. Cf. K. V. Rangaswami Aiyangar, *Aspects of the Pol. and Soc. System of Manu*, p. 132.

It is difficult to say how far these laws were put into effect. Perhaps they may have been the suggestions of a fanatic and were rarely if ever put into practice.[1]

In cases of assault and similar crimes the punishments prescribed for the śūdras are very harsh. It is provided that the very limb with which a man of low caste (*antyajaḥ*) hurts a man of the highest caste (*śreṣṭhaḥ*) shall be cut off.[2] Here Kullūka takes *antyaja* in the sense of śūdra,[3] which agrees with a similar rule of earlier times.[4] The term *śreṣṭha* refers to brāhmaṇas and not to the men of three higher orders, such as is sometimes understood.[5] In a verse Manu states that he who raises his hand or a stick shall have his hand cut off; he who in anger kicks with his feet shall have his foot cut off.[6] Probably this also refers to the offences of the śūdra against the brāhmaṇa. It is further laid down that if a man of the lowest birth (*apakṛṣṭajaḥ*) tries to place himself on the same seat with a person of high caste (*utkṛṣṭaḥ*), he shall be branded on his hip and banished, or the king shall cause his buttock to be gashed.[7] The *apakṛṣṭaja* stands for the śūdra and the *utkṛṣṭa* for the brāhmaṇa.[8] Similarly if out of arrogance the śūdra spits on a brāhmaṇa, the king shall cause both his lips to be cut off; if he urinates on him, the penis; if he breaks wind against him, the anus.[9] Again, if the śūdra lays hold of the hair of a brāhmaṇa, the king should unhesitatingly amputate his hands, likewise if he takes him by the feet, the beard, the neck, or the scrotum.[10] Perhaps to cover all such cases, Manu lays down a general rule that the king shall inflict on a base-born śūdra, who intentionally gives pain to brāhmaṇas, various corporal punishments

1. Basham. *Wonder that was India*, p. 80.
2. *Manu*, VIII. 279.
3. Kull. on Manu, VIII. 279.
4. *Gaut. Dh. S.*, XII. 1; This rule also occurs in the *AŚ*.
5. *SBE*, xxv, 303.
6. *Manu*, VIII. 280.
7. *Ibid.*, VIII. 281.
8. Kull. on *Manu*, VIII. 28. Medhā. and Govindarāja concur with Kull. (*SBE*, xxv, 303).
9. *Manu*, VIII. 282.
10. *Ibid.*, VIII. 283.

which cause terror.[1] Giving pain to the brāhmaṇas is interpreted as causing him physical pain or stealing his property.[2]

Most of the provisions enumerated above are directed against the śūdras offending against the brāhmaṇas. Even the mere existence of these provisions in the law-book shows that relations between the highest and the lowest varṇas were very strained. We have hardly any evidence to determine whether such provisions were carried out. The *Mahāvastu*, however, informs us that sometimes severe bodily tortures were inflicted on the hired labourers in order to make them work. This text states that some people cause these workers to be shackled with fetters and chains, ordering the hands and feet of many to be pierced, and the nose, flesh, sinews, arms and back of many to be slit five or ten times.[3] The *Saddharmapuṇḍarika* refers to a young man of good family bound in wooden manacles.[4] Therefore it is small wonder if śūdra offenders were subjected to corporal punishments, but whether the penal laws of Manu were literally applied to them is open to doubt.

Harsh punishments are, however, not prescribed in the case of people of equal castes assaulting each other. It is laid down that he who breaks the skin of an equal or draws blood from him shall be find 100 paṇas; he who cuts a muscle six niṣkas, and he who breaks a bone shall be banished.[5] According to Rāghavānanda this rule refers to śūdras assaulting śūdras.[6]

For the expiation of the sin of murder Manu prescribes the performance of the lunar penance, which varies in length according to the varṇa of the murdered person. A penance lasting for three years is prescribed in the case of the murder of

1. *Ibid.*, IX. 248.
2. Kull. on *Manu*, IX. 248.
3. *Mahāvastu*, i, 18· Senart has the term *hastinagaḍādibhiḥ*, but Bailey reads it as *hadio*, which also occurs in *Divya.*, pp. 365 and 435 in the sense of fetters (*SBB*, xvi, 15, fn. 2). The term *harahīgorahī*, is used in Maithilī in the sense of wooden shackles.
4. P. 289.
5. *Manu*, VIII. 284.
6. *SBE*, xxv, 304.

a brāhmaṇa and a penance for 2¼ months in the case of the murder of a śūsdra.[1] For killing a śūdra Manu prescribes a wergeld of ten cows and a bull,[2] such as is found in the earlier law-books. But he adds that this fine is to be paid to a brāhmaṇa.[3] Similarly, like the earlier lawgivers, he prescribes the same penance for killing a śūdra as for killing a number of small animals and birds.[4] Such provisions leave no doubt that Manu attaches very little importance to the life of a śūdra. Curiously enough, in one provision of Manu's rules regarding murder there is no trace of varṇa distinctions. If the case involves the death of a member of any varṇa, a falsehood may be spoken and the sin arising therefrom may be expiated by making offering to the Sarasvatī.[5] Manu also declares that slaying women, śūdras, vaiśyas and kṣatriyas is a minor offence, causing loss of caste.[6] But this rule is probably merely meant to emphasise the importance of the life of a brāhmāṇa.

Manu holds that the higher the varṇa, the greater is the crime in committing theft; the guilt of a śūdra is considered the smallest,[7] for the habit of stealing is thought to be more usual with him.

In the law of inheritance Manu upholds the old rule of giving the tenth part of property to the śūdra son of a brāhmaṇa, even when the father has no son by wives of the higher castes.[8] There also recurs the old idea that the śūdra son of a brāhmaṇa, a kṣatriya or a vaiśya is not entitled to any share; whatever is allotted to him by his father becomes his share;[9] a śūdra can be regarded as a kinsman but not an heir.[10] As regards

1. *Manu*, XI. 127, cf. 129-31.
2. *Ibid.*, XI. 128-31.
3. *Ibid.*, XI. 131.
4. *Manu*, XI. 132, 141. This rule shows a discrepancy between the religious and 'secular' punishments of Manu and other lawgivers, for according to secular provisions a wergeld of ten cows and a bull is prescribed for killing a śūdra.
5. *Manu*, VIII. 104-5.
6. *Ibid.*, XI. 67.
7. *Ibid.*, VIII. 337-38.
8. *Ibid.*, IX. 151-154.
9. *Ibid.*, IX. 155.
10. *Ibid.*, IX. 160.

inheritance among the śūdras, even if there be a hundred sons, their shares shall be equal.[1] Thus, only the śūdra sons of the higher caste people were not always certain of receiving shares. Generally, members of the śūdra varṇa enjoyed the right to property. This can be also inferred from another law, according to which property stolen by thieves must be restored by the king to the members of all the varṇas.[2]

Manu's laws of adultery do not discriminate so much against śūdra women as against śūdra men. If a brāhmaṇa approaches unguarded women of the three lower varṇas, he shall be fined 500 paṇas; for a similar crime against an antyaja woman the fine shall be raised to a thousand paṇas.[3] The same fine shall be imposed on a kṣatriya or a vaiśya if he has intercourse with a guarded śūdra woman.[4] If a brāhmaṇa dallies with a vṛṣalī for a night, he removes that sin in three years, by subsisting on alms and by daily muttering sacred texts.[5] While most of these laws are meant to preserve the purity of the brāhmaṇa by preventing moral lapses on his part, they make it clear that Manu also protects the purity of the śūdra woman. This is in keeping with his principle that women of all the four varṇas should be protected.[6]

But the rule of Manu that people should not converse with the wives of others does not apply to some sections of the śūdras such as actors and singers, for they live on the intrigues of their wives.[7] Nevertheless, those who converse with these and women slaves under the charge of a master are required to pay a small fine.[8] Buddhist and Jain nuns are also included in this category,[9] for they were probably recruited from the lower orders, and, like monks, were looked upon as śūdras.[10] Manu

1. *Ibid.*, IX. 157.
2. *Ibid.*, VIII. 40.
3. *Ibid.*, VIII. 385.
4. *Ibid.*, VIII. 383.
5. *Ibid.*, XI. 179.
6. *Manu*, VIII. 359.
7. *Ibid.*, VIII. 361-62.
8. *Ibid.*, VIII. 363.
9. *Ibid.*
10. Jayaswal, *Manu and Yājñavalkya*, pp. 167-68.

prescribes the most severe punishment for a śūdra male adulterer. The śūdra who has intercourse with an unguarded woman of the twice-born caste shall lose the part offending and all his property; in the case of such an offence against a guarded woman he shall lose everything, even his life.[1] Here the term twice-born (*dvijāti*) seems to refer to the brāhmaṇa, for the two following rules provide punishments for kṣatriya and vaiśya offenders against a brāhmaṇa woman.[2] But if these two offend against a guarded brāhmaṇī who is the wife of an eminent brāhmana, they shall be also punished like a śūdra or be burnt in a fire of dry grass.[3] It may be recalled that in this case Kauṭilya provides the punishment of death by burning only for the śūdra offender,[4] although Vasiṣṭha provides similar punishments for kṣatriya and vaiśya offenders as well.[5] A passage of Manu is taken to mean that in such a case the śūdra shall be punished with death.[6] Since the death penalty for the śūdra adulterer is generally corroborated by other sources, the provision of Manu may not have been ineffective.

Manu's laws regarding slavery throw considerable light on the civic status of the śūdras. According to Kauṭilya the śūdra sons of āryan parents cannot be reduced to slavery. But although Manu allows shares in the inheritance of family property to śūdra sons, he does not refer to this practice. He is the first to enunciate the principle that slavery is the eternal destiny of a śūdra. But this applies only to relations between the brāhmaṇas and the śūdras. Manu states that a śūdra, whether bought or unbought, should be reduced to slavery because he is created by God for the service of a brāhmaṇa.[7] In the next verse he adds that a śūdra cannot be released from

1. *Manu*, VIII. 374.
2. *Ibid.*, VIII. 375-76.
3. *Ibid.*, VIII. 377.
4. *AŚ*, IV. 13.
5. *Vas. Dh. S.*, XXI. 2-3.
6. *Manu*, VIII. 359 with the comm. of Kull. The terms used is *abrāhmaṇa*, which is taken in the sense of śūdra by Kull.
7. *śūdrantu kārayeddāsyaṃ krītamakrītameva vā*; *dāsyāyaiva hi sṛṣṭo'sau brāhmaṇasya svayambhuvā. Manu*, VIII. 413.

servitude because servitude is innate in him.[1] As compared to the śūdras, the members of the twice-born castes cannot be reduced to slavery. If a brāhmaṇa compels men of the twice-born castes to work as slaves, he shall be fined 600 (paṇas) by the king.[2] In this connection Kauṭilya provides a graded scheme of fines; the highest fine of 48 paṇas is provided by him for enslaving a brāhmana.[3] Manu does not refer to such distinctions but provides a far heavier fine for enslaving the people of the three upper varṇas.

Even in the law-book of Manu, all the śūdras are not treated as slaves.[4] The legal distinction between a śūdra and a slave is clearly recognised by Manu, who refers to the son of a śūdra by a dāsī or by a woman slave of his slave.[5] Thus, though the slave may have been generally recruited from the śūdra varṇa, sometimes the śūdras themselves owned slaves. But the distinction between the śūdra and his slave was not so wide as that between the twice-born and his slave. According to Manu, if permitted by the father, the son of a śūdra by a woman slave could take a share of the inheritance.[6] But this is not provided in the case of similar sons of the twice-born. Incidentally, the above law of Manu shows that slaves enjoyed the right to property. According to the comment of Kullūka on a passage of Manu, when the master is abroad, for the sake of his family the slave can represent him in business transactions, which the master cannot rescind.[7] At another place, however, this is denied by Manu; sale made by one not the real owner is declared invalid.[8] It has been pointed out earlier that on

1. *na svāminā nisṛṣṭo'pi śūdro dāsyādvimucyate; nisargajaṃ hi tattasya kastasmāttadapohati. Manu*, VIII. 414. This is treated by Medhātithi as a glorified exaggeration (*arthavāda*), but probably it better indicates conditions in the time of the commentator than that of Manu.

2. *Manu*, VIII. 412.

3. *AŚ*, III. 13.

4. This question has been dealt with in detail by G. F. Ilyin, "Śūdras und Sklaven in den altindischen Gesetzbüchern" *Sowjetwissenschaft Gesellschaftswissenschaftliche Abteilung*, 1952, No. 2. pp. 105-108. Cf. Senart, *op. cit.*, 103.

5. *dāsyāṃ vā dāsadāsyāṃ vā yaḥ śūdrasya suto bhavet. Manu*, IX. 179.

6. *Ibid.*

7. Here the term *adhyadhīna* means a dāsa according to Kull. *Manu*, VIII. 167.

8. *Manu*, VIII. 199.

failure of competent witnesses even slaves and servants could give evidence. All this would show that even the slaves had some status in law.

In some sense domestic slaves were treated as members of the family. Manu enjoins the head of the household not to enter into discussions with his parents, sister, daughter-in law, brother, wife, son, daughter and dāsa.[1] Stating the reason for this he points out that wife and son are parts of the body of the householder,[2] that the daughter deserves kindness, and that the class of slaves forms his own shadow. Hence Manu instructs that, even if these people insult the householder, he should calmly put up with them.[3] Does this suggest that the old family solidarity suffered a temporary break-down ? For it sounds curious that this lawgiver should ask the master to pocket the insults given by his slaves.

But the slaves and the hired labourers did not enjoy the same rights as the citizens. This can be inferred from the conditions obtaining in the republican states of the Mālavas and the Kṣudrakas. Commenting on a passage of Pāṇini Patañjali states that the sons of the Kṣudrakas and the Mālavas are respectively known as Kṣaudrakyas and Mālavyas, but this does not apply to the sons of their slaves and labourers.[4]

Manu's provisions regarding the politico-legal position of the śūdras are mostly based on the similar rules of the older authorities. Of his new provisions some were directed against the foreign rulers and followers of heterodox sects who were condemned as śūdras, and others against the śūdras as such. The provisions of the later type mainly relate to śudras offending against brāhmaṇas. But even in this respect Manu's policy of gross discrimination against the śūdras could not make any appreciable headway. He not only retains the old provision of wergeld for the life of a śūdra but also prescribes a fine of 12

1. IV. 180.
2. IV. 184.
3. IV. 185.
4. *idaṃ tarhi kṣaudrakāṇāmapatyam mālavānāmapatyamiti. atrāpi kṣaudrakyaḥ mālavya iti naitatteṣām dāse vā bhavati karmakare vā.* Pat. on *Pā,* IV. 1.168. Cf. *Kāśikā on Pā.,* V. 3.114.

paṇas for the brāhmaṇa abusing a śūdra—a provision which is not to be found in the earlier law-books. It is significant that in the second century A.D. the Sātavāhana ruler Gautamīputra Śātakarṇi (A.D. 106-130) claims to have restored order out of the confusion of the four varṇas by conciliating the brāhmaṇas and the śūdras (*avaras*).[1] This alignment of the varṇas was directed by the brāhmaṇa ruler against the kṣatriyas,[2] who perhaps belonged to the foreign ruling dynasties.

Manu's provisions regarding the social position of the śūdras are largely the re-mastications of the views of the older authorities. But he introduces certain new discriminations against them. He recounts the mythical story of creation which gives the lowest place to the śūdras.[3] He also repeats the old law prescribing different forms of greetings (presumably used by a brāhmaṇa) in relation to the members of the four varṇas.[4] But he adds that a brāhmaṇa who does not know the form of returning salutation must not be saluted by a learned man because he is like a śūdra.[5] We learn from Patañjali that in returning greetings śūdras were addressed differently from non-śūdras. Thus an elevated tone was not to be used in addressing śūdras. The term *bho* (a vocative particle) was to be used in addressing a rājanya or a vaiśya[6] but not a śūdra. Hence varṇa distinctions were reflected even in the formation of grammatical rules. Manu provides that a śūdra can be respected if he has reached the tenth decade of his life[7] But such a rule can have covered only a very limited number of śūdras.

Manu introduces varṇa distinctions even in the ceremony of naming the child, which naturally emphasises the low position of the śūdra. According to him a brāhmaṇa's name

1. *dijāvara kuṭūba vivadhanasa...vinivatita cātuvaṇa saṃkarasa.* Nāsik Cave Inscription of Vāsiṣṭhiputra Puḷumāvi, ll. 5-6 (D. C. Sircar, *Select Inscriptions*, i, 197).

2. *Ibid.*

3. *Manu*, I. 31.

4. *Ibid.*, II. 127.

5. *Ibid.*, II. 126.

6. *bho rājanyaviśāṃ vā.* Pat. on *Pā.*. VIII. 2.82-83.

7. *Manu*, II. 137. Cf. Gautama who declares that a śūdra is worthy of respect on reaching the age of eighty.

should denote something auspicious, a kṣatriya's name power, a vaiśya's name wealth and a śūdra's name something contemptible.[1] As a corollary to this he states that the titles of the members of the four varṇas should respectively imply happiness, protection, prosperity and service.[2] We have no evidence that this practice was widely followed, but Manu's provisions with regard to names show that the members of the lower orders were generally objects of contempt in brāhmaṇical society. Thus the word *vṛṣala* used for the śūdra was a term of abuse and opprobrium. While illustrating a rule of Paṇini regarding the formation of the *samāsas* Patañjali states that "like the female slave" or "like the vṛṣali" are terms of abuse,[3] suggesting thereby that śūdras and slaves were considered despicable elements in society. The vṛṣala was placed in the category of the thief, and both aroused brāhmaṇical hostility.[4] We also learn that the vṛṣala, the dasyu and the thief were treated as contemptible people.[5]

The company of the śūdra was considered contaminating for a brāhmaṇa. Manu states that a brāhmaṇa who lives in the company of the most excellent people and shuns all low people becomes most distinguished; by the opposite conduct he is degraded to the position of śūdra.[6] He reproduces the provision that the snātaka should not travel with the śūdras.[7] Manu recalls the old rule that if the vaiśyas and śūdras come to the house of a brāhmaṇa as guests, out of compassion they should be permitted to take their food along with the servants.[8] Manu provides that the snātaka should not eat the food of a śūdra.[9] In a long list of those whose food should not be taken by the snātaka are

1. *Manu* II. 31.
2. *śarmavadbrāhmaṇasya syādrājño rakṣāsamanvitam; vaiśyasyapuṣṭisaṃyuktaṃ śūdrasya preṣyasaṃyutam. Manu.* II. 32. Kull. comments that these titles should be respectively *śarman*, *varman*, *bhūti* and *dāsa*.
3. Pat. on *Pā*., VI. 2.11.
4. Pat. on *Pā*., II. 2.11 and III. 2.127.
5. Pat. on *Pā*., V. 3.66; cf. Pat. on *Pā*., III. 1.107-8.
6. *Manu*, IV. 245.
7. *Ibid*., IV. 140 He, however, uses the word *vṛṣala* in the place of *śūdra*.
8. *Manu*, III. 112.
9. *Ibid*., IV. 211.

blacksmiths, niṣādas, stage-players, goldsmiths, basket-makers, trainers of hunting dogs, distillers and vendors of spiritous liquors (śauṇḍikas), washermen and dyers.[1] It is further stated that the food of a king impairs the vigour of the snātaka, the food of a śūdra his excellence in sacred learning, the food of a goldsmith his longevity and that of a leather-cutter (*carmāvakartinaḥ*) his fame.[2] Curiously enough, along with the food of the various sections of the śūdra community, the food of the king is also considered detrimental to the welfare of the snātaka. Manu further adds that the food of an artisan destroys the offspring of the snātaka, that of a washerman his physical strength and the food of the tribal groups and harlots excludes him from the higher worlds.[3] If he takes the food of any of these people unintentionally, he must fast for three days; but if he has done so intentionally, he must perform a difficult penance known as the *kṛcchra*.[4] It seems that in all these references the snātaka probably means a Vedic student from the brāhmaṇa varṇa. The result of these restrictions, if enforced, would be to prevent all social contacts between the lower orders and the educated brāhmaṇas. Manu lays down that the learned brāhmaṇa must not take the cooked food of a śūdra who does not perform the rites of *śrāddha*, but on failure of all other means of subsistence he might accept raw grain sufficient to maintain him for one night.[5] But such a rule is not valid in abnormal times. Manu cites several examples of the distinguished sages who took forbidden food in time of distress.[6] Thus hungry Viśvāmitra, who could distinguish between right and wrong, was ready to eat the haunch of a dog, receiving it from the hands of a caṇḍāla.[7] Generally the food of the śūdras was accepted in normal times. Manu lays down that, among śūdras, one may eat the food of his share-cropper, a friend of his family, his cow-herd, his slave and his

1. *Ibid.*, IV. 215-16.
2. *Ibid.*. IV. 218.
3. *kārukānnaṃ prajāṃ hanti balaṃ nirṇejakasya ca; gaṇānnaṃ gaṇikānnaṃ ca lokebhyaḥ parikṛntati. Manu*, IV. 219.
4. *Manu*, IV, 222.
5. *Ibid* , IV. 223.
6. *Manu*, X. 106-8.
7. *Manu*, X. 108.

barber.[1] Patañjali informs us that the plates of carpenters, washermen, and blacksmiths could be used after proper cleaning.[2] This would suggest that in matters of food there were relations of give and take between the members of the higher varṇas and these sections of the śūdra community. To eat the leavings of the śūdras was considered a great sin. It is stated that he who has eaten the leavings of women and śūdras should remove the impurity by drinking barley gruel for seven days and nights.[3] Perhaps this rule applies to the brāhmaṇa. Similarly a brāhmaṇa who drinks water left by a śūdra should expiate his sin by drinking water in which kuśa grass has been boiled for three days.[4] Manu's provisions throw some light on the dietary habits of the śūdras. The twice-born should perform the *cāndrāyaṇa* penance if he eats dried meat, mushrooms growing on the earth and meat about the origin of which he has no knowledge, or which had been kept in a slaughter-house.[5] Similarly if the twice-born takes the meat of carnivorous animals, boars, camels, cocks, crows, human beings and asses, he should perform a very difficult penance known as the *taptakṛcchra*.[6] If in these references the dvija is taken as a member of the first three varṇas, it would imply that śūdras were free to take all varieties of meat. Commenting on a passage of Manu Kullūka states that, by eating garlic and other kinds of forbidden roots, the śūdra cannot commit an offence leading to loss of caste.[7] This would suggest that garlic, onion and various kinds of meat were regarded as the legitimate food of the members of the lower orders.

1. The possessive pronoun does not occur in the text, but Kull. interprets the passage to apply only to a man's own servants. This seems to be more in the spirit of Manu than if it were taken as referring to all slaves, sharecroppers etc. *Manu*, IV, 353. The term *ārdhikaḥ* has been wrongly translated as "labourer in tillage" in *SBE*, xxv, 168. The cow-herd is used in the sense of an *ābhīra* in the *Mahābhāṣya* of Patañjali.
2. Pat. on *Pā.*, II. 4.10.
3. *Manu*, XI. 153.
4. *Ibid.*, XI. 149 with the comm. of Kull.
5. *Ibid* , XI. 156.
6. *Ibid.*, X. 157.
7. *Manu*, X. 126. Rāghavānanda also includes the act of keeping a slaughter-house with this.

It seems that the vaiśyas and śūdras followed forms of marriage which were different from those of the higher varṇas. Manu quotes the opinions of authorities, according to whom the first four forms of marriage, i.e. the *brahma*, the *daiva*, the *ārṣa*, and the *prājāpatya* are prescribed for the brāhmaṇa, the *rākṣasa* for the kṣatriya and the *āsura* for the vaiśya and the śūdra.[1] He adds that the brāhmaṇa can also follow the *āsura* and the *gāndharva*, the kṣatriya can also practise the *āsura*, *gāndharva* and the *paiśāca* and so also the vaiśya and the śūdra.[2] Thus the kṣatriyas are distinguished from the vaiśyas and śūdras only by the provision that they can practise the *rākṣasa* form of marriage. But perhaps in this case the main object of Manu is to demarcate the brāhmaṇas from the three other varṇas. In regard to the two lower varṇas, the real position is reflected in the statement quoted by Manu and also occurring in the *Ādi Parvan*[3] that the *āsura* (marriage by purchase) of the bride usually prevails among the vaiśyas and śūdras. Manu ordains that the *āsura* and *paiśāca* forms of marriage must not be practised.[4] Kullūka comments that this rule applies to the brāhmaṇas and the kṣatriyas,[5] which suggests that these two forms of marriage were especially meant for the two lower varṇas.

Manu's rules regarding the *strīdhana* differ according to the forms of marriage. It is said that, if the wife dies without leaving any issue in the *āsura*, *rākṣasa* and *paiśāca* forms of marriage, the *strīdhana* belongs to her mother and father, i.e. to her parents' family and not to her husband, as is the case in the first four and the *gāndharva* forms of marriage.[6] This would show that matrilineal elements had some importance in the forms of marriage practised by the vaiśyas and śūdras.

Manu declares that *niyoga* (levirate) cannot take place in marriages that are performed according to the Vedic mantra.[7]

1. *Manu*, III. 24.
2. *Ibid.*, III. 23.
3. Ch. 67. 11.
4. *Manu*, III. 25.
5. Kull. also says that the *rākṣasa* form of marriage is prescribed for the vaiśyas and śūdras. Comm. to *Manu*, III. 25.
6. *Manu*, IX. 196-97 with the comm. of Kull.
7. *Ibid*, IX. 65.

Since these mantras are not permitted in the marriages of the śūdras,[1] it is clear that *niyoga* was confined mainly to the śūdras. This can be inferred from a further statement of Manu, who asserts that widow remarriage and levirate are regarded as beastly practices by the twice-born people learned in the śāstras.[2] Jolly thinks that Manu's views on the questions of *niyoga* and widow remarriage are contradictory,[3] for he approves of them in some passages and condemns them in others. But these passages can be easily reconciled if we bear in mind that Manu's approval of *niyoga* and widow remarriage is meant for the śūdras and his condemnation of these is meant for the members of the three upper varṇas. The prevalence of the above mentioned practices among the śūdras would show that women were not so dependent in their community.

As regards the inter-varṇa marriage, Manu quotes the old dictum, which permits the members of a higher varṇa to marry the woman of a lower varṇa.[4] But he adds that, if twice-born men wed women of their own and of the other lower varṇas, the seniority, status and habitation of these wives must be settled according to the order of the varṇas.[5]

Manu, however, detests the idea that a śūdra woman should be the first wife of either a brāhmaṇa or a kṣatriya. According to him there is no precedent for this in any ancient story.[6] Probably the śūdra wives of the people of the higher varṇas had a very low status. Patañjali informs us that the *dāsi* and the *vṛṣali* were meant for satisfying the pleasures of the people of higher classes.[7] Manu declares that the twice-born men who wed śūdra wives soon degrade their families and children to the status of a śūdra.[8] According to Kullūka this rule applies to all the three upper varṇas.[9] In support of his statement Manu quotes the

1. *Vas. Dh. S.*, I. 25.
2. *ayaṃ dvijairhi vidvadbhiḥ paśudharmo vigarhitaḥ. Manu*, IX. 66.
3. Jolly, *Hindu Law and Custom*, p. 155.
4. *Manu*, III. 13.
5. *Ibid.*, IX. 85.
6. *Ibid.*, III. 14.
7. Pat. on *Pā.*, II. 3. 69 and I. 2. 43.
8. *Manu.* III. 15.
9. Comm. to *Manu.* III. 15.

views of several authorities. According to Atri, if a brāhmaṇa marries a śūdra woman, he becomes an outcaste; according to Śaunaka a kṣatriya is reduced to this position on the birth of a son; and according to Bhṛgu a vaiśya becomes an outcaste if he has male offspring by a śūdra wife alone.[1] But Manu very strongly disapproves of the idea of a brāhmaṇa having intercourse with a śūdra woman. Such a person, in his opinion, will sink into hell after his death. If he begets a child by her, he will lose the rank of a brāhmaṇa[2] and, in absence of issue other than śūdras, his family will quickly perish.[3] For the śūdra son of a brāhmaṇa, though alive, is a corpse, and hence he is called a pāraśava.[4] There can be no expiation for the man who drinks the moisture of a śūdra's (*vṛṣali*) lips, is tainted by her breath, and begets a son on her.[5] The context shows that this prohibition was meant for the brāhmaṇas only.[6]

Manu mentions the old mixed castes such as the niṣāda,[7] the pāraśava, the ugra, the āyogava, the kṣattṛ, the caṇḍāla, the pukkasa,[8] the kukkuṭaka, the śvapāka and the veṇa,[9] who are said to have originated from the intermixture of the varṇas. He ascribes a similar origin to a long list of new castes. Since his list counts as many as 61 castes, their consolidation in Chapter X seems to have been the work of about the fifth century A.D.[10] However they are enumerated here for the sake of clarity. A brāhmaṇa begets on the daughter of an ugra an āvṛta, on the daughter of an ambaṣṭha an ābhīra, and on the woman of the

1. *Manu*, III. 16. with the comm. of Kull.
2. *Ibid.*, III. 17.
3. *Ibid.*, III. 64.
4. *Ibid.*, IX. 178.
5. *Ibid.*, III. 19.
6. *Ibid.*, III. 17-19.
7. Even during this period we hear of the country of the Niṣādas (Pat. on *Pā.*, IV. 2. 104; Junāgarh Rock Inscr. of Rudradāman I, l. 11 (Sircar, *Select Inscrs.*, i, 172).
8. *Manu*, (XII. 55) states that a slayer of a brāhmaṇa shall enter the womb of a caṇḍāla or a pukkasa.
9. *Manu*, X, 8-9, 12, 16, 18, 19. By now some of the old castes had become hereditary, for we hear of the sons of the niṣādas and caṇḍālas (Pat. on *Pā.*, IV. 1.97.)
10. See Appendix I.

āyogava caste a dhigvaṇa.[1] Further, on an āyogava woman the dasyu begets a sairandhra, the vaidehaka a maitreyaka, the niṣāda a mārgava or a dāśa who is also known as a kaivarta.[2] On a vaidehaka woman the caṇḍāla begets a pāṇḍusopāka and the niṣāda an āhiṇḍaka.[3] On a woman of the vaidehaka caste the niṣāda also begets kārāvara; and a vaidehaka begets an andhra on a kārāvara woman and a meda on a niṣāda woman.[4] A niṣāda woman bears to a caṇḍāla a son called the antyāvasāyin, who is despised even by those who are excluded from the fourfold varṇa system (*bāhyas*).[5] Manu further states that the sūta, the vaidehaka, the caṇḍāla, the māgadha, the kṣattṛ and the āyogava beget on women of similar castes issues who are more despicable, more sinful than their fathers, and are excluded from varṇa society.[6] He adds that *bāhyas* and *hīnas* (low people) produce fifteen kinds of low castes[7] on woman of higher castes. Although Manu does not enumerate these castes by name, they seem to have been covered by the list that has been given above.

The above-mentioned castes were to be distinguished by their occupations.[8] The caṇḍālas, śvapākas and antyāvasāyins were engaged for executing criminals, and were given their clothes, beds and ornaments.[9] The niṣādas lived by fishing, and the medas, andhras, madgus and cuñcus were employed in hunting wild animals.[10] Kṣattṛs, ugras and pukkasas are described as engaged in the catching and killing of animals living in holes.[11] Apparently all of these were backward aboriginal tribes, who retained their occupations even when they were absorbed

1. *Manu*, X ' .
2. *Ibid*., X. 33-34.
3. *Ibid*., X. 37.
4. *Ibid*., X. 36.
5. *Ibid*., X. 32.
6. *Ibid*., X. 26-29.
7. *pratikūlaṃ vartamānā bāhyā bāhyatarānpunaḥ; hīnā hīnānprasūyante varṇānpañcadaśaiva ca*. *Manu*., X. 31. In his comm. Kull. tries to show that the total of such castes was thirty. This may have been a later development.
8. *Manu*. X. 40.
9. *Ibid*., X. 56; cf. *Mahāvastu*, ii, 73.
10. *Manu*, X. 48.
11. *Ibid*., X. 49.

in brāhmaṇical society. Manu informs us that some of the mixed castes pursued important crafts. The āyogava practised wood work;[1] and the dhigvaṇa and the kārāvara worked in leather,[2] and the pāṇḍusopāka dealt in canes.[3] The mārgava or the dāśa subsisted by working as a boatman and was known as the kaivarta by the inhabitants of Āryāvarta.[4] The veṇas played on drums,[5] and the sairandhra was considered skilled in adorning and attending on his master. The latter, though not a slave, lived like a slave or subsisted by snaring animals.[6] The maitreyaka is described as a sweet-tuned fellow, who rang a bell at the appearance of dawn and was constantly engaged in praising great men.[7]

Some low castes of the above type are also mentioned in a Buddhist source. It is stated that the followers of the Buddha or the Bodhisatta shall have nothing to do with the caṇḍālas, kaukkuṭikas (poulterers), saṃkarikas (pork butchers), śauṇḍikas (sellers and vendors of spirituous liquors),[8] maṃsakas (butchers), mauṣṭikas (boxers), naṭa-nartakas (actors and dancers), jhallas and mallas (wrestlers).[9] These people were despised by the Buddhists on account of their association with cruel and unpuritanical activities.

Most of the mixed castes enumerated by Manu were untouchable. After stating the functions of the niṣādas, āyogavas, medas, andhras, cuñcus, madgus, kṣattṛs, pukkasas, dhigvaṇas and veṇas Manu ordains that they should live outside villages near famous trees and burial grounds on mountains and in groves.[10]

1. *Ibid.*, X. 48.
2. *Manu,* X. 36, 49. Incidentally this shows that leather work had become an important craft, for three categories of workers, namely the carmakāra, the dhigvaṇa and the kārāvara, were engaged in it.
3. *Ibid.*, X. 37.
4. *Ibid.*, X. 34.
5. *Ibid.*, X. 49.
6. *Ibid.*, X. 32.
7. *Ibid.*, X. 33.
8. Tr. of this term as mutton butchers does not seem to be accurate. *SBE*, xxi, 438.
9. The list also includes the Ājīvikas, Nirgranthas and Lokāyatikas. *Saddharmapuṇḍarīka*, pp. 180-81, 311-12; cf. Bose, *op. cit.*, ii, 463-64. A cow butcher and his apprentice is mentioned in the *Mahāvastu*, ii, 125.
10. *Manu*, X. 49-50.

This shows that these tribal people lived outside brāhmaṇic settlements. Certainly the caṇḍālas and śvapacas lived outside. Food vessels used by them were discarded for ever. Their sole property consisted of dogs and donkeys; they took their food in broken dishes, used ornaments of iron and clothes of dead people, and wandered from place to place.[1] They were not permitted to appear in towns and villages at night, where they could work only during the day.[2] Manu provides that the caṇḍālas and śvapacas should be distinguished by marks at the king's command.[3] Rāghavānanda's explanation that the caṇḍālas should be branded on the forehead and other parts of the body is not corroborated by any contemporary evidence. Possibly the caṇḍāla and śvapacas were required to put on some kind of uniforms to distinguish them from the rest of the people.[4] They could not enter into any transactions with others regarding marriage, debt, loan etc., which could take place only with the members of their own castes. Manu ordains that members of the higher varṇas should not give them even grain with their own hands.[5]

But in particular Manu wants to avoid all contact between the brāhmaṇas and the untouchables. He lays down that a snātaka (generally a brāhmaṇa) should not stay with the caṇḍālas, pukkasas, antyas and antyāvasāyins.[6] Among those who should not look at the brāhmaṇa at the śrāddha ceremony are the caṇḍālas, village pigs, cocks, dogs etc.[7] Manu further declares that, if a brāhmaṇa either has intercourse with caṇḍāla or antya women or takes their food, he shall fall from his

1. *Manu*, X. 49-50. *Bālacarita*, II. 5; *Avimāraka*. VI. 5-6. Pusalker, *Bhāsa—A Study*, pp. 358 and 391.
2. *Manu*, X. 54-55.
3. ...*cihnitā rājaśāsanaiḥ*. *Manu*, X. 55.
4. Medhātithi takes these marks in the sense of "axes, adzes and so forth used for executing criminals and carried on the shoulder". Govindarāja explains them as 'sticks and so forth,' and Sarvajñanārāyaṇa as 'iron ornaments, peacock feathers and the like', *SBE*. xxv, 415, fn. 55). Cf. Bose, *op. cit.*, ii, p. 437.
5. Kull. says that this should be done through servants. *Manu*, X. 53-54.
6. *Manu*, IV. 79.
7. *Ibid.*, III. 239.

brāhmaṇahood. But if he does these things intentionally, he shall be reduced to their status.[1] This would imply that such connections of non-brāhmaṇas with the caṇḍālas were not strongly disapproved.

Whether the untouchables and the mixed castes were regarded as śūdras by Manu is not clear. Manu categorically states that there are only four varṇas,[2] which may imply that the mixed castes were included in the śūdra varṇa. The myths of their origin show that they were supposed to have śūdra blood in their veins. At one place in Manu the antyaja is explained as a śūdra by Kullūka.[3] But the term antyaja is also used by Manu in the sense of a caṇḍāla.[4] The mixed castes such as the sūta, the vaidehaka, the caṇḍāla, the māgadha, the kṣattṛ and the āyogava are known as *bāhyas*, who are regarded by the commentators as people outside the fourfold varṇa system.[5] Manu distinguishes an antyaja from a śūdra in connection with his penalties for the crime of adultery,[6] and an antyāvasāyin from a śūdra in his law of evidence. But Patañjali defines *niravasita* śūdras as caṇḍālas and mṛtapas, whose food vessels could not be used by the people of the higher varṇas;[7] this suggests that these untouchables were considered śūdras. Manu also uses the term *apapātra* (i.e. those whose vessels could not be used) for such śūdras.[8] Thus it seems that the mixed castes and the untouchables were being absorbed as inferior śūdras, who were distinguished from the ordinary śūdras by their separate habitations, backward culture and primitive religious beliefs.

Manu's provisions regarding the boycott of the food, company

1. *Ibid.*, II. 276.
2. X. 4.
3. *Manu*, VIII. 279.
4. *Ibid.*, IV. 6. According to later sources the term *antyaja* indicates rajakas, carmakāras, naṭas, burudas, kaivartas, bhillas and medas. Parāśara and Atri quoted in K. V. Rangaswami Aiyangar, *Some Aspects of the Hindu View of Life according to the Dharmaśāstra*, pp. 115-16.
5. *Manu*, X. 29-31 with the comm. of Medhā. Govindarāja and Kull.
6. *Manu*, VIII. 385.
7. *yairbhukte pātraṃ saṃskāreṇāpi na śudhyati te niravasitāḥ.* Pat. on *Pā.*, II. 4.10.
8. *Manu*, X. 51.

and women of śūdras apply mainly to the brāhmaṇas.[1] We observe a similar social distance between the brāhmaṇa and the vṛṣala in the *Mahābhāṣya* of Patañjali. Thus while the brāhmaṇa has white teeth, the vṛṣala has black;[2] the brāhmaṇa gets a high seat but the vṛṣala a low seat.[3] A person can indulge in illicit and disreputable dealings towards the vṛṣalī and dāsī, but he should behave with due respect towards a brāhmanī.[4]

It is argued by Bhandarkar that the vṛṣalas formed a community consisting of people from all the four varṇas after the pattern of the āryan community.[5] But generally the vṛṣala was identical with the śūdra. Thus while the Dharmasūtras enjoin the snātaka not to travel with śūdras, Manu instructs him not to travel with vṛṣalas.[6] His denunciation of connections between a brāhmaṇa and a vṛṣalī occurs in the context in which he bans all connections between a brāhmaṇa and a śūdra.[7] Although nowhere in the *Mahābhāṣya* the term vṛṣala distinctly refers to a śūdra,[8] the similar status of the vṛṣalī and dāsī[9] and the proverbial poverty of the vṛsala[10] show that the vṛṣala was no better than a śūdra. Like the term śūdra, the term vṛṣala was also used indiscriminately to cover barbarians and heretics. But commonly vṛṣala signified a member of the fourth varṇa, and hence the contrast between the brāhmaṇa and the vṛṣala in the *Māhābhāṣya* should be taken in the sense of that between the brāhmaṇa and the śudra.

Manu reproduces the old injunction confining Vedic studies to the twice-born.[11] In contrast to them the śūdras are called *ekajāti*, i.e. having one birth.[12] The first birth of the āryan is

1. The terms brāhmaṇa and śūdra are used to cover the whole population in the *Mahāvastu*, i, 188.
2. Pat. on *Pā.*, II. 2.8,11.
3. Pat. on *Pā.*, II. ? 11.
4. Pat. on *Pā.*, I. 3.55.
5. *Some Aspects of Ancient Indian Culture*, pp. 51 and 54.
6. IV. 140.
7. *Manu*, III. 19.
8. S. K. Bose, *IC*, ii. 596-97.
9. Pat. on *Pā.*, II. 3.69 and I. 2.48.
10. Pat. on *Pā.*, I.2.47 and VI. 3.61.
11. II. 165.
12. *Manu*. X. 4.

from his natural mother, but the second birth takes place on the tying of the girdle of muñja grass.[1] Therefore a twice-born man who, not having studied the Veda, applies himself to other occupations is reduced to the condition of a śūdra, and his descendants also meet the same fate.[2] The presence of the śūdra is to be scrupulously avoided while the study of the Veda goes on.[3]

Notwithstanding these provisions, we hear of some teachers instructing śūdras. Manu provides that he who instructs śūdra pupils or learns from a śūdra teacher should not be invited at the *śrāddha*.[4] It is not clear whether the śūdra teacher or pupils refer to heretics. In a list of ten kinds of people who may receive education from the teacher occurs the name of the *śuśrūṣu*, who is taken by Kullūka as a servant (paricāraka),[5] and perhaps may refer to a śūdra.

But generally the śūdra seems to have been deprived of education. Like Vasiṣṭha, Manu ordains that nobody should give advice to a śūdra or should explain the law to him.[6] He strengthens this provision by enacting that a person who acts to the contrary shall sink into the Asamvṛta hell together with the person whom he instructs.[7]

In the religious sphere the śūdra continued to be deprived of the right to Vedic sacrifice.[8] It is said that the śūdra cannot suffer loss of caste; he is not worthy to receive the sacraments and has no right to follow the dharma of the āryans.[9] A twice-born should not associate his śūdra wife with the performance of rites.[10] If he does this foolishly, he should be regarded

1. *Ibid.*, II. 169-70.
2. *Manu*, II. 163. Cf. II. 172, X. 110. It is suggested that the *upanayana* of girls and śūdras was done without a formal ceremony (Rangaswami Aiyangar, *Social and Political Aspects of the System of Manu*, p. 145), but there seems to be no evidence for this.
3. *Manu*, IV. 99 and 108.
4. III. 156.
5. *Manu*, II. 109.
6. *Ibid.*, IV. 80.
7. *Ibid.*, V. 81.
8. Pat. on *Pā.*, IV. 1.93.
9. *Manu*, X. 126.
10. *Ibid.*, IX. 86.

despicable as a caṇḍāla.[1] Perhaps this rule refers to the brāhmaṇas. It is also laid down that a brāhmaṇa should not beg from a śūdra anything required for the sacrifice; if he does so, he will be born as a caṇḍāla after death.[2]

But there was a class of priests who ministered to the religious needs of the śūdras. Manu states that those who officiate as priests for a śūdra by obtaining wealth from him and offering an *agnihotra* are censored by the *brahmavādins* (reciters of the Veda) as śūdra *ṛtvijas* (priests), and considered ignorant.[3] Commenting on a passage of Manu Kullūka states that the śūdras can perform minor domestic sacrifices (*pākayajñas*).[4] We learn from Bhāsa that śudras worshipped the deities without mantras.[5] Manu avers that the virtuous śūdras obtain praise if they emulate the habits of the good, but they should do so without reciting the Vedic texts.[6] He further provides that the śūdras can offer water to their ancestors, like the members of the three upper varṇas. In this connection he states that the Sukālins are the manes of the śūdras and Vasiṣṭha their progenitor.[7] All this would suggest that Manu invests the śūdras with some religious rights which they did not enjoy in the Mauryan or the pre-Mauryan period.

The emergence of Vaiṣṇavism as an important sect during this period offered the śūdras an option, and they could get rid of some religious disabilities imposed on them by the brāhmaṇical system. The cult of Viṣṇu promised salvation to vaiśyas, śūdras and women. The Greek and Kuṣāṇa princes who had turned Vaiṣṇava may have adopted a more liberal religious policy towards the śūdras. This is possibly the reason why the princes of foreign connections ruling in India are dubbed śūdras in the epics and Puraṇas.

Manu lays down the same moral code for the members of all the four varṇas. They should practise non-injury, truth,

1. *Ibid.*, IX. 87.
2. *Ibid.*, XI. 24.
3. *Ibid.*, XI. 42-43.
4. *Ibid.*, X. 126.
5. *Pratimā.*, III. 5.
6. *Manu*, X. 127.
7. *Ibid.*, III. 196-98. Vasiṣṭha appears as a lawgiver in *Manu*, VIII. 140 and as one of the ten Prajāpatis in *Manu*, I. 35.

non-stealing, purity, sublimation of passions, and freedom from spite, and should beget children on their wives only.[1] But from the religious point of view he considers women and śūdras as the most impure sections of society. They are to be avoided by a sacrificer engaged in the *cāndrāyaṇa* vow.[2] He prescribes less rigorous rites of purification for them.[3] A śūdra should keep himself pure by shaving once a month and, like the vaiśyas, should observe rites of purification in cases of death and birth.[4] But he endorses the view of the old lawgivers that a vaiśya's period of impurity lasts for 15 days and that of a śūdra for a month.[5] He adds that at the end of the period of impurity a brāhmaṇa can become pure by touching water, a kṣatriya by touching the animal on which he rides and his weapons, a vaiśya by touching his goad or the nose-string of his oxen and a śūdra by touching his staff.[6] Manu also provides that a dead brāhmaṇa should not be carried by a śūdra, because if he defiles the burnt offering by his touch the deceased does not reach heaven.[7] Thus he maintains the distinction between a śūdra and a brāhmaṇa even after the latter's death.

If the descriptions of the Kali age in the Purāṇas are taken even as a faint indication of the conditions prevailing during the pre-Gupta period,[8] it would appear that the śūdras openly defied the existing social system. The excesses committed by the śūdras are described in the *Kūrma Purāṇa*: "The foolish śūdra officials of the king force the brāhmaṇas to give up their seats and beat them. The king dishonours the brāhmaṇas in the Kali on account of the changing times, and the śūdras occupy high seats among the brāhmaṇas. The brāhmaṇas, who are less educated in the Vedas and are less fortunate and

1. *Manu*, X. 63.
2. *Ibid.*, XI. 224.
3. *Ibid.*, V. 139. Patañjali places dāsa and bhāryā in the same category (Pat. on *Pā.*, II. 1.1).
4. *Manu*, V. 140.
5. *Ibid.*, V. 83.
6. *Ibid.*, V. 99.
7. *Ibid.*, V. 104.
8. Hazra, *Studies in the Purāṇic Records on Hindu Rites and Customs*, pp. 208-10.

powerful, honour the śūdras with flowers, decorations and other auspicious things. Though thus honoured, the śūdras do not cast even a glance at the brāhmaṇas. The brāhmaṇas dare not enter the houses of the śūdras but stand at the gate for an opportunity to pay respect to them. The brāhmaṇas, who depend upon the śūdras for their livelihood, surround them, when they are seated in vehicles, in order to praise them and teach them the vedas".[1] A somewhat similar picture is presented in the *Matsya Purāṇa*, which prophesises that the dharma of the Śrutis and Smṛtis will become very lax and the varṇāśrama dharma will be destroyed. It deplores that the people will be of mixed origin, the śūdras will sit with the brāhmaṇas, eat and perform sacrifices with them, and pronounce mantras with them.[2] The *Vāyu Purāṇa* and the *Brahmāṇḍa Purāṇa* state that in the Kali age the śūdras act as brāhmaṇas and *vice versa*. They inform us that the śūdras are respected by everybody, and that, unprotected by the kings, the brāhmaṇas depend for their livelihood upon the śūdras.[3]

Probably the above statements refer to conditions in the early Christian centuries. They do not seem to apply to the times of Aśoka, who, with all his zeal for Buddhism, cannot be charged with such gross intolerance towards the brāhmaṇas, as is represented in the Purāṇic statements. Although the insertion of the description of the Kali age in the *Kūrma Purāṇa* is ascribed to the period A.D. 700-800,[4] it looks back to post-Mauryan times. Some of the passages in this description are exactly the same as can be found in the earlier texts of the *Vāyu* and the *Brahmāṇḍa*.[5] In an inscription of the first half of the fifth century A.D. the Pallava ruler Siṃhavarman is described as ever ready to save the dharma from the sins of the Kali age.[6] This may suggest

1. *Kūrma P.*, Ch. 30, pp. 304-05.
2. *Matsya P.*, Ch. 272. 46-47. ff.
3. *Vāyu P.*, Ch. 58 38-49. *Brahmāṇḍa P.*, Pt. ii, Ch. 31. 39-49.
4. Hazra, *op. cit.*, p. 178.
5. Portions dealing with the Kali age in these Purāṇas are ascribed to A.D. 200-275 by Hazra (*op. cit.*, pp. 174-75).
6. *kaliyugadoṣāvasanna-dharma uddharaṇa-nitya sannaddhasya. EI.* viii. Inscr. No. 15, I. 10.

that the conception of the Kali age was not very old.[1] As pointed out earlier, the mention of the mlecchas and of the intermingling of various peoples in the description of the Kali age better suits conditions obtaining in the post-Mauryan period. The Purāṇic statements that the foreign rulers will kill the brāhmaṇas and seize the wives and wealth of others is generally applied to this period,[2] and is in consonance with the spirit of similar allegations in the *Yuga Purāṇa*.[3]

The descriptions of the Kali age, which are in the form of complaints and prophetic assertions made by the brāhmaṇas,[4] cannot be brushed aside as figments of imagination. They depict the pitiable plight of the brāhmaṇas on account of the activities of the Greeks, Śakas and Kuṣāṇas. It is likely that their invasions caused an upheaval among the śūdras, who were seething with discontent. Naturally they turned against the brāhmaṇas, who were the authors of discriminatory provisions against them. How long and in which part of the country this social convulsion prevailed is difficult to determine for lack of data. But it seems that the intense hostility of the brāhmaṇas towards the heretical 'śūdra' kings was on account of the latters' fraternization with the śūdras. The servile position of the śūdras as slaves and hired labourers may have been undermined by the policy of the foreign rulers such as the Śakas and Kuṣāṇas, who were not committed to the ideology of varṇa-divided society.

The condition of society during the post-Mauryan period was perhaps similar to that which followed the collapse of the Old Kingdom in Egypt, when for some time the masses fought against the priests and nobles, and played havoc with the established

1. Pargiter thinks that the Kali age begins from the time of the Bhārata battle, but the description of the sins of the Kali age at the end of an age (yugānte) seems to refer to the period of chaos between the fall of the Mauryan and the rise of the Gupta empires.

2. Jayaswal, *Hist. of Ind.* (A.D. 150-350), pp. 151-52.

3. *Ibid.*, p. 46. *Yuga Purāṇa*, 95 ff. Tarn doubts whether the picture in the *Yuga P.* applies to the results of the Greek conquest. *The Greeks in Bactria and India*, p. 456.

4. A similar literary style was adopted by the Hebrew prophets in describing the fall of Assyria.

order. Therefore Manu's provisions were meant to combat the forces of disintegration, which followed the break-up of the Mauryan empire, rather than to undo the measures of Aśoka. His strong emphasis on the servile nature of the śūdra was obviously necessitated by the latter's refusal to work. He enjoins the king to compel the vaiśyas and śūdras to work,[1] which shows that the masses did not feel sharing any common interest with the members of the two higher varṇas. Manu ordains that the king should maintain the varṇa-dharma, for the state which is sullied by the intermixture of varṇas perishes together with its inhabitants,[2] i.e. the established order is destroyed. Such measures are broadly analogous to the decrees issued by the Roman empire in the third century A.D., commanding people of various callings to stick to their trades. But Manu also applies some spiritual sanctions. If the śūdra fails in his duty, he is born as a cailāśaka (a kind of goblin feeding on moths);[3] but if he performs it loyally, he gets a higher birth next time.[4]

Manu provides a number of safeguards against the hostile activities of the śūdras. In contrast to Kauṭilya, he lays down that the king should settle in a country chiefly peopled by the āryans,[5] for the kingdom having majority of śūdras (*śūdra-bhūyiṣṭha*) soon perishes.[6] Manu confines the protection of the state only to the people who live like āryans.[7] He further states that those non-āryans (i.e. śūdras) who wear marks of āryans should be treated as thorns and removed without delay.[8] In particular the mixed castes (mostly śūdras) were considered non-āryans who were cruel and violent.[9] All these statements of Manu betray his

1. *Manu*, VIII. 418.
2. *Ibid.*. X. 61.
3. *Manu*, XII. 72.
4. *Ibid.*, IX. 337.
5. *Manu*, VII. 69. It is said that the country should be *anāvilam*, which is explained by commentators (Nār. and Nand.) as 'free from defilement such as a mixture of the castes'. (*SBE*, xxv, 227).
6. The commentators' interpretations that this refers to the predominance of śūdra judges or administrative officers seem to be gratuitous.
7. *Manu*, IX. 253.
8. *Ibid.*, IX. 260.
9. *Ibid.*, X. 57-58.

complete distrust of the śūdras and his consequent anxiety to guard against their hostile activities, which were either apprehended or actually took place in times of foreign invasion. Manu probably has such situations in mind when he ordains that, if the members of the three upper varṇas are hindered in the performance of their duties on account of the outbreak of revolution, they should take up arms.[1] In the context of the description of conditions at the end of the Kali age the *Vāyu Purāṇa* refers to the exploits of Pramiti (an incarnation of god Mādhava), who raised an army of armed brāhmaṇas and set out to annihilate the various peoples such as the mlecchas and the vṛṣalas.[2] This may be taken as a faint echo of violent struggle between the brāhmaṇas on the one hand, and the śūdras and foreign rulers on the other. This was natural, for the vṛṣalas were regarded as the breakers of the established order[3] and not its preservers. Manu's elaborate provisions for punishing śūdras offending against brāhmaṇas are attributed to his hostility chiefly against the learned śūdra.[4] But his measures as a whole show that he was not less hostile to the śūdra masses.

The descriptions of the Kali age in the Purāṇas and the violent anti-śūdra measures of Manu point to a prolonged social crisis, which seems to have been caused by the oppression of the rulers. The Purāṇas repeatedly state that oppressed with taxes, famine, drought, etc., the people will perish.[5] It is further stated that they would suffer from hunger, thirst and diseases.[6] The *Āraṇyaka Parva* states that out of the fear of the burden of taxes peasants would earn their livelihood by thieving on a

1. *śastraṃ dvijātibhirgrāhyaṃ dharmo yatroparudhyate : dvijātināṃ ca varṇānāṃ viplave kālakārite. Manu,* VIII. 348. This provision is also found in *Vas. Dh. S.*, but not in such clear terms (III. 24.25).

2. Quoted in Patil, *Cultural History from the Vāyu Purāṇa* pp. 74-75. The author thinks that this description applies to the early centuries of the Christian era preceding the Gupta age (p. 128).

3. *vṛṣo hi bhagavān dharmastasya yaḥ kurute hyalam, vṛṣalaṃ taṃ vidurdevāstasmaddharmaṃ na lopayet. Manu,* VIII. 16. This provision is also repeated in the *Śanti P.*, but is not to be found in earlier brāhmaṇical texts.

4. Jayaswal, *Manu and Yājñavalkya*, pp. 91-92.

5. *anāvṛṣṭyā vinaṃkṣayanti durbhikṣakarapīḍitāḥ...prajāḥ. Bhag. P.*, XII.2.10.

6. *Ibid.*, XII. 2.11.

large scale, by donning the garb of *munis*, and by taking to trade.[1] Referring to the Kali era the Purāṇas add that the people would seize the crops and clothes belonging to others.[2] The *Viṣṇu Purāṇa* states that suffering intensely on account of oppressions caused by taxes and famine the unhappy peasants would flee to those regions which produce rich crops of wheat and barley.[3]

There is no doubt that besides natural calamities oppressive taxation played a significant part in creating such a situation. The imposition of heavy taxes is attributed to the rulers in several Purāṇas. The *Viṣṇu* and *Brahmāṇḍa* state that the king would live on taxes such as *bali*, *bhāga* and *śulka*; but they would not peotect the prople; they would be concerned only with their own safety.[4] The *Viṣṇu* adds that in the Kali era the king would seize the property of the people.[5] It is obvious that the good principles of taxation set forth in the *Śānti Parvan* and elsewhere, which stress that people should be taxed to the extent which keeps them alive, were not followed by the rulers with the result that the vaiśya peasants were completely done with. Since many of the śūdras were attached to the vaiśyas as labourers, oppressive taxation also affected them deeply. It is in this context that we can appreciate Manu's desperate provision that under no circumstances should the vaiśyas and śūdras be allowed to deflect from their duties otherwise the whole world will be thrown into chaos.

In the earlier periods the main distinction lay between the śūdras and three upper varṇas. Although this distinction is retained by Manu as a matter of form, his work shows a far

1. *karabhayāt puṃso gṛhasthāḥ parimoṣakāḥ, punicchadmākṛticchannā vāṇijyamupajīvate.* Cr. edn., III. 186.40; the term *paripoṣakāḥ* occurs in Ms Śl. Kl.

2. *sasyacorā bhaviṣyanti tathā cailāpihāriṇaḥ. Brahmāṇḍa P.* (ed. J. L. Shasri), I. 2. 31. 60; *Vāyu P.* (ed. S. R. Acharya), I. 40.60 makes slight changes in wording.

3. *durvikṣakarapīḍābhiratīvopadrutā janāḥ* (Gita Press, V.S. 2009), VI. 1.38. Incidentally it seems that the *Viṣṇu Purāṇa* speaks of conditions prevailing in the rice-producing area.

4. *arakṣitāro harttāraśśulkavyājena pārthivaḥ, Viṣṇu P.*, VI. 1.34; *na rakṣitāro bhoktāro balibhāgasya pārthivāḥ, svarakṣaṇa parāyaṇāḥ. Brahmāṇḍa P.*, I. 2.31.48.

5. *hāriṇo janavittānaṃ samprāpte tu kalau yuge.* VI. 1.34.

stronger tendency towards the approximation of the vaiśyas and śūdras in matters of legal provisions, food and marriage. The development was probably due to the fact that large numbers of vaiśyas were being thrown into the ranks of the śūdras. The *Viṣṇu Purāṇa* states that in the Kali age the vaiśyas will give up agriculture and trade, and will take to servitude and mechanical arts,[1] and the prevailing castes will be those of the śūdras.[2] That the traditional vaiśya varṇa was gradually disappearing is evident from a passage of Manu. He attributes the quality of truth (sattva) to the brāhmaṇa and activity (rajas) to the kṣatriya;[3] the śūdras and mlecchas are cast together as representatives of the dark quality *madhyamā tāmasī gati* produced by actions in a former life,[4] but there is no mention of vaiśyas in this connection. This may suggest that the vaiśyas were being lost in the śūdra masses.

Hopkins states that some of the provisions of Manu imply antagonism between the two upper varṇas on the one hand, and the two lower varṇas on the other.[5] In this conflict it seems that the upper varṇas were led by the brāhmaṇas, and the lower varṇas were led by the śūdras. There is indication of subdued friction between the śūdras and the other varṇas even in the earlier periods. But in the post-Mauryan period it assumed acute and violent forms. In a study of Manu it has been claimed that economic inequality and friction could hardly arise in a society planned on Indian lines.[6] But this is not borne out by the nature of relations subsisting between the varṇas on the basis of Manu. The latter clearly states that a śūdra should not be permitted to amass wealth, for he gives pain to the brāhmaṇas.[7]

1. *Viṣṇu P.*, VI. 1.36.
2. *śūdraprāyāstathā varṇā bhaviṣyanti kalau yuge*. *Ibid.*, VI. 1.51.
3. *Manu*, XII. 46-48.
4. *Ibid.*, XII. 43.
5. Hopkins, *Mutual Relations of the Four Castes*, p. 78, cf. p. 82.
6. K. V. Rangaswami Aiyangar, *Aspects of the Social and Pol. System of Manu*, pp. 151-52. He admits that the *nītiśāstras* occasionally "have a fling at millionaires" (p. 159).
7. *Manu*, X. 129.

But it would not be fair to hold that Manu's diatribes against the śūdras mark the nadir of their fortunes during the post-Mauryan period. These should be taken in the nature of desperate measures, which were suggested to maintain the old form of society threatened by the appearance of new forces. Even the law-book of Manu could not ignore several changes in the position of the śūdras, which had appeared perhaps as a result of their struggle against the brāhmaṇas, the advent of new peoples and developments in arts and crafts.

Notwithstanding Manu's insistence on the servitude of the śūdras, they do not appear as slaves and labourers on the same scale as in the pre-Mauryan and Mauryan periods. We do not hear of big individual or state farms being worked with slave and hired labour. Presumably slaves and hired labourers working on the Mauryan state farms were now in the process of being transformed into tax-paying agriculturists. Manu is the first writer explicitly to describe the śūdra as a sharecropper,[1] a fact which can be only deduced from the *Arthaśāstra* of Kauṭilya. While the sharecropper (*ardhasitika*) retains only $\frac{1}{8}$th or $\frac{1}{4}$th portion of the produce in the *Arthaśāstra*, in Manu he seems to retain half of the produce (*ārdhikaḥ*).[2] There seems to have been an increase not only in the share of the sharecroppers, but also in their numbers. Instead of the paid officials of the *Arthaśāstra* Manu gives a list of graded officers who are to be remunerated by grants of land.[3] In the absence of references to slaves employed in agriculture, we may presume that these plots of land were cultivated by sharecroppers and hired labourers. Perhaps no text other than Manu shows such a great accession to the numerical strength of the śūdras. In order to assimilate numerous aboriginal tribes and foreign elements Manu made a far greater use of the fiction of *varṇa-saṃkara* (intermixture of varṇas) than was done by his predecessors. In the majority of instances the mixed castes were lumped with the śūdras[4]

1. IV. 253.

2. *AŚ*, II.23; *Manu*, IV. 253. While the sharecropper in the *AŚ* receives land from the state, in Manu he receives it from the individual.

3. *Manu*, VII. 119. Here we have an important germ of feudalism.

4. K. V. Rangaswami Aiyangar, *Aspects of the Soc. and Pol. System of Manu*, p. 108.

in respect of their hereditary duties. But the new śūdras do not seem to have been recruited as slaves and hired labourers like their old counterparts. They pursued their old occupations and were possibly taught new methods of agriculture,[1] which gradually turned them into tax-paying peasants. Thus while the aborigines benefited from the knowledge of civilised life imparted to them by brāhmaṇical society, the latter could overcome its internal weaknesses by the addition of new producing masses.

The formation of new guilds of artisans and the rise of new crafts betoken changes of considerable importance,[2] not only in the economic life of the period, but in the position of the śūdras. With the disappearance of the all-powerful Mauryan state they helped to secure the comparative independence of artisans, therefore leading to some improvement in their status, which is evident from epigraphic records of numerous donations made by them to the Buddhists. The economic policy of some rulers also indirectly helped to improve the position of the śūdras. The Śaka ruler Rudradāman, a supporter of varṇa society,[3] claims to have made the repair of the Sudarśana lake without imposing any forced labour upon his subjects.[4] This must have meant a great boon to śūdra slaves and labourers who were usually subjected to corvée.

The literary evidence for the rise of new crafts and guilds can be linked up with the numismatic evidence and the testimony of foreign writers regarding trade between Rome and India, which was at its height during the first two centuries of the Christian era,[5] especially in the Sātavāhana territory. This remarkable increase in the volume of trade must have softened the rigours of the caste system at least in the trading-ports[6] and

1. Kosambi, *JAOS*, lxxv, 41.

2. Existence of independent handicrafts is generally regarded as an important feature of feudal society in medieval Europe.

3. Junāgarh Rock Inscr. of Rudradāman I, 1.9.

4. *Ibid.*, 1.16.

5. The problem has been discussed in Warmington, *The Commerce between the Roman Empire and India.* For recent archaeological evidence see Wheeler, *Rome beyond the Imperial Frontiers*, Chs. 12-13.

6. Sixteen of the coastal towns are singled by Ptolemy as *emporia*, Wheeler, *op. cit.*, p. 151.

some other inland towns, and thus may have improved the social position of the lower orders.

The advent of foreign peoples in this period served to loosen the shackles of the varṇa system. The number of the Greeks Śakas and Parthians may not have been great, but numerous finds of the Kuṣāṇas, such as coins, terracottas and sculptures scattered over the whole of Northern India, suggest that they came in considerable numbers. This naturally caused displacement of existing populations and led to the foundation of new settlements, thereby promoting mobility during the first century of the Christian era. Since the caste system basically rests on a static way of life, these ethnic upheavals may have undermined the privileges of the higher varṇas and thus favourably affected the position of the śūdras.

Similarly we notice some improvement in the śūdra's legal and political status. Manu's punishment of a brāhmaṇa abusing a śūdra is significant,[1] for in the Dharmasūtras the brāhmaṇa goes scot-free. Again, the fact that the brāhmaṇa ruler Gautamīputra Śātakarṇi felt it necessary to court the support of the *avaras*[2] shows the importance that was being accorded to them in the second century A.D.

Lastly, Manu's mention of Vasiṣṭha as the progenitor of the śūdras points to their better social and religious position.[3] The fact that the śūdras could perform the *nāmadheya* (naming) ceremony[4] shows that they gained in religious status. This may have also improved on account of the liberal religious outlook of the Kuṣāṇa rulers. Being mainly Śaivites and Buddhists rather than supporters of the orthodox brāhmaṇism, they were probably better disposed towards the lower classes. Similar results may have been produced in the Sātavāhana dominions, where Buddhism undoubtedly enjoyed an important influence during the first and second centuries A.D.

1. VIII. 268.
2. Nāsik Cave Inscr. of Vāsiṣṭhīputra Pulumāvi, ll. 5-6 (D. C. Sircar, *Select Inscrs.*, i, 197).
3. III. 196-98.
4. *Manu*, II. 30-31.

These signs of change in the position of the śūdra permit us to conjecture that the old society which treated him as a helot saddled with numerous disabilities had begun to decline and was being partly replaced by a new society which gave him a better position—a process that was carried further in the Gupta period. The repeated mention of the end of an age (*yugānta*) suggests the destruction of values on which the old society was based. Thus for some time the idea of birth, which was seen as the basis of varṇa society, was completely undermined. While describing the conduct of the foreign invaders the *Viṣṇu Purāṇa* prophesises that during their rule property alone will confer rank, wealth alone will be the source of dharma, and liberality will constitute dharma.[1] These new values possibly also infected the kingdoms of indigenous rulers, and were as much the outcome of foreign conquests as of internal crisis in the varṇa system. The nature of social crisis as known from the descriptions of the Kali age in the *Mahābhārata* and Purāṇas and some signs of change in the position of the śūdras suggest that the social formation which treated him as a helot and saddled him with numerous disabilities was in the throes of dissolution. Society was faced with a state of *varṇasaṃkara* or the collapse of the varṇa system, which disorder really implied non-payment of taxes and refusal of religious gifts by the vaiśyas and non-performance of serving functions by the śūdras. It also may have meant the changed outlook of śūdra artisans. To meet the situation it was necessary to devise measures of both coercion and concession, and more importantly, to think of new ways of collecting surplus produce and surplus labour for maintaining the religious and administrative apparatus, Manu's general attitude of intense hostility towards the śūdras and even the vaiśyas is therefore understandable; so is the emphasis on the central importance of *daṇḍa* or coercive power found in both the law-book of Manu[2] and in the *Śānti Parvan*.[3] Some religious concessions were made

1. *tataścārtha evābhijanahetur dhanamevāśeṣadh armahetuḥ....dānameva dharmahetuḥ āḍhyataiva sādhutvahetuḥ*. *Viṣṇu P.*, IV. 24.21-24; cf. *Yuga P.* 95-112.

2. VII. 14-32.

3. Cr. Edn., 15.2.9, 12-13.

to the śūdras even by Manu, and in order to pay the religious functionaries and fiscal authorities a few land grants were made even in the first two Christian centuries. But it was only in Gupta times that these two processes assumed significant dimensions.

CHAPTER VII

PEASANTHOOD AND RELIGIOUS RIGHTS

(*circa* A.D. 300—600)

The Smṛtis of Viṣṇu, Yājñavalkya, Nārada, Bṛhaspati and Kātyāyana[1] constitute the main source for the study of the position of the śūdras in this period. Of these the *Yājnavalkya* seems to have been the most important because of the authority it came to enjoy in Northern India in subsequent times. Perhaps its provisions reflect more faithfully than do the other Smṛtis the developments in society during the Gupta period. This law-book either undoes or ignores the extremist measures of Manu against the śūdras, and provides the punishment of branding and banishing even for the brāhmaṇas.[2]

We can only guess the regions to which the lawgivers belonged. Yājñavalkya probably flourished in Mithilā,[3] and Nārada seems to have been from Nepāl.[4] Other lawgivers also may have lived in the north, and hence their works reflect the conditions obtaining mainly in Northern India.

These Smṛtis expand the texts of the Dharmasūtras, and in many cases reproduce the verses of Manu.[5] New information

1. Kane gives the following dates for these Smṛtis: *Viṣṇu* A.D. 100-300, *Yājñavalkya* A.D. 100-300. *Nārada* A.D. 100-400, *Bṛhaspati* A.D. 300-500, *Kātyāyana* A.D. 400-600. *Hist. Dh. S.*, ii, pt. I. p. XI. Although *Viṣṇu* and *Yāj.* seem to be earlier, roughly all these law-books can be treated as authorities for the Gupta period.

2. *Yāj.*, II. 270; *Viṣṇu*, V. 3. Hopkins thinks that this is scarcely possible to be true of *Yāj.* (*Mutual Relations of the Four Castes*, p. 31), but this is consistent with *Yāj's* popular attitude in several matters.

3. Hopkins, *CHI*, i, 279.

4. *Ibid.*, 280.

5. In its original form the *Bṛhaspati Smṛti* may have been read as a running commentary on Manu's Code. *GOS.* No. LXXV, Introd., p. 118.

can be obtained only from the variants, which do not always have direct bearing on the subject of our study.

The information gleaned from the Smṛtis is sometimes corroborated and supplemented by the Smṛti sections of the *Mahābhārata* and the Purāṇas. Hopkins holds that masses of didactic matter were intruded into the epic between 200 B.C. and A.D. 200.[1] This seems to be true of several verses of the *Śānti Parvan*, which are exactly similar to those in Manu. But variants in the *Śānti Parvan* and the *Anuśāsana Parvan* seem to be more in line with the Smṛti sections of the Purāṇas, which belong to a later period. Hopkins himself thinks that the swollen *Anuśāsana Parvan* was separated from the *Śānti* and recognised as a separate book in the period A.D. 200-400.[2] There is no reference to the Smṛti contents of the Purāṇas in the pre-Christian era.[3] The chapters dealing with the duties of the varṇas in the *Viṣṇu*,[4] the *Mārkaṇḍeya*,[5] the *Bhaviṣya*,[6] and the *Bhāgavata*[7] Purāṇas may be roughly assigned to the Gupta period.

A characteristic feature of the Smṛti writings of this period is their Vaiṣṇavite leanings. This is noticeable particularly in the *Viṣṇu Smṛti*, the *Bṛhaspati Smṛti*,[8] the *Viṣṇu Purāṇa*,[9] and the *Matsya Purāṇa*.[10] Probably the worship of Kṛṣṇa and the influence of Vaiṣṇavism account for the more liberal views that are so largely represented in the great epic.[11] As will be shown later, the Vaiṣṇavite tendencies liberalised the brāhmaṇical attitude towards the śūdras, who were granted narrow but definite rights in the sphere of religion.

1. Hopkins, *The Great Epic of India*, pp. 397-98.
2. *Ibid.*, Cf. *CHI*, i, 258.
3. Hazra, *Purāṇic Records on Hindu Rites aud Customs*, p. 5.
4. *Ibid.*, p. 175.
5. *Ibid.*, p. 174.
6. *Ibid.*, p. 188.
7. Probably the first half of the sixth century A.D. *Ibid.*, p. 177.
8. *GOS*, No. LXXXV, Introd., p. 173.
9. Hazra, *op. cit.*, p. 19.
10. *Ibid.*, p. 51. In the *Brahmāṇḍa Purāṇa* there are a few chapters which indicate the influence of Vaiṣṇavism (*Ibid.*, p. 18.)
11. Cf. Hopkins. *Ethics of India*, p. 241.

Information supplied by the works of Kālidāsa and Śūdraka is also in the spirit of the Smṛtis. Kālidāsa is a portrayer of varṇāśrama ideals,[1] and the same seems to be true of Śūdraka.[2] The Buddhist works *Laṅkāvatāra Sūtra* and *Vajrasūci* also supply some information about the position of the śūdras. The former was compiled before A.D. 443,[3] but the date of the latter is not so certain. It does not seem to be the work of Aśvaghoṣa, who flourished in the post-Mauryan period, for it does not find place in the list of his works mentioned by the Chinese pilgrim I-tsing.[4] The Chinese translation, done between A.D. 973-981, ascribes it to the Buddhist logician Dharmakīrti, who in all probability flourished in the fifth century A.D.[5] Quotations from the *Manu Smṛti* in the *Vajrasūci* show that the latter belonged to a later period. The major Buddhist and Jain[6] commentaries, which probably belong to this period, also give some incidental references about the subject of our study.

Technical works such as the *Nītisāra* of Kāmandaka, the *Nāṭyaśāstra* of Bharata,[7] the *Kāmasūtra* of Vātsyāyana,[8] the *Amarakośa* of Amarasiṃha and the *Bṛhat Saṃhitā* of Varāhamihira[9] throw welcome light on the conditions of the śūdras during this period.

1. Dasgupta and Dey, *Hist. of Sansk. Lit.*, Introd. p. XXX.
2. It is said that Śūdraka was a great brāhmaṇa minister. J. Charpentier, *JRAS*, 1923, pp. 596-97.
3. *Suzuki*, *Laṅkāvatāra Sūtra*, Introd., p. XLIII.
4. Dasgupta and Dey, *Hist. of Sansk. Lit.*, p. 71.
5. Dasgupta and Dey, *op. cit.*, p. 532, fn. Keith ascribes him to the 7th century A.D. (*HSL*, Preface, p. XXII).
6. Motichandra has used them for describing the dress and costumes in the Gupta period (*Bhāratīya Veśa-bhūṣā*, Ch. ix).
7. The third cen. A.D. seems to be the probable date of this work. (*The Age of Imperial Unity*, p. 270). Cf. 2nd cen. A.D. (M. Ghosh, *Nāṭyaśāstra*, Tr., Introd., p. LXXXVI); Also see Dasgupta and Dey, *Hist. of Sansk. Lit.*, p. 522.
8. Schmidt assigns it to the 2nd cen. B.C. (Quoted in Dasgupta and Dey, *Hist. of Sansk. Lit.*, p. 645) and H. P. Sastri to the first cen. A.D.; but Banerjee Sastri, Chakladar, Jolly and Winternitz ascribe it to the 3rd-4th cens. A.D. (*Soc. Life in Anc. India*, pp. 33-37). Chakladar thinks that Vātsyāyana flourished in western India (*Ibid.*, p. 96).
9. Varāhamihira is ascribed to the period A.D. 505-587, and all his works are placed in the middle of sixth cen. A.D.

Some information can also be gleaned from those portions of the *Hayaśirṣa Pañcarātra* and the *Viṣṇudharmottara Purāṇa* which deal with iconography. Although the former seems to have been a work of the Gupta period,[1] the latter seems to have been a compilation of post-Gupta times, and hence can be used only as a secondary piece of evidence.

Inscriptions do not mention the śūdras as a varṇa, but land grants repeatedly refer to the tax-paying peasants and artisans and indicate the process through which aboriginal tracts were annexed to brāhmaṇical society. A few epigraphs speaks of the artisans' guilds. All this helps us to determine the nature of changes in the social and economic conditions of the śūdras.

The familiar maxim that the duty of the śūdra is to serve the three other varṇas[2] recurs in the texts of the Gupta period. Just as in Manu, it is claimed that he should particularly serve the brāhmaṇas.[3] In the *Śānti Parvan* a ruler boasts that in his kingdom the śūdras duly serve and wait upon the other three orders without any malice.[4]

The *Anuśāsana Parvan* holds that the śūdras are workers (*karmakaras*)[5] and states that there would be no workers if there were no śūdras.[6] There is no doubt that a considerable section of the śūdras continued to be employed as wage earners, for all the eleven synonyms for wages occur in the *śūdra-varga* of the *Amarakośa*.[7] Similarly names of various types of hired labourers and servants are also listed in the same section. There are four names for wage earners, two for carriers, two for porters and eleven for domestic servants (*bhṛtyas*).[8]

The bhṛtakas (wage earners) were divided by Nārada and Bṛhaspati into three categories : i.e. those who served in the

1. Banerjea, *Development of Hindu Iconography*, pp. 28-29.
2. *Kāmandakīya Nītisāra*, II. 21; *ŚP*, 60. 26; 92. 2; *Anu. P.* (SE), 9. 18; *Bhāg. P.*, XI. 17.19; *Bhav. P.*, i, 44.27; *Mārk. P.*, 28. 3-8; *Viṣṇu P.* III. 8.32 and 33.
3. *Āśvamedhika P.* (SE), 97.29.
4. Ch. 78. 17.
5. *Anu. P.* (SE), 208.34.
6. *Ibid.*, 208. 33.
7. *AK*, II. 10. 38-39.
8. *AK*, II. 10. 15-18.

army, those who were engaged in agriculture and those who carried loads from place to place.[1] The first were considered the best, the second the middle, and the third the lowest type of workers.[2]

Although the porters and carriers were considered the lowest type of workers, they seem to have been the nonetheless important sections of labourers, for provisions relating to the conditions of their work occupy some space in the law-books of the period. These carriers were mostly employed by the merchants and were held responsible for the ware placed under their charge, except in the case of losses caused by fate or the state.[3] The porters could be variously punished for giving up their work at various stages. Nārada lays down that one who abandons merchandise, which he had agreed to convey to its destination, shall give a sixth part of his wages;[4] he shall be compelled to pay twice the amount of his wages, if he raises difficulty at the time of starting[5] —a rule which is also supported by Yājñavalkya.[6] But according to the other provisions of the latter lawgiver if the porter gives up his work after having started it, he shall pay $\frac{1}{7}$, if on the way, and if in the midway the whole of it.[7] The corresponding obligation on the hirer to pay wages to the porter does not seem to have been so effective. Nārada ordains that a merchant who does not take a conveyance or beasts for draught or burden, after having hired them, shall be made to pay $\frac{1}{4}$ of the hire; and the whole if he leaves them halfway.[8] This provision applies only to the owners of conveyances or animals most probably to the cart-owners cum drivers, and not to the human beings who acted as beasts of burden. Nevertheless, the parallel Nepalese version, which is considered as true reading,[9] states

1. *Nārada*, V. 23; *Bṛhaspati*, XV. 12 and 13.
2. *Ibid.*
3. *Viṣṇu*, V. 155-56; *Yāj.*, II. 197; *Nār.*, VI. 9.
4. VI. 6-7.
5. VI. 3.
6. *Yāj.*, II. 198.
7. *Ibid.*
8. VI. 7.
9. *SBE*, xxxiii, 140-41.

that, if the porter strikes work through the fault of his employer, he shall be rewarded for as much as has been finished by him.[1]

We have some idea of the wages of the workers who were employed as agricultural labourers and cowherds. Yājñavalkya, Nārada and Kātyāyana repeat the rates of payment as precribed in the *Arthaśāstra* of Kauṭilya. According to this a cultivator should get $\frac{1}{10}$ of the crop, a herdsman $\frac{1}{10}$ of the butter and pedlar $\frac{1}{10}$ of the sale proceeds as his wages.[2] Such a statement seems to be conventional in nature, and does not take into account the changes in wages during the Gupta period. These can be deduced from variant passages found in the *Śānti Parvan* and the law-books of Nārada and Bṛhaspati. As regards the wages of a herdsman the *Śānti Parvan* states that, if he keeps six kine for others, he should get the milk of one cow.[3] It adds that for keeping a hundred cows a pair of animals will be given to the herdsman.[4] Nārada gives a lower rate of remunertion. For tending a hundred cows a heifer shall be given as wages every year, for tending 200 cows a milch cow shall be given, and in both cases the cowherd shall be allowed to milk all the cows every eighth day.[5] This works out at the rate of the milk of one cow for tending eight cows and modifies Nārada's statement in which he lays down the conventional rate of $\frac{1}{10}$ of butter as wages for a herdsmen. Contemporary Jain sources show that these provisions were often approximately followed in practice. We hear of a herdsman who was given the whole milk of a cow or a buffalo on the eighth day.[6] In another case the remuneration is much higher; a cowherd received $\frac{1}{4}$ of the milk produced as his wages.[7] Thus there was a definite advance in the wages of herdsmen. Moreover, provisions for the possession of animals indicate the relatively independent status of the herdsman, who was supposed to own his own house and patch of land for fodder.

1. *Ibid.*, fn. on VI. 6.
2. *AŚ*, III. 13; *Yāj.*, II. 194; *Nār.*, VI. 2.3; *Kātyā.*, verse 656.
3. Ch. 60. 24.
4. *Ibid.*
5. *Nār.*, VI. 10.
6. *Piṇḍa Niryukti*, pp. 368-369.
7. *Bṛhatkalpa Bhāṣya*, 2. 358.

The *Śānti Parvan* and the *Bṛhaspati Smṛti* lay down higher rates of wages for agricultural labourers than the other texts of around this period. Thus, according to the former, if a cultivator is supplied with seeds and other accessories, he may take a seventh part of the yield.[1] Bṛhaspati is more liberal. According to him the workers engaged in cultivation (*sīra-vāhakas*) should be given $\frac{1}{4}$ of the produce if they are provided with food and clothing.[2] If they work without being given food and clothing by their employer, they should be given $\frac{1}{3}$ of the produce.[3] Obviously these provisions apply to the agricultural labourers and not to the sharecroppers who supplied their own seeds, oxen and implements. There is no justification for the view that the *sīra* land was identical with the *sītā* land of Kauṭilya.[4] While the *sītā* was crown land, the *sīra* was in the possession of individuals, who employed labourers for its cultivation.[5]

The rates of payment prescribed by Brhaspati suggest that towards the end of the Gupta period wages of agricultural labourers were doubled Further, the fact that they worked without the provision of food and clothes indicates the rise of a new stratum of labourers, who possessed resources to meet their requirements and were consequently less dependent on their employers. Thus it is clear that during this period there was a definite increase in the wages of herdsmen and agricultural labourers, which meant consequent improvement in the economic position of a considerable number of śūdras.

There is also some information about the condition of domestic servants. The *Kāmasūtra* informs us that, in addition to food and drink, servants (*bhṛtyas*) should receive their wages monthly or annually.[6] The *Śānti Parvan* emphasises that the śūdra servant must be maintained by masters of the three higher varṇas.[7] But it repeats the old rule that he should be given worn

1. *ŚP*, 60. 25. The *Śānti Parvan* provisions refer to the vaiśya herdsmen and agricultural labourers, but they may have applied to the śūdras as well.
2. *Bṛ.*, XVI. 1-2.
3. *Ibid.*
4. Pran Nath, *Eco. Cond. in Anc. India*, p. 158.
5. Cf. *s. v.* sir, Wilson, *A Glossary of Judicial and Revenue Terms*, p. 485.
6. *Kāma. S.*, IV. 1.33 & 42 with comm.
7. ... *avaśya bharaṇīyo hi varṇānāṃ śūdra ucyate. Śānti P.*, 60. 31.

out umbrellas, turbans, beds and seats, shoes and fans, and torn clothes by the twice-born.[1]

The *Śānti Parvan* repeats the myth that the śūdra was created by Prajāpati as the *dāsa* of the three other varṇas.[2] And hence he is required to practise the *dāsa-dharma.*[3] But this does not mean that all the śūdras were slaves. On account of the prevalence of slavery[4] some of the śūdras may have been slaves. But they were not slaves employed in producing activities. Although Nārada mentions fifteen kinds of slaves,[5] both he and Bṛhaspati make it clear that they are employed only in impure work.[6] This consists in sweeping the gateway, the privy, the road, removing the leavings of food, ordure, wine etc. and rubbing the master's limbs or shampooing the secret parts of his body.[7] On the other hand those engaged in producing activities, namely agricultural labourers or porters, are looked upon as doing pure work.[8] Therefore there is hardly any evidence of slaves being employed in production, either by individuals or by the state, such as we find in the pre-Mauryan and Mauryan periods.

The period shows a number of other signs which indicate the general weakening of the institution of slavery and the increasing freedom of the śūdras from the obligation to serve as slaves. As it is shown earlier, Kauṭilya's laws of manumission of slaves generally apply to those who are born of āryan parents or are āryans themselves. But Yājñavalkya introduces a very important

1. *Ibid.*, 60. 32-33.
2. *Ibid.*, 60. 27.
3. *Anu. P.*, (*SE*) 208. 34.
4. There is a simile of sale and purchase of slaves in a Gupta inscr. (*CII*, iii, No. 6, l. 2.). The *Br.* refers to the *dāsalekhyam,* a deed for the sale of slaves (VI. 7). In the *Mṛcchakaṭika* slavery was in vogue as an institution permitted by the state (*IHQ*, v, 307).
5. *Nār*, V. 26-28. Of these slaves *some are slaves improperly called* according to the citation in the *Vivādārṇava-setu*, where it is attributed to Bṛhaspati (H. T. Colebrooke, *A Digest of Hindu Law*, ii, 12). Six classes of slaves seem to have been mentioned in contemporary Jain works (Jain, *Life in Ancient India as Depicted in Jain Canons*, p. 107).
6. *Nār.*, V. 5; *Bṛ.*, XV. 15-16.
7. *Nār.*, V. 6-7.
8. *Ibid.*, V. 23-25.

principle when he asserts that nobody can be reduced to slavery without his consent; such a person has to be emancipated.[1] According to the commentary of Jagannātha Tarkapañcānana this means that a śūdra, a kṣatriya or a vaiśya employed in servile work without his own consent shall be released by the king.[2] Thus the above provision completely reverses Manu's precept, which provides for the forcible enslavement of a śūdra.[3]

In the earlier texts members of the three upper varṇas or their sons born of śūdra wives cannot be reduced to slavery. But there is no indication of such a special privilege for the twice-born in the Smṛtis of the Gupta period. Yājñavalkya, Nārada and Kātyāyana state that slavery should take place in the natural (*anuloma*) order of the varṇas and not in the reverse (*pratiloma*) order, that is to say, a slave should be of lower varṇa than his master.[4] Kātyāyana, however, makes the claim that slavery is provided for the three lower varṇas and not for the brāhmaṇas.[5] Nevertheless, these provisions imply that the śūdras were no longer singled out for enslavement.

Nārada and Bṛhaspati strongly deprecate the attitude of the wretch who, being independent, sells himself.[6] The *Anuśāsana Parvan* states that a person should not sell others; how much more one's own children.[7] Although rules for manumission of slaves (especially āryan) are found in Kauṭilya, the ceremony for their emancipation is first laid down by Nārada.[8] All this may have undermined the slave system.

Nārada states that in local disputes a class of people known as the *vargins* may be called as witnesses in cases concerning

1. *balāddāsīkṛtaścaurairvikrītaścāpimucyate. Yāj.*, II. 182.
2. Colebrooke, *op. cit.*, ii, p. 25.
3. This theory is, however, repeated by *Kātyā.*, verse 722.
4. *Yāj.*, II. 182-83; *Nār.*, V. 39; *Kātya.*, verse 716.
5. Verse 715. Cf. *Viṣṇu*, V. 154.
6. *vikrīṇīte svatatntro yaḥ samātmānaṃ narādhamaḥ, sa jaghanyatamaḥ tu eṣāṃ so'pi dāsyānna mucyate. Nār.*, V. 37; *Br.*, XV. 243.
7. *Anu. P.*, 45. 23 quoted in Kane, *Hist. Dh. S.*, ii, pt. I, p. 182.
8. *Nār.*, V. 42-43. Cf. rules of manumission in *Kātyā.*, verse 715. Nārada, however, adds that certain classes of slaves cannot be manumitted (V. 29) except by the favour of the owner.

their respective classes.[1] According to Kâtyâyana, among those to whom the term *vargin* applies are the leaders (*nāyakas*) of dāsas.[2] Thus the prevalence of organisation among slaves may have further weakened the institution of slavery.

There seems to be, however, sufficient evidence of the existence of women slaves, who served as maid-servants in the houses of the wealthy. The word *dāsīsabham* (multitude of women slaves) is used in the *Amarakośa* as an illustration of words showing multitude.[3] Jain works of the period show that numerous female slaves and maid-servants were recruited from tribal peoples.[4]

For the rest, the general condition of the slaves remained unchanged in the Gupta period. They could be beaten, put in fetters,[5] and were considered unreliable.[6] They had no status in law,[7] and were treated as an item of property either to be owned in common[8] or to be divided among the coparceners.[9] Nārada and Kâtyâyana repeat the dictum of Manu that the dāsa has no right to property,[10] but Kâtyâyana also states that the master is not entitled to that money which the slave gets by selling himself openly.[11]

In spite of all this the general weakening of slavery during the Gupta period seems to be evident. After the conquests of Samudra Gupta and Candra Gupta II we do not come across any large-scale wars in Gupta times. Therefore the possibility

1. Quoted in *Dharmakośa*, i, pt. I, p. 299.
2. *Kātyā.*, verse 350.
3. *AK*, III. 5.27.
4. Jain, *op. cit.*, pp. 362-65. The *Bṛhatkalpa Bhāṣya-gāthā* refers to three *nāpita-dāsīs* (6094).
5. Ghoshal, *The Classical Age*, p. 558., *Kātyā.*, verses 962-63., *Mṛcchakaṭika*. VIII. 25.
6. *Mṛcchakaṭika* (Karmarkar's edn.), p. 309.
7. *Kātyā.*, verse 92.
8. *Viṣṇu*, XVIII. 44.
9. *Kātyā.*, verse 882; *Bṛ.* (SBE), XXV. 82-83.
10. *Nār.*, V. 41; *Kātyā.*, verse 724.
11. Verse 724. This could not have been possible without the consent of the master. Kane prefers the reading of the *Vivādacintāmaṇi*, *Kātyā.*, p. 267. fn. on verse 724.

of acquiring slaves through conquest seems to have been exhausted. The system of slavery was further undermined because of the shrinkage of the market. In Greece and Rome, where it prevailed on a wide scale, it was connected with the money market. This was also partly true of India. The wide use of metallic money facilitated the sale and purchase of slaves for about a thousand years from about *circa* 500 B.C. But the paucity of coins from towards the end of the sixth century may have weakened the practice of dealing in slaves. Although the category of purchased slaves (*krita dāsa*) exists in the later law-books, their number may not have been very large. Similarly lesser use of money would mean less of moneylending and reduce the number of those who were held as pledge or mortgage and made slaves. However, metallic money seems to have decreased markedly only towards the end of the sixth and the beginning of the seventh century. And this phenomenon itself was a consequence of the decline of trade and towns[1] and the rise of a new type of economy in which various services were paid through land grants, and the donated villages came to form some kind of new, self-sufficient economic units catering to their own needs as well to those of the beneficiaries.[2]

A significant factor which contributed to this development was the fragmentation of land through the processes of partitions and gifts. The laws of inheritance as laid down in the Dharmaśāstra, the *Arthaśāstra* of Kauṭilya, and the law-books of Manu and even of Yājñavalkya never refer to the partition of landed property, which, is mentioned for the first time in the codes of Nārada[3] and Bṛhasapati.[4] This may suggest that in the middle or towards the end of the Gupta period big joint families, owning large stretches of land, began to break into smaller units. Once the principle of the partition of land was recognised, the increasing density of population in the fertile river valleys of Northern India, after the earlier phases of

1. R. S. Sharma, "Decay of Gangetic Towns in Gupta and post-Gupta Times", *Joural of Indian History*, Golden Jubilee Volume, pp. 135-50.

2. *Ibid.*, *Indian Feudalism*, Ch. I.

3. *Nār.*, XIII. 38.

4. *Bṛ.*, XXVI. 10, 28, 43, 53 & 64.

settlements, was bound to accelerate the pace of the fragmentation of arable plots of land. The pressure of population on land is indicated by an epigraphic record of the 5th cen. A.D., which shows that it was not possible to obtain 1½ *kulyavāpa* of land at one place in northern Bengal; it had to be purchased in smaller plots at four different places.[1] The purchase was made for the purpose of making gifts, of which we have numerous examples during this period. Land grants, made to the brāhmaṇas and temples, further helped the process of fragmentation. We no longer hear of large plots of 500 *karisas* or of the state farms of the Mauryan period. Epigraphic references to arable units of one *kulyavāpa* or of 4, 2 and 1 *droṇavāpas* do not suggest big plots.[2] According to Pargiter a *kulyavāpa* was a little larger than an acre.[3] But if the *kulyavāpa* measure of land prevalent in the Cachār district of Assam be considered identical with the *kulyavāpa*,[4] the area of the latter would be about 13 acres. Since one *kulya* is equal to 8 *droṇas*, it would appear that the average plots of land in north Bengal varied from seven acres to three acres. During the same period a survey of the land grants made by the Maitraka rulers of Valabhī in Gujarat shows that the average plot of land did not exceed two or three acres in size.[5] Naturally smaller holdings made it uneconomical to employ a large number of śūdra slaves and labourers. While some may have been employed in twos or threes, others may have been dispensed with.

It has been suggested that during the Gupta period land grants to brāhmaṇas served to promote village settlements by private enterprise.[6] This may have been the case in the undeveloped areas in Central and South India. Possibly either the waste and undeveloped land was settled with surplus śūdra population, for the old peasants would not like to shift from

1. *EI*, xx, Inscr. No. 5, ll. 5-11; S. K. Maity, *The Economic Life of Northern India in the Gupta Period*, pp. 50-51.
2. *EI*, xx, Inscr. No. 5. ll. 5-11.
3. *IA*, xxxix, 215-16.
4. *Bhāratavarsha*, 1349, pt. I, p. 384 (quoted in *History of Bengal*, i, 652).
5. Krishnakumari J. Virji, *Ancient History of Saurashtra*, pp. 246-47, 267ff.
6. Kosambi, *JAOS*. lxxv, 237.

settled areas, or aboriginal cultivators were enrolled as śūdras in the brāhmaṇical social organisation. Although in the traditional social hierarchy śūdras were required to serve as slaves and hired labourers, the new śūdras were either peasants or sharecroppers. Hence in Gupta and post-Gupta texts it became necessary to call them cultivators.

The traditional view that vaiśyas were peasants recurs in the literature of this period.[1] In the *Amarakośa* words for cultivators are listed in the *vaiśya-varga* (section).[2] But there are reasons to think that śūdras were also becoming peasants. Like Manu, Viṣṇu and Yājñavalkya show that land was rented out to the śūdra for crop.[3] This would suggest that the practice of leasing land to śūdra sharecroppers was growing stronger. Gradually they established permanent possession over the land. A Pallava land grant of this period (A.D. 250-350) informs us that four sharecroppers (*ārdhikaḥ*) remained attached to the land even when it was gifted away to brāhmaṇas.[4] The grant also mentions the transfer of two kolikas,[5] who may have been peasants or agricultural labourers of the Kol tribe.[6] Another Pallava land grant of the same period speaks of the transfer of a plot of four *nivartanas* cultivated by a person called Atuka,[7] who may also have been a sharecropper. This would suggest that at least in some cases the śūdra sharecroppers of the state could not be dispossessed of the land even when it was transferred to others.

Nārada includes the *kināśa* (peasant) among those who are

1. *ŚP*, 60. 24-26, 92. 2.

2. *AK*, II. 9. 6.

3. *Manu*, IV. 253 and *Viṣṇu*, LVII. 16 use the term *ārdhikaḥ*, but *Yāj.*, I. 166, uses the term *ardhasīrikaḥ*.

4. *EI*, i, Inscr. No. 1. l. 39. The term *ārdhikaḥ* has been wrongly rendered by Bühler as a labourer (*Ibid.*, p. 9).

5. The *kulikas* are mentioned as a people in *Bṛ.* (Saṃskāra, 404). They also appear in a list of peoples in a Pāla inscription of the 11th cen A.D. *EI*, xxix, Inscr. No. 1, l. 39.

6. The Kols are an important group of aboriginal people of the Muṇḍā stock in Chotānāgpur.

7. *EI*, viii. Inscr. No. 12, l. 6.

not fit to be examined as witnesses.[1] Asahāya, a commentator of the 7th cen. A.D.,[2] explains the term *kināśa* as a 'śūdra'.[3] This interpretation seems to be correct, for next to the *kināśa* the son of a śūdra wife is also declared by Nārada to be an incompetent witness.[4] This shows that śūdras were probably considered as peasants. This is also corroborated by Bṛhaspati, who provides a very severe corporal punishment for the śūdra, acting as a leader in boundary disputes relating to fields.[5] It is obvious that they could lead these disputes only as owners of fields. The *Mārkaṇḍeya Purāṇa* defines the village as a settlement where śūdras are numerous and cultivators thrive.[6] Some of these cultivators may have been śūdras. Kātyāyana lays down that, if a person cannot pay his debt, he should be made to work it off; if he is unable to work, he should be sent to jail. But this law applies only to the members of the three lower varṇas who are cultivators, and not to the brāhmaṇas.[7] The *Bṛhat Saṃhitā* states that the outbreak of fire in the south would cause pain to the ugras and vaiśyas, and its outbreak in the west to the śūdras and cultivators.[8] This may suggest that śūdras and cultivators were regarded as closely connected with one another. Thus the above references indicate that śudras were gradually becoming peasants.

The land grants of this period, made in Central India, repeatedly refer to the tax-paying *kuṭumbins* and *kārus* (artisans).[9] Land transactions from Bengal mention the names of the

1. *Nār.*, I. 181.
2. *The Age of Imperial Unity*, p. 299.
3. *kīnāśaḥ śūdraḥ kadaryo vā.* Comm. to *Nār.*, I. 181.
4. *Nār.*, I. 181.
5. *yadi śūdro netā syāt ... Bṛ.*, XIX. 6.
6. *tathā śūdrajalaprāyaḥ svasamṛddhikṛṣībalāḥ Mārk. P.*, 49. 47. Cf. Refs. to śūdra villages in the *Anuśāsana Parvan*, Ch. 68 (quoted in Bandyopadhyaya, *Economic Life and Progress in Ancient India* p. 329).
7. ... *karṣakān kṣatraviṭśūdraān samahīnāṃstu dāpayet. Kātyā.*, verses 479-80. The context here shows that the term *karṣakān* qualifies the phrase *kṣatraviṭ-śūdrān*. In his translation Kane treats the term *karṣakān* as an independent noun (Tr., verses 479-80), but this does not seem to fit in with the tenor of the passage, which introduces *karṣakān* between the terms *brāhmaṇa* and *kṣatraviṭśūdrān*. cf. *Kātyā.*, verse 586.
8. *Bṛ. Saṃ.*, 31. 3.4.
9. *CII*, iii, Inscr. No. 60, l. 12; No. 27, l. 6; No. 26, l. 6.

kuṭumbins who are informed of the gifts or the sale of land.[1] It is beyond doubt that the *kārus* were śūdras. This applies also to the *kuṭumbins*. The latter have been taken as cultivators[2] or houseslaves.[3] It is also suggested that the *kuṭumbins* belonged to the professional artisan classes who cultivated land as a subsidiary means of livelihood.[4] But it seems that, in contrast to the *kārus*, the *kuṭumbins* were cultivating householders. In the early Pāli texts they appear as householders of substance,[5] and may have been vaiśyas. In the *Arthaśāstra* of Kauṭilya the share-cropping *kuṭumbins* have been taken as śūdras by T. Ganapati Sastri.[6] The tax-paying cultivator families of the Gupta period may have included both vaiśyas and śūdras. But the position seems to have changed substantially in subsequent times. The kurmis, who constitute a numerous cultivating caste in West Bengal, Bihar and U.P. and are placed in the category of śūdras, seem to correspond to the *kuṭumbin*. The same is true of the kunbi caste found in Maharashtra and parts of Madhya Pradesh.

Again, if the interpretation of the term *uparikara* as a tax levied on temporary peasants is accepted,[7] it would appear that the dāsas and karmakaras, who worked in the fields of the state or of the individual proprietors in the early period, were now being temporarily provided with lands.

Perhaps it was on account of the rise in the number of cultivators, pressure of the increasing population on land, and the inability of the new peasant to pay higher taxes, that the burden of land revenues was reduced from $\frac{1}{4}$th to $\frac{1}{6}$th of the produce.[8] Bṛhaspati lays down that the king should take $\frac{1}{6}$, $\frac{1}{8}$, or $\frac{1}{10}$th of the produce according to the nature and yield of cultivation.[9]

1. D. C. Sircar (ed.) *Select Inscriptions*, i, Bk. III, no. 40A, line 5. no. 42, line 3.
2. Fleet, *CII*, iii, p. 123.
3. Kielhorn, *EI*, iii, 314.
4. Pran Nath, *op. cit.*, p. 157.
5. *s. v.* kuṭumbika, *Pāli-Eng. Dict.*
6. *AŚ*, i, 13.
7. Fleet, *CII*, iii, p. 98; Ghoshal, *Hindu Revenue System*, pp. 191, 210. For other views see Barnett, *JRAS*, 1931, p. 165; Sircar, *Select Inscrs.*, i, p. 266, fn. 5.
8. *Raghuvaṃśa*, XVII. 65; *Nār.*, XVIII. 48; *Bṛ.*, Āpaddharma, 7.
9. *Bṛ.*, I. 43-44. In the text the term *kīnāśa* is used, which, according to the comment of Asahāya on Nār. I. 131, means a śūdra.

In the first half of the 7th cen. A.D. Hsüan Tsang describes śūdras as a class of agriculturists,[1] a description which is confirmed by the *Narasiṃha Purāṇa*, where agriculture is laid down as the duty of the śūdras.[2] But it seems that this significant development took place during Gupta times. The view that the farmer population was largely composed of śūdras[3] seems to be more true of the Gupta period than of earlier times. Perhaps never in any earlier period was there such a great accession to the numerical strength of the śūdras. In order to assimilate numerous aboriginal tribes and foreign elements Manu made a far greater use of the fiction of *varṇasaṃkara* (intermixture of varṇas) than was done by his predecessors. In the majority of instances the mixed castes were lumped with the śūdras[4] in respect of their hereditary duties. But the new śūdras do not seem to have been recruited as slaves and hired labourers like their old counterparts. They pursued their old occupations and were probably taught new methods of agriculture,[5] which gradually turned them into tax-paying peasants. Thus while the aborigines benefited from the knowledge of civilised life imparted to them by brāhmaṇical society, the latter could overcome its internal weaknesses by the addition of new producing masses.

It is possible to risk a hypothesis about the process which led to the peasanthood of the śūdras. Around the third century A.D. the vaiśya-śūdra social formation was afflicted with a deep social crisis. The crisis is clearly reflected in the descriptions of the Kali age in those portions of the Purāṇas which belong to the third and fourth centuries A.D. Emphasis on the importance of coercive mechanism (*daṇḍa*) in the *Śānti Parva* and description

1. "The fourth class is that of the śūdras or agriculturists; these toil at cultivating the soil and are industrious at sowing and reaping". Watters, *On Yuan Chwang's Travels in India*, i, 168.

2. *Narasiṃha Purāṇa*, 58. 10-15. This Purāṇa was known to Al-Birūni (Sachau, i, 130), and hence its latest compilation may be placed in the 10th cen. A.D.

3. Hopkins presumably uses the word 'slaves' in place of śūdras. *CHI*, i, p. 268.

4. K. V. Rangaswami Aiyangar, *Aspects of the Soc. and Pol. System of Manu*, p. 108.

5. Kosambi, *JAOS*, lxxv, 41.

of anarchy (*arājakata*) in the epics possibly belong to the same age and point to the same crisis. The Kali age is characterised by *varṇasaṃkara*, i.e., intermixture of varṇas or social orders, which implies that vaiśyas and śūdras, i.e., peasants, artisans and labourers either refused to stick to the producing functions assigned to them or else vaiśya peasants declined to pay taxes and the śūdras refused to make their labour available. Since collection of taxes by royal officers was made difficult, religious and probably administrative services began to be remunerated through land grants. The process created a class of landlords between the king and the peasants who were mostly vaiśyas in the settled areas, and thus downgraded the vaiśyas. Similarly when tribal chiefs created difficulties, brāhmaṇas were planted in the tribal areas through land grants. In the backward and aboriginal areas the grants to brāhmaṇas and others led to the spread of iron-plough agriculture, preservation of cattle, spread of agricultural calendar, diffusion of the knowledge of *āyurveda* medicine and thus contributed to increase in overall agricultural production and also to the submission of the tribals to the state. In the process the grants brought to the brāhmaṇical fold a large number of aboriginal peasants who came to be ranked as śūdras. Śūdras therefore began to be called peasants and agriculturists in early medieval texts.

It may be suggested, very tentatively, that this transition was facilitated by the use of iron on an extensive scale. The *Amarakośa* gives seven names for iron and two names for iron rust,[1] and a Buddhist commentary of the period makes a detailed classification of metals.[2] The *Amarakośa* also gives five names for ploughshare,[3] which may indicate ready supply of this most important agricultural implement and intensive cultivation of land. Without a plentiful supply of such implements former dāsas, karmakaras, aboriginal peoples and the growing number of new families among the higher varṇas could not have carried

1. *AK*, II. 9. 98 and 99.
2. *Vibhaṅga Aṭṭhakathā*. p. 63 quoted in *s. v.* loha in *Pāli-Eng. Dict.* As is evident from the Mehrauli Iron Pillar of Candra, the technical knowledge in iron-working reached its high watermark during this period.
3. *AK*, II. 9. 13.

on agriculture. That there was plentiful supply of iron tools can be inferred from the export of iron goods to the Roman empire in the first two Christian centuries where it had to be eventually banned. The art of making steel had started about from *c.* 200 B.C.;[1] and so widespread had become the use of iron objects that now it was being used for non-utilitarian purposes. The greatest example of such use is the Mehraulī iron pillar. Unfortunately no attention has been paid to the excavation of various phases of village settlements in Northern India, which might throw light on the extent of the use of iron agricultural implements during earlier times. For the lawgivers inform us that hired labourers were supplied with implements, which had to be returned to the masters at the end of the work.[2] But these labourers could not become agriculturists without their own implements, which were probably provided for them by the growing iron industry of the period.

During this period śūdra artisans maintained their importance. The earlier lawgivers permit arts and crafts to the śūdras only when they fail to earn their livelihood through the service of the three higher varṇas, but this condition is now waived,[3] and handicrafts are included in the normal occupations of the śūdras.[4] These crafts are defined by Bṛhaspati as working in gold, base metals, wood, thread, stone and leather.[5] The *Amarakośa* list of craftsmen, which occurs in the *śūdra-varga*, gives two names each for general artisans, heads of their guilds, garland makers, washermen, potters, bricklayers, weavers, tailors, painters, armourers, leather workers, blacksmiths, shell-cutters and workers in copper.[6] The list gives four names for goldsmiths and five names for carpenters.[7] Amara also includes

1. Information from H. C. Bharadwaj of Banaras Hindu University.
2. *Yāj.*, II. 193; *Nār.*, V. 4.
3. This view, however, is repeated in the *Bhāg. P.*, XI. 18. 49.
4. *Kām. N. S.*, II. 21; cf. IV. 54-56; *Mārk. P.*, 28. 3-8; *Viṣṇu P.*, III. 8. 32-33; *Yāj.*. I. 120: *Viṣṇu*, III. 5; *śūdrasya ... sarvaśilpāni*, *Bṛ.*, Saṃskāra, verse 530.
5. *Bṛ.*, XIII. 33.
6. *AK.*, II. 10. 5-10.
7. *Ibid.*, II. 10. 8 and 9.

players on drums, water, flute and *vīṇā*,[1] actors, dancers and tumblers in the *śūdra-varga*.[2] Thus the list would suggest that all varieties of arts and crafts were practised by śūdras.[3]

The old provision that artisans should work for a day in a month for the king is repeated by Viṣṇu.[4] This rule continued to work in practice, for an inscriptions of the sixth century A.D. in Western India states that forced labour (*viṣṭi*) should be imposed on smiths, chariot-makers (*rathakāras*) barbers and potters by the elders (*vārikeṇa*)[5]. Vasiṣṭha states that no taxes should be imposed on the earnings of craftmanship.[6] In post-Mauryan times, however, taxes seem to have been confined to weavers only,[7] but during this period there began the practice of levying taxes from the artisans. The *Śānti Parvan* lays down that artisans and traders should be taxed after taking into account conditions of production and the nature of their crafts. Assessment may be made on the basis of the number of commodities produced, and taxes may be collected in kind.[8] It is beyond doubt that artisans paid taxes to the state, for this fact is repeatedly mentioned in the inscriptions of this period. A Pallava inscription of A.D. 446 from Southern India informs us that blacksmiths, leather workers, weavers and even barbers paid taxes to the king.[9] All this testifies to the material progress and growing importance of some sections of śūdra artisans. The commentary on a passage of the *Kāmasūtra* suggests that a śūdra

1. *Ibid.*, II. 10. 13.
2. *Ibid.*, II. 10. 12.
3. Some of these people such as garland makers, goldsmiths, washermen, actors, dancers etc. are also mentioned in the *Kāmasūtra* (I. 4.28, V. 2. 12, VI. 1.9), probably providing for the luxuries of the *nāgaraka*.
4. *Gaut. Dh. S.*, X. 31-33, *Vas. Dh. S.*, XIX. 28: *Manu*, VII, 138; *Viṣṇu* III. 32.
5. It is not clear whether this was done for the sake of the king or the village elders. *JRASB*, series III. xvi, p. 121, Law No. 72.
6. XIX. 37.
7. Supra, ch. VI.
8. *ŚP.*, 88. 1-12. Note on 12 in Cr. Ed., *Rāja Dharma*, Pt. II, Fas. 19, p. 668. Cf. 87. 16-77.
9. *EI.* xxiv, Inscr. No. 43, ll.18-19. The inscr. also refers to the imposition of the marriage tax, a custom which prevailed till recent times in Northern India.

could accumulate earnings through the occupations of craftsmen, actors, etc. and could thus become a *nāgaraka*, i.e. a respectable and dignified citizen.[1]

Provisions for the payment of taxes show that artisans were no longer employed and controlled by the state in the same manner as they were in the Mauryan period. Probably artisans living in the capital[2] were attached to the king. But the frequent mention of artisans in villages shows that they were far more numerous in the rural areas, where they lived and worked more or less independently.

The strengthening of the guilds contributed to the growing importance of artisans. Guilds (*śreṇis*) came to be regarded as the constituent elements in the organisation of capitals or towns.[3] Evidently these were the associations of artisans[4] and traders. While the earlier law-books and the *Arthaśāstra* of Kauṭilya enjoin the king to pay respect to the customs of the guilds (*śreṇidharma*),[5] those of the Gupta period instruct the king to enforce the usages prevalent in the guilds.[6] Bṛhaspati lays down that whatever is done by the heads of guilds towards other people, in accordance with prescribed regulations, must be approved by the king, for they are declared to be the appointed managers of affairs.[7] He also warns that, if the usages of localities, castes and *kulas* are not maintained, the people will get discontented and wealth will suffer thereby.[8] Thus it seems that the guilds were free to act in whatever way they liked, and the king was bound to accept their decision.[9] In other words they

1. I. 4. 1.
2. *Bṛ*. I. 34. This is also provided in the *Arthaśāstra* of Kauṭilya.
3. *AK*, II. 8. 18.
4. There are references to the guild of artisans (śilpisaṃgha) in the *Raghuvaṃśa* XVI. 38 and to masons under the master-builder in the *Pañcatantra*, pp. 4-5.
5. *Gaut.*, XI. 21-22; *Manu*, VIII. 41 and 46; Mookerji, *Local Government in Ancient India*, pp. 125-31.
6. *Nār.*, X. 2; cf. *Viṣṇu*, V. 168 uses the term *saṃvid*; *teṣāṃ vṛttiṃ pālayet*, *Yāj.*, II. 192, cf. I. 361.
7. *Bṛ*., XVII. 18.
8. *Ibid.*, I. 126.
9. Majumdar, *Corporate Life in Ancient India*, p. 62.

seem to have been more or less independent units of production, practically free from the control of the state. They continued their old functions of receiving money as deposits, paying interest on them and obviously investing them in their trades, as would appear from an inscription of the guild of oil-pressers of Indore in the fifth century. A.D.[1] Such activities naturally promoted their material prosperity, which is evident from the construction and the repair of the temple of the Sun by the silkweavers of Mandasor in the fifth century A.D.[2] It would be wrong to think that when the power of the brāhmaṇical priesthood began to predominate guilds began to decline.[3] Not only the increasing power of the guild was recognised by brāhmaṇical lawgivers, but the two guilds mentioned in the inscriptions of the Gupta period were either patronised by the brāhmaṇas or had brāhmaṇical associations.[4]

The rules governing the relations between the employer and the employees indicate some improvement in the position of various categories of workers, who were recruited from the śūdra community. We have seen that in the case of non-performance of work Kauṭilya prescribes a fine of 12 paṇas, which comes to from five to twenty times the amount of wages prescribed by him.[5] But most lawgivers of the Gupta period provide a fine of double the amount of wages, in case the worker does not perform his work after having taken his wages.[6] Bṛhaspati, however, prescribes an additional fine according to the ability of the worker.[7] Viṣṇu ordains that, if a worker does not complete his work, he should pay all his wages to the employer and a fine of 100 paṇas to the king.[8] But this provision of his is counterbalanced by another, which lays down similar punishment for the employer if he dismisses the worker when the

1. *CII*, iii, Indore Copper-plate Inscr. of Skanda Gupta (A.D. 465).
2. *CII*, iii, Inscr. No. 18, pp. 80-85.
3. Narsu, *Essence of Buddhism*, p. 141.
4. In the *tailaka śreṇi* of Indore money was desposited by a brāhmaṇa, and the silkweavers erected temple to the Sun, a brāhmaṇical deity.
5. *AŚ*, III, 14; Supra, p. 168.
6. *Yāj.*, II. 193; *Nār.*, VI. 5; *Bṛ.*, XVI. 5-6.
7. *Bṛ.*, XVI. 5.
8. *Viṣṇu*, V. 153-5 4.

work is incomplete.[1] In this connection Bṛhaspati introduces certain provisions which are not found in the other law-books of the period. In one of them he just uncritically takes over the rule of Manu that, if the worker does not carry out his stipulated work out of pride although he is physically fit, he shall forfeit his wages and be subjected to a fine of eight kṛṣṇalas.[2] But this lawgiver adds that, in case the worker does not complete his work, he shall be deprived of his wages and proceeded against in a court of law.[3] Like Viṣṇu, Bṛhaspati safeguards the interests of the workers by stating that, if the employer does not pay wages to a worker who has completed his work, he shall be awarded proper punishment by the king.[4] Nārada adds that in such a case the employer shall be compelled to pay the wages with interest.[5] This was obviously meant to enforce his general rule, which makes it obligatory on the master to pay regular wages, as agreed upon, to the servant hired by him.[6] Reference has already been made to another provision of his, which states that, if the porter strikes work through the fault of the employer, he shall be rewarded for as much as has been done by him.[7] It is likely that this rule may have been extended to other classes of workers.

The provisions regarding herdsmen stress their duty of protecting the cattle under their charge,[8] but in the case of loss of animals they are not to be punished with death, as is provided by Kauṭilya. Bṛhaspati, however, states that, if the cattle under the charge of herdsmen cause damage to standing crops, they shall be beaten.[9]

1. *Ibid.*, V. 157-58.
2. *Manu*, VIII. 215; *Bṛ.* XVI. 4 and 8. In another version of *Bṛ.* we have two hundred paṇas instead of eight kṛṣṇalas (*SBE*, xliii, 345, fn. on *Bṛ.* XVI. 15).
3. XVI. 3.
4. XVI. 11.
5. Nepalese version, *SBE*, xxxiii, 140-41, fn. on VI. 7.
6. VI. 2.
7. Nepalese version, *SBE*, xxxiii, 140-41, fn. on VI. 7.
8. *Nār.*, VI. 11-17: *Bṛ.*, XVI. 10, 12-17.
9. XVI. 17.

Thus, on the whole, the punishments for non-performance of work in the Gupta period are not so severe as in the Mauryan period; and there are some provisions which safeguard the interests of the workers in case the employer does not pay wages or is unfair towards them. Further, a law-book of this period prescribes incentive rewards for workers. Kauṭilya recommends rewards only for weavers,[1] but Yājñavalkya lays down that the employer should pay more if the worker turns out more work than what is expected of him.[2] Therefore the provisions dealing with the relations between the employers and employees in the Gupta period leave the impression that, compared to the state of affairs in earlier times, such relations were humane and liberal and consequently were expected to improve the material condition of those members of the śūdra community who lived on wages.

In the Gupta period trade appears as one of the normal functions of the śūdras. Yājñavalkya states that, if the śūdra cannot maintain himself by the service of the twice-born, he can become a trader.[3] Bṛhaspati allows him to trade in all articles as one of his normal occupations.[4] The Purāṇas also state that a śūdra can carry on buying and selling[5] and can subsist on the profits of trade.[6] Bṛhaspati lays down that a śūdra partner in business should pay $\frac{1}{6}$ of the profits to the king, a vaiśya $\frac{1}{8}$, a kṣatriya $\frac{1}{10}$ and a brāhmaṇa $\frac{1}{20}$.[7] This would show that conditions for the śūdra traders were not so favourable as in the case of the members of the higher varṇas. Moreover, good śūdras were not expected to deal in some commodities such as wine.[8] But it is certain that śūdras could carry on trade, and in this respect the brāhmaṇical lawgivers obliterated the distinctions not only between them and the vaiśyas, but in some

1. *AŚ*, II. 23.
2. II. 195.
3. *Yāj.*, I. 120.
4. ...*vikrayaḥ sarvapaṇyānāṃ śūdradharma udāhṛtaḥ Bṛ.*, Saṃskāra, verse 530.
5. *Mārk. P.*, 28. 3-8.
6. *Viṣṇu P.*, III. 8. 32-33.
7. *Bṛ.*, XIII. 16.
8. *Bhaviṣyat P.*, I. 44. 32.

cases between them and the first two varṇas. Generally the śūdra traders may have served as pedlars. The lawgivers of the period repeat the *Arthaśāstra* rule that a pedlar should get $\frac{1}{10}$ of the sale proceeds,[1] but the *Śānti Parvan* raises this to $\frac{1}{7}$.[2] Perhaps this change indicates the position in the Gupta period.

As artisans and traders the śūdras played an important part in promoting trade and industry, which continued to be generally steady during this period.[3] What is more important, the Gupta period witnessed the rise of śūdra peasants, who sustained and expanded the agrarian economy of the country.

But in comparison to the members of the higher varṇas the śūdras continued to have a lower standard of living. The housing rules laid down by Varāhamihira provide that a brāhmaṇa should have a house of five rooms, a kṣatriya of four, a vaiśya of three and a śūdra of two. In every case the length and breadth of the main room should vary in the order of the superiority of the four varṇas.[4] Such a rule may have been observed only by orthodox brāhmaṇas, but it shows that members of the lower varṇas were not expected to enjoy better housing conditions.

During this period also we hear of śūdra rulers such as those in Saurāṣṭra, Avanti, Arbuda and Malwa. Along with them are mentioned the traditional Śūdra, Ābhīra[5] and Mleccha

1. *AŚ.*, III. 13; *Yāj.*, II. 194; *Nār*, VI. 2-3.; *Kātyā.*, verse 656.

2. *ŚP*, 60. 25. Although in the *ŚP* wage is provided for the vaiśya pedlar, it may have applied to the śūdras as well.

3. This is evident from detailed rules about partnership which appear for the first time in the *Yāj.* It is significant that, unlike Kauṭilya and *Manu*, (VII. 206-10), *Yāj.* (II. 265) states the law of partnership for merchants and foreign traders first, and adds that the same principles shall apply to priestly partnerships and to that of agriculturists and artisans. Similarly the foreign trade of the period made it necessary for Nārada to say that contracts of loans entered into in foreign countries were to be governed by the laws of the place of contract (*Nār.*, I. 105-06). Cf. Jayaswal, *Manu and Yājñavalkya*, pp. 198 and 211. The *Bṛhatkathā* of Guṇāḍhya, a work of about A.D. 500 (Keith, *Hist. of Sansk. Lit.*, p. 268), deals not so much with kings as with merchants, traders, seafarers and handicraftsmen (*Ibid.*).

4. *Bṛhat Saṃhitā*, 52. 12-13.

5. The *Amarakośa* distinguishes between *śūdrī* who is the wife of a śūdra, and *śūdrā* who is a woman of the śūdra tribe. The woman of the Ābhira tribe is called *mahāśūdrī*. *AK*, II. 6·13.

rulers, who all are described as reigning in the regions of Sindhu and Kashmir, and are assigned by Pargiter to the fourth century A.D.[1] But they were labelled śūdras not because they arose from the fourth varṇa, but because these tribal and foreign rulers did not patronize the brāhmaṇas and did not follow the brāhmaṇical dharma.[2] In a drama, however, there is the example of a cowherd who became a king.[3] When Yājñavalkya repeats the old injunction that a *snātaka* should not accept presents from a king who is not a kṣatriya he has probably such rulers (either tribal or śūdra) in mind.[4] But in course of time these rulers received brāhmaṇical recognition and were turned into respectable kṣatriyas.

As regards the appointment of ministers, Yājñavalkya and Kāmandaka repeat the old view that they should possess noble birth (*kulīnaḥ*) and knowledge of the Vedas,[5] which rules out the possibility of śūdras being selected as ministers. But the *Śānti Parvan* breaks new ground when it provides for a body of eight *mantrins* of whom four should be brāhmaṇas, three loyal, disciplined and obedient śūdras, and one a sūta.[6] We do not know whether such a precept was followed, but it shows a significant change in the brāhmaṇical attitude towards the śūdras.

There is no sign of such a liberal attitude in the appointment of judges and councillors (*sabhyas*). Yājñavalkya lays down that the king should administer justice with the assistance of learned brāhmaṇas who can act as judges in the case of the inability of the king to do so.[7] Kātyāyana adds that, if a brāhmaṇa is

1. Pargiter, *DKA*, p. 55.
2. *Ibid.*
3. Case of Āryaka who was a *gopāladāraka* (*Mṛcchakaṭika*, VI. 11). This is doubtful, for Gopāla may also be taken as a proper name.
4. *Yāj.*, I. 141.
5. *Manu*, VII. 54; *Kām. N. S.*, IV. 25; *Yāj.*, XIII. 312. Cf. *Kām. N. S.*, V. 68-70. *Kātyā.*, verse 11, lays down that the *amātya* should be a brāhmaṇa.
6. *ŚP*, 85. 7-10. The passage, which provides for a body of 37 *amātyas* of whom four should be brāhmaṇas, eight kṣatriyas, twenty-one vaiśyas, three śūdras and one sūta (*ŚP.* (Cal.), 85-7-11), does not occur in the critical Edn. of the *ŚP*.
7. *Yāj.*, II. 1-3; cf. *Bṛ.*, I. 67.

wanting either a kṣatriya or a vaiśya should be appointed a judge, but a śūdra should be carefully avoided,[1] a view which is also upheld by Bṛhaspati in regard to the appointment of the *sabhyas*.[2] The latter also repeats the warning of Manu that the kingdom, strength and treasury of the ruler who carries on his work with the assistance of the śūdras (*vṛṣalas*) suffer destruction.[3]

At the district level, however, the head of the artisans, who was a śūdra, had some share in the work of administration. The two Dāmodarpur copper-plate inscriptions dated A.D. 433 and 438 represent the *prathamakulika* Dhṛtimitra as a member of the district council of Koṭivarṣa (in north Bengal), which was in charge of a kumārāmātya.[4] The term *kulika* has been interpreted variously as a senior town judge[5] or a merchant.[6] But such interpretations are not supported by early texts. The term *kulika* is probably identical with the *kulaka* of the *Amarakośa*, which means the head of the artisans and occurs in the *śūdra-varga* of that work.[7] The term also seems to have been used in the sense of an artisan by the *Nārada Smṛti*, which includes the *kulika* in the list of false witnesses.[8] Therefore the *prathamakulika* was the first among the *kulikas*,[9] i.e. the head of he guilds of artisans, and as such had a place in the advisory council of the district of Koṭivarṣa in north Bengal. Probably the same practice was followed at the district headquarters of Vaiśālī, where we find individual seals of two *prathamakulikas*.[10]

1. Verse 67.
2. I. 79.
3. *Bṛ.*, I. 72.
4. *EI*, xv, p. 130.
5. Jayaswal, *Hindu Polity.*, Pt. i, p. 53; Pt. ii, p. 105.
6. T. Bloch, *ASR*, 1903-04, p. 104.
7. *kulakaḥ syāt kulaśreṣṭhaḥ*. *AK*, II. 10.5. Diksitar accepts this interpretation (*Gupta Polity*, p. 257).
8. *Nār.*, I. 187. It seems that old prejudices against śūdra witnesses continued during this period.
9. Eighteen seals of *kulikas* (head of companies of artisans) have been discovered at Basārh (Vaiśālī). *ASR*, 1903-04, pp. 114-16.
10. *ASR*, 1903-04, p. 117. In the 10-11th cent. A.D. the *kulika* appears as a minor officer in the Chambā state along with the *śaulkika*, *gaulmika* and others (Vogel, *Antiquities of Chamba State*, Pt. I, Inscr, No. 15. ll. 8-9). The *mahāpāndhākulika* is also mentioned with the *śaulkika*, *gaulmika* and others in

The association of the head of the guilds of artisans with the administration of the district was in keeping with their growing importance, which is also reflected in a Jain work of the period, which describes the *vaḍḍhai* or an architect as one of the fourteen jewels.[1] All this suggests some improvement in the civic status of the śūdra artisans.

Generally the śūdras continued to perform minor administrative tasks. Kāmandaka repeats the view of Kauṭilya that domestic servants should act as spies in reporting the activities of high state officials.[2] Nārada provides that the caṇḍālas, executioners (*vādhakas*) and similar persons should be employed in tracking down thieves inside the village, and that those living outside the village should search for them outside.[3]

In the judicial administration the old discriminations generally continued. Bṛhaspati provides that witnesses should belong to respectable families and regularly perform religious rites as prescribed in the Vedas and the Smṛtis.[4] This naturally excludes the śūdras. The provision that śūdras should appear as witnesses only for śūdras is repeated by the lawgivers of this period.[5] Kātyāyana lays down that the case against the accused should be proved by witnesses who are similar to him in caste. A litigant of a lower caste should not establish his case by the evidence of witnesses of higher castes.[6] Nārada's list of false witnesses includes jugglers, public dancers, sellers of spirituous liquors, oil pressers, elephant drivers, leather workers, caṇḍālas, śūdra peasants (*kināśas*), sons of śūdra women and outcastes (*patitas*).[7] But Nārada also moderates the old provision regarding varṇa witnesses by providing that members of all the varṇas

an inscription of A.D. 1031 from Gorakhpur in Uttar Pradesh (*EI*, vii, Inscr. No. 9, 1.34). Possibly *kulikas* and *mahāpāndhākulikas* were officers collecting taxes from guilds of artisans.

1. *Jambuddivahannatti*, 3.55 (p. 229).
2. XII. 44-45.
3. XIV. 26.
4. V. 38.
5. *Yāj.*, II. 69; *Kātyā.*, verse 341; *Nār.*, I. 154, uses the term irreproachable śūdra.
6. Verse 348.
7. I. 178, 181-185.

can appear as witnesses in the cases of all the varṇas.[1] In certain cases such as adultery, theft, defamation and assault anybody could act as a witness.[2] In boundary disputes relating to houses and fields Bṛhaspati permits peasants, artisans, hired labourers, herdsmen, hunters, gleaners, diggers of roots, and *kaivartas* (fishermen) to act as witnesses[3] as a matter of course. This seems to be a significant development, for Yājñavalkya allows such a concession only to herdsmen, peasants and foresters in boundary disputes confined to fields.[4] The corresponding provision in Manu is of a still more limited nature. It is only in relation to boundary disputes between villages that Manu permits hunters, fowlers, herdsmen, fishermen, root-diggers, snake-catchers, gleaners and foresters to act as witnesses and that only on failure of witnesses from the two or four neighbouring villages.[5] Bṛhaspati's provisions for witnesses who mostly belonged to the śūdra caste make an important concession to the śūdras, which is in accord with their new position as peasants and artisans. This was an important right, for boundary village disputes were naturally expected to be more frequent than any other type of disputes.

The lawgivers of the period, however, retain the different warnings administered to the members of the different vraṇas at the time of their giving evidence, the most severe warning being prescribed for the śūdra witness.[6]

Varṇa distinctions in ordeals, which are not found in Manu,[7] are laid down by the lawgivers of this period.[8] Yājñavalkya states that the ordeals of fire, water or poison should be administered to the śūdra and that of the balance to the brāhmaṇa;[9] he does not mention kṣatriyas and vaiśyas in this connection. But three other lawgivers lay down that a brāhmaṇa

1. I. 154.
2. *Yāj.*, II. 72.
3. XIX. 26-27.
4. *Yāj.*, II. 150.
5. VIII. 258-60.
6. *Viṣṇu*, VIII. 20-23; *Nār.*, I. 199.
7. VIII. 114-16.
8. *Yāj.*, II. 98; *Bṛ.*, VIII. 12.; *Kātyā.*, verse 422.
9. II. 98.

should be tested by the balance, a kṣatriya by fire, a vaiśya by water, and a śūdra by poison.[1] But here again Kātyāyana provides the alternative that all these ordeals can be administered to the members of all the varṇas, except that of poison, which cannot be administered to the brāhmaṇa.[2] Nārada also gives the alternative rule that the ordeal of poison can be administered to the kṣatriyas, vaiśyas and śūdras.[3] Viṣṇu states that this ordeal cannot be administered to a brāhmaṇa,[4] as is done by Nārada and Kātyāyana.[5] Viṣṇu prescribes different kinds of oaths, and ordeal by sacred libation for the śūdra, according to the value of deposit denied, or of the theft or robbery.[6] If the vaule exceeds half a suvarṇa, the judge may administer to the śūdra any of the four ordeals, namely balance, fire, water or poison.[7] But although Viṣṇu gives detailed rules about the application of these four ordeals,[8] he does not prescribe them for different varṇas as other lawgivers do. Perhaps some consideration was shown to the brāhmaṇas to whom poison could not be administered, otherwise varṇa distinctions in matters of ordeal did not prevail. The practice of ordeal by water obtained in Western India, probably in the kingdom of the Sātavāhanas, in the third century A.D.,[9] but there is nothing to show that it was confined to the members of any particular varṇa. It seems, however, that special types of ordeals prevailed among the tribal peoples and foreigners, who were being absorbed in the lower ranks of brāhmaṇical society. Therefore Kātyāyana lays down that the king should observe the ordeals peculiar to the untouchables (*aspṛśyas*), low people (*adhamas*), slaves and mlecchas.[10]

1. *Nār.*, I. 334-35; *Bṛ.*, VIII. 12; *Kātyā.*, verse 422.
2. Verse 422. Kātyāyana also does not permit the ordeals of fire, water and poison to those who deal with these things (v. 424).
3. I. 322.
4. IX. 27.
5. *Nār.*, I. 335, *Kātyā.*, verse 422.
6. IX. 3-10.
7. *Viṣṇu*, IX. 11.
8. *Ibid.*, IX, X, XI and XII.
9. Bardesanes quoted by Johannes Strobaios (A.D. 500), McCrindle, *Anc. India as Described in Classical Literature*, pp. 172-74.
10. Verse 433.

Manu provides that petitions should be entertained by the court in the order of the varṇas,[1] but this rule does not seem to have been mentioned by the lawgivers of this period. Nevertheless, varṇa distinctions are maintained in civil laws. Thus in the lawsuits requiring deposit of sureties Kātyāyana makes a distinction between the twice-born and the śūdras. On failure to provide surety, a twice-born person should be merely guarded by the warders, but the śūdras and others should be kept confined and fettered.[2] But irrespective of varṇa considerations, he provides the same fine of eight paṇas for all those who break the restraint and run away.[3] He also adds that while in restraint there should be no obstruction to the performance of daily obligatory rites in the case of the members of all the four varṇas.[4]

The laws of inheritance continue to have the provision of giving the smallest share to the śūdra son[5] of a higher caste person. Viṣṇu fixes the share of the śūdra son of a brāhmaṇa in various circumstances,[6] and lays down the liberal rule that, if the twice-born father has a śūdra son, he can inherit one half of his property.[7] But Bṛhaspati repeats the old view that even an excellent and obedient śūdra son of a man having no other male issue shall receive only a maintenance.[8] It is said that the son of the twice-born from a śūdra woman is not entitled to a share in landed property.[9] But at one place the *Anuśāsana Parvan* emphasises that the śūdra son must receive property,[10] a provision which is generally corroborated by the law-books of this period.

1. VIII. 24.
2. *dvijātiḥ pratibhūhīno rakṣyaḥ syād bāhyacāribhiḥ; śūdrādīnpratibhūhīnān bandhayennigaḍena tu. Kātyā.*, verse 118.
3. Verse 119.
4. *Ibid.*
5. *Yāj.*, II. 125; *Bṛ.*, XXVI. 41-42; *Anu. P.*, (SE) 82.18 & 21, (NE) 47.18 & 21.
6. XVIII. 38-39
7. *Viṣṇu*, XVIII. 32.
8. *Bṛ.*, XXVI. 125. Cf. *Anu. P.*, (SE) 85.15, (NE) 47.15.
9. *Bṛ.*, XXVI. 122.
10. *Anu. P.*, (SE) 19.82, (NE) 47.19.

It is provided that the property of the śūdra shall be equally divided among his sons.[1] Yājñavalkya states that the son of a śūdra from a slave shall receive a share in property if the father desires so.[2] The *Anuśāsana Parvan* adds that this share should be the tenth part of the property.[3]

The old provision making for different rates of interest for the four different varṇas recurs in the two law-books of this period.[4] But Yājñavalkya modifies this by stating that whatever is agreed upon may be paid as interest.[5]

The law of treasure-trove is based on considerations of varṇa. According to the lawgivers, if the brāhmaṇa finds treasure, he may take the whole of it.[6] Viṣṇu adds that in such a case the kṣatriya should make over $\frac{1}{4}$ to the king and the brāhmaṇa each, and retain the remaining half; a vaiśya should give $\frac{1}{4}$ to the king, $\frac{1}{2}$ to the brāhmaṇa and should retain $\frac{1}{4}$ for himself; a śūdra should divide the find into twelve parts, give five parts each to the king and the brāhmaṇa, and should retain $\frac{1}{6}$ for himself.[7] Although the śūdra's share in the treasure-trove is the smallest, it is double the share of the labourer as provided by Kauṭilya.[8] How far the laws regarding treasure-trove worked is difficult to say. A Jain text refers to a king who confiscated the treasure-trove discovered by a merchant but honoured a brāhmaṇa who discovered a similar treasure-trove.[9]

Generally Nārada, and in some cases Bṛhaspati, repeat the cruel corporal punishments against śūdras offending against brāhmaṇas.[10] Bṛhaspati states that a śūdra should not be subjected to pecuniary punishments but to beating, chaining and

1. *Ibid.*, (SE) 82.57, (NE) 47.56.
2. *Yāj.*, II. 133.
3. *Anu. P.*, (SE) 84.18.
4. *Yāj.*, II. 37; *Viṣṇu*, VI. 15.
5. II. 38.
6. *Viṣṇu*, II. 58; *Yāj*, II. 34-35; *Nār.*, VII. 6-7.
7. *Viṣṇu*, III. 59-61.
8. *dvādaśamāṃśa bhṛtakah*. *AŚ*, IV. 1.
9. *Niśītha Cūrni*, 20. p. 281. Quoted in Jain, *op. cit.*, p. 62.
10. *Nār.*, XV & XVI. 22, 23-25, 26-28. Introd. to Plaint, II. 37.

ridicule.[1] Bṛhaspati is particularly harsh on the *pratilomas* (i.e. those born of higher caste mothers and lower caste fathers) and the *antyas* (untouchables), whom he considers the dregs of society. If they offend against brāhmaṇas, they should be beaten and never amerced in a fine.[2] The same provision occurs in Nārada in regard to the śvapacas, medas, caṇḍālas, elephant-drivers, dāsas etc.[3] Nārada adds that in these cases the offended parties should punish the offenders themselves, for the king has nothing to do with the penalty to be inflicted on the guilty.[4] This is an important indication of the weakening of state power. The rule that if a brāhmaṇa abuses a śūdra he must pay 12½ paṇas as a fine is repeated in the law-books of this time.[5] But Bṛhaspati adds that this applies only to the case of virtuous śūdras; no offence is imputable to a brāhmaṇa for abusing a śūdra devoid of virtue.[6] Probably this refers to the untouchable sections of the śūdras, who in such cases had no redress in law. But in this respect other sections of the śūdras enjoyed legal protection against offences committed by the members of the three higher varṇas.[7]

Although it is stated that the śūdras should be subjected to corporal punishments, the scale of punishments, which is provided by Bṛhaspati for śūdras abusing vaiśyas, kṣatriyas and brāhmaṇas,[8] does not give any indication of this. Fa-hsien informs us that in the Middle Kingdom the king governed without decapitation or other corporal punishments.[9] This may be an exaggeration but suggests that corporal punishment was used less frequently than before, a factor which worked in favour of the śūdras. Although Yājñavalkya accepts the principle of varṇa

1. *tāḍanaṃ bandhanaṃ caiva tathaiva ca viḍannakam; eṣa daṇḍo hi śūdrasya nārthadaṇḍo bṛhaspatiḥ. Bṛ.* IX. 20. The word *viḍambanam* in Ms. Ia according to Rangaswami Aiyangar's classification gives a better reading than *viḍannakam.*
2. *Bṛ.*, IX. 18.
3. XV-XVI. 11-14.
4. *Nār.*, XV-XVI. 13.
5. *Manu,* VIII. 267-69; *Nār.*, XV & XVI. 16; *Bṛ.*, XX. 12.
6. XX. 13.
7. *Bṛ.* XX. 10.
8. *Ibid.*, XX. 16.
9. J. Legge. *A Record of Buddhistic Kingdoms*, p. 43.

legislation,[1] he does not repeat the Draconian measures of Manu against offending śūdras. In one of his provisions regarding assault there is no trace of varṇa distinctions. He states that, if both parties threaten with arms, the punishment shall be the same to all.[2] But if a non-brāhmaṇa causes pain to a brāhmaṇa, he shall be deprived of his limb.[3] It is not clear whether this law applies to śūdras assaulting brāhmaṇas.

Viṣṇu provides the highest amercement for connection with a woman of one's own caste, and the second amercement for adultery with a woman of the lower caste.[4] Curiously enough he lays down the punishment of death (unless the term *vadhya* be taken in the sense of beating) for adultery with a woman of one of the lowest castes.[5] But this is in conflict with another provision of his, according to which a brāhmaṇa guilty of intercourse with a caṇḍāla woman for a night can remove his guilt by subsisting upon alms and constantly repeating the *gāyatri* for three years.[6] It is to be noted, however, that the severe punishment prescribed by Manu against a śūdra committing adultery with a twice-born woman is not mentioned in any law-book of this period.

The law-books of this period do not provide for the discriminatory scale of compensation for the murder of the members of the four varṇas. Viṣṇu, however, introduces such a scale of penances for the expiation of the sin of murder. Thus a person guilty of killing a brāhmaṇa, a kṣatriya, a vaiśya or a śūdra should perform the *mahāvrata* penance respectively for 12, 9, 6 and 3 years.[7] There is nothing to show that such penances were enforced, but they reflect the relative importance of the life of the members of the four varṇas. Nevertheless, Viṣṇu and Yājñavalkya regard the murder of a kṣatriya, a vaiśya, or a śūdra

1. II. 206.
2. *parasparaṃ tu sarveṣāṃ śastre madhyamasāhasaḥ. Yāj.*, II. 216.
3. *Yāj.*, II. 215. In the text the term *piḍanam* is explained by Vijñāneśvara as beating etc.
4. V. 40-41.
5. *antyāgamane vadhyaḥ. Viṣṇu*, V. 41.
6. *Viṣṇu*, LIV. 9.
7. *Ibid.*, L. 6 & 12-14.

as a crime of the fourth degree (*upapātaka*),[1] and according to the former the guilty are required to perform the *cāndrāyaṇa* or *parāka* penances, or to sacrifice a cow.[2] Such a provision places the śūdra on a footing of equality with the vaiśya and the kṣatriya, and emphasises the special position of the brāhmaṇa. A passage in one of the manuscripts of the *Śānti Parvan* also betrays this tendency. It states that, if a kṣatriya, a vaiśya, or a śūdra kills a brāhmaṇa, either his eyes should be taken out or he should be killed; but if the offender is a brāhmaṇa, he should be banished.[3] Another passage from the same manuscript states that the brāhmaṇa who is guilty of sinful actions and is a murderer or a thief among the *vipras*, and a kṣatriya, a vaiśya or a śūdra guilty of killing the brāhmaṇas, should be deprived of their eyes.[4] Thus there is no mention of varṇa distinctions in this case.

It seems that varṇa distinctions in the administration of the criminal law were undermined in the Gupta period. An inscription of the 6th century A.D. in Western India does not mention varṇa punishments for defamation, assault and injury.[5] Fa-hsien informs us that in Mid-India every criminal was fined according to the gravity of his offence,[6] which suggests that the offender was not punished according to his varṇa. It is likely that in the administration of the criminal law the brāhmaṇa was shown some favour, but the śūdra was not singled out for harsh punishments in the same manner as we find in earlier times.

1. *Viṣṇu*, XXXVII. 13, 34; *Yāj.*, II. 236.
2. *Viṣṇu*, XXXVII. 35. The provision for sacrificing a cow is evidently very ancient, and we cannot believe that it was followed in Gupta times. No doubt Viṣṇu took it over uncritically from a much earlier source.
3. *Ms. D7s* (acc. to Cr. Edn. classification), verse 45. In the *Mṛcchakaṭika* (IX. 39) the presiding judge recommends the exemption of the brāhmaṇa Cārudatta from the death penalty. For such immunity also see *Kātyā.*, verse 483.
4. *Ms. D7s* (acc. to Cr. Edn. classification), verse 55.
5. *JRASB*, Series III, xvi, p. 118.
6. S. Beal, *Travels of Fa-hien*, pp. 54-55. Giles also gives a similar translation (*Travels of Fa-hisen*, pp. 21), but Legge translates that "criminals are fined according to the circumstances (of each case)" (*A Record of Buddhistic Kingdoms*, p. 43), which may suggest varṇa distinctions.

Nārada upholds the old view that, in case of theft, the brāhmaṇa's guilt is the highest and that of the śūdra the lowest.[1] This was perhaps based on the principle that a brāhmaṇa should acquire and practise the full measure of dharma, a rājanya $\frac{3}{4}$ dharma, a vaiśya $\frac{1}{2}$ dharma and a śūdra $\frac{1}{4}$ dharma. The heaviness or lightness of sins for purposes of expiation of each of the four varṇas should be determined upon this principle.[2] Kātyāyana also seems to think of theft when he provides that a kṣatriya or a brāhmaṇa should be awarded double the punishment which is provided for a śūdra.[3] The fact that the vaiśyas are not mentioned in this connection shows that they were becoming merged with the śūdras. But all this would suggest that śūdras were considered habitual thieves, an inference which is also corroborated by the *Amarakośa*, in which words for thieves and *dasyus* are listed in the *śūdra-varga*.[4]

The *dasyus* are repeatedly mentioned in the *Śānti Parvan* as enemies of the king, always threatening the peace and tranquillity of the realm.[5] Probably this refers to enemies outside the state and not to the śūdras. For it is provided that, if the troubles created by the dasyus cause the intermixture of varṇas, brāhmaṇas, vaiśyas, and śūdras — all can take up arms.[6] It is argued that, be he a śūdra or be he a member of any other order, he who becomes a raft on a raftless current, a means of crossing where means there are none, certainly deserves respect in every way.[7] The person who protects helpless men against the dasyus deserves to be worshipped by all as if he were a kinsman.[8] The *Dhanurveda Saṃhitā*[9] lays down that, while the members of the

1. *Manu*, VIII. 337 & 8; *Nārada*, Appendix (Theft), Pariśiṣṭa, 51 & 52.
2. *ŚP*, 36. 28-29.
3. Verse 485.
4. *AK*, II. 10. 25-26. Cf. *Anu. P.*, (SE) 143.21, (NE) 94. 21.
5. *ŚP*, 12.27, 25-11, 67.2, 76.5, 88.26, 90.8, 98.8, 101.3.
6. *ŚP*, 79. 17-18, *abhyutthite dasyubale kṣatrārthe varṇasaṃkare; ... brāhmaṇo yadi vā vaiśyaḥ, śūdro vā rājasattama; dasyubhyo'tha prajā rakṣeddaṇḍaṃ dharmeṇa dhārayan* ... *Ibid.*, 79.34-36.
7. *ŚP*, 78.37.
8. *Ibid.*, 78.38.
9. Although this work is ascribed to Vasiṣṭha, its style is not similar to that of the law-book of Vasiṣṭha. But the importance which it attaches to archery may suggest that the work was compiled not later than the Gupta period.

three upper varṇas can ordinarily take up arms, the śūdra can do so only in times of danger.[1] But it adds that a brāhmaṇa should use a bow, a kṣatriya a sword, a vaiśya a lance and a śūdra a mace.[2] Thus the above references clearly show that śūdras were conceded the right to bear arms. This indicates a very significant change in their civic status, for the early lawgivers do not permit them to bear arms. The new development links up with the transformation of śūdras into peasants, and shows that the old apprehension of their getting completely out of hand no longer exercised the minds of the upholders of the varṇa system. It seems that śūdras were actually enrolled in the army. In a drama of this period two army officers are represented as belonging respectively to the castes of barbers and leather workers.[3]

But concessions made to śūdras did not bring about the complete cessation of internal conflict between the varṇas. There are at least nine verses in the *Śānti Parvan* stressing the necessity of combination and harmony between the first two varṇas,[4] which probably indicate some combined opposition on the part of the vaiśyas and śūdras. It is complained that at one stage the śūdras and vaiśyas, acting most wilfully, began to unite themselves with the wives of brāhmaṇas.[5] There are several references which suggest that the śūdras were especially antagonistic to the existing order. The *Anuśāsana Parvan* avers that śūdras are destroyers of the king, and hence a wise ruler should not be complacent towards this danger.[6] A long passage of the *Āśvamedhika Parvan*, which partly reproduces a similar passage from the *Vasiṣṭha Dharmaśāstra*, characterises the śūdras as hostile, violent, boastful, short-tempered, untruthful, extremely greedy, ungrateful, heterodox, lazy and impure.[7]

1. *Dhanurveda Saṃhitā*, verse 3.
2. *Ibid.*, verse 8.
3. Cases of Vīraka and Candanaka in the *Mṛcchakaṭika*, VI. 22 & 23.
4. *ŚP*. 73.9, 74.4, 5, 8, 10, 28, 32, 75.13,22.
5. *ŚP*, 49.60-61.
6. *śūdrāḥ pṛthivyāṃ bahavo rājñāṃ bahuvināśakāḥ*; *tasmātpramādaṃ suśroṇi na kuryāt paṇḍito nṛpaḥ*. *Anu. P.*, (SE) 214. 58.
7. *Vas. Dh. S.*, IV. 24; *Āśvamedhika P.*, (SE) 118. 17-20. The *Amarakośa* (II. 10.3) characterises the śūdras as lazy and dexterous (*dakṣa*).

Similarly, like Manu, the *Śānti Parvan* defines a vṛṣala (i.e. a śūdra) as one who defies the established order (dharma).[1] The hostile attitude of the śūdra can be also inferred from a passage of the *Nārada Smṛti*. It declares that, if the king does not exercise the power of the sword (*daṇḍa*), brāhmaṇas, kṣatriyas and vaiśyas will all abandon their work, but the śūdras will surpass all the rest.[2] Yājñavalkya repeats the provision of Kauṭilya that the śūdra who pierces the eyes of others,[3] pretends to be a brāhmaṇa, and acts against the king should be fined a sum of 800 paṇas.[4] Certain sections of śūdras such as actors, gamblers, keepers of gaming houses and other persons of this kind are considered sources of disorder to the state, for they cause harm to the better classes of subjects (*bhadrikāḥ prajāḥ*).[5] A passage from a manuscript of the *Śānti Parvan* ordains that dāsas and mlecchas should be dealt with through the same agencies, and that force should be used against the caṇḍālas and mlecchas.[6] All this suggests that the old antagonism between śūdras and the ruling classes continued in some form or other, but it probably lost in intensity thanks to the provisions for śūdra ministers, the association of the head of the guilds of artisans with the work of the district administration, the lessening of varṇa distinctions in the administration of law, and finally the recognition of the śūdras' right to bear arms in times of emergency.

The old fiction about the origin of the four varṇas[7] continues to be repeated, but the *Vāyu* and *Brahmāṇḍa* Purāṇas affirm the statement of Manu that Vasiṣṭha was the progenitor of the śūdras,[8] which means lending legitimacy to their improved social status.

1. *ŚP*, 91. 12-13.
2. *Nār.*, XVIII. 14-16.
3. Acc. to *Viramitrodaya*.
4. *Yāj.*, II. 304. *Manu* (IX. 224) provides the punishment of death for a *dvijaliṅgin śūdra* (who pretends to be a brāhmaṇa), but he does not refer to his opposition to the king in this connection.
5. *ŚP*, 89. 13-14. Kauṭilya does not permit such people to enter new settlements. *AŚ*, II. 1.
6. *Ms. D7s* (acc. to Cr. Edn. classification), verse 20.
7. *Yāj.*, III. 126.
8. *Vā. P.*, ii. 11.90; *Brahmāṇḍa P.*, iii. 10.96.

The association of the four colours white, red, yellow and black respectively with the four varṇas shows their relative social status.[1] In representing the actors, the *Nāṭyaśāstra* prescribes red for the brāhmaṇa and the kṣatriya,[2] and dark or deep blue for the vaiśyas and śūdras.[3] This work also lays down that in the auditorium a white pillar should be erected for marking seats for the brāhmaṇas, a red pillar for the kṣatriyas, a yellow pillar for the vaiśyas and a blue-black pillar for the śūdras.[4] Gold and ear ornaments should be thrown at the foot of the brāhmaṇa pillar, copper at the foot of the kṣatriya pillar, silver at the foot of the vaiśya pillar and iron at the foot of the śūdra pillar.[5] Such provisions are similar to the fiction invented by Plato that philosophers were made of gold, warriors of silver, and agriculturists and artisans of brass and iron.[6]

The rule that only the śūdra should bear the title of *dāsa*[7] does not seem to have been followed. Thus the name of an ancestor of Ravikīrti, a brāhmaṇa, was Varāhadāsa;[8] and the name of a ruling chief of the Sanakānīkas, who was a feudatory of Candra Gupta II, was Mahārāja Viṣṇudāsa.[9] The *Nāṭyaśāstra* ordains that in a drama the names of the brāhmaṇas and kṣatriyas should indicate their *gotra* and functions, those of traders their generosity, and those of servants different kinds of flowers.[10] It is not clear why the śūdras were to be named after flowers.

The rule that different terms should be used in enquiring about the health of different varṇas does not seem to have

1. *Vā. P.*, App. No. 818. Quoted in Patil, *Cultural History from the Vāyu Purāṇa*, p. 304. This distinction also occurs in the *Śānti Parvan*.
2. In another manuscript the *gauḍa* (fair) colour is prescribed.
3. *Nāṭyaśāstra*, XXI. 113. Black is also recommended for the Pañcālas, Śūrasenas, Māgadhas, Aṅgas, Vaṅgas and Kaliṅgas (*Ibid.*, XXI. 112).
4. *Ibid.*, II. 49-52.
5. *Ibid.*, II. 55.
6. *The Republic* (Jowett's Tr.), pp. 126-27.
7. *Viṣṇu*, XXVII. 6-9.
8. *CII*, iii, No. 35 (dated A.D. 533-34), ll. 9-12.
9. *Ibid.*, No. 3 (dated A.D. 401-02), ll. 1-2; cf. Fleet, *op. cit.*, p. 11, fn. 1.
10. XVII. 95-99.

been emphasised during this period. But the *Nātyaśāstra* provides that in the drama a mode of address indicating command should be used in conversing with servants of both sexes, artisans and mechanics.[1] This shows that low caste people were addressed contemptuously. In the *Mṛcchakaṭika* abusive expressions such as "sons of slave women", "sons of concubines" and "bastards" are used in addressing low class people.[2]

The *Nāṭyaśāstra* also prescribes a different kind of gait and movement for the portrayal of menial servants on the stage. According to this text one of their sides or the head or a hand or a foot should be lowered, and their eyes should move to different objects.[3] Such behaviour suggests lack of confidence and shows that members of the lower orders were not encouraged to hold their heads high in the company of their masters.

Yājñavalkya states that an elderly śūdra deserves respect.[4] Unlike the early lawgivers, he does not insist that vaiśya and śūdra guests should be made to work and then fed with the servants. He provides, however, that guests should be received and fed in the order of their varṇas.[5] But his provision that a guest should not be turned away in the evening and should be offered whatever is available[6] is not confined to the members of any particular varṇa. The Dharmasūtra rule of providing food to caṇḍālas at the end of the Vaiśvadeva ceremony is repeated during this period,[7] and slaves, śvapacas and beggars are added to this list.[8]

The texts of the period repeatedly state that a brāhmaṇa should not accept the food of a śūdra, for it reduces his spiritual

1. XVII. 73.
2. *Mṛcchakaṭika*, Act I, p. 5. Act II, pp. 63-64. Some of these terms such as *chiṇāliāputta* are still used in Bihār.
3. *...nīcādi ceṭādinām*. XII. 146-48.
4. *Yāj.*, I. 116. Unlike Gautama, he does not fix the age limit of eighty years.
5. *Ibid.*, I. 107.
6. *Ibid.*
7. *Āp. Dh. S.*, II. 4.9.5; *Bau. Dh. S.*, II. 3.5. 11.
8. *Yāj.*, I. 103; *Anu. P.*, (SE) 154.22, 250.15.

strength.[1] The *Śānti Parvan* does not allow the brāhmaṇa to take the food of carpenters, leather workers, washermen and dyers.[2] According to Yājñavalkya the food of the śūdras and outcastes (*patitas*) is not permitted to a snātaka.[3] He further specifies that a snātaka should not take the food of a stage-player, a bamboo worker, a goldsmith, a weapon seller, an artisan, a tailor, a dyer, one whose living is by dogs, a butcher, a washerman or an oilmaker.[4] There also begins the tendency to ban the food of some śūdras for the kṣatriyas. It is said that a kṣatriya must eschew food given by those śūdras who are addicted to evil ways and who partake of all manner of food without any scruple.[5] The *Anuśāsana Parvan* declares that the man who takes food from a śūdra swallows the very abomination of the earth, drinks the excretions of the human body, and partakes of the filth of all the world.[6] Perhaps this is meant to deter the brāhmaṇas from adopting such a course. Penances are provided for the purification of the brāhmaṇa who accepts the food of śūdras or eats in the company of vaiśyas and kṣatriyas.[7]

The rules for the boycott of the śūdra's food have a very limited application. They mostly apply either to the brāhmaṇas or to the snātakas, who may have been chiefly brāhmaṇas. Even the brāhmaṇa is permitted to take milk and curd at the house of a śūdra.[8] Further, if the brāhmaṇa is unable to procure food from the twice-born for his livelihood, he may accept it from a śūdra.[9] Yājñavalkya repeats Manu's rule that among the śūdras, a snātaka can take food from his herdsman,

1. *Āśvamedhika Parvan*, (SE) 110.17-20, 61.44-45; *Bṛhaspati*, Śrāddha Khaṇḍa, verse 43.
2. *ŚP*, 37. 22-23. The term *raṅgajīvinaḥ* may indicate either a dyer or an actor.
3. I. 160.
4. *Yāj.*, I. 161-65. The term *cākrika* may mean an oilmaker, a potter, or a coachman.
5. *Anu. P.*, (NE) 135. 2-3, (SE) 198. 3.
6. *Ibid.*, (NE) 135.5, (SE) 198.5.
7. *Ibid.*, (NE) 136.20-22, (SE) 199. 20-22.
8. *Āśvamedhika P.*, (SE) 110.24.
9. *Ibid*, 110.32.

a friend of the family, his slave, his barber, his sharecropper and one who surrenders himself to him for the sake of maintenance.[1] Bṛhaspati also provides that food can be accepted from slaves and domestic servants.[2]

The idea that a twice-born should eat or touch the leavings of the śūdra's food was considered horrible, and appropriate penances were provided for the expiation of the sin.[3]

There is no evidence of forbidding accepting water from certain śūdra castes, except in the case of the caṇḍālas and other untouchables The *Mṛcchakaṭika* informs us that the same well was open to the śūdras and brāhmaṇas.[4]

Yājñavalkya prohibits certain kinds of food for the twice-born. The twice-born is not permitted to take wine. Penances are provided for the brāhmaṇa wife if she violates this rule,[5] but according to Vijñāneśvara these are not necessary if a śūdra wife drinks wine.[6] Drinking seems to have been a vice specially associated with the śūdras, for the list of words for spirituous liquor and various processes of its preparation and for intoxication are enumerated by Amara in the *śūdra-varga*;[7] words for gambling are also listed in the same section.[8] In the *Pañcatantra* a drunken weaver is represented as beating his wife.[9] Yājñavalkya also forbids the use of the milk of a cow in heat, within ten days of the birth of her calf, and of one without a calf; as also of a camel, a single-hoofed animal, a woman, a wild animal or a sheep.[10] An oblation intended for gods, sacrificial viands, *śigru* (a kind of horseradish), unhallowed meat, fungi, carnivorous animals, and a number of birds such as the parrot, the swan, the *vaka*, the *cakravāka* etc. are declared uneatable for the twice-born,[11] and penances are provided for the expiation of the

1. I. 166.
2. XV. 19.
3. *Bṛhaspati*, Prāyaścitta, verses 34, 86-88, Ācāra, verse 87.
4. I. 32.
5. *Yāj.*, III. 255-56.
6. Comm. to *Yāj.*, III. 255-56.
7. *AK*, II. 10. 39-43.
8. *Ibid.*, II. 10. 44-46.
9. *Pañcatantra*, p. 15.
10. *Yāj.*, I. 170.
11. *Ibid.*, I. 171-173.

sin arising out of the violation of the rule in some cases.[1] Yājñavalkya further states that, among the five-clawed animals, the twice-born should not take the porcupine, alligator, tortoise, hedgehog and the hare; he also specifies the four varieties of fish which a twice-born should take.[2] He prohibits the eating of roots, onion, garlic, village pig, mushroom and leek; those who violate this rule should perform the *cāndrāyaṇa* penance.[3] Fa-hsien informs us that onion and garlic were taken only by the caṇḍālas.[4] Yājñavalkya lays down that the person who compels a śūdra to partake of the prohibited food shall be subjected to half the punishment involved in the first amercement, which shall increase if the offence is committed against the members of the higher varṇas.[5] This would suggest that certain items of food were tabooed even for the śūdras, but these are not specified by Yājñavalkya. On the other hand the list of food items prohibited for the twice-born clearly implies that they could be taken by the śūdras. The *Bṛhaspati Smṛti* states that in the Middle Kingdom labourers and artisans eat the meat of cows,[6] which shows that even the strong brāhmaṇical propaganda against cow slaughter did not always succeed in stopping this old practice among the masses of the people. This can also be inferred from a didactic anecdote, probably inserted in the *Vāyu Purāṇa* during this period. It relates that Pṛṣadhra, son of Manu Vaivasvata, ate the flesh of his preceptor's cow, upon which the sage Cyavana cursed him to become a śūdra.[7] Thus the above discussion would show that the food habits of śūdras were somewhat different from those of the members of the twice-born varṇas.

Family life is enjoined for a śūdra in the same manner as for

1. *Ibid.*, I. 175-76.
2. *Ibid.*, I. 177-78.
3. *Ibid.*, I. 176.
4. Legge, *A Record of Buddhistic Kingdoms*, p. 43.
5. II. 296.
6. *madhyadeśe karmakarāḥ śilpinaśca gavāśinaḥ. Bṛ*, p. 21, verse 128. Ambedkar argues that beef-eating was one of the root causes of the origin of untouchability (*The Untouchables*, Ch. IX), but there is nothing to show that these artisans and labourers were regarded as untouchables.
7. Quoted from *Vā. P.* in Patil, *op. cit.*, p. 38.

a member of any other varṇa.[1] But the śūdras continue to have their own marriage practices.[2] The *Anuśāsana Parvan* states that the marriage of the three higher varṇas has to be accomplished through the joining of hands with the mantras, but the marriage of the śūdras is accomplished through sexual intercourse.[3] A Jain source refers to a *svayaṃvara* hall at Tosalī, where a slave girl selected her husband from an assembly of slave boys.[4] Several references suggest that in the śūdra community women continued to be comparatively freer than in the higher classes Commenting on a passage of Yājñavalkya, Viśvarūpa is of the opinion that the Smṛti texts about *niyoga* refer to śūdras,[5] and supports his view by quoting two verses of Vṛddha Manu and a *gāthā* of the *Vāyu Purāṇa*.[6] In the case of the absence of the husband it was far easier for a śūdra wife to secure dissolution of the marriage tie and take another husband than in the case of the wives of the other three varṇas. In such a case the *Anuśāsana Parvan* prescribes a waiting period of only one year for the śūdra wife.[7] But Nārada, who specifies the waiting periods for vaiśya, kṣatriya and brāhmaṇa wives, declares that no such definite period is prescribed for a śūdra woman whose husband is gone on a journey.[8] Again, the repetition of the provision that wives of herdsmen, oilmakers, distillers etc. are responsible for the payment of debts incurred by their husbands[9] shows that these śūdra women did not always depend for their livelihood on their menfolk.

Viṣṇu states that, if a girl is not married after she has attained maturity, she should be considered to be a degraded woman.[10]

1. *Mārk. P.*, 69. 72 quoted in Hazra, *op. cit.*, p. 232.

2. The *Anuśāsana Parvan* (NE 44.9, SE 79.9) repeats the old rule that the *āsura* and *paiśāca* forms of marriage should not be performed, presumably by the twice-born.

3. *uttamānāṃ tu varṇānāṃ mantravatpāṇisaṃgrahaḥ; vivāhakaranaṃ cāhuḥ śūdrāṇāṃ saṃprayogataḥ. Anu. P.*, (SE) 249.9.

4. *Bṛhatkalpa Bhāṣya*, 2. 3446 quoted in Jain, *op. cit.*, p. 159.

5. *evaṃ tācchūdrāṇāṃ niyogādhikāraḥ uktaḥ* on *Yāj.*, I. 69, Kane, *Hist. Dh. S.*, ii, pt. I, 604.

6. Texts quoted in Kane, *Hist. Dh. S.*, ii. pt. I. pp. 604-05.

7. *Anu. P.*, (SE) 149. 15-16.

8. XII. 100.

9. *Yāj.*, I. 48; *Kātyā.*, verse 568.

10. *Viṣṇu*, XXIV. 41.

The commentator Nandarāja observes that this rule applies to young women of the lower castes only,[1] but there is nothing in the text to warrant such an assumption.

The view that members of the higher varṇas can take wives from the members of the lower varṇas is expressed in the texts of this period also.[2] But there also recurs the idea that wives from the lowest order, i.e. śūdras, are to be espoused for the sake of pleasure.[3] The *Kāmasūtra* does not differentiate the maid servants, *kumbhadāsis* (maid servants employed in carrying water or harlots?) and wives of washermen and weavers from the prostitutes.[4] According to this work intercourse with a śūdra woman is neither prohibited nor considered wise.[5] Vātsyāyana commends marriage within one's own varṇa.[6] In particular, the idea that the brāhmaṇa should wed a śūdrā, or have intercourse with her or beget sons on her, is strongly discounted in the texts of the period.[7] But there are cases of deviations from this rule. In the *Mṛcchakaṭika* the brāhmaṇa Cārudatta marries the prostitute Vasantasenā, although this is done with the special permission of the king.[8] The same drama represents the brāhmaṇa Śarvilaka as marrying his slave Madanikā.[9] The literature of the period also supplies instances of kṣatriyas marrying śūdra women.[10]

That marriages between the members of the higher varṇas were not altogether absent is also suggested by the repetition of the

1. *SBE*, vii, 109, fn. 41.
2. *Nār.*, XII. 4-6; *Anu. P.*, (NE) 44.11, (SE)79.11.
3. *Anu. P.*, (NE) 44.12 & 13.
4. VI. 6.54 with comm.
5. *Kāma. S.*, I. 5.3.
6. *Ibid.*, III. 1.1.
7. *Yāj.*, I.56-57; *Bṛ.*, Āpaddharma, verse 47, Saṃskāra, verse 375-77; *Anu. P.*, (NE) 44. 13, 47. 8-9; *Āśvamedhika Parvan*, (SE) 117.10. If a person has intercourse with a *pukkasī*, he is purified by performing the *parāka* penance. *Bṛ.*, Prāyaścitta, verse 70.
8. *Mṛ. Kaṭ.*, Act. X.
9. An epigraphic record of the 8th cen. A.D. informs us that the maternal ancestor of the ruler Lokanātha, who was a brāhmaṇa, begot a son (*pāraśava*) on a śūdra wife. *EI*, xv, p. 301.
10. *Mālavikāgnimitra*, I, p. 10; Jain, *op. cit.*, pp. 155-56

theory of the origin of the mixed castes [1] It has been suggested earlier that Manu's list of the mixed castes given in the tenth chapter of his law-book probably belongs to the fifth century A.D. The *Anuśāsana Parvan* enumerates fifteen old mixed castes,[2] and introduces four new castes of māṃsas, svâdukaras, kṣaudras saugandhas, who are represented to have been born from māgadhī mothers through wicked men of the four varṇas.[3] There is also mention of the madranābhas, who are supposed to have been derived from the niṣâdas and described as riding on cars drawn by asses.[4] The vrātya is defined not as one who has fallen from the duties of the twice-born, but as one who is begotten upon a kṣatriya woman by a śūdra,[5] and is placed in the category of the caṇḍāla.[6] It is also stated that a vaidya is begotten by a śūdra on a vaiśya woman.[7] This is typical of the low esteem in which physicians were held in early times. The *Amarakośa* introduces a new caste māhiṣas, who are described as the issues of kṣatriyas from vaiśya (aryā) women. Probably they were identical with the Māhiṣakas, who appear as degraded śūdras along with the Draviḍas, Kaliṅgas, Pulindas, Uśīnaras, Śakas, Yavanas and Kāmbojas.[8] If we add the seven additional mixed castes known from the *Anuśāsana Parvan* to those known from Manu, the number will come to sixty-eight. Though the theory of the origins of new castes through the intermixture of varṇas was fanciful, by this time it may have influenced the course of social developments; for even in our times such cases are noticeable in Eastern Nepāl.

The law-books of the period retain the distinction between the śūdras and untouchables. Thus Yājñavalkya lays down that a śūdra who has intercourse with a caṇḍāla woman is reduced to her position.[9] Śūdras and śvapakas are mentioned separately

1. *Yāj.*, I. 91-94; *Nār.*, XII., 108, 111 and 113; *Amarakośa*, II. 10. 1-4.
2. *Anu. P.*, (NE) 48. 5-27, (SE) 84. 17.
3. *Ibid.*, (NE) 47.22, (SE) 83. 22.
4. *Ibid.*, (NE) 47.23, (SE) 83.23.
5. *Ibid.*, (SE) 49.9.
6. *Ibid.*, (SE) 84.28.
7. *Ibid.*, (NE) 49.9.
8. *Ibid.*, (Cal), 33. 21-23.
9. II. 294.

in several texts.[1] But in the *Amarakośa* mixed castes and untouchables are looked upon as part of the śūdra community. Ten mixed castes, the karaṇa, the ambaṣṭha, the udgra (probably ugra), the māgadha, the māhiṣa, the kṣattṛ, the sūta, the vaidehaka, the rathakāra and the caṇḍāla are included in the *śūdra-varga* of that work.[2] The vaidehaka (trader) is, however, listed in the *vaiśya-varga* also.[3]

Amara gives ten names for caṇḍālas, some of which such as *plava*, *divākīrti*, *janaṅgama* are rarely mentioned in the earlier texts,[4] which may suggest an increase in the number of this untouchable caste. This can be also inferred from the fact that while the caṇḍālas are not mentioned by the Greek writers of the earlier period, they attracted the special attention of Fa-hsien.[5]

The ḍombas, who came to form a numerous section of the untouchables in Northern India in subsequent times, seem to have appeared as a caste in the Gupta period. The Jain sources describe them as a despised class.[6] They were probably one of the aboriginal tribes, who were assimilated to the lower orders of brāhmaṇical society. Wild tribes such as the Kirātas, Śabaras, and Pulindas, along with the Mlecchas, are included in the *śūdra-varga* of the *Amarakośa*,[7] which shows that large masses of tribal population were being absorbed in the śūdra community.

During this period there seems to have been not only an increase in the number of the untouchables but also some intensification in the practice of untouchability. The *Bṛhaspati Smṛti* provides a penance for removing the sin arising out of touching a caṇḍāla.[8] Fa-hsien informs us that, when the caṇḍālas enter the gate of a city or a market-place, they strike

1. *Kātyā.*, verse 351. *Āśvamedhika Parvan*, (SE) 116.19.
2. *AK*, II. 10. 1-4.
3. *Ibid.*, II. 9.78.
4. *Ibid.*, II. 10.20.
5. Legge, *A Record of the Buddhistic Kingdoms*, p. 43.
6. *Vyavahāra Bhāṣya*, 3. 92; *Niśītha Cūrṇi*, 11, p. 747 quoted in Jain, *op. cit.*, p. 360.
7. *AK*, II. 10.21.
8. *Bṛ.*, Prāyaścitta, verses 49-50. A penance is also provided for a *rajasvalā*, if she is touched by a śvapāka (*Ibid.*, Prāyaścitta, verse 87).

a piece of wood to give prior notice of their arrival so that men may know and avoid them.[1] The *Mārkaṇḍeya Purāṇa* provides a purificatory rite for the person who looks at an *antyaja* or an *antyāvasāyin*.[2] But the practice of untouchability was observed mainly in respect of the caṇḍālas. There is no direct evidence that the ḍombas were regarded as untouchables. Similarly there is nothing to show that the carmakāras, who came to be looked upon as untouchables in later times, were regarded as such during this period.

There is not much new information about the occupations of the mixed castes and untouchables. Manu's rule that these castes are to be recognised by their occupations recurs in the *Anuśāsana Parvan*.[3] The caṇḍālas continued to be employed in the work of cleaning streets, working in the cremation grounds, executing criminals and tracking down thieves at night.[4] Hunting constituted an important occupation of the lower sections of the śūdras. Curiously enough, the *Amarakośa* catalogues not only fowlers and hunters in the *śūdra-varga*,[5] but also ordinary dogs, dogs trained for chase, village hogs, and deer wounded on the right side;[6] so also are mentioned snare, net, rope and cage for trapping birds in the same section.[7] Fa-hsien informs us that the caṇḍālas are fishermen and hunters, and sell flesh and meat.[8] But the caṇḍālas are mentioned by Kālidāsa as separate from the fowlers and fishermen although they all belong to the same class.[9] Thus in this period the caṇḍālas do not seem to have been primarily hunters though hunting may have been one of their subsidiary occupations A Jain source states that the medas used to hunt animals day and night with bow and arrow.[10]

1. Legge, *op. cit.*, p. 43.
2. 25. 34-36.
3. *Anu. P.*, (NE) 47. 29-30, (SE) 83. 29-30.
4. *Mahāvaṃsa*, X. 93. *Vyavahāra Bhāṣya*, 7. 449-462, p. 79; *Nār.*, XIV. 26.
5. *AK*, II. 10.14.
6. *Ibid.*, II. 10.22-24.
7. *Ibid.*, II. 10.26-27.
8. Legge, *op. cit.*; p. 43. Giles translates the term *caṇḍāla* as 'foul men (lepers)' *op. cit.*, p. 21.
9. Upadhyaya, *India in Kālidāsa*, p. 170.
10. *Bṛhatkalpa Bhāṣya*, gāthā 2766.

We also learn that the śvapākas cooked the flesh of dogs and sold bow strings.[1]

There is some information about the manners, customs and religious beliefs of the mixed castes, especially of the caṇḍālas. Iron objects were the chief ornaments of the mixed castes,[2] who lived outside village settlements. A caṇḍāla is represented as besmeared with the dust raised by dogs and asses.[3] Fa-hsien informs us that only the caṇḍālas drink intoxicating liquor and eat onions or garlic,[4] which shows that they were particularly addicted to these practices. Being hunters and fowlers, they were naturally habitual meat-eaters.[5] A Buddhist source declares that those who eat meat are born again and again in the families of the caṇḍālas, pukkasas and dombas.[6] It adds that, when a dog sees even from a distance the persons who desire to take meat, he is terrified with fear, thinking "they are death-dealers, they will even kill me".[7]

Singing, presumably for the entertainment of the people, seems to have been an important occupation of the ḍombas.[8] They lived on singing and selling winnowing baskets and similar articles.[9] The *Amarakośa* includes *caṇḍālikā*, a kind of vulgar lute, in the *śūdra-varga*,[10] which may suggest that the caṇḍālas also had some share in providing popular entertainment.

The ḍombas and the mātaṅgas had their own deities known as the Yakṣas (Jakkhas).[11] A Jain source informs us that the shrine of the Jakkhas of the mātaṅgas was built on the bones of humun beings who had died recently.[12] This practice was

1. *Vyavahāra Bhāṣya*, 3. 92; *Niśītha Cūrṇi*, 11, p. 747 quoted in Jain, *op. cit.*, p. 360.
2. *Anu. P.*, (NE) 47.32, (SE) 83.32.
3. *Ibid.*, (NE) 101. 3. (SE) 158.4.
4. Legge, *op. cit.*, p. 43.
5. Cf *Mṛcchakaṭika*, X.
6. *Laṅkāvatārasūtra*, p. 258.
7. *Ibid.*, p. 246.
8. They were a caste of degraded musicians, representing early inhabitants of Northern India. Jain. *op. cit.* p. 360.
9. Jain, *op. cit.*, pp. 144-45.
10. II. 10. 31-32.
11. Jain, *op. cit.*, pp. 220-22. Songs about *Jaṭṭas* and *Jaṭṭis* are still prevalent among the people of the 'low' castes in Bihār.
12. *Āvaśyaka Cūrṇi*, II. p. 294, quoted in Jain, *op. cit.*, p. 222.

probably the result of the caṇḍāla's association with the cremation grounds.

The untouchables, and the caṇḍālas in particular, are portrayed in very disparaging terms. It is stated that the *antyāvasāyins* are characterised by impurity, untruth, theft, heterodoxy, useless quarrels, passions, wrath and greed.[1] Ferocity appears as a special trait of the caṇḍāla's character. In the *Mṛcchakaṭika* the caṇḍālas argue that they are not caṇḍālas, though born in their family, but caṇḍālas and sinners are those who persecute a virtuous man.[2] A Buddhist text contends that, if a brāhmaṇa does not cultivate truth, asceticism, sublimation of passions, and compensation for all beings, he is like a caṇḍāla.[3] In the same spirit it is provided that by serving kine and brāhmaṇas, practising the virtues of abstention from cruelty, compassion, truthfulness of speech and forgiveness, and, if need be, by saving others by laying down their very lives, persons of the mixed castes can achieve success.[4]

For the first time the *Śānti Parvan* declares that all the four varṇas ought to hear the Veda,[5] and that a person ought to acquire knowledge even from a śūdra.[6] Such injunctions are in sharp contrast to those of Manu, which provide very severe punishments in such cases. The precepts of the *Śānti Parvan* may have been thwarted by the deep-rooted prejudice against allowing Vedic education to the śūdras,[7] but the recitation of the epics and Purāṇas was certainly open to the śūdras. The *Bhāgavata Purāṇa* states that instead of the Veda the *Mahābhārata* is provided for women and śūdras.[8] It is not clear whether the *Mahābhārata* was to be read or only to be heard by the śūdras.

1. *Bhāg. P.*, XI. 17.20, cf. VII. 11.30.
2. X. 22.
3. *Vajrasūcī*, (S), verse 16, p. 5.
4. *Anu. P.*, (NE) 47. 33-35, (SE) 83. 33-5.
5. *śrāvye ca caturo varṇān. Mbh.*, XII. 328.49 quoted in Hopkins, *The Religions of India*, p. 425.
6. *prāpya jñānam ... śūdrādapi. Mbh.*, XII. 319.87 ff. quoted *ibid.*
7. *Mārk. P.*, XXI. 31; *Nāṭyaśāstra*, I. 14.
8. *strīśūdradvijabandhūnāṃ trayī na śrutigocarāḥ; karma śreyasi mūḍhānāṃ śreya evaṃ bhavediha; iti bhāratamākhyānaṃ kṛpayā muninā kṛtam. Bhag. P.*, I. 4.25; I. 4.29.

In the case of the Purāṇas, however, the *Bhaviṣyat Purāṇa* states that they should never be studied by the śūdras, but should be heard by them.[1] Possibly the religious practice of narrating stories from the Purāṇas and epics to all sections of the people for their edification and salvation originated in the Gupta period.

Nāṭyaśāstra or dramatics was another branch of learning which was brought within the reach of the śūdras. This is declared to be the fifth Veda, which was composed out of the elements of the four Vedas and which men of all castes should enjoy.[2] Moreover, the two philosophical systems of Yoga[3] and Sāṃkhya,[4] which probably took their final form during the Gupta period, were also open to the śūdras.[5] The fact that the Veda formed one of the sources of proof according to the Sāṃkhya system was not inconsistent with that system being made available to all; similarly the epic, which contains Vedic quotations, was equally open to śūdras to hear.[6]

The Gupta period also provides instances of educated śūdras. A passage of Yājñavalkya suggests the existence of the teachers of servants.[7] In the *Mṛcchakaṭika* the judge reprimands Śakāra: "A low caste fellow, you are talking of the sense of the Vedas, yet your tongue has not fallen off."[8] The existence of such śūdras is also attested by the *Vajrasūcī*, which speaks of the śūdras who are learned in the vedas, grammar, *mimāṃsā*, *sāṃkhya*, *vaiśeṣika*, *lagna* etc.[9] This statement does not refer to the Buddhists but to the śūdras proper, for the Buddhists were condemned as śūdras in the brāhmaṇical idiom but not in that of

1. *...śrotavyameva śūdreṇa nādhyetavyaṃ kadā cana*. *Bhav. P.*, i, I. 72.
2. *Nāṭyaśāstra*, I. 12 & 13.
3. The *Yoga-sūtra* of Patañjali is probably not older than the 3rd cen. A.D. Keith, *The Sāṃkhya System*, p. 57.
4. Īśvarakṛṣṇa, the author of the *Sāṃkhya-kārikā*, was an earlier contemporary, according to Chinese evidence, of Vasubandhu, who lived in all probability about A.D. 300. *Ibid.*, p. 57.
5. *Ibid.*, p. 100.
6. Keith, *The Sāṃkhya System*, p. 100.
7. *bhṛtakādhyāpakaḥ*. *Yāj.*, I. 223.
8. *vedārthān prākṛtastvaṃ vadasi na ca te jihvā nipatitā*. IX. 21.
9. *Vajrasūcī*, (M), p. 4.

the Buddhists. Jayaswal argues that learned śūdras and the śūdras talking Sanskrit, referred to in Buddhist texts, were sons of the brāhmaṇas through śūdra women.[1] This is probable, but some advanced sections of the śūdras, who tried to uplift their brethren, may have been educated.

There is no doubt, however, that, compared to the members of the upper varṇas, the śūdras functioned at a low cultural level. Thus in the dramas women and low caste people always speak Prākrit, the tongue of the vulgar, in contrast to the refined tongue of the higher class characters who speak Sanskrit.[2] The *Nāṭyaśāstra* provides, however, that queens, courtesans and women artistes may use Sanskrit according to circumstances.[3] Sometime distinction was made even in the use of the dialects of Prākrit; Śaurasenī was used for persons of good position in the drama while Māgadhi was reserved for those of low rank.[4] The *Nāṭyaśāstra* assigns local dialects (*vibhāṣās*) to various tribes and occupations such as those of the caṇḍālas, pulkasas etc.[5] All this would suggest that members of the lower orders did not receive literate education, which would enable them to speak the refined tongue Sanskrit.

It is contended that as a student of military science the śūdra passed through the ceremony of the *upanayana*, which was accompanied by the recital of Vedic mantras,[6] but there is no reference to such a rite in the *Dhanurveda Saṃhitā*. Probably as artisans the śūdras continued to have vocational or technical training in their family or under outside experts, but this remained divorced from literate learning. Nevertheless, it is clear that the texts of the Gupta period not only take a liberal view of the education of the śūdras but also testify to the existence of some educated śūdras.

The old maxim that the śūdras have no religious rights is repeated in this period. It is argued[7] that their sacrifice consists

1. *Manu & Yājñavalkya*, p. 241.
2. *Nāṭyaśāstra*, XVII. 37.
3. *Ibid.*, XVII. 39.
4. Keith, *HSL*, p. 31.
5. XVII, 54-56.
6. Mookerji, *Ancient Indian Education*, p. 347.
7. *Yāj.*, III. 262; *Anu. P.*, (SE) 149. 13; cf. *ŚP*, 70.5.

in performing the service of the three higher varṇas.[1] In keeping with this attitude Nārada states that consecrated water should not be given to atheists, vrātyas and slaves.[2] But Viṣṇu provides that under certain circumstances a śūdra has to undergo the ordeal by sacred libation (*kośa*).[3] There also appear other indications of changes in the religious position of the śūdras. The *Mārkaṇḍeya Purāṇa* assigns the duties of making gifts (*dāna*) and performing sacrifices (*yajña*) to the śūdra.[4] There is no doubt that the śūdras were conceded the right to perform the five great sacrifices (*pañcamahāyajñas*).[5] Manu does not clearly state this, but Yājñavalkya makes it explicit that a śūdra can perform five sacrifices with the *namaskāra* mantra.[6] Hopkins is not correct when he says that this statement does not appertain to the śūdras,[7] for it is corroborated by other sources.[8] While Manu regards initiation into sacrifice (*yajñadikṣā*) as one of the births of the twice-born,[9] this special privilege is not mentioned in the corresponding passage of Yājñavalkya.[10] This is in consonance with the latter's liberal attitude, which allows sacrifice to the śūdras. The *Śānti Parvan* unequivocally declares that the *trayi* (three Vedas) allows the śūdra the use of *svāhākāra namaskāra* and *mantra*, and adds that with the help of the first two he can perform the *pākayajñas*, after being formally consecrated.[11] In justification of this reform the precedent of the śūdra Paijavana is cited. It is said that in ancient times he

1. *śūdrā paricārayajñāḥ...Anu. P.*, (SE) 147. 1. Cf. *Brahmāṇḍa P.*, II. 29.55.
2. I. 332.
3. IX. 10.
4. 28. 7-8.
5. *Brahmāṇḍa P.*, III. 12. 19. These five devotional acts were *brahmayajña, pitṛyajña, daiva, bali*, and *nṛyajña*. *Manu*, III. 69-70.
6. *Yāj.*, I. 121.
7. Hopkins, *Mutual Relations of Four Castes* p. 36, fn. 1.
8. *Brahmāṇḍa P.*, III. 12. 19.
9. *Manu*, II. 169.
10. *Yāj.*, I. 39.
11. *svāhākāranamaskārau mantraḥ śūdre vidhīyate*; *tābhyāṃ śūdra pākayajñairyajet vratavānsvayam*. *ŚP*. 60. 36. The central group of MSS distinguishes between the *yajña* allowed to the śūdra and that to the twice-born. It denies the use of *svāhākāra, namaskāra* and *mantra* to the śūdra, but permits him to perform the *pākayajñas* without a *dīkṣā vrata*. Critical Notes on *ŚP*, 60. Rājadharma,

performed one of the *pākayajñas*, and according to the rules of the *aindrāgni* (a one-day sacrifice) he made the gift of a hundred thousand vessels full of rice (*pūrṇapātras*).[1] This reminds us of similar practices of modern social reformers who hunt out old precedents in favour of widow marriage, divorce etc. While allowing domestic sacrifices to the śūdras the *Śānti Parvan* makes the important assertion that all the varṇas enjoy the right to perform sacrifices provided they possess faith.[2]

As an important corollary to the śūdra's right to sacrifice follows his right of performing penances. Yājñavalkya lays down the *cāndrāyaṇa* penance for the śūdras, who are obviously covered by the use of the term *avakṛṣṭa* by him.[3] This provision is considered to be an interpolation,[4] but it is in keeping with the liberal attitude of Yājñavalkya and a similar provision in the *Bṛhaspati Smṛti*, which prescribes the *prājāpatya* penance for the śūdra in the case of his snapping the thread of a brāhmaṇa.[5]

The *Bṛhaspati Smṛti* provides the sacraments of *karṇavedhana* (ear-boring).[6] and *cūḍākaraṇa*[7] (tonsure) for the śūdras. The first ceremony is not mentioned in the Gṛhyasūtras, but the second, which is prescribed by them[8] and is confined by Manu[9] to the twice-born, is now extended to the śūdras. It may be noted that the performance of *saṃskāras* or sacraments confers some prestige on a person and raises his status in brāhmaṇical society. It establishes his identity as a respectable member of

Pt.II, Fascicule 19, pp. 660-661. The *pākayajñas* are also recommended for all the *dasyus* (*ŚP*, 65. 21-22), which shows that these were being extended to the people outside brāhmaṇical fold. Cf. *Bṛhaspati*, Saṃskāra, verse 529.

1. *ŚP.*, 60. 37-38.
2. *...yajño manīṣayā tāta sarvavarṇeṣu bhārata; ... tasmātsarveṣu varṇeṣu śraddhāyajno vidhīyate. ŚP*, 60. 39-43, cf. 51-52. The term *sarvavarṇa* is glossed as *traivarṇika* by the comm. Cn (according to the classification of the Critical Edn.). Fascicule, 19, pp. 660-61.
3. *Yāj.*, III. 262.
4. Gampert, *Die Sühnezeremonien in der Altindischen Rechtsliteratur*, p. 94.
5. *Bṛ.*, Prāyaścitta, verse 60.
6. *Bṛ.*, Saṃskāra, verse 101. But the metal of the needle for piercing ears differs according to the varṇa of the child (*Ibid.*).
7. *Ibid.*, Saṃskāra, verse 154 (a).
8. R. B. Pandey, *Hindu Saṃskāras*, p. 161.
9. *cūḍākarma dvijātīnāṃ sarveṣāmeva dharmataḥ. Manu*, II. 35.

society, and is a probable recognition of ritualistic citizenship. Since the śūdra ranks came to contain a large number of peasants in Gupta times and came to acquire the same status as that of the vaiśyas, we notice a corresponding change in their religious status. More than anything else the process is reflected in the gradual increase of the *saṃskāras* to be performed by them. The Gṛhyasūtras or the texts on domestic rites, which mostly belong to pre-Maurya times, do not permit any sacrament to a śūdra; nor are these allowed to him in any pre-Gupta text. But the process starts in Gupta times, in which the number of sacraments in general shot up to at least sixteen or even more. The problem of accommodating the new śūdras in the brāhmaṇical system becomes so important that a new Gṛhyasūtra called the *Vaijavāpa Gṛhyasūtra* is prepared for this purpose. Literally it means the text dealing with the sowing of seeds, a function performed by both the vaiśyas and śūdras. Mentioned in the *Tantravārttika* of Kumārila Bhaṭṭa,[1] the text is earlier than the seventh century.[2] But it cannot be treated as one of the earliest Gṛhyasūtras; it seems to have been compiled in Gupta or post-Gupta times.

According to the *Vaijavāpa Gṛhyasūtra* a śūdra can perform conceiving ceremony (*niṣeka*), ceremony for getting a son in the third month of conception (*puṃsavana*), parting of the hair ceremony (*sīmantonnayana*), birth ceremony (*jātakarma*), naming ceremony (*nāmakaraṇa*), taking the child out of the house (*niṣkramaṇa*), cereal eating ceremony (*annaprāśana*) in the sixth month after birth, and tonsure (*caula*).[3] All these ceremonies are to be performed, without mantras and at the time prescribed for them.[4] It is interesting that all these sacraments are connected more or less with birth and were to be performed by the twice-born also. This shows the great importance of child birth not only to members of the three higher varṇas but also to the lowest varṇa. Obviously more working hands were

1. P. V. Kane, *Hist. Dh. S.*, i, 596.
2. *Ibid.*, v, Pt. II, chronological Table (p. xiii) assigns Kumārila-bhaṭṭa, author of the *Tantravārttika*, to A.D. 650-700.
3. *DK.* iii, Pt. I, 28; cf. 29.
4. *amantrakāṇi yathākālamupadiṣṭāni. Ibid.*

needed in Gupta and post-Gupta times to look after the expanding agrarian economy, and emphasis lay on production rather than on sterilisation.

However in the *Vaijavāpa* list marriage is not included as one of the sacraments meant for the śūdras. This is done in the *Harihara Bhāṣya*, a commentary of the 13th-14th centuries.[1] Commenting on the statement of the *Brahma Purāṇa* that a śūdra is always entitled to the marriage sacrament. Harihara repeats the eight *saṃskāras* mentioned by *Vaijavāpa* and adds *vivāha* to it.[2] Another commentator Jayapāla (16th century)[3] also speaks of nine *saṃskāras* allowed to the śūdras.[4] This number is raised to twelve by Sārṅgadhara, quoted in a work of the 17th century.[5] Sārṅgadhara however does not specify the twelve sacraments extended to the śūdras. Either he has in mind three additional ones or his list of twelve includes a few which are not listed by others who prescribe nine sacraments. In any case what is significant is a marked increase in the number of rituals to be performed by the śūdras.

Some medieval commentators draw a line between pure (*sat*) and impure śūdras and prescribe rituals only for the former.[6] Thus Gadādhara, a commentator of the sixteenth century,[7] prescribes twelve *saṃskāras* for pure śūdras, and only marriage for impure śūdras.[8] Possibly Sārṅgadhara's sacraments are ordained for the pure śūdras, but he clearly prescribes five sacraments for mixed castes.[9] According to him the twice-born are entitled to sixteen, the śūdras to twelve, and the mixed castes (*miśrajātinām*) to five.[10] Apparently in this case mixed castes refer to untouchables, who seem to have played an important role in the expanding agrarian feudal economy and

1. *Ibid.*, p. 10, entry no. 139.
2. *Ibid.*, 59.
3. *Ibid.*
4. *Ibid.*
5. *Ibid.*, 62.
6. *Ibid.*, 60.
7. *Ibid.*
8. *Ibid.*
9. *Ibid.*
10. *Ibid.*, 62.

were apparently in a position to meet the costs incurred in these rituals.

From the third century onwards several texts emphasise that the śūdras can perform a number of rituals including the *saṃskāras*;[1] the only condition is that these have to be done without mantras,[2] which obviously belong to the Vedic texts. For it is recognised in the *Padma Purāṇa* that the rituals of the dvijas follow the śruti (*śrautam*), and those of the śūdras follow the *smṛti* (*smārtaṃ*).[3] The fact that the śūdras are not allowed to utter the Vedic mantras does continue a religious hiatus between them and the twice-born, but this is more formal than real. For in early medieval times some Smārta mantras find their way into the Vedic mantras.[4]

But the crucial development to be noted is not the non-recitation of the Vedic mantras but the performance of the *saṃskāras*. And since the sacraments had to be performed it was laid down by several early medieval authorities such as Vyāsa,[5] Marīci[6] and the *Varāha Purāṇa*[7] that a brāhmaṇa should be employed for reciting the mantras; it is not clear whether this was done within the hearing of the śūdra sacrificer.

Altogether in Gupta and post-Gupta times we encounter a large number of rituals which are to be performed by the śūdras. Some of these are in the form of *pākayajñas*, which involve the feeding of the brāhmaṇas. Others are in the nature of rites connected with maternity, birth, marriage, funeral rites, etc., and are called *saṃskāras*. Still others are in the nature of rites for acquiring longevity and are called *pauṣṭikakarmāṇi*.[8] An early medieval lawgiver permits *pūrta*-dharma, i.e. charity,

1. *DK*, iii, Pt. I, 28, 35-36, 43, 46, 54, 56-57, 59.
2. *Ibid.*, 35, 43, 47, 56.
3. *Ibid.*, 59.
4. P. V. Kane, op. cit., v, Pt. II, 920; iv, 440, fn. 984.
5. *amantrasya tu śūdrasya vipro mantreṇa gṛhyate* quoted in *DK*, iii, Pt. I, 54.
6. *Ibid.*, 56.
7. *Ibid.*, 57.
8. *Mbh.* quoted in *DK*, iii, Pt. I, 36; The *Bṛhat Saṃhita* states that the *Sāṃvatsara* (astrologer) should be well-versed in the *śāntika* and *pauṣṭika* rites. Quoted in P. V. Kane, *Hist. Dh. S.*, V, i, 349.

social service, etc., to the śūdra but without Vedic rites.[1] It is likely that rites meant for warding off the threat and evil effects of the planets were also prescribed for the śūdras. All these rituals taken together betoken a tremendous change in the religious position of the śūdras towards the end of the ancient and the beginning of the early medieval period.

Several texts of the period deny ascetic life to the śūdra. Kālidāsa deliberately repeats the *Rāmāyaṇa's* condemnation of the śūdra ascetic Śambūka[2] who, in his opinion, threatened the security of the established order by trying to acquire merit through asceticism. He commends the punishment of death inflicted on Śambūka by Rāma; and he argues that as a result of this the śūdra obtained the position of the virtuous which he could not secure even by his severe austerity, for this was being done in violation of the rules of his class.[3] But on the question of the relation between the varṇas and the āśramas the *Śānti Parvan* adopts a different attitude. It insists that a brāhmaṇa should go through the four āśramas, but does not make this obligatory on the three other varṇas,[4] who, however, cannot adopt the life of an ascetic.[5] This implies that a śūdra, if he so desires can enter the first three āśramas, the fourth being closed not only to him but also to the vaiśya and the kṣatriya. But Kātyāyana refers to the śūdra ascetic who is to be punished by the king if he forsakes the order of the saṃnyāsins.[6] Yājñavalkya provides that śūdra ascetics should not be fed in the worship of the gods and the ancestors.[7] This may refer either to Jain and Buddhist monks or to ascetics from the śūdra varṇa.

An important indication of improvement in the religious status of the śūdra is to be found in some provisions regarding

1. Quoted in Kane, ibid., V, ii, 949, fn, 1532.

2. Probably the story of the death of Śambūka at the hands of Rāma, which reflects the attitude of Manu, was inserted in the *Rāmāyaṇa* (Uttarakāṇḍa, Chs. 74-76) in the post-Mauryan period.

3. *Raghuvaṃśa*, XV. 53; cf. *Anu. P.*, (SE) 270.11.

4. *ŚP*, 63. 9-11; Cr. note on 63.9. Fasc, 19, p. 662.

5. *ŚP*, 63. 12-14.

6. *Kātyā.*, verse 486. The *Mārk. P.* also mentions śūdra ascetics (22.19), but we have no idea of the time to which they belong.

7. *Yāj.*, II. 235.

the making of images. While enumerating the constituents suitable for preparing clay for this purpose, a Vaiṣṇavite text lays down that men of all castes can make images.[1] This shows that the śūdras could make and worship images, made of the same material as the members of the other varṇas. Another text of the period, however, prescribes varṇa distinctions in the selection of wood to be used for making images, and accordiugly four varieties of wood are provided for the four varṇas respectively.[2] A similar rule occurring in a post-Gupta Vaiṣṇavite Upapurāṇa ordains that in making temples and images white wood is auspicious for the brāhmaṇas, red for the kṣatriyas, yellow for the vaiśyas, and black for the śūdras.[3] In making images, the same text recommends stones of these four colours for the four varṇas respectively.[4] In spite of these varṇa distinctions in regard to the selection of wood and stone, the texts dealing with iconography leave no doubt that the śūdras could make and worship images.

It is laid down that a brāhmaṇa should not accompany the corpse of a śūdra to the pyre; if he does so, he is purified by bathing, touching fire and eating ghee.[5] The old rule providing for the highest period of impurity in the case of death in a śūdra's family is maintained by several texts of the period.[6] But in such a case Yājñavalkya prescribes one month for an ordinary śūdra and fifteen days for a pious (*nyāyavartin*) śūdra, thus placing the latter in the rank of the vaiśya.[7] Vaiśyas and śūdras are also placed in the same category in connection with the observance of fasts. It is provided that the vaiśyas and śūdras should observe fast for only one night.[8] If from folly they

1. Passage quoted by Gopālabhaṭṭa from the *Hayaśirṣa Pañcarātra* in the 18th vilāsa of the *Haribhaktivilāsa*, and reproduced in Banerjea, *Development of Hindu Iconography*, p. 227, fn. 1.

2. *Bṛhat Saṃhitā* (*Sudhākara Dvivedī's edn.*), 89. 5-6.

3. *Viṣṇudharmottara Mahāpurāṇa*, iii. 89. 12.

4. *śuklā śastā dvijātīnāṃ kṣātriyānāṃ ca lohitā, viśaṃ pīta hitā kṛṣṇā śūdrānāṃ ca hitapradā. Ibid.*, iii. 90.2.

5. *Yāj.*, III. 26.

6. *Brahmāṇḍa P.*, III. 14. 86-87; *Viṣṇu P.*, III. 13.19; *Bṛ.*, Aśauca, verse 39.

7. III. 23.

8. *Anu. P.*, (NE) 101. 11-12, (SE) 163. 11-12.

observe fasts for two or three nights, these do not lead to their advancement.[1] On special occasions, however, they can perform fasts for two nights.[2] But sometimes it is also asserted that only the brāhmaṇas and ksatriyas can observe the vow of fasts.[3]

Bṛhaspati lays down that in the case of still birth (*janmahāni*) a brāhmaṇa is purified in 10 days, a kṣatriya in 7 days, a vaiśya in 5 days and a śūdra in 3 days.[4]

The impurity of women and śūdras in relation to ceremonial occasions is also maintained by the texts of this period.[5] In some cases penances are provided for seeing śūdras and outcastes (*patitas*), who are considered to be as impure as dogs.[6] Penances are also provided for the kṣatriya student who comes into contact with a vaiśya or a śūdra, and for the vaiśya student who comes into contact with a śūdra.[7]

The *śrāddha* rites, as laid down in the Gṛhyasūtras, are not prescribed for a śūdra,[8] but the texts of this period clearly allow these rites to a śūdra.[9] He can perform not only the ordinary (*sādhāraṇa*) śrāddha but also the extraordinary (*vṛddhi*) śrāddha,[10] in which offerings are made to dead ancestors on special occasions such as the birth of a son.[11] We further learn that after death *Prājāpatya* is the heaven assigned to the brāhmaṇas who perform the ceremonies, *Aindra* to the kṣatriyas who do not flee in battle, *Māruta* to the vaiśyas who carry out their duties, and *Gāndharva* to the śūdras who are engaged in menial service.[12]

1. *Ibid.*
2. *Ibid.*, (NE) 101. 13, (SE) 163.2.
3. *Ibid.*, (NE) 106.2, (SE) 163.2.
4. *Bṛ.*, Aśauca, verses 34-35. Certain sections of people such as artisans, cultivators, physicians, slaves of both sexes, barbers, kings, and brāhmaṇas learned in the *śrutis* were always considered pure. *Yāj.*, III. 28-29; *Bṛ.*, Aśauca, verse 9.
5. *ŚP.*, 36.35.
6. *Bṛ.*, Ācāra, verse 37.
7. *Bṛ.*, Prāyaścitta, verses 74-75.
8. Pandey, *op. cit.*, p. 439.
9. *Yāj.*, I. 121; *Vā. P.*, ii. 13.49.
10. *Matsya P.*, 17. 63-64.
11. *Ibid.*, 17.70.
12. *Mārk. P.*, 49, 77-81; *Viṣṇu, P.*, I. 6. 34-35.

The śūdras could make offerings of water and other things to their *pitaras*, who are referred to by the epithet *Sukālin* in the Purāṇas[1] and are described as dark in colour.[2] But, unlike the members of the three higher varṇas, who are described as sons of the ṛṣis, the śūdras are not supposed to have any *pravaras*.[3]

Since śūdras and women were not permitted to offer *homa* which could be done only with the Vedic mantras,[4] the newly growing practices of *pūjā*[5] and *vrata* were open to them. Persons of all castes including śūdras were entitled to perfom *vratas*. According to Devala, a lawgiver of A.D. 600-900,[6] men of all varṇas are certainly released from sins by practising vows, fasts, temperance and selfmortification.[7] Although the *vratas* number seven hundred in the thirteenth century *Caturvargacintāmaṇi* of Hemādri,[8] many of them find place in those portions of the Purāṇas which belong to the sixth and seventh centuries.[9] It has been calculated that as many as twenty-five thousand verses in the Purāṇas deal with *vratas*.[10] Of course the major portion may be early medieval, but the importance of the vows for the śūdra peasant castes and others from Gupta times cannot be ignored.

It seems that the vows were incorporated in the Purāṇas to wean away the people from tāntric influences,[11] and in the process many tāntric and non-āryan rituals were brāhmaṇised. The *vratas* came to occupy a large place in the religious life of the

1. *Brahmāṇḍa P.*, III. 10. 96-99; *Vāyu P.*, ii. 11.90. *Mārk. P.*, 96.23.
2. *Mārk. P.*, 96. 36.
3. *Brahmāṇḍa P.*, II. 32.90, 121-22.
4. P. V. Kane, *Hist. Dh. S.*, v. Pt. I, 32-33.
5. For the origin and growth of this practice see Suvira Jaiswal, *Origin and Development of Vaiṣṇavism*, Ch. V.
6. P. V. Kane, op. cit., v. Pt. II, Chronological Table, xiii.
7. *vratopavāsaniyamaiḥ śarīrottāpanaistathā, varṇāḥ sarvepi mucyante pātakebhyo na saṃśayaḥ*. Quoted in ibid., p. 51, fn. 123.
8. P. V. Kane, op. cit., v. Pt. I, 47.
9. R. C. Hazra, op. cit., pp. 176, 182, 183, 188.
10. P. V. Kane, op. cit., v. Pt. I, 57. On the basis of Kane we can count as many as 1256 *vratas, utsavas*, etc. (ibid., 253-462), but this list has been prepared on the basis of many late medieval texts by him. Kane thinks that if properly sifted the number would be much smaller than 1000.
11. R. C. Hazra, op. cit., pp. 225-26.

peasantry and consumed a good amount of their time and earnings. Probably in the beginning some of these could be performed by the peasants themselves, but gradually the brāhmaṇas intervened for which they had to be paid. Several *vratas* involved *homa* which could be performed only by the brāhmaṇas.[1] Since most vows were *tithi vratas*,[2] people also needed the help of astrologers who could tell the exact duration of lunar days. Generally the brāhmaṇa acted as both priest and astrologer.

The process by which the religious rights of the śūdras were enlarged and they were brought firmly within the ambit of the brāhmaṇical way of life seems to have reached its culmination in late medieval time. Between the fourteenth and the seventeenth century we have a spate of books dealing with the contents and the manner of the rituals to be performed by the śūdras. These are *Śūdradharmabodhini* of Madanapāla written in the Delhi region in the fourteenth century,[3] *Śūdrācāracintāmaṇi* of Vācaspatimiśra written in Mithila in the fifteenth century,[4] *Śūdrācāraśiromaṇi* by Kṛṣṇaśeṣa written in the sixteenth century in western India,[5] *Śūdrakṛtyatattva* of Raghunandana written in Bengal in the sixteenth century,[6] and *Śūdrakamalākara* of Kamalākarabhaṭṭa written in Banaras in the first half of the seventeenth century.[7] It seems that the texts meant for standardising the religious duties and observances to be performed by the śūdras were written even earlier. For example the *Śūdrapaddhati* of Apipāla, a work written earlier than A.D. 1500,[8] was based on an earlier work composed by Somamiśra,[9] which may have been earlier than A.D. 1300. A text called *Śūdrācāra* was based on extracts dealing with the duties of the śūdras found in the Purāṇas.[10]

It is significant that similar texts dealing with the duties of the three higher varṇas are rarely found. Apparently in all

1. P. V. Kane, op. cit., v. Pt. I, 52, fn.130.
2. *Ibid.*, 56.
3. P. V. Kane, *Hist. Dh. S.*, i, See 93 (381-89), and fn. 940.
4. *Ibid.*, Sec. 98 (399-406).
5. *Ibid.*, 641, 686-87.
6. *Ibid.*, Sec. 102 (416-19) with fn. 1018.
7. *Ibid.*, Sec. 106 (432-37) with fn. 1092.
8. *Ibid.*, 680.
9. *Ibid.*, 640.
10. *Ibid.*, 641.

general texts on the Dharmaśāstras emphasis lay on the duties of the twice-born. But the fact that it was found necessary to lay down and systematise the religious duties and conduct of the śūdras shows the enormous importance attached to them as a community in medieval times. However the clear beginnings of this whole process are found in Gupta times.

An important religious development of this period is the emphasis on the śūdra's right of making gifts.[1] Charity is declared to be the best course for a śūdra, by performing which he gains all his ends.[2] A śūdra who practises truth and sincerity, honours *mantra* and brāhmaṇas, and makes gifts attains heaven and even brāhmaṇahood in the next birth.[3] In a special vow known as the *anaṅgadāna-vrata*, prescribed for prostitutes, it is provided that a brāhmaṇa should recite the Vedic *mantras* while accepting the cow of a prostitute, who was normally thought of as a śūdra.[4] We are further told that a Śaivite prostitute named Līlāvatī and a śūdra goldsmith made gifts, as a result of which the former attained the region of Śiva (*śivamandiram*) after death and the latter became a paramount sovereign named Dharmamūrti.[5] A Buddhist commentary of the 5th century A. D. provides instances of at least a dozen persons of the lower orders who enjoyed the pleasures of heaven and the joys and comforts of the Buddhist *vimānas* as a result of their gifts to the Buddha, the Bhikṣus or the Saṃgha.[6] Thus the doctrine of gift was common to both the Buddhist and brāhmaṇical systems.

There is no evidence to show that any vigorous propaganda was made by the brāhmaṇas to popularise the piety of making gifts earlier than the time of the *Yājñavalkya Smṛti*.[7] With the

1. *Mārk. P.*, 28. 3-8.
2. *dānena sarvakāmāptirasya sañjāyate. Matsya P.*, 17. 71.
3. *Anu. P.* (SE) 217. 13-15. For the importance of gifts in expiating sins see Hazra, *Purāṇic Records on Hindu Rites and Customs*, p. 250.
4. ...*ka idaṃ kasmādāditi vaidikaṃ mantramīrayat. Mat. P.*, 69. 51-54. Chs. 69-72 on vows corresponding to 70-71 of Jivānanda's edn. have been assigned by Hazra to A.D. *c.* 550-650 (*op. cit.*, p. 176).
5. *Mat. P.*, 91. 23-32.
6. Calculated on the basis of B.C. Law's summary of the *Vimānavatthu* comm. in *Heaven and Hell*, pp. 36-45.
7. Hazra, *op. cit.*, p. 247.

law-book of Bṛhaspati the doctrine of salvation through gifts reached its high watermark.[1] The fact that this doctrine was repeatedly emphasised in connection with the śūdras may suggest that they were in a position to make gifts which was in accord with the change in their economic position.

The provisions for the performance of sacrifices, penances, *śrāddhas* and various other rites by the śūdras presuppose the employment of brāhmaṇas, who were the recipients of the gifts made on these occasions. Even a śūdra is allowed to accept gifts, but the merit of the donor increases according to the varṇa of the person accepting gifts.[2] The repeated condemnation of the priests who officiate at the rites performed by the śūdras[3] not only betrays old prejudices against these priests, but also suggests that the practice of engaging them was becoming more frequent. Unlike Manu,[4] Yājñavalkya does not condemn śūdra priests (*ṛtvijs*). The *Vajrasūcī* avers that brāhmaṇas are to be found even in the families of the kaivartas, rajakas (washermen) and caṇḍālas, among whom the rites of cūḍākaraṇa, muñja, daṇḍa (staff), kāṣṭha (wood) etc. are performed.[5] This suggests that the brāhmaṇas officiated as priests even for the lowest sections of the śūdras. The *Vajrasūcī* also states that kṣatriyas, vaiśyas and śūdras are seen sacrificing and officiating at sacrifices, studying and teaching, and accepting gifts.[6] This development, if true, may indicate a spirit of revolt in certain sections of the people against the brāhmaṇical monopoly of priestly functions. Several movements of such a type have taken place in more recent times.

While the champions of Buddhism continued to argue against birth as the basis of varṇa,[7] the growth of certain reforming ideologies, especially the creed of Vaiṣṇavism, secured a large measure of religious equality for the śūdras. Vaiṣṇavism reached its high watermark in the Gupta period, when we find numerous

1. K. V. Rangaswami Aiyangar, *Bṛhaspati*, Introd., p. 162.
2. *Bṛ.*, Saṃskāra, verse 288.
3. *Viṣṇu*, LXXXII. 14 & 22; *ŚP.*, Ms. Ds 5; *Brahmāṇḍa P.*, III. 15.44.
4. *Manu*, XI. 42.
5. *Vajrasūcī*, (BB), p. 7.
6. *Ibid.*, (O), p. 4.
7. *Ibid.*, (EE) and (GI), pp. 8 & 9.

epigraphic, numismatic and sculptural records testifying to its unparalleled influence not only in Northern India but even in parts of Southern and Western India.[1] The doctrines of this sect, as propounded in the didactic sections of the *Mahābhārata* and Purāṇas, show that, unlike the old orthodox form of brāhmaṇism, Vaiṣṇavism did not keep the śūdras and untouchables at a distance, but extended to them the privilege of knowing God and attaining liberation.[2] The Vaiṣṇava texts never fail to emphasise that women and śūdras can attain emancipation through their devotion to Kṛṣṇa, Nārāyaṇa or Vāsudeva.[3] Bhagavān is represented as claiming that the whole world from the brāhmaṇa to the śvapāka is purified if devoted to Him.[4] A śvapāka possessed of sincere faith and devotion is considered dearer to God than a brāhmaṇa endued with other qualities but lacking in faith.[5] If a person of low birth utters the name of God only once, he is liberated from bondage.[6] It is asserted that "brāhmaṇas learned in the Vedas regard a virtuous śūdra as the effulgent Viṣṇu of the universe, the foremost one in all the worlds".[7] Those who disregard the śūdra devotees of Viṣṇu are condemned to hell for ten million (koṭi) years.[8] Hence a wise person should not disregard even a caṇḍala devotee of Viṣṇu.[9] Through devotion to Viṣṇu a rājanya obtains victory, a brāhmaṇa learning, a vaiśya wealth and a śūdra happiness.[10]

A similar assertion is made with regard to all the four varṇas if they recite the hymns dedicated to Mahādeva.[11] If vaiśyas, women and śūdras listen to the story of the Dakṣa-Śiva conflict

1. K. G. Goswami, "Vaiṣṇavism", *IHQ*, xxxi, 132.
2. Raychaudhuri, *The Early History of the Vaiṣṇava Sect.*, p. 117.
3. *Bhagavat Gītā*, IX. 32; *Bhāg. P.*, VII. 7. 54-55; XI. 5.4.
4. *Bhāg. P.*, III. 16.6.
5. *Ibid.*, III. 33. 7.
6. *Ibid.*, V. 1. 35. cf., *Āśvamedhika P.*, (SE) 117. 2.
7. *vaidehakaṃ śūdramudāharanti dvijā mahārāja śrutopapannāḥ; ahaṃ hi paśyāmi narendra devaṃ viśvasya viṣṇuṃ jagataḥ pradhānam. ŚP.* (Cal.), 296. 28. The use of the term *vaidehaka* as an adjective of śūdra shows a decline in the status of traders.
8. *Āśvamedhika P.*, (SE) 116.21.
9. *Ibid.*, 116.22.
10. *Ibid.*, 116. 31.
11. *Anu. P.*, (NE) 18.81, (SE) 49.81.

from the brāhmaṇas, they receive a place in the Rudra-loka.[1] Like the members of the three higher varṇas, a śūdra devotee of Śiva is also promised the status of Gaṇapati provided he is not a drunkard.[2] Thus it would appear that Śaivism also kept its doors equally open to the śūdras.

Tantricism, which was connected with both Vaisṇavism and Śaivism, also did not recognise varṇa distinctions in matters of religion. The *Jayākhya-saṃhitā*, a Tantra work of the fith century A.D.,[3] permits members of all the four varṇas to be initiated into Tantricism, preferably by a brāhmaṇa;[4] if a brāhmaṇa is not available, worthy members of the kṣatriya, vaiśya and śūdra varṇas can act as initiators for their respective classes, or for people of lower classes.[5]

Vaiṣṇavism, and to some extent Śaivism, counted many followers among the members of the ruling class in the Gupta period, but we have hardly any means of ascertaining the extent of the influence of these sects among the lower orders. It is suggested that in Vaiśālī the artisan class was considerably influenced by Vaiṣṇavism, for two craftsmen (kulikas) bear the name of Hari.[6] This may have been the case at other places also.

Under the influence of the reforming creeds the religious texts of the period shift the emphasis from the observance of rites and sacraments to that of good conduct, which determines the social status of a person. It is stated that neither the performance of the *agnihotra* nor the knowledge of the Veda is of any avail,[7] for the gods are satisfied through good conduct which is

1. *Vāyu P.*, i, 30. 18.

2. *Ibid.*, ii, 39. 352-54. In the Appendix to the *Vāyu Purāṇa*, in a story a barber named Maṅkha installs an image of Gaṇeśa Kṣemaka at Vārāṇasi. Patil, *op. cit.*, p. 38.

3. On paleographical grounds this work has been placed about A.D. 450. B. Bhattacharya, *Jayākhya-saṃhitā*, Foreword, p. 34.

4. *Jayākhya-saṃhitā*, 18. 3-5.

5. *su (sa ?) jātīyena śūdreṇa tādṛśena mahādhiyā; anugrahābhiṣekau ca kāryau śūdrasya sarvadā. Ibid.*, 6-9.

6. K. G. Goswami, *IHQ*, xxxi, 125.

7. Several provisions, however, stress the necessity of observing the rites, especially on the part of the brāhmaṇa. If he does not say his prayers. or perform the *agnihotra*, and takes to the duties of a trader or a cultivator,

fostered by the Śrutis; brāhmaṇas who do not maintain good conduct (*śila*) should be regarded as śūdras.[1] A person bereft of good conduct (*śila*) should not be honoured; on the other hand even a religious śūdra should be honoured.[2] A śūdra not only may become a non-regenerate (*asaṃskṛta*) dvija, but he should be revered like a regenerate person, if he is "pure of heart, and of subdued senses",[3] since "not birth, nor sacrament, nor learning, nor stock (*santatiḥ*) make one regenerate, but only conduct".[4] The argument that even a śūdra of good conduct can attain brāhmaṇahood in the next birth is repeatedly advanced in the didactic sections of the *Mahābhārata* and the Purāṇas,[5] and is also reproduced in the *Vajrasūci*.[6]

Appropriate anecdotes are cited to support the above theory. In the *Vana Parvan* occurs the legend of the brāhmaṇa ṛṣi Kauśika who was taught the duties of the varṇas and code of moral conduct to be followed by them by a dharma-knowing fowler.[7] It is claimed by the *dharmavyādha* of Mithilā that he served elders and superiors, always spoke the truth, never envied anybody, used to make gifts according to his means, and lived upon what was left after the service of the gods, the guests and his dependents. He never spoke ill of any one and he hated none.[8] It is argued that this anecdote is Buddhistic,[9] but the

he is reduced to the position of a śūdra or vṛṣala. *Anu. P.*, (NE) 104. 19-20; (SE) 161.20, (SE) 217. 10-12; *Āśvamedhika Parvan*, (SE) 116. 11-12; cf. *ŚP*, XII. 63. 3-5; Non-observance of the religious rites and *saṃskāras* such as keeping fire, *upanayana*, vows etc., and officiating for non-sacrificing people as well as serving the śūdras are regarded as so many *upapātkas* for a brāhmaṇa. *Yāj.*, III. 234-242.

1. *Āśvamedhika Parvan*, (SE) 116. 5-6.
2. *Anu. P.*, (NE) 48. 48, (SE) 83.47.
3. *yastu śūdro dame satye dharme ca satatotthitaḥ; taṃ brāhmaṇamahaṃ manye vṛttena hi bhaveddvijaḥ. Vana P.* (Cal.), 215. 13.
4. ...*na yonirnāpisaṃskāro na śrutaṃ na ca santatiḥ. ... Anu. P.* (Cal.), 143. 46-50. Cf. *Vana Parvan* (Cal.), 181. 42-43.
5. *Anu. P.* (Cal.), 143.51; *ŚP* (Cal.), 189.8; *Vana P.* (Cal.), 180. 25-26, cf. 35-36; *Bhaviṣya P.*, I. 44.31; cf. *Bhāg. P.*, VII. 11.35.
6. *Vajrasūci*, (KK), verse 43, p. 10.
7. *Vana Parvan* (Cal.), 205.44; 206. 10-25.
8. *Ibid.*, 206. 20-22.
9. Holtzman, *Neunzehn Bücher*, p. 86, quoted in Hopkins, *Religions of India*, p. 425.

tenor of the fowler's statement is quite in keeping with Vaiṣṇavite doctrines, and provides a good example of acculturation. Even the Buddhistic argument in the *Vajrasūci* that Vyāsa, Kauśika, Viśvāmitra and Vasiṣṭha all were lowborn but came to be regarded as brāhmaṇas on account of their conduct in this world[1] is apparently derived from the old tradition embodied in the Purāṇas.

But the influence of the reforming sects should not be exaggerated. Vaiṣṇavism was utilised by the ruling classes to maintain the bases of the varṇa divided society. Vaiśyas, women and śūdras are condemned as people of low origin.[2] It is asserted that nothing offers salvation to the śūdra excepting the service of the twice-born and devotion to Viṣṇu.[3] This is more or less a corollary of the theory of *karma*, and of the general belief in the imperative necessity of performing the duties of the order in which a person is born. It seems that members of the lower orders were made to believe in this doctrine by the brāhmaṇical ideologies.[4] In the *Mṛcchakaṭika* a bullock-cart driver refuses to carry out his master's orders to kill Vasantasenā on the ground that: "Destiny and sins made me a slave at birth; I do not wish to fall again into the same misfortune, and therefore I shall refuse to commit a crime".[5] Such a belief naturally prevented the masses of the people from looking for the causes of their miseries in the actions of human agencies.

It is difficult to dilate upon the origin of the numerous rituals, vows, *utsavas*, *saṃskāras*, etc., that appear in the Smṛtis, epics and the Purāṇas. They were derived from diverse sources such as ancient texts, various tribes and regions, and different artisanal and agricultural practices. Several of these rituals were derived from the reforming sects. In Gupta and post-Gupta times they were better recognised, brāhmanised, systematised

1. *Vajrasūci*, (G), verses 9 & 10, p. 2, cf. (Y), verse 27, p. 7.

2. *Gītā*, IX. 32. Even the Dharmavyādha believes that service is prescribed for the śūdras (*karma śūdre....*).

3. *dvijaśūṣrūṣaṇaṃ dharmaḥ śūdrāṇāṃ bhaktito mayi...Āśvamedhika Parvan*, (SE) 118. 15-16.

4. *Manu*, IX. 335.

5. *jeṇa hmi gabbhadāśe viṇimmide bhāadheadośehim. ahiaṃ ca na kiṇīśśaṃ teṇa akajjaṃ palihalāmi. Mṛcchakaṭika*, VIII. 25, Karmarkar's Tr., p. 232.

and consolidated into the Smārta texts for the use and acculturation of a large number of expanding peasantry which was being brought into the 'Hindu' fold as śūdras and also for their observation by the womenfolk. Some rituals were as old as pre-Maurya times set forth in the Gṛhyasūtras and meant only for the twice-born. We may recall that in later Vedic times the śūdras possessed certain religious rights, which they enjoyed as original members of the āryan tribes. As the tribal element was weakened and slaves, domestic servants, agricultural labourers, etc., came to be called śūdras, they lost these rights. Now in Gupta and post-Gupta times a good many of the śūdras became peasants or vice-versa, and so a few rights enjoyed by the upper varṇas including the vaiśyas were not only extended to them, but the religious practices of aboriginal peasants brought to the śūdra fold through the mechanism of land grants were also incorporated in the omnibus brāhmaṇical system and made respectable. Anyway we notice a sharp contrast between the saddling of the śūdras with religious disabilities in post-Vedic times on the one hand and conferring religious rights on them in the early Christian centuries and enlarging their scope and content in early medieval times on the other. This contrast, in our opinion, can be explained in terms of changes in the nature of the socio-economic formation in Gupta and post-Gupta times.

But there is no doubt that during the Gupta period the religious rights of the śūdras were enlarged, and in respect of several ceremonies they were placed on a level with the members of the three higher varṇas. It is argued that moved by selfish interests the brāhmaṇas wanted that a large section of people should observe brāhmaṇical rites,[1] which consequently led to the spiritual betterment of the śūdras. But the same selfish interest of the brāhmaṇas may equally well have existed in earlier periods, when there is not much evidence for such a development. Perhaps the reasons for the broadening of the religious rights of the śūdras lay in the improvement of their material conditions, which enabled them to perform sacraments and sacrifices by paying for priests. For the ability to sacrifice was rightly believed to be intimately connected with the ability

1. Ghurye, *Caste and Class*, p. 95.

to pay.[1] Roughly speaking, the developments in the religious position of the śūdras during the Gupta period may be compared to what happened in Egypt at the beginning of the Middle Kingdom, when certain funerary rites, hitherto confined to the Pharaohs and nobles, were extended to the masses of the people.[2] But this was accompanied by improvements in their economic conditions,[3] a fact which seems to be also true of the position of the śūdras in the Gupta period.

The Gupta period witnessed momentous changes in the status of the śūdras. Not only was there an increase in the rates of wages paid to hired labourers, artisans and pedlars, but slaves and hired labourers were gradually becoming sharecroppers and peasants. This change is broadly reflected in the politico-legal position of the śūdras. The admonitions of the *Śānti Parvan* advocating the appointment of śūdra ministers[4] may not be taken seriously, but certainly the heads of the guilds of artisans were associated with the work of the district government, and in times of emergency the śūdras were conceded the right to bear arms. The rigours of the varṇa legislation were softened, and probably some of the harsh measures against the śūdras were annulled. The religious rights of the śūdras were considerably enlarged. Social degradation undoubtedly took place in the case of the untouchables, who were regarded as śūdras only theoretically, but for all practical purposes were marked out as a separate community. But it would be wrong to think that other sections of the śūdras were socially degraded in the Gupta period.[5] There is no evidence for this in regard to food and marriage practices. As regards education, the śūdras were definitely conceded the right of hearing the epics and the Purāṇas, and sometimes even the Veda. Considered as a whole, the economic, politico-legal, social and religious changes in the position of the śūdras during the Gupta period may be regarded as marking a transformation in the status of that community.

1. *Anu. P.*, (SE) 164. 2-3, (NE) 107. 2-3.
2. Murray, *The Splendour that was Egypt*, p. 185.
3. Moret aud Davy, *From Tribe to Empire*, p. 222.
4. *ŚP*, 85. 7-10.
5. As does Ghurye, who is of the opinion that in the period A.D. 300 to A.D. 1000 the śūdra became socially more degraded (*Caste and Class*, p. 94).

CHAPTER VIII

CHANGE AND CONTINUITY

The main phases in the history of the śūdras, from their earliest appearance to *cir.* A.D. 600, may be roughly indicated. The early Vedic society was primarily pastoral in which tribal elements predominated. Although we come across artisans, agriculturists, priests and warriors even in the earlier portions of the *Ṛg Veda*, the society of Āryans in this period was basically tribal, pastoral and egalitarian. Spoils of war and cattle constituted the main forms of wealth and in the absence of a strong food-producing economy they could not generate such surplus as would fully support priests and warriors. It was possible to have high ranks based on age, seniority, experience and personal qualities, but not social classes based on the exploitation of social surplus. It was therefore a pre-class society, which provided little scope for the formation of a serving order in the form of the śūdras. Princes and priests had women slaves for domestic service, but their number may not have been large. It seems that towards the end of the Ṛg Vedic period the defeated and dispossessed sections of the Āryan and non-Āryan tribes were reduced to the position of śūdras. Both inter-tribal and intra-tribal conflicts contributed to their numbers. But their ranks really swelled on account of the transformation of the pastoral society into an agricultural society in the upper Gangetic basin. For carrying on agricultural operations labourers were needed, and many of them were the poor cousins of "Aryan" priests, princes and peasants. Since originally a considerable number of śūdras formed part of the Āryan community, they retained several tribal rights, especially religious, in later Vedic society. On the basis of the fiction of belonging to the same tribe these rights may also have been extended to non-Āryan śūdras. That the śūdras could participate in certain Vedic ceremonies had something to do with the nature of the later Vedic economy. Although it was food-producing and agricultural, agricultural technology was primitive. The use of iron was known, but confined mainly to war. Problems of clearance were very difficult, and large plots needing the help of numerous labourers could not be formed. The result was that the peasants did not produce much over and above the needs of their daily subsistence. Naturally taxes and tributes could not be collected regularly, and differentiation between those who laboured and produced on the one hand and those who lived as parasites and managers of production on the produce of peasants and labourers on the other could not be intensified. The beginnings of class society were still weak, and at such a stage the position of the śūdras tended to be ambiguous.

When iron tools came to be used for handicrafts, large-scale clearance and field cultivation, conditions were created for the transformation of the tribal, pastoral, egalitarian Vedic society into a full-fledged agricultural and class-divided social order in the sixth century B.C. Once the forested areas of the middle Gangetic basin were cleared with the iron axe and brought under the iron ploughshare, one of the most fertile parts of the world was opened to settlement. Probably through gifts made by the community for services rendered to it or through their own machinations princes and priests managed to bring under contol large stretches of land, which they could not cultivate themselves, even ordinary peasant families needed occasional help from outside in their fields. In a well-established agricultural society, when families come to acquire resources which they are unable to exploit on their own, they usually procure labour power by force of arms[1] and perpetuate its supply by force of law and custom. To this they add the compulsion generated by religion and ideology. What is unique in the case of ancient Indian society is the fact that these different elements of compulsion, physical and ideological, were interwoven into a social texture called the varṇa system. The imperial expansion of Magadha and the other powers resulted in territorial aggrandisement and in the social subjection of a large number of people who not only had to pay taxes but also to provide labour power. The labouring masses who did not pay taxes were presumably placed in the category of śūdras.

1. M. I. Finley, *The Ancient Economy*, p. 66.

Once labour was made available by means of force, law, religion and ideology were pressed into the service of the ruling orders to regularise the system so that labour supply could be maintained and augmented. The Dharmasūtras made a clear distinction between the twice-born and the śūdra by stating that the latter was meant for serving the three higher varṇas. Various kinds of social distinctions were drawn between the two on the same ground by the law-books. The śūdras were excluded from Vedic sacrifices and investiture with the sacred thread which were considered to be the ritualistic hallmarks of an ārya or twice-born. A clear line was drawn between mental and manual labour. The denial of Vedic education to the śūdra implied that he was condemned to physical labour. He was saddled with economic, politico-legal, social and religious disabilities. All this could be justified on the basis of his mythical origin from the feet of the creator. This is similar to Aristotle's justification of slavery on the ground that some people are born to obey and others to command. He asserts that the first become slaves, and the second citizens.

The śūdra is considered identical with the slave, although only a section of śūdras may have been legally slaves. Therefore it is wrong to render the word "śūdra" by "slave", as has been done by Hopkins.[1] In spite of the use of money slaves were used on a limited scale, and the private use of land still remained submerged under clan and joint family rights. The clans which formed higher varṇas held landed property in common, so also did they hold labourers in common to work on the land. It is not correct to characterise the śūdra as a serf, as is done in the *Vedic Index*[2], for a serf means a person whose service is attached to the soil and who is transferred along with it.

By and large, the śūdra community was subjected to a kind of "generalized slavery".[3] Some Pāli texts and the *Arthaśāstra* of Kauṭilya attest the employment of the slaves in agricultural and other types of production by the state and the individuals, but

1. Hopkins, *CHI*, i, 268.
2. *VI*, ii, 389.
3. This idea has been taken from Berdichewsky, "Anthropology and the Peasant Mode of Production" in Bernardo Berdichewsky, ed., *Anthropology and Social Change in Rural Areas*, Mouton, 1979, p. 17.

the slave mode of production was not typical of ancient India. The main producers were the vaiśyas, organised in village communities, who paid taxes to the royal collectors. Their producing activities were supplemented by the śūdras who also served as domestics in the households of the higher varṇas. Manu therefore stated that a śūdra should be reduced to slavery, either through purchase or otherwise. But even between 500 B.C. and A.D. 300 the śūdras were not numerous enough to form the main prop of production. They were considered slaves and subordinates of the higher varṇas in the general sense of these terms. Their "generalized slavery" meant that they could be called by the king for various kinds of work including porterage, construction, etc. Various artisanal activities are included under the term "forced labour" (*viṣṭi*) in the *Arthaśāstra* of Kauṭilya. These were performed by the *dāsas* and *karmakaras* and others, who apparently belonged to the śūdra community.

Tribal practices suggest that the Vedic chief could mobilise communal labour for the good of the kin-ordered community. But when he was transformed into a powerful king with taxes and army he could divert the communal labour to his own advantage. With the division of the community into social classes this kind of forced labour could not be levied from all its members. It was confined to a segment called the śūdras, who consisted of both Vedic and non-Vedic peoples. The śūdras were therefore placed in a state of "generalized slavery" under which they were forced to supply their physical labour to the households of the three higher communities. They were not expected to pay taxes; only those śūdras who served as artisans had to work for a day every month for the king.

The śūdra is called helot, but such a characterisation cannot be made without reservations. The helots could be occasionally recruited in the army, but Kauṭilya alone prefers recruitment of the vaiśyas and śūdras on the ground of their numerical strength. Manu is dead against the enrolment of the śūdras, the apprehension being that they might turn their arms against their recruiters. More importantly, the helots lay under the general control of the state which was identical with the citizenry of Sparta. However although the śūdras were considered to be the subordinates of the twice-born comprising the three higher varṇas, the vaiśyas who were mainly peasants could not be regarded as identical with the state power. Further, the agrarian production of Sparta was run primarily by the servile class of helots, but in India independent peasants called vaiśyas played a vital role in agriculture. Helotry is called undeveloped slavery; in a sense śūdrahood can be called undeveloped helotry, for the śūdras were not so thoroughly under the control of the state as the helots were.

The śūdras' servitude assumed different forms. They served as domestic servants and slaves, agricultural slaves, hired labourers and artisans. A writer condemns them as incapable of constructive efforts,[1] but, undoubtedly the śūdra skill and labour, together with the agricultural surplus produced by the vaiśya peasants, provided the material basis for the development of ancient Indian society, which in this sense was a vaiśya-śūdra formation.

In the Mauryan period, the tendency to employ śūdra labour in agriculture reached its climax, and never before or after did the state exercise so much control over the slaves, hired labourers and artisans. This was the period when slaves were used in production on a large scale by the state. They were possibly recruited from the lowest order in society, although the Kaliṅga and similar wars may have been an important source. But the direct control of the servile order by the state was an interlude in India's social history probably confined to the middle Gangetic plains. It was not followed later. The view that in the *Arthaśāstra* of Kauṭilya the śūdras were regarded as āryas[2] and as such could not be reduced to slavery is not sustained by a close examination of the passages in question.[3] And Aśoka's attempt to abolish varṇa distinctions in the administration of justice probably irritated the brāhmaṇas, but did not benefit the lower orders.

The post-Mauryan period (*cir.*200 B.C.-A.D.300), especially the third century A.D. marks a critical stage in the position of the śūdras. Manu's fanatical anti-śūdra measures and the Purāṇic

1. Valvalkar, *Hindu Social Institutions*, pp. 327-28.
2. R. P. Kangle. *The Kauṭilīya Arthaśāstra*, Pt. II, p. 271, fn. 1.
3. *AŚ*, III. 13.

denunciations of the śūdras for their anti-brāhmaṇical activities indicate a phase of bitter social conflicts and tensions, which was perhaps aggravated by the intervention of the non-brāhmaṇical foreign elements and the increasing importance of artisans. Probably as a result of this conflict, the disappearance of the strong state power of the Mauryas, and the rise of new arts and crafts we notice signs of change in the position of the śūdra. The first two Christian centuries were an age of crafts, commerce, gold and copper coins, trading ports and inland towns. For crafts and commerce the period of the Kuṣāṇas and Sātavāhanas seems to have been as unique as that of the Mauryas for agrarian expansion under the aegis of the state. In no other period of early history India's international trade thrived so much. Naturally the artisans came to the fore, as can be inferred from the epigraphic records of their guilds and donations. Free from state control the guilds could function effectively, and a large number of towns could provide alternative sources of livelihood to oppressed members of the lower orders from the countryside. On the other hand the descriptions of the Kali age suggest a prolonged social crisis caused by the refusal of the two lower varṇas to perform their functions. It was overcome by a policy of coercion and conciliation. Manu's anti-śūdra measures reflect coercion, but he also grants them some concession. The śūdras were given a few minor religious rights.

In the Gupta Period (*cir.* A.D. 300 - *cir.* 600) the śūdras gained some religious and civic rights, and in many respects were placed on a par with the vaiśyas. The bracketting of the vaiśyas and śūdras is not unknown in the earlier texts, but it becomes more frequent in the texts of the post-Mauryan and Gupta periods, and considered in the light of other developments it carries a new significance during the Gupta period. Apparently the status of the vaiśya was degraded towards servitude, that of the śūdra raised towards freedom. Numerous land grants made to the brāhmaṇas in the developed areas tended to depress the position of the old peasants by creating a class of intermediaries between them and the king.[1] Possibly this was

1. The earliest epigraphic evidence for land grants can be traced back to the first century B.C. (Sircar, *Select Insrciptions*, i, p. 188, Inscr. no. 82, line 11), but such grants become common in Gupta period.

the result of a prolonged social conflict which made it difficult to collect taxes from the vaiśyas and labour from the śūdras. Priests and administrators therefore had to be paid through grants of land. Land grants to brāhmaṇas in the undeveloped areas added to the number of śūdras, for aboriginal peasants were recruited into the brāhmaṇical social organisation as śūdras. In the earlier periods the service of the śūdras consisted in supplying labour to the higher varṇas, but from the Gupta period onwards their service and subordination consisted in supplying part of their produce as artisans and traders, and particularly as peasants. The theoretical position about their servitude still continued, but its practical content underwent a change. Of course the śūdras did not cease to be slaves, domestic servants, craftsmen and agricultural labourers, but now their ranks were dominated by peasants, though of a servile nature.

We may consider the position of the śūdras in the economic system on the one hand and their social and ritualistic status on the other. Religious disabilities imposed on them in *c*.500-200 B.C. persisted mostly till *c*. A.D. 300, so long as this category consisted mainly of slaves, artisans, domestic servants and agricultural labourers. But when large numbers of aboriginal peasants began to multiply the śūdra ranks and when the slave element in agrarian production declined substantially, giving way to less servile workers, the social and ritualistic status of the śūdras, as laid down in the Dharmasūtras, became incongruous with their new role in production. This anachronism was gradually removed by enlarging the existing religious rights of the śūdras, by conferring on them more such rights in Gupta and post-Gupta times. At the same time the śūdra community was kept divided by throwing a good many tribal and artisans into the order of untouchables. Those who still continued in their old servile position and were further reinforced by the growing number of untouchables came to be known ritually *asat* or impure śūdras, and their religious conduct was accordingly laid down. Apparently peasant castes supplemented by some artisans accounted for the pure or *sat* śūdras, and the untouchables consisting of agricultural labourers and some low artisanal occupations stood for the impure śūdras or mixed (*miśra/saṃkara*) castes, which clearly marked the social configuration of Gupta and post-Gupta times. A late chapter of Manu mentions more than sixty mixed castes. They resulted from the process of consolidating continuous conquests through the mechanism of land grants by which numerous tribes annexed to the brāhmaṇical order were converted into śūdra castes. Tribals at lower stages of culture were made untouchables, whose number shot up suddenly and became considerable enough to attract the attention of the Chinese travellers. From towards the end of the Gupta period onwards the decline of crafts and commerce added to the number of castes, for guilds lost mobility and tended to become rigid, hereditary organisations.

Changes in the position of the śūdras in the period of our study did not alter the status of their basic servility. They cannot be called slaves, but they functioned as substitutes for slaves. Except in the period from about 500 B.C. to A.D. 300 in northern India slaves were not an important element in production. On the other hand the śūdras supplied the main labour power to an economy in which land, cattle and other instruments of production lay under the effective control of the three higher orders who constituted some kind of ārya citizenry. Very roughly the twice-born comprising the first three social estates in India can be compared to citizens of Greece and Rome, and the śūdras to their non-citizens. The varṇa system was not only an instrument for regulating social relations, but what is more significant, a mechanism for carrying on production and distribution and consequently for governing the relations between different classes involved in these processes. As a mechanism for the appropriation of surplus produce and labour by those who were not directly and primarily engaged in production, the varṇa system of ancient India roughly served the same purpose as the citizenship system in classical antiquity. The Dharmaśāstras gave it the same legal validity as was enjoyed by the scheme of citizenship in Greece and Rome. But there were two differences. First, the varṇa system was presented under a religious garb while the citizenship system was given mainly a politico-legal garb. Secondly, although the vaiśyas were "citizens" till Gupta times they continued to be the principal taxpayers as peasants on account of which they had to function as primary producers. Unlike the Indian system the social formation of classical antiquity did not provide for a large segment of producing citizens. This is however not to ignore the perpetual tensions and conflicts that raged between rich and poor citizens, between patricians and plebians in classical antiquity. In the Indian structure whatever may have been the nature of tensions and conflicts within the ārya body of citizenry, for a long time the myth of the twice-born was successfully cultivated to keep the community of śūdras in isolation from the vaiśya peasants. Their form of servility underwent a significant change probably on account of a social crisis in around the third century A.D. but the element of servitude continued. For a long time the śūdras supplied surplus labour as slaves, artisans and agricultural labourers; from Gupta times onwards they supplied surplus produce as peasants and supplemented it with occasional forced labour. Since the social fabric of ancient India was based on the vaiśya tax and the śūdra labour, it may be called a vaiśya-śūdra society, but from the ideological and ritualistic point of view it may be called a brāhmaṇical society.

Low caste men are called robbers and murderers, and considered guilty of thefts, burglaries and even sedition. The śūdras are called cruel, liars and backbiters, and represented as enemies of the brāhmaṇas. But there is no direct reference to their revolt like the one to the revolt of the Śākya slaves.

In spite of the servile status and miserable conditions of the śūdra masses, particularly in pre-Gupta times, there is hardly any direct evidence of śūdra revolts. However references to their violent anti-brāhmaṇical activities appear during the second and third centuries A.D. The epic and Purāṇic descriptions of the Kali age and statelessness (*arājakatā*), which focus on social convulsions and mixing of the social orders (*varṇasaṃkara*) and highlight the manifestation of the śūdra antagonism towards the brāhmaṇa, may be taken as echoes of śūdra revolts, but their exact time and place cannot be fixed. In comparison with the slave revolts in Rome, occasional and sporadic anti-state activities of the śūdras are insignificant. The śūdras may have contributed to people's wrath called *janapada-kopa*[1] and *prakṛti-*

1. *AŚ.*, I. 13.

kopa[1]. It is suggested that the lower vaiśyas constituted the middle class ('petty bourgeoisie'), which held the balance between the śūdra and dvija classes.[2] The use of the term dvija classes is inaccurate, for the vaiśyas were also regarded as such. But even the fact of the vaiśyas acting as a stabilising sector between the first two varṇas on the one hand and the śūdras on the other can be true only of the period before the beginning of the Christian era, when the two lower varṇas began to approximate to one another. By the Gupta period they practically lost their independent identities.

We may, however, suggest some other reasons to explain the comparative calmness of the śūdras in ancient Indian society. It seems that money economy had not developed in India to the extent to which it had in Greece[3] and Rome, and hence notwithstanding the theoretical servitude of the śūdras, very few of them could be reduced to slavery through failure to pay debts, which was a major source of slavery in Greece.[4] Except in the pre-Mauryan and Mauryan periods, there is very little evidence of the employment of agricultural slaves. Slavery was mostly domestic, under which there subsisted intimate relations with the master, and the slaves formed not a sharply marked class, but merely the lowest rung of the household ladder.

In the case of oppression the śūdra labourers may have taken refuge[5] among the free tribal population, or have migrated from one state to another. The oppressed seem to have offered passive resistance; we have hardly any concrete instance of revolt or active resistance. Further, in contrast to the brāhmaṇas and kṣatriyas, the śūdras were not a well-organised, closed community, capable of making any combined efforts against their masters. As time passed, they fragmented into numerous subcastes of unequal social status, which went on multiplying through the accession of numerous tribes. It is suggested that

1. *Ibid.*, V. 6, VII. 6. Eva Ritchle presented a paper on this subject to IV World Sanskrit Conferences, Weimar 1979.
2. Bose, *op. cit.*, ii, 486-87.
3. Cf. Thomson, *Studies in Ancient Greek Society*, ii, pp. 194-96.
4. Cf. Solon's Debt Laws towards the beginning of the sixth century B.C.
5. A case of the desertion of the Pāñcāla kingdom by the oppressed subjects is reported in a Jātaka.

in the *Amarakośa*, craftsmen such as garland makers, potters, masons, weavers, tailors, painters etc. are noted in an approximately descending order.[1] The theory of the origin of mixed castes through hypergamy (*pratiloma*) was cleverly used to create a hierarchy of degraded śūdra castes, separated by ideas of purity and pollution from one another,[2] with the result that they found it difficult to make a common cause. The division between the pure (*sat*) and impure (*asat*) śūdras became marked from Gupta times onwards.

There is no doubt that among the śūdras domestic servants, sharecroppers, herdsmen and barbers were regarded as higher in the social scale than most other types of śūdras, for their food could be taken even by the brāhmaṇa master.[3] Greater weakness of the lower orders lay in their division into śūdras and untouchables, which appeared in the time of Pāṇini, was perpetuated in later times and accentuated in the Gupta period. The śūdras gained in status not only through their levelling up with the higher varṇas but also through their exaltation above the untouchables, so that, with a class of people lower than they, they might satisfy their sense of vanity in the brāhmaṇical hierarchy.

And, lest perchance the discontented śūdras resorted to arms, the lawgivers prescribed a consistent policy of keeping them disarmed, which was possibly modified in the Gupta period.

A powerful factor which helped to preserve the essentials of the varṇa system and thus to keep the śūdras down was the indoctrination of the masses in the theory of *karma* and of the bad consequences following the non-performance of the varṇa or *jāti* duties ordained by gods. It is argued that since the masses were widely educated and endowed with critical acumen, they could not believe in the natural superiority of the

1. Kosambi. *JOR*, xxiv, 61.

2. "... *pratiloma* is a convenient intellectual device for generating various disapproved categories, assigning them degraded positions, and ideologically explaining and rationalising why so many groups in the caste hierarchy are placed in low or downtrodden positions." S. J. Tambiah, "From Varṇa to Caste through Mixed Unions," in Jack Goody (ed.), *The Character of Kinship*, p. 207.

3. *Yāj*., I. 166.

higher varṇas,[1] but there is no basis for such a wild claim. On the contrary, the minds of the labouring masses were so strongly enchained by the brāhmaṇical ideology that both direct coercion against the śūdras and violent revolts on their part were made extremely difficult.

But the brāhmaṇical ideologues were not always the slaves of their theories. Considerations of birth did not prevent them from inventing suitable kṣatriya genealogies for aboriginal and foreign chiefs.[2] Probably the few adventurous śūdras, who may have risen to influential status from time to time, were neatly fitted into the brāhmaṇical system as kṣatriyas, so that they could defend the dominance of the higher varṇas with the usual enthusiasm of new converts. The traditional account of the brāhmaṇa Kauṭilya's support to the śūdrā-born Candragupta shows that such developments were not impossible.

The Jains, Buddhists and Ājīvikas were condemned as śūdras, who could be admitted to the fold of those sects without any discrimination. Their influence may have been felt especially in the period from B.C. 500—A.D. 300 and seems to have been confined to artisan śūdras; Buddhism, the strongest of all, did not admit slaves and debtors to the saṃgha. The impact of Vaiṣṇavism was felt in post-Mauryan and more particularly in Gupta times, but the worship of Viṣṇu was exploited by the brāhmaṇas to maintain the principle of social stratification and economic discrimination involved in the varṇa system. Tantricism admitted women and śūdras to its *cakra* or ordination and popularised the folk and aboriginal cult of the mother goddess towards the end of the Gupta period and in post-Gupta times, but it soon came to develop a religious hierarchy, typical of a feudal society, giving the lowest place to its lay devotees. The reforming sects responded to the religious aspirations of the various sections of the śūdras at one stage or the other. The Jain and Buddhist sects catered to the needs of śūdra artisans, and the śaivite, vaiṣṇavite and tantric sects (although all early

1. K. V. Rangaswami Aiyanger, *Aspects of the Social and Political System of Manusmṛti*, p. 134.

2. This process has continued even to recent times. *Census of India*, 1891, 13 (Madras), p. 213. Quoted in *ZDMG*, 1, 510.

medieval sects were affected by tantricism) catered to the needs of śūdra peasants, but none of them could substantially alter the servile position of the fourth varṇa. None of the reforming religious movements of Buddhism, Jainism, Śaivism and Vaiṣṇavism questioned the fundamental theory of *karma*, which provided the doctrinal basis of the brāhmaṇical social order They tried to contain social discontent rather than channalise it into revolutionary directions. By promising religious equality in place of other forms of equality they helped to reconcile the lower orders to the existing social system. The spirit of protest against social inequities, which marked these movements in their earlier stages, withered away in course of time, and they identified themselves with the essentials of the varṇa organisation. Thus the complex of all these factors helped to maintain the comparative calmness of the śūdras and to secure their permanent servitude.

APPENDIX I

DATE OF THE *Manu Smṛti* WITH SPECIAL REFERENCE TO THE TENTH CHAPTER

The time bracket 200 B.C.—A.D. 200 suggested by Bühler for the *Manu Smṛti* covers a period of four hundred years.[1] Jayaswal substantially delimits this period and ascribes Manu to the period of the brāhmaṇical 'counterrevolution' in the age of the Śuṅgas.[2] But a careful study of the law-book of Nārada (fifth-sixth century) would show that the brāhmaṇas are given equally, if not more, important privileges by that lawgiver. A comparison of some technical terms used in Manu with those found in inscriptions also suggests a late date for this law-book.

Although the Yavanas mentioned by Manu and identical with the Indo-Greeks lose their importance in the early centuries of the Christian era this is not true of the Śakas, Pahlavas, and Ābhīras who continue to hold ground in north-western India during that period. Of course inscriptions do not mention the Parthians beyond the first century A.D., but they attest the existence of the Śakas till the end of the fourth century and that of the Ābhīras from the second to the fourth centuries. Curiously enough Manu speaks of a mixed caste called maitra;[3] they may be identified with the Maitrakas of Valabhī, who appear in inscriptions in the fifth century although as a tribe they may have existed earlier.

Two mixed castes meda and andhra bracketted together in the tenth chapter of Manu[4] appear in the same form in Pāla inscriptions.[5] The ambasṭhas, who appear mentioned as a mixed

1. *SBE*, xxv, Introd., pp. CXIV-CXVIII.
2. *Manu and Yājñavalkya*, pp. 25-32; cf. Kane, *Hist. Dh. S.*, ii, p. XI. Ketkar (*History of Caste*, p. 66) argues that the work belongs to A.D. 272-320.
3. The earliest inscription of the Maitrakas belongs to A.D. 502, but they appear to have been the feudatories of the Guptas in the fifth century.
4. X. 49-50.
5. *EI*, iii, no. 36, ll. 5-6, 22-23.

caste in earlier texts, are described by Manu as physicians, a function associated with them in early medieval times.[1] The most striking thing about the tenth chapter of Manu is the sudden jump in the number of mixed castes to over sixty from about twenty in the earlier law-books. Since this is not found in any other smṛti, it makes the tenth chapter of Manu suspect. On the other hand the number of the mixed castes increases in such later texts as the *Skanda Purāṇa* and the *Brahmavaivarta Purāṇa*. Manu's number exceeds 100 if we add to it the list of mixed castes given in the *Brahmavaivarta Purāṇa*.[2] All this might suggest that the tenth chapter of Manu is very late because none of these Purāṇas seem to have existed before *c.* A.D. 700.[3]

The provision for land gift in the fourth chapter of Manu may suggest its contemporaneity with the Smṛtis and inscriptions of the early Christian centuries. Manu recommends gift of land and points out the merit of granting it,[4] which is touched on only in some Dharmasūtras. But it is in consonance with the teachings of the *Śānti Parvan*, of Viṣṇu,[5] Yājñavalkya[6] and Bṛhaspati.[7] We have a section called *bhūmidānapraśaṃsā* in the *Anuśāsana Parva*.[8] The later text and the *Viṣṇudharmottara Purāṇa*[9] (eighth century) declare the gift of land to be the best of all the gifts. But Manu holds a different view. According to him the gift of the Veda or learning (*brahmadāna*) is superior to all the other gifts including that of land.[10] Manu does not favour the acceptance of land by a brāhmaṇa on the ground that such *pratigraha* destroys the merit of the recipient.[11] This obviously

1. D. C. Sircar, *Studies in the Society and Administration of Ancient and Medieval India*, i, 107-8.
2. *Brahma Khaṇḍa*, X. 14-136.
3. R. C. Hazra, *Studies in Purāṇic Records on Hindu Rites and Customs* (2nd edn., Delhi, 1975), pp. 165-67.
4. IV. 230.
5. *Viṣṇu*, Chs. 91-92, quoted in *SBE*, xxv, 165 fn.
6. I. 210-11.
7. I. 8.
8. Cr. edn.. Ch. 61.
9. III. 93.13.
10. IV. 233.
11. IV. 188-89.

points to a situation in which land grants had become the order of the day, and Manu's model of a puritan brāhmaṇa was in danger of being subverted. But the practice being widespread, Manu reluctantly allows a brāhmaṇa to accept land; provided untilled (*akṛta*) land is preferred to tilled (*kṛta*) land.[1] The epigraphic reference to the faint beginning of land grant can possibly be pushed back to the first century B.C., but clear evidence belongs to the second century A.D. in Maharashtra under the Sātavāhana rulers. However Manu's law-book was applicable to the Āryāvarta, where we have hardly any instance of land grant in the first two-three centuries of the Christian era. It seems that by the fourth century or so the practice may have become common enough to have invited the attention of Manu. His recommendation regarding acceptance of the uncultivated land reminds us of the grant of *khila* or *aprahata* land to the brāhmaṇa according to the principle of *bhūmicchidranyāya*,[2] mentioned first in inscriptions of the fifth century. Manu also uses the term *kūṭa-śāsana* in the sense of forged land grant,[3] which term is used in the law-books of Gupta times and in a land grant of Harṣavardhana.[4] All this helps us to fix the lower limits for dating his law-book.

Although Manu recommends payment of lower class servants in cash or paṇa, he is the first lawgiver to ordain that fiscal and administrative functionaries should be paid by grants of land,[5] a provision also repeated by Bṛhaspati.[6] This again reminds us of the situation in which both religious and non-religious services are paid through land grants. Direct epigraphic corroboration of non-religious grants is not available because these were recorded on such perishable material as piece of cloth or the bark of the birch tree, but we have a few instances of land grants to secular parties in the fifth century.[7] The term

1. X. 114.
2. *CII*, iii, no. 31, ll. 7-11, 13.
3. IX. 232.
4. *EI*, vii, no. 22, l. 10.
5. VII. 115-20.
6. Quoted in *Vyavahāramayūkha* (tr. P. V. Kane & S. G. Patwardhan), pp. 25-27.
7. *Indian Feudalism*, pp. 13-14.

daśagrāmi used by Kauṭilya and *daśagrāmapati* by Manu[1] is however mentioned first in a Pāla inscription of the ninth century.[2]

In his law of inheritance Manu recommends that the *kīnāśa* or cultivator should go to the eldest son of a brāhmaṇa.[3] This would suggest that certain cultivators or cultivating tenants were attached to the family lands, and although division of landed property is not explicitly recommended by Manu, it is difficult to think of cultivators in isolation from the land they tilled. A Pallava Prākṛt copper plate charter of about A.D. 250-350 transfers sharecroppers to a beneficiary along with the land.[4] The allied provision in Manu therefore may not have been of an earlier date.

The establishment of a military unit called *gulma* for two to five villages in backward areas appears as a device in Manu.[5] Its head can be identified as *gulmika* or *gumika* mentioned in a Pallava Prākrit inscription of the middle of the fourth century A.D.[6] But *gaulmika* clearly appears in inscriptions of Bihar and Bengal in the fifth century,[7] and repeatedly in the list of royal officers mentioned in later Chamba, Pāla and Sena grants.[8]

The divinity of kingship is a distinctive feature of the lawbook of Manu, who assigns the attributes of eight gods to the king.[9] The Kuṣāṇa and Sātavāhana inscriptions introduce the idea of royal divinity,[10] but the Gupta epigraphs provide a more convincing counterpart for the ideas of Manu. The Allahabad inscription of Samudra Gupta, possibly belonging to the middle of the fourth century, compares the king to four gods.[11] This

1. VII. 115.
2. *EI*, xxix, no. 13, ll. 28-29; the term used is *daśagrāmika*.
3. IX. 150.
4. *EI*, i, no. 1, l. 39.
5. VII. 114.
6. *Sel. Inscrr.*, i, Bk. III, no. 65, l. 5; the term *gumika* is used. Sukthankar reads *gāmika* as *gumika* in a Sātavāhana inscription of the first half of the third century A.D. *ibid.*, p. 212, fn. 6.
7. *CII*, iii, no. 12, l. 29.
8. N. G. Majumdar, *Inscriptions of Bengal*, iii (Rajshahi, 1929), 184.
9. VIII 4-8.
10. *Sel. Inscrr.*, i, Bk. II, nos. 40, 41, 44, etc., cf no. 86.
11. Line 26.

suggests that the order of eight gods found in Manu may have developed later. Similarly the term *daivata* applied by Manu to the brāhmaṇa[1] is applied as *paramadaivata* to Gupta kings first in the Bengal inscriptions of the fifth century.[2] All this would indicate a late date for chapters VII, IX and XI of Manu where these ideas occur. On the other hand the term *akṣayanidhi* used by Manu in the sense of perpetual deposit[3] occurs as *akṣayanivi* in the second century inscriptions[4] of the Kuṣāṇas and Sātavāhanaṣ and is found later in several land grants.

Some indication of the date can be given on the basis of the references to coins in Manu. For various offences Manu prescribes fines in paṇas, and there is no doubt that the age of the Kuṣāṇas and Guptas saw an extensive use of coins. The standard Kuṣāna gold coin weighed 144 grains, which seems to be the equivalent of 80 *kṛṣṇalas* or *rattis* for a *suvarṇa* (coin) given in Manu.[5] But the rate of interest recommended by Manu is higher than the rate in a Nasik inscription of the second century A.D.[6]

In the second century, inscriptions of Gautamīputra Sātakarṇi and Rudradāman emphasise the preservation of varṇas as one of the main royal functions. This aspect is also stressed by Manu, who is very keen on avoiding *varṇasaṃkara*. All this may point to a date around A.D. 200 for the earlier portions of Manu. But an epigraphic examination of some of the other contents of Manu would place them in the fifth century or even later. We can therefore suggest a revised time bracket, between A.D. 220 and 400. This fits in with the dating of the *Śānti Parvan* in which some of Manu's verses exactly occur; it is difficult to say who borrowed from whom. However the tenth chapter, which deals with over five dozen mixed castes, may belong to late Gupta or even post-Gupta times.

1. IX. 317; XI. 84.
2. *Sel. Inscrr.*, i, Bk. III, nos. 18-19.
3. VII. 83.
4. *Sel. Inscrr.*, i, Bk. II, no. 49, l. 11; no. 58, l. 1.
5. VIII. 134.
6. VIII. 139-42; *Sel. Inscrr.*, i, Bk. II. no. 58, ll. 1-3.

APPENDIX II

PROLIFERATION OF SERVILE AND PEASANT CASTES

The later Vedic texts speak of four varṇas, a few non-Aryan tribals such as the Niṣādas and Andhras, and of about a dozen craft groups. All these find place in the *puruṣamedha* described in the Yajus texts. The object of this sacrifice was to establish some kind of rapport between the patriarchal 'Aryans' living on cattle-rearing and plough-agriculture and matrilineal non-Aryans engaged in hunting and hoe-cultivation. The *puruṣmedha* was evidently a religious mechanism for bringing the divergent orders, occupations and non-Aryan peoples under one umbrella. But these tribes and occupations did not assume the characteristics of caste in the brāhmaṇical sense. Another device introduced in later Vedic times to absorb the non-Aryan peoples in the brāhmaṇical fold was the theory of the vrātya. Vrātyas, as later explained by Kauṭilya and Manu, were originally dvijas who came to be regarded as 'second class citizens' because of their deviation from *vrata* or vow. The Magadhas, originally a people who settled down in Magadha, belonged to this category, and their king appears as a vrātya ruler in later Vedic texts. But the vrātya also included many other peoples. It was a package term used by the brāhmaṇas to cover such tribal people in the eastern zone as lived on hoe-cultivation, producing some kind of primitive maize called *gavedhuka*,[1] which served as their food and the fodder of their cattle. They seem to have been a matrilineal people. Rudra, the god of animals, was the god of the vrātyas, who knew neither ploughing nor trading. The vrātyas were possibly the black-and-red ware people who used microliths and some copper implements in the pre-iron age in eastern U.P., Bihar and Bengal, and lived on fish and rice. However their material

1. K.P. Chattopadhyaya, *The Ancient Indian Culture Contacts and Migrations* (Calcutta, 1970), p. 28.

equipment does not suggest large settlements in the thickly forested areas of the Gaṅgā basin. Evidently the vrātya people consisted of several tribes such as the Niṣādas, Punjiṣṭhas and others whose names are not mentioned. Members of a clan headed by its chief may have lived together for six generations, and at a time they may have numbered 200.[1] A clan was collectively admitted to later Vedic peasant society through the ritual known as *vrātyaṣṭoma*, and gradually it settled down to plough agriculture and developed as a caste. Some names mentioned in Manu may look back to much earlier times, but all this is speculative.

With the establishment of a full-fledged agrarian economy based on iron-plough agriculture the 'Aryan' society went on expanding through conquests, and the problem of tribal acculturation assumed important dimensions in pre-Maurya times when we find at least sixteen large territorial kingdoms in northern India inhabited by the standard four orders and numerous new tribes. The spread of iron technology in eastern U.P. and Bihar, the beginnings of trade and commerce, the use of coins and the rise of towns in the Gaṅgā basin naturally gave rise to many crafts, whose practitioners had to be given place in the brāhmaṇical social framework. Hence the Dharmasūtras evolved the theory of the *anuloma* and *pratiloma*, namely, the mixed castes formed as a result of miscegenation between men of the higher varṇas and women of the lower varṇas and vice versa. The number of such castes arose gradually. The Dharmasūtras mention twenty-four mixed castes, and Kauṭilya specifies sixteen; all of whom except vrātya are common to the Dharmasūtra list, which raises the total number of mixed castes to twenty-five. Obviously the list does not include all the crafts, twenty-eight of which are mentioned in the *Digha Nikāya* and eighteen of which seem to have been organized into guilds conventionally known as the *aṣṭādaśa śreṇi* in early Pāli texts.[2] The craft guilds did not develop into rigid

1. *Ibid.*, pp. 25-26.

2. The number eighteen is latter applied to *tīrthas* (officers in the *Arthaśāstra* of Kauṭilya), *parihāra* (immunities), *parvans* and *askṣauhiṇīs* in the *Mahābhārata*, to *Purāṇas* and so on. Its multiple thirty-six appears in early medieval times to enumerate varṇas.

castes so long as there was plentiful use of money, thriving towns meeting the needs of their rural hinterlands and vice versa, and expanding trade and commerce from about the fifth ceutury B.C. to about the fifth century A.D. The economic set-up made room for considerable mobility in the case of craftsmen and merchants for whom the taboos regarding food and marriage habits had to be relaxed.

But when we come to Manu's tenth chapter, ascribable to late Gupta times, we have the remarkable spectacle of sixty-one mixed castes, most of them being the products of *pratiloma* or hypogamous unions. Later Hsuan Tsang notices so many mixed castes that he finds it difficult to describe them. Manu offers two explanations for their origin. First he takes recourse to the vrātya theory, which was modified in post-Vedic times. Baudhāyana identifies vrātya with the *varṇasaṃkara* and the third book of the *Arthaśāstra* of Kauṭilya roundly supports this view.[1] According to Kauṭilya the vrātyas are sons begotten by impure men of any of the four orders on a woman of lower caste.[2] Manu also characterises the vrātya as a mixed caste but excludes the śūdras from the process of producing the vrātyas. In addition to assigning a mixed origin to the vrātya both Kauṭilya and Manu call him a deviant from the established religious practice. According to Manu a twice-born (*dvijāti*) produces on a similar woman (*savarṇā*) those who do not observe *vrata* (*avratān*), and these people, who are not entitled to the sacred thread ceremony, are called vrātya.[3] The vrātya brāhmaṇa produces on a brāhmaṇa woman Bhūrjakaṇṭaka, Āvantya, Vāṭadhāna, Puṣpadha and Śaikha.[4] The progeny of the rājanya vrātya from a kṣatriya woman consist of the Jhallas, Mallas, Licchavis, Naṭas, Karaṇas, Khasas and Draviḍas.[5] From the vaiśya vrātya on a vaiśyā are produced Sudhanvā, Ācārya, Kārūṣa, Vijanma, Maitra and Sātvata.[6] Thus Manu enumerates in all eighteen vrātya mixed castes. Although divided into three categories of brāhmaṇa,

1. *AŚ*, III. 7.
2. According to Kangle's translation of *AŚ*, III. 7 vrātyas are produced by impure men of three higher varṇas on women of the same varṇa.
3. X. 20.
4. X. 21.
5. X. 22.
6. X. 23.

kṣatriya and vaiśya, they are all reduced to the position of śūdras inasmuch as they are not entitled to *upanayana* and consequently Vedic studies. In addition to these vrātya castes, Manu enumerates twelve kṣatriya castes who were reduced to śūdrahood on account of abandoning their rituals and lack of contact with the brāhmaṇas.[1] These are Pauṇḍraka, Audra, Dravida, Kāmboja, Yavana, Śaka, Pārada, Pahlava, Cīna, Kirāta, Darada and Khasa.[2] They are as good as vrātyas, for they are also distinguished by the lack of *upanayana*. Since two mixed castes mentioned in the second list are also found in the first list, the total number of the vrātya and semi-vrātya castes comes to twenty-eight.

It is difficult to identify all the twenty-eight *jātis* ethnically, linguistically, geographically and occupationally. The Āvantya (people of Avanti), and Vāṭadhāna (mentioned as a people in the *Mahābhārata*) definitely belong to the category of tribes and peoples, and at least the former lived in the Malwa area. The Sātvata tribe also belonged to western India, and if we identify the Maitra with the Maitraka, which is grammatically a diminutive of the former, the Maitra belonged to Valabhī situated in the Kathiawar region of Gujarat. The Mallas lived in earlier times in the foothills of the Himalayas, and in Gupta times the Licchavis had set up their rule in Nepal, where they made land grants to the brāhmaṇas. The Jhallas may have been their neighbours, and were probably the remnants of a tribe. The title *jhalla* is still prevalent, and we have a district called Jhalawar in Rajasthan. The Pauṇḍrakas belonged to north Bengal, the Auḍras to Orissa, and the Draviḍas to south India, and all the three are mentioned by Manu in the same geographical order. Similarly a set of foreign peoples – the Yavana, Śaka, Pārada and Pahlava – is mentioned in a neat geographical and chronological order which also includes the borderline Kāmbojas; they all belonged to north-western India. We have another group of local and foreign peoples belonging to northern and eastern India. They are mixed together as Cīna, Kirāta, Darada and Khasa; many of these find place in the *Mahābhārata*, and the

1. X. 43-44.
2. Ibid.

Khasas are also mentioned as a people in Pāla inscriptions along with the Hūṇa and Kulika. Karūṣa can be identified as a people of the forested area of Bihar covering the districts of Sasaram and Palamau. All told nineteen out of the twenty mixed castes of Manu appear to be indigenous or foreign tribes, mostly living in the periphery of the Āryāvarta or Brahmāvarta which was the area of the Aryan culture according to Manu. Thus the myth of the vrātyahood or the status resulting from the loss of ritual was invented to facilitate the admission of local and foreign tribes as non-dvija members of society. However these members enjoyed varying degrees of respectability as degraded brāhmaṇas, kṣatriyas, vaiśyas and śūdras.

Of the remaining nine vrātya castes mentioned by Manu bhūrjakaṇṭaka, puṣpadha,[1] śaikha and ācārya seem to be degraded priests or followers of different religious sects which tended to crystallize into castes. Naṭas and karaṇas are occupational groups; sudhanvā may have been a group of archers, while vijanma literally means an illegitimate child. Thus the vrātya theory was used by Manu on a large scale to cover all categories — ethnic, occupational and territorial — which had been assimilated in brāhmaṇical society as castes. It is likely that the tenth chapter of Manu, which theorises about the legitimisation of these peoples as castes, is a work of about the fifth century by when all these tribes had been assimilated into brāhmaṇical society.

The second explanation given by Manu for the origin of numerous castes is the extension of the theory of *anuloma* and *pratiloma*, an idea which also forms part of the vrātya theory. More than thirty castes are accounted for by means of this theory. The origins of a good many of these are explained in the Dharmasūtras, and in several cases the varṇasaṃkara theory applied by Manu runs counter to them. The inconsistencies involved in accounting for the varṇasaṃkara origin of the same caste in different ways by different lawgivers including Manu have been brought out in an article.[2] They demonstrate that

1. The bhūrjakaṇṭaka may have something to do with the Bhojaka, first mentioned in the *Aitareya Brāhmaṇa*.

2. Vivekananda Jha, "Varṇasaṃkara in the Dharmasūtras : Theory and Practice", *Journal of the Economic and Social History of the Orient*, xiii (1970), 273-88.

this theory was fictitious. Whether it is deviation from prescribed varṇa duties or the miscegenation between the varṇas or both the relentless logic of the four original varṇas is being imposed on all the castes. But it seems that many of the mixed castes had nothing to do with the four orders in either sense. The explanation has to be sought in certain historical processes.

The non-Sanskritic names of many of these mixed castes and their description as tribes or occupations at different places suggests that these were older tribes and occupations improvised into castes. We may possibly identify eighteen remnants of the older tribes in this Manu's list of mixed castes. These are: Ābhīra, Āhiṇḍaka, Ambaṣṭha, Andhra, Caṇḍāla, Cuñcu, Dāśa, Kaivartta, Madgu, Mādhuka, Māgadha, Mārgava, Meda, Niṣāda, Pukkusa, Sairindhra, Vaidehaka, and Veṇa. The remaining thirteen, namely, āvṛta, āyogava, carmakāra, dhigvaṇa, kukkuṭaka, kārāvara, karaṇa, kṣattā, maitreyak, pāṇḍusopāka, pāraśava, sūta, śvapāka, and ugra might indicate occupation.[1] Antyāvasāyin, though defined as a separate mixed caste in Vasiṣṭha and Manu, seems to have been an omnibus term applied to all the untouchables.

The total number of vrātya and mixed castes mentioned by Manu comes to sixty-one, and, if we add the four broad orders, it comes to sixty-five. This list includes practically all the mixed castes mentioned in the Dharmasūtras and the *Arthaśāstra* of Kauṭilya. These are ambaṣṭha, antyāvasāyin, āyogava, bhṛjjyakaṇṭha, caṇḍāla, karaṇa, kṣattā, kukkuṭaka, māgadha, niṣāda, pāraśava, pukkusa or paulkasa, sūta, śvapāka, ugra, vaidehaka or vaideha, veṇaor vaina, and yavana. Dauṣmanta, dhīvara, kṛta, kuśīlava, mahiṣya, and mūrdhāvaṣikta are the mixed castes who are mentioned in the earlier lists but do not find place in Manu's catalogue, although naṭa in Manu may correspond to kuśīlava in Kauṭilya. Vrātya appears as a mixed caste in Kauṭilya, but Baudhāyana and Manu treat it as a generic term, and Manu places twenty-eight mixed castes in this category. However the important thing to note is more than doubling of

1. The problem of occupational untouchables has been discussed by Vivekananda Jha in his Patna University Ph. D. thesis, Untouchables in Early India, Ch. III.

the mixed castes in Manu. In the earlier law-books altogether their number is twenty-five, but in the tenth chapter of Manu it rises to over sixty. The lists in either case may not be exhaustive, but they unmistakably reflect the trend towards the multiplication of castes.

In post-Gupta times the number of 'mixed' castes goes on steadily multiplying, and from the numerical point of view Manu's list is not very much different from the one given in the tenth chapter of the Brahma khaṇḍa of the *Brahmavaivarta Purāṇa*, attributable to the tenth century. The latter counts seventy-two mixed castes, of which many are common to Manu. However the additional castes, mentioned in this Purāṇa, comprise about fifty tribes and craft groups who do not appear in Manu.

It is obvious that we can neither accept Manu's explanation of the proliferation of castes nor its further projection in later texts. Then how did this number increase? Since many of the mixed castes were originally tribes, we have to find out the circumstances under which they were made part of the caste system. As stated earlier, conquest and territorial expansion brought the caste or varṇa-based rulers into contact with the tribal, aboriginal people all over the country. Since the established values regarding property, social orders and patriarchal family were not shared by the tribal people who did not understand the language of the ruling class, by persisting in their old ways of life they created troubles for these rulers. Aśoka had to face difficulties, and he tried to convert them to civilized life by propagating principles of dharma among them. He claims to have achieved success, but we have no idea of its extent.

The society which received the tribals in pre-Manu times and the methods through which it assimilated them changed after the age of Manu. Although the earlier society was varṇa-divided, it was not sharply marked by unequal distribution of land leading to the establishment of strong private rights in it. Independent peasants formed the backbone of the society which was also served by a considerable amount of trade and commerce, a good many thriving towns and handicrafts, and a widespread use of metallic money. The tribals therefore were annexed to a four-tier society, and several of them were absorbed as kṣatriyas and vaiśyas. The vrâtya list of Manu does not speak of any specific śūdra caste. On the other hand it specifies twelve second-class ksatriya castes (all of them being originally tribal peoples, foreign and indigenous) and six vaiśya castes tribes. The number of the brāhmaṇa vrātya castes is five, out of whom only two appear to be remnants of original tribes. It seems that the vrātya theory meant for according recognition to tribals annexed to brāhmaṇical society had started much earlier, and if Manu's vrātya examples are taken as marking the climax of the old process, it would appear that most tribals were given place in the second and third strata of society, in other words as warriors and peasants.

The mechanism for absorbing tribals involved the support of brāhmaṇa priests and Buddhist monks who received gifts consisting of cash money supplemented by grants of pieces of land. This can be said on the basis of epigraphic evidence from western Maharashtra and in the Sanchi and Bharhut areas. The nature of gift was determined by the medium of exchange prevalent in *circa* B.C. 200-A.D. 500. The Buddhist missionaries, like the *dharmamahāmātras* of Aśoka, must have played an important part in propagating Buddhist social ethics among the tribal people. This ethic emphasised the values of patriarchal family, individual property, respect towards elders, monks, priests, etc., preservation of cattle wealth, and respect for kṣatriyas and brāhmanas, for according to the later Buddhist texts the Buddha was born only in the two higher varṇas. It was in this phase that a good portion of Maharashtra and Gujarat was acculturated, and, because of the strength of the four-strata system, in these areas almost all the four orders came to be established.

Cash grants were supplemented by grant of pieces of land, mostly belonging to the royal demesne (*rājakaṃ khetam*) in western Maharashtra where we have the earliest inscriptional evidence. Villages also began to be granted, but such grants transferred the royal revenues in the donated areas and not their ownership. In any case in Gupta and post-Gupta times the mechanism of gift-making changed materially. Cash endowments were replaced mainly by land endowments, and Buddhist receivers by brāhmaṇa beneficiaries.

Later rulers, instead of deputing *dharmamahāmātras* or *antamahāmātras*, adopted the practice of planting brāhmaṇas in the tribal areas through land grants. Between the second and fifth centuries brāhmaṇas were granted land in good numbers in the Deccan — in Andhra Pradesh and Maharashtra. Land grants to brāhmaṇas on a considerable scale appear in Madhya Pradesh in the fourth-fifth centuries, in Orissa in the fifth-seventh centuries, in West Bengal and Bangladesh during the same period, in Assam in the seventh century and in Himachal Pradesh and Nepal in the fifth-seventh centuries. To the sixth-seventh centuries belong an appreciable number of grants issued to brāhmaṇas by the Maitraka princes of Valabhī in Gujarat. In short in the fourth-seventh centuries large-scale land grants were made to members of the priestly order in the outlying, peripheral, backward (and in some cases mountainous), and aboriginal areas such as Andhra Pradesh, Assam, Bengal, Gujarat, Himachal Pradesh, Madhya Pradesh, Maharashtra, and Nepal. In some cases the number of landed beneficiaries was quite large. In the fifth century 1000 brāhmaṇas were endowed with land in one district by a charter by Pravarasen II.[1] In the seventh century, 205 brāhmaṇas were granted land through a single charter in Assam, and 100 brāhmaṇas through a single charter in the wild tracts of the Tipperah district of Bangladesh. In the same century 23 brāhmaṇas in one case and 12 in another received lands in the Cuttack area, and in the following century 200 brāhmaṇas were given lands in the Balasore district of Orissa.[2]

Since the priestly beneficiaries were endowed with almost all the fiscal rights and privileges which were enjoyed by the kings, they were faced with the problem of collecting regular share of the produce, levying forced contributions such as food, fuel, grass, timber, etc., and imposing forced labour called *viṣṭi* or *piḍā*. If necessary they could lease their land and fiscal rights to others and replace one set of peasants by another. They had

1. D. C. Sircar (ed.), *Sel. Inscr.*, i, Bk. III, no. 62, ll. 19-20.

2. For more instances see B. P. Mazumdar, "Collective Landgrants in Early Medieval Inscriptions", *JAS*, x (1968), 7-17.

also the authority to punish offences against family and property. Although in many cases the villagers were instructed to carry out the orders of the beneficiaries and in some cases specifically transferred to them, these provisions in themselves would not help the brāhmaṇas unless these were constantly enforced. But for enjoying all these fiscal and economic concessions and maintaining law and order the brāhmaṇas did not possess any administrative apparatus. In a way they appeared as the enjoyers of a good portion of the produce but did not have the coercive machinery to compel the peasants and artisans to produce. What they mainly possessed was the strength of refined rituals and the ability to propagate the varṇa ideology and convert the people to it. For various civil and criminal offences the Smṛtis prescribe not only fines and punishments enforceable by the government but also elaborate penances (*prāyaścittas*), which obviously were enforced by the brāhmaṇas. But these would not mean anything to the tribals who did not subscribe to the varṇa system and the values associated with it. The brāhmaṇas therefore accelerated the age-old practice of converting the tribes into castes within their established social framework. This is the reason why the lists of Manu and of the late Purāṇas disclose a large number of mixed castes, all śūdras, whose tribal origins can be detected without difficulty.

In backward areas the land grant economy led to the accession of numerous tribes as varṇasaṃkara śūdras; in settled areas it led to the loss of mobility at the lower levels. The loss of mobility was further caused by the decline of foreign trade. One of the reasons of the flourishing trade in the first two centuries of the Christian era was the establishment of stability over large areas on account of the Han, Kuṣāṇa and Iranian (Arṣasid) empires, all of which carried trade with one another and the Roman empire. The first three empires disappeared in the middle of the third century,[1] and decline set in in the Roman empire a century later. Trade with the eastern Roman empire continued in a depleted form in Gupta times, for some Byzantine coins of the fifth-sixth centuries have been found in India. But this

1. Michael Loewe, "Aspects of World Trade in the First Seven Centuries of the Christian Era", *JRAS*, no. 2 (1971), 177.

trade sharply declined from the sixth century. One of the reasons was the acquisition of knowledge of silk by the Byzantium which ceased to depend for its silk on India from the seventh century. Even earlier we have an indication of sharp fall in silk production in western India, for in the middle of the fifth century a guild of silk weavers migrated from the Nausari-Broach region, the hinterland of the Gujarat ports, to Mandasor in Malwa where they gave up their old vocation and proliferated into the occupations of archers, story tellers, religious expounders (teachers), astrologers, warriors, and ascetics.[1] Obviously all these trades were non-productive. On account of fall in demand for trade similar things may have happened to other craft guilds engaged in petty commodity production.

Decline of trade in the western world and central Asia was not offset by trade with China and South-East Asia, which possibly in the third-fourth centuries, supplied gold to India in return for beryl, cotton fabrics and sugar. During the rule of the Wei dynasty (A.D. 220-265) the Chinese learnt from Indians the art of making from stone coloured glass which could be passed off as beryl.[2] Soon after the sixth century A.D. they learnt cotton cultivation and the manufacture of textiles from Central Asia and South-East Asia, where it was introduced through Indian contacts.[3] They also learnt the art of making sugar from Magadha in the reign of the Tạng Emperor Tai-tsang (A.D.627-649).[4] Hence by the seventh century or so China and South-East Asia ceased to depend on India for the supply of sugar, cotton goods and precious stones. This, therefore, undermined Indian trade in this direction. What India supplied later consisted mainly of perfumes and elephant tusks.

Commercial decline is also indicated by progressive decline in the pure gold content of the Gupta gold coins as compared with those of the Kuṣāṇas. The Vāsudeva coins have 118 grains of pure gold, the Candragupta-Kumāradevī coins 109, certain Samudra Gupta coins have 105-04, other Samudra Gupta-Candra

1. *Sel. Inscr.*, i, Bk. III, no. 24, verses 16-19.

2. Tan Chang, "Ancient China's Quest for Indian Products", *The Sunday Statesman*, Magazine Section, 6 April 1969.

3. *Ibid.*

4. *Ibid.*

Gupta II coins have 99-98, the Archer coins of Kumāra Gupta I have 92, the similar coins of Skanda Gupta have 79-67, and those of the successors of Narasiṃha Gupta have 73-54 grains.[1] Thus by the middle of the fifth century the pure gold content of the Gupta coins is reduced to almost half the gold content of the Kuśāṇa coins. By the end of the sixth century gold coins almost disappear and become rare for about four hundred years. In western India under the Śakas and Guptas we have a good number of silver coins which were apparently used for trade in that area, but they practically disappear in post-Gupta times. All this must have meant a great setback to heavy commercial transactions.

Medium and petty transactions, especially internal, could be carried on through copper coins, but we have very few copper coins after Candra Gupta II. Imitations of Kuṣāṇa copper coins have been found in certain parts of the country, but their number is limited as compared to those of the Kuṣāṇas. Paucity of coins therefore indicates substantial shrinkage of the internal market from the middle of the fifth century.

The decline of trade and petty commodity production is further underlined by the decay of urban settlements in Gupta times and their desertion in the post-Gupta period. Excavated urban sites in north India show a constant improvement in structures from about the fifth century B.C. to about the third century A.D., the Kuṣāṇa levels providing the most flourishing phase. In Pakistan the Kuṣāṇa phase is so thriving that it is called the golden age of that country. But when we come to Gupta levels in northern India, we notice that Kuṣāṇa bricks are re-used in their buildings. In post-Gupta times most excavated sites were abandoned, for we have little or no signs of habitation. This is also attested by Hsüan Tsang. Although his observations are confined to the decay of the Buddhist towns, their number is considerable, and in many cases his statement can be substantiated archaeologically.[2] The decay of towns therefore would mean less activity for crafts and commerce.

1. Based on S. K. Maity, *Economic Life of North India in Gupta Period* (Calcutta, 1957), Appendix III, p. 202 and Table I (c) on p. 205; also see my "Indian Feudalism Retouched", *The Indian Historical Review*, i (1974), 322-23.

2. R. S. Sharma, "Decay of Gangetic Towns in Gupta and Post-Gupta Times," *Journal of Indian History*, Golden Jubilee Volume, 1973 pp. 135-50.

Coupled with the practice of land grants the decay of trade created conditions for reversion from semi-commodity production to some kind of natural economy in which people were mainly attached to the lands and all remunerations were made through land grants and grant in the share of produce. Although for acquiring lands the brāhmaṇas moved from one place to the other, artisans and merchants did not have to move. Social intercourse in the form of marriage and interdining was confined to a small circumference, and it is prescribed that a brāhmaṇa should not give his daughter to a person who lives at a long distance. On account of loss of mobility, territorial and occupational, at the lower levels of society in a purely agrarian economy guilds of artisans based on occupation tended to fossilize into castes. This may have been particularly true of the settled older areas.

The decline of crafts and commerce lessened the importance of traders and craftsmen and hardened the attitude of landed classes — brāhmaṇas and kṣatriyas — towards them. Craftsmen working in bamboo and leather were placed in the category of untouchable castes. But the basic factor that explains the increase in the number of mixed, śūdra castes also operated in the case of the conversion of the tribal peoples and in the fossilization of craft occupations. It was the expansion of land grant economy, and the introduction of feudal localism in which everybody had to stick to his land, village, master or client. Clients and masters might change, but not their artisans and peasants. This changelessness, which was the result of a society which practically stopped petty commodity production, prepared the climate for the perpetuation and proliferation of castes.

It seems that in earlier times artisans sold their products in the market and were paid in cash. But in the beginning of the sixth century in addition to a share in the produce land grants became an important mode of paying them. We have indirect indication of service grants in a sale deed recorded on a copper plate of A.D. 507 from Rajshahi district in Bangḷadesh. In defining the plots of land granted to brāhmaṇas, the plots of land belonging to the neighbouring cultivators are mentioned in detail. This list also includes many artisans. We hear of the field belonging to kālāka,[1] which may be identical with kaulika or weaver. There is clear mention of the ground belonging to a carpenter called Viṣṇuvarddhaki,[2] and to a vaidya or physician.[3] We come across three plots of land each belonging to three persons whose names end in vilāla,[4] who are thought to have been a mechanic caste like carpenter.[5] In addition to this we also come across *ja(jo)lāri-kṣetra*,[6] which may possibly belong to a weaver. Similarly the term *vi(ḍu)ggurika-kṣetra*[7] might mean a field belonging to a *vāgurika* or a hunter. Although in some of these cases identification of artisans is doubtful, there is no doubt that service grants were given to artisans and others. This coupled with the practice of remunerating their services in kind would naturally make them attached to their plots of land and make their movements difficult. It would hasten the process of the conversion of crafts into castes and contribute to the growth of the *jajmāni* system.

1. *Sel. Inscr.*, i, Bk. III, no. 37, line 25.
2. *Ibid.*, l. 19.
3. *Ibid.*, l. 22.
4. *Ibid.*, ll. 19, 21-22, 28.
5. *Ibid.*, p. 345, fn. l.
6. *Ibid*, l. 24.
7. *Ibid.*, l. 26.

BIBLIOGRAPHY

Sources consulted for more than one chapter

A. ORIGINAL

Epics

Mahābhārata,

(Cal. Edn.) Ed. N. Siromani and others, *BI*, Calcutta, 1834-39. Tr. K. M. Ganguly. Published by P. C. Roy, Calcutta, 1884-96.

(Kumbhakonam Edn.) Ed. T. R. Krishnacharya and T. R. Vyasacharya, Bombay, 1905-10.

(Critical Edn.) Ed. Various hands, Poona, 1927-1966. Unless otherwise stated the references are to this edition.

The Jaya-Saṁhitā i.e. *The Ur-Mahābhārata*, 2 volumes, Redactor, Keshavram K. Shastree, Ahmedabad, 1977.

Rāmāyaṇa of Vālmīki,

Ed. Kāśīnāth Pāṇḍurang, 2 pts., Bombay, 1888.

Purāṇas

Agni Purāṇa,

Tr. M. N. Dutt, 2 vols., Calcutta, 1903-4.

Bhāgavata Purāṇa,

Bombay, 1905.

Bhaviṣya Purāṇa,

Bombay, 1910.

Brahmāṇḍa Purāṇa,

Bombay, 1913.

Mārkaṇḍeya Purāṇa.

Ed. Rev. K. M. Banerjee, *BI*, Calcutta, 1862. Tr. F. E. Pargiter, Calcutta, 1904.

Matsya Purāṇa,

Ed. Jivananda Vidyaṣagara, Calcutta, 1876.

The Purāṇa Text of the Dynasties of the Kali Age, Tr. F. E Pargiter, Oxford, 1913.

Vāyu Purāṇa, Ed. R. L. Mitra, 2 vols., *BI*, Calcutta, 1880-88.

Viṣṇu Purāṇa with the comm. of Śrīdharasvāmi, Ed. Jivananda Vidyasagara, Calcutta, 1882. Tr. H. H. Wilson, 5 vols., London, 1864-70.

Inscriptions

D. C. Sircar, *Select Inscriptions Bearing on Indian History and Civilization*, i, Calcutta, 1942.

B. DICTIONARIES AND REFERENCE BOOKS

W. H. Gilbert, *Caste in India* (Bibliography), Pt. I, Cyclostyled copy, Washington, 1948.

Laxmanshastri Joshi, *Dharmakośa*, Vol. i (in three parts), Wai, Dist. Satara, 1937-41; Vol. III, pt I. Wai, 1959.

H. G. Liddell and R. Scott, *A Greek-English Lexicon*, 2 vols., Oxford, 1925-40.

G. P. Malalasekera, *A Dictionary of Pali Proper Names* 2 vols., London, 1937-8.

A. A. Macdonell and A. B. Keith, *Vedic Index of Names and Subjects*, 2 vols., London, 1912.

Monier Monier-Williams, *A Sanskrit-English Dictionary*, Oxford, 1951.

J. Muir, *Original Sanskrit Texts*, i, London 1872.

T. W. Rhys Davids and W. Stede, *Pali-English Dictionary*, PTS, London, 1921.

H. H. Wilson, *A Glossary of Judicial and Revenue Terms etc.*,. London 1885.

C. HISTORIES OF INDIAN LITERATURE

S. N. Dasgupta and S. K. De, *A History of Sanskrit Literature* (Classical Period), vol. i, Calcutta, 1947.

A. B. Keith, *A History of Sanskrit Literature*, Oxford, 1928.

B. C. Law, *A History of Pali Literature*, vol. i, London, 1933.

Albrecht Weber, *The History of Indian Literature*, Tr. from 2nd German Edn. by J. Mann and T. Zachariae, London, 1876.

M. Winternitz, *A History of Indian Literature*, Vol. i, Tr. from German by Mrs. Ketkar, Calcutta.

„ „ *Geschichte der Indischen Literatur*, Vols. ii-iii. Leipzig, 1920.

D. GENERAL WORKS

K. Antonova, G. Bongard-Levin & G. Kotovsky, *A History of India*, BOOK I, Moscow, 1979.

L. D. Barnett. *Antiquities of India*, London, 1913.

A. L. Basham, *The Wonder that was India*, London, 1954.

M. I. Finlay, *The Ancient Economy*, University of California Press, 1973.

Raymond Firth (ed.), *Themes in Economic Anthropology*, London, 1975.

Max Gluckman, *Politics, Law and Ritual in Tribal Society*, Basil Blackwell, 1977.

Maurice Godelier, *Perspectives in Marxist Anthropology*, Cambridge, 1977.

D. D. Kosambi, *An Introduction to the Study of Indian History*, Bombay, 1956.

Lawrence Krader (ed. & tr.), *The Ethnological Notebooks of Karl Marx*, Assen, 1972.

Gunnar Landtman, *The Origin of the Inequality of the Social Classes*, London, 1938.

Christian Lassen, *Indische Alterthumskunde*, 4 vols., Leipzig, 1847-1861.

R. C. Majumdar, H. C. Raychaudhuri and K. K. Datta, *An Advanced History of India*, London, 1948.

R. C. Majumdar and A. D. Pusalker, *The Vedic Age*, London, 1951.

,, ,, ,, *The Age of Imperial Unity*, Bombay, 1951.

K. A. Nilakanta Sastri, *The Mauryas and Satavahanas*, Bombay, 1957.

H. C. Raychaudhuri, *Political History of Ancient India*, 6th Edn., Calcutta, 1953.

E. J. Rapson, *The Cambridge History of India*, Vol. i, Cambridge, 1922.

Walter Ruben, *Einführung in die Indienkunde*, Berlin, 1954.

V. A. Smith, *Early History of India*, 4th Edn. revised by S. M. Edwardes, Oxford, 1924.

Emmanuel Terray, *Marxism and Primitive Societies*, New York, 1972.

E. SECONDARY WORKS MAINLY ON SOCIAL AND ECONOMIC LIFE IN ANCIENT INDIA

K. V. Rangaswami Aiyangar, *Some Aspects of the Hindu View of Life according to Dharmaśāstra*, Baroda, 1952.

A. S. Altekar, *Education in Ancient India*, Banaras, 1934.

B. R. Ambedkar, *Who were the Shudras*? (How they came to be the Fourth Varna in the Indo-Aryan Society), Bombay, 1946.

„ „ *The Untouchables* (Who were they? And why they became Untouchables?), New Delhi, 1948.

A. Baines, *Ethnography*, Strassburg, 1912.

Narayanchandra Bandyopadhyaya, *Economic Life and Progress in Ancient India*, Calcutta, 1945.

N. N. Bhattacharya, *Ancient Indian Rituals and Social Content*, Delhi, 1975.

S. C. Bhattacharya, *Some Aspects of Indian Society from 2nd Century* B.C. *to 4th Century* A.D., Calcutta, 1178.

G. M. Bongard-Levin, "Some Problems of the Social Structure of Ancient India", *History and Society*: *Essays in Honour of Professor Niharranjan Ray*, Calcutta, 1977, pp. 199-227.

Atindranath Bose, *Social and Rural Economy of Northern India* (*cir.* 600 B.C.-200 A.D.), 2 vols., Calcutta, 1945.

Devraj Chanana, "Ideological Aspects of Slavery in Ancient India", *Journal of the Oriental Institute*, viii, 1959.

„ „ *Slavery in Ancient India*, English edn., Delhi, 1960.

Moti Chandra, *Geographical and Economic Studies in Mahābhārata*, Lucknow, 1945.

„ „ *Sārthavāha*, Patna, 1953.

K. P. Chattopadhyaya, *The Ancient Indian Culture Contacts and Migrations*, Calcutta, 1970.

K. L. Daftari, *The Social Institutions in Ancient India*, Nagpur, 1947.

S. A. Dange, *India from Primitive Communism to Slavery*, Bombay 1949.

Santosh Kumar Das, *The Economic History of Ancient India*, Calcutta, 1944.

J. D. M. Derrett, *Religion, Law and State in Ancient India*, London, 1968.

M. G. Dikshit, *History of Indian Class*, Bombay, 1969.

Bhupendranath Dutt, *Studies in Indian Social Polity*, Calcutta, 1944.

N. K. Dutt, *Origin and Growth of Caste in India*, Vol. i, (*c*. B.C. 2000-300), London, 1931.

U. N. Ghoshal, *Contributions to the History of Hindu Revenue System*, Calcutta,1929.

G. S. Ghurye, *Caste and Class in India*, Bombay, 1950.

L. Gopal, "Slavery in Ancient India" *JAHRS*, xxvii, 70-89.

R. C. Hazra, *Studies in the Purāṇic Records on Hindu Rites and Customs*, Dacca, 1940.; 2nd edn., Delhi, 1975.

E. W. Hopkins, "Position of Ruling Caste in Ancient India", *JAOS*, xiii, 57-376.

J. H. Hutton, *Caste in India*, Oxford, 1951.

Jagdish Chandra Jain, *Life in Ancient India as Depicted in the Jain Canons*, Bombay, 1947.

P. C. Jain, *Labour in Ancient India*, New Delhi, 1971.

Suvira Jaiswal, *Caste in the Socio-Economic Framework of Early India*, Presidential Address, Section I, Indian History Congress, 38th Session, Bhubneshwar, 1977.

,, *Origin and Development of Vaiṣṇavism* (*c*. 200 B.C.—A.D. 500), Delhi, 1967.

,, ,, "Some Recent Theories of the Origin of Untouchability: A Historiographical Assessment," *Indian History Congress, Proceedings of the Thirty-ninth Session*, Hyderabad, 1978, 218-229.

K. P. Jayaswal, *Hindu Polity*, 2 pts., Calcutta, 1924.

,, ,, *Manu and Yājñavalkya*, Calcutta, 1930.

D. N. Jha, "Social Changes in Ancient India", *Economic and Political Weekly*, xiv, No. 35, 1 September 1979, 1499-1500.

Vivekanand Jha, "From Tribe to Untouchable: The Case of the Niṣādas" *Indian Society: Historical Probings*, ed. R. S. Sharma and V. Jha.

,, ,, "Stages in the History of Untouchables," *IHR*, ii, 14-31.

,, ,, "Untouchables in Early Indian History," Ph. D. Thesis, Patna University, 1972.

,, ,, Varṇasaṃkara in the Dharmasūtras", *JESHO*, xiii, 273-88.

J. Jolly, *Hindu Law and Custom*, Calcutta, 1928, Tr. S. K. Das from the German Edn. of 1896.

P. V. Kane, *History of Dharmaśāstra*, Vol. ii, Poona, 1941.

S. V. Ketkar, *The History of Caste in India*, New York, 1909.

D. D. Kosambi, *The Culture and Civilization of Ancient India in its Historical Outline*, London, 1965.

B. C. Law, *Tribes in Ancient India*, Poona, 1943.

R. C. Majumdar, *Corporate Life in Ancient India*, Calcutta, 1922.

R. K. Mookerji, *Ancient Indian Education*, London, 1940.

,, ,, *Local Government in Ancient India*, Oxford, 1920.

Pran Nath, *A Study in the Economic Condition of Ancient India*, London, 1929.

Robert A. Padgug, "Problems in the Theory of Slavery and Slave Society," *Science and Society*. xl, No. 1, 1976, 3-27.

Jaimal Rai, *The Rural-Urban Economy and Social Changes in Ancient India*, Varanasi, 1974.

Dev Raj, *L'Esclavage dans l' Inde ancienne d'apres les Textes Palis et Sanskrits*, Pondichery, 1957.

H. Risley, *The People of India*, London, 1915.

Walter Ruben. *Die Lage der Sklaven in der altindischen Gesellschaft*, Berlin, 1957.

,, ,, *Die okonomische und Soziate Entwicklung Indiens*, Berlin, 1959.

Walter Ruben, Uber die *Fruhesten Stufen der Entwicklung der altindischen Śūdras*, Berlin, 1965.

,, ,, *Die gesellschaftliche Entwicklung im alten Indien*, II. Die Entwicklung von Staat und Recht, Berlin, 1968.

,, ,, *Kulturigeschichte Indiens*, Berlin, 1978.

B. A. Saletore. *The Wild Tribes in Indian History*, Lahore, 1935.

K. M. Saran, *Labour in Ancient India*, Bombay, 1957.

Emile Senart, *Caste in India*, Tr. Denison Ross from the French Edn. *Les Castes dans l' Inde* (Paris, 1896), London, 1930.

R. N. Sharma, *Brahmins Through the Ages*, Delhi, 1977.

R. S. Sharma, *Aspects of Political Ideas and Institutions in Ancient India*, 2nd Edn., Delhi, 1968.

,, ,, *Indian Feudalism*, (*c.* A.D. 300-1200) 2nd Edn., Delhi, 1980.

,, ,, *Ancient India*, 2nd Edn., New Delhi, 1980.

,, ,, *Social Changes in Early Medieval India* (*c.* A.D. 500-1200), Reprint, New Delhi, 1981.

,, ,, "The Kali Age: A Period of Social Crisis", in S. N. Mukherjee, Ed., *India: History and Thought, Essays in Honour of A. L. Basham*, Calcutta, 1982, pp. 186-203.

,, ,, *Material Culture and Social Formations in Ancient India*, Delhi, 1983.

,, ,, *Perspectives in Social and Economic History of Early India*, 1983.

,, ,, *Urban Decay in India* (*c.* 300-*c.* 1000), Delhi, 1987.

,, ,, *Origin of the State in India*, Bombay, 1989.

,, ,, Ed., *A Survey of Research in Social and Economic History of India*, Delhi, 1987.

Romila Thapar, *Social History of Ancient India*, New Delhi, 1978.

G. P. Upadhyay, *Brāhmaṇas in Ancient India*, New Delhi, 1979.

P. H. Valavalkar, *Hindu Social Institutions*, London, 1939.

Max Weber, *The Agrarian Sociology of Ancient Civilization*, London, 1976.

Lynn White, Jr., *Medieval Religion and Technology*, California, 1978.

CHAPTER I

Historiography and Approach

R. G. Bhandarkar, *Collected Works*, Ed. N. B. Utgikar and V. G. Paranjpe, 4 vols., Poona, 1927-33.

V. S. Bhattacharya, "The Status of the Śūdras in Ancient India", *Vishwa Bharati Quarterly*, 1924.

H. T. Colebrooke, *Miscellaneous Essays*, Ed. E. B. Cowell, 2 vols., London, 1873.

J. C. Ghosh, *Brahmanism and the Sudra*, Calcutta, 1902.

Mountstuart Elphinstone, *The History of India*, London, 1841.

N. B. Halhed, *A Code of Gentoo Laws*, London, 1776.

Alfred Hillebrandt, "Brahmanen und Śūdras", *Festschrift für Karl Weinhold*, Breslau, 1896, pp. 53-57.

William Jones, *Institutes of Hindu Law or the Ordinances of Manu* (Tr.), Calcutta, 1794.

James Mill, *The History of India*, Vols. i and ii, 2nd edn., London 1820.

Raja Rammohun Roy, *The English Works*, 3 vols., Ed. J. C. Ghosh, Calcutta, 1901.

Swami Dayananda Sarasvati, *Satyārthaprakāśa*, Ajmer, Saṃvat, 1966.

B. K. Sarkar, *The Positive Background of Hindu Sociology*, Allahabad, 1937.

Chitra Tiwari, *Śūdras in Manu*, Delhi, 1963.

CHAPTER II

ORIGIN

ORIGINAL SOURCES

Atharva Veda (of the Paippalādas), Ed. Raghu Vira, Lahore, 1936-41.

Atharva Veda Saṃhitā (School of the Śaunakas), Ed. C. R. Lanman, Tr. W. D. Whitney, *HOS*, vii and viii, Harvard University, 1905. Ed. R. Roth and W. D. Whitney, Berlin, 1856. With the comm. of Sāyaṇa, Ed. S. Pāṇḍurang, Paṇḍit, 4 vols., Bombay, 1895-98. Tr. R. T. H. Griffith, 2 vols., Banaras, 1916-17. Unless otherwise stated the references are to the Śaunaka recension.

Bhaviṣyatkathā by Dhanapāla, Ed. C. D. Dalal and P. D. Gune, *GOS*, xx, Baroda, 1923.

J. W. McCrindle, *Ancient India as Described by Ptolemy*, Calcutta, 1885.

,, ,, *The Invasion of India by Alexander the Great*, Westminster, 1893.

Ṛg Veda Saṃhitā with the comm. of Sāyaṇa, 5 vols., Vaidika Samshodhan Mandal, Poona, 1933-51. Tr. of the first six Maṇḍalas, H. H. Wilson, London, 1850-7 Tr. in German, K. F. Geldner, *Der Rig-Veda*, HOS, xxxiii-xxxvi, Cambridge, Massachusetts, 1951-1257.

Vedānta-Sūtra of Bādarāyaṇa with the comm. of Śaṅkarācārya, 2 vols., *BI*, Calcutta, 1863. Tr. George Thibaut, *SBE*, xxxiv, Oxford, 1890.

SECONDARY WORKS

H. W. Bailey, "Iranian Arya and Daha," *Transaction of the Philological Society*, London, 1959.

D. R. Bhandarkar, *Some Aspects of Ancient Indian Culture*, Madras, 1940.

V. S. Bhattacharya Sastri, "Śūdra", *IA*, li, 137-9.

T. Burrow, *The Sanskrit Language*, London, 1955.

Jarl Charpentier, *Brahman*, Uppsala, 1932.

V. Gordon Childe, *The Aryans*, London, 1926.

" " *New Light on the Most Ancient East*, London, 1954.

Georges Dumezil, *Flamen-Brahman*, Paris, 1935.

" " "La Prehistoire Indo-Iranienne des Castes", *Journal Asiatique* (Paris), ccxvi, 109-130.

R. C. Dutt, *A History of Civilization in Ancient India*, Calcutta, 1891.

R. Ghirshman, *Iran* (Pelican Series), 1954.

N. N. Ghosh, "The Origin and Development of Caste System in India", *IC*, xii, 177-191.

Hermann Grassmann, *Wörterbuch zum Rig-Veda*, Leipzig, 1873.

Robert Heine-Geldern, "Archeological Traces of Vedic Aryans", *Journal of the Indian Society of Oriental Art* (Calcutta), vi, 87-115.

G. J. Held, *The Mahābhārata: An Ethnological Study*, London and Amsterdam, 1935.

P. V. Kane, "The Word *Vrata* in the *Ṛgveda*", *JBBRAS*, NS xxix, 1-28.

D. D. Kosambi, "Brahmin Clans," *JBBRAS*, lxxiii, 1953, 202-8.

,, ,, ,, "Early Brahmins and Brahminism" *JBBRAS*, NS, xxiii, 39-46.

,, ,, "On the Origin of Brahmin Gotras", *JBBRAS*, NS, xvvi, 21-80.

,, ,,. "Early Stages of the Caste System in Northern India" *JBBRAS*, NS, xii, 32-48.

Dharmanand Kosambi, *Bhagvān Buddha*, Tr. from Marathi into Hindi by Shripad Joshi, Delhi, 1956.

B. B. Lal, "Protohistoric Investigation" *AI*, No. 9.

,, ,, " The Indo-Aryan Hypothesis vis-a-vis. Archaeology", Cyclostyled copy of a paper read at the Seminar on "Ethnic Problems of the Early History of the Peoples of Central Asia and India in the Second Millennium B.C." held at Dushanbe (USSR) from 17 to 22 October 1977.

E. Mackay, *Early Indus Civilizations*, 2nd Edn.. London, 1948.

F. E. Pargiter, *Ancient Indian Historical Tradition*, London, 1922.

Louis Renou, *Vedic India*, Calcutta, 1957.

R. Roth, "Brahma und die Brahmanen," *ZDMG*, i, 66-86.

W. Ruben, "Indra's Fight against Vṛtra in the Mahābhārata", *S. K. Belvalkar Felicitation Volume* (Banaras, 1957), 113-26.

Robert Shafer, *Ethnography of Ancient India* (on the basis of the *Mahābhārata*), Wiesbaden, 1954.

R. S. Sharma, "Conflict, Distribution and Differentiation in Rigvedic Society ", *IHR*, iv, No.1, 1977, 1-12..

" " " Forms of Property in the early Portions of the *Ṛgveda*", *Essays in Honour of Prof. S.C. Sarkar*, New Delhi, 1976, pp. 39-50.

E. L. Stevenson, *Geography of Claudius Ptolemy*, New York, 1932.

Suryakanta, "Kīkaṭa, Phaliga and Paṇi", *S.K. Belvalkar Felicitation Volume*, 43-44.

J. Wackernagel, "Indoiranisches", *Sitzungsberichte der Koniglich Preussischen Akademie der Wissenschaften*, 1918, pp. 380-411.

R. E. Mortimer Wheeler, *The Indus Civilization* (Suppl. vol. to *CHI*, i), Cambridge, 1953.

Viśva-Bandhu Śāstrī, *A Vedic Word-Concordance*, Lahore, 1944.

CHAPTER III

TRIBE VERSUS VARṆA (*c.* 1000—*c.* 500 B.C.)[1]

ORIGINAL SOURCES

Aitareya Brāhmaṇa with the comm. of Sāyaṇa, Ed. T. Weber, Bonn, 1879. Tr. Martin Haug, Bombay, 1863.

Āpastamba Śrautasūtra with the comm. of Rudradatta, Ed. Richard Garbe, 3 vols., Calcutta, 1882-1902. Ed. and Tr. W. Caland, 3 vols., Gottingen-Leipzig-Amsterdam, 1921-1928.

Bṛhadāraṇyaka Upaniṣad with the comm. of Śaṅkarācārya, Tr. Swami Madhavanand, Almora, 1950.

Bṛhad-devatā attributed to Śaunaka, Ed. and Tr. A. A. Macdonell, *HOS*, v and vi, Harvard, 1904.

Chāndogya Upaniṣad, Text, Tr. and Annotation, Emile Senart, Paris, 1930.

Drāhyāyaṇa Śrautasūtra with the comm. of Dhanvin, Ed. J. N. Reutter, London, 1904.

Gopatha Brāhmaṇa, Ed. Dienke Gaastra, Leiden, 1919.

Jaiminīya Brāhmaṇa of the Sāma Veda, Ed. Raghu Vira and Lokesh Chandra, Nagpur, 1954.

Das Jaiminiya Brāhmaṇa in Auswahl, Ed. and Tr. into German, W. Caland, Amsterdam, 1919.

Jaiminīya Śrautasūtra, Ed. and Tr. into German, D. Gaastra, Leiden, 1906.

Jaiminīya or Talavakāra Upaniṣad Brāhmaṇa, Ed. Rama Deva, Lahore, 1921.

Kāṇva Saṃhitā of the Śukla Yajur Veda, Ed. Madhava Sastri, Banaras, 1915.

Kapiṣṭhala-Kaṭha Saṃhitā, Ed. Raghu Vira, Lahore, 1932.

Kāṭhaka Saṃhitā, Ed. Leopold von Schroder, Leipzig, 1900-1910.

1. Books assigned to a period do not necessarily belong to it or deal only with it. It is also difficult to have a clear-cut point for beginning or ending a period.

Kātyāyana Śrautasūtra with the comm. of Karkācārya, Ed. Madanmohan Pathak, Banaras, 1904.

Lāṭyāyana Śrautasūtra with the comm. of Agnisvāmi, Ed. Anandacandra Vedāntarāgeśa, *BI*, Calcutta, 1872.

Maitrāyaṇi Saṃhitā, Ed. Leopold von Schroder, Leipzig, 1923.

Nighaṇṭu and Nirukta, Ed. and Tr. Lakshman Sarup. Text, University of Punjab, 1927. Eng. Tr. and Notes, Oxford, 1921.

Rg Veda Brāhmaṇas: *Aitareya and Kauṣitaki Brāhmaṇas*. Tr. A. B. Keith, *HOS*, xxv, Harvard, 1920.

Śāṅkhāyana Brāhmaṇa, *ASS*, No. 35, 1911.

Śāṅkhāyana Śrautasūtra, Ed. A. Hillebrandt, *BI*, Calcutta, 1888.

Śatapatha Brāhmaṇa (Mādhyandina recension), Ed. V. Sharma Gauḍa and C. D. Sharma, Kasi, Saṃvat, 1994-7.

Satyāṣāḍha (*Hiraṇyakeśin*) *Śrautasūtra* with the comm. of Mahādeva, *ASS*, 1907.

Taittiriya Brāhmaṇa of the Black Yajur Veda, with the comm. of Sāyaṇa, Ed. R. L. Mitra, 3 vols., Calcutta, 1859-70.

Taittiriya Saṃhitā, Ed. A. Weber, *Indischen Studien*, Band 11 and 12, Leipzig, 1871-2. Tr. A. B. Keith, *HOS*, xviii and xix, Harvard, 1914.

The Thirteen Principal Upaniṣads, Tr. R. E. Hume, Oxford, 1931.

Vājasaneyi Saṃhitā (Mādhyandina recension) with the comm. of Uvaṭa and Mahīdhara, Ed. Wāsudev Laxmaṇ Shāstrī Paṇśīkar, Bombay, 1912.

Vārāha Śrautasūtra, Ed. W. Caland and Raghu Vira, Lahore, 1933.

Zend-Avesta, pt. I Vendīdād, Tr. James Darmesteter, *SBE*, iv, Oxford, 1880.

SECONDARY WORKS

A. C. Banerjea, "Studies in the Brāhmaṇas", Ph. D. Thesis, London University, 1952.

Jogiraj Basu, *India of the Age of the Brāhmaṇas*, Calcutta, 1969.

M. Bloomfield, *The Atharvaveda*, Strassburg 1899.

H. M. Chadwick, *The Heroic Age*, Cambridge, 1912.

R. G. Forbes, *Metallurgy in Antiquity*, Leiden, 1950.

Wilhelm Geiger, *Civilization of the Eastern Iranians in Ancient Times*, Tr. from the German by D. D. Poshotan Sanjānā, Vol. i, London, 1885.

U. N. Ghoshal, *Historiography and Other Essays*, Calcutta, 1944.

U. N. Ghoshal, *Hindu Public Life*, Pt. I, Calcutta, 1944.

J. Gonda, *The Ritual Sūtras*, Wiesbaden, 1977.

A. Hillebrandt, "Zur vedischen Mythologie und Volkerbewegung." *ZII*, Band 3, Leipzig, 1925.

A. A. Macdonell, *A Vedic Grammar for Students*, Oxford, 1916.

J. Muir, "Relation of the Priests to the other Classes of Indian Society in the Vedic Age," *JRAS*, NS, ii (1866), 257-302.

Emile Benveniste, *Indo-European Language and Society*, London, 1973.

G. C. Pande, *Studies in the Origins of Buddhism*, Allahabad, 1957.

R. S. Sharma, "Class Formation and its Material Basis in the Upper Gangetic Basin (*c.* 1000-500 B.C.)", *IHR*, ii. No 1, 1975, 1-13."

" " "The Later Vedic Phase and the Painted Grey Ware Culture," *History and Society: Essays in Honour of Professor Niharranjan Ray*, Calcutta, 1978, pp. 133-41.

George Thomson, *Studies in Ancient Greek Society*, i, London, 1949.

Vibha Tripathi, *The Painted Grey Ware: An Iron Age Culture of Northern India*, Delhi, 1975.

S. V. Venkateswara, *Indian Culture through the Ages*, Pt. I, London, 1928.

A. Weber, "Collectanea über die Kastenverhaltnisse in den Brāhmaṇa und Sūtra", *Indische Studien*, x, 1-160.

" " "Der erste Adhyāya des ersten Buches des Śatapatha-Brāhmaṇa", *ZDMG*, iv, 289-304.

Heinrich Zimmer, *Altindisches Leben*, Berlin, 1879.

CHAPTER IV

SERVILITY AND DISABILITIES (*c.* 600—*c.* 300 B.C.)

ORIGINAL SOURCES

A. Brāhmaṇical

Āpastamba Dharmasūtra, Ed. G. Bühler, Bombay, 1932.

Āśvalāyana Gṛhyasūtra with the comm. of Haradattācārya, Ed. T. Gaṇapati Śāstrī, Trivandrum, 1923.

Baudhāyana Gṛhyasūtra, Ed. R. Shamasastry, Mysore, 1927.

Baudhāyana Dharmasūtra, Ed. E. Hultzsch, Leipzig, 1884.

Gautama Dharmasūtra, Ed. A.S. Stenzler, London, 1876, with the comm. of Maskarin, Ed. L. Srinivasacharya, Mysore, 1917.

Pāṇini-Sūtra-Pāṭha and Pariśiṣṭas with Word Index, compiled by S. Pathak and S. Chitrao, Poona, 1935.

Pāraskara Gṛhyasūtra, Bombay, 1917.

Śāṅkhāyana Gṛhyasūtra, Ed. H. Oldenberg in *Indische Studien,* xv, pp. 13f.

Vaśiṣṭha Dharmaśāstra, Ed. A. A. Führer, Bombay, 1916

Trs. of the Gṛhyasūtras of Śāṅkhāyana, Āśvalāyana, Pāraskara, Khadira, Gobhila, Hiraṇyakeśin and Āpastamba by H. Oldenberg in *SBE,* xxix and xxx, Oxford, 1886-92.

Trs. of the Dharmasūtras of Āpastamba, Gautama, Vaśiṣṭha and Baudhāyana by G. Bühler in *SBE,* ii and xiv, Oxford 1879-82.

B. Buddhist

Aṅguttara Nikāya, Ed. R. Morris and E. Hardy, 5 vols., PTS, London, 1885-1900. Tr. i, ii and v by F. L. Woodward, and iii and iv by E. M. Hare, PTS, London, 1932-36.

Digha Nikāya, Ed. T. W. Rhys Davids and J.E. Carpenter, 3 vols., PTS, London, 1890-1911. Tr. T. W. Rhys Davids 3 vols., *SBB,* London, 1899-21.

Jātaka with commentary, Ed. V. Fausböll, 7 vols. (Vol. 7, Index, by D. Anderson) London, 1877-97. Tr. Various hands, 6 vols., London, 1895-1907.

Majjhima Nikāya, Ed. V. Trenckner and R. Chalmers, PTS, 3 vols., London, 1888-1896. Tr. Lord Chalmers, 2 vols., *SBB,* London 1926-7.

Vinaya Piṭaka, Ed. H. Oldenberg, 5 vols., London, 1879-83. Tr. I. B. Horner, 5 pts., *SBB,* London, 1938-52.

C. Jain.

Antagaḍa-Dasāo and *Aṇuttarovavāiya-Dasāo*, Ed. P. L. Vaidya, Bombay, 1932. Tr. L. D. Barnett, London, 1907.

Āyāraṅga Sutta of the Śvetāmbara Jainas, Ed. H. Jacobi, PTS, London, 1882.

Kalpasūtra of Bhadrabāhu, Ed. H. Jacobi, Leipzig, 1879.

Ovāiya (or *Aupapātikasūtra* with Abhayadeva's comm., Ed. Muni Hemasâgara, Āgamodaya Samiti publication.

Sthānāṅga Sūtra with the comm. of Abhayadeva, Ed. Veṇīcandra Suracandra, 2 vols., Bombay, 1918-20.

Sūyagaḍam, Ed. P. L. Vaidya, Bombay, 1928.

Uttarādhyayanasūtra, Ed. Jarl Charpentier, Uppsala, 1922.

Uvāsagadasāo, Ed. A.F. Rudolf Hoernle, Calcutta, 1890.

SECONDARY WORKS

V. S. Agrawala, *India as known to Pāṇini*, Lucknow, 1953.

V. M. Apte, *Social and Religious Life in the Gṛhyasūtras*, Bombay, 1954.

N. C. Banerjee, "Slavery in Ancient India" *The Calcutta Review* (Aug. 1930), pp. 249-265.

A. L. Basham, *History and Doctrines of the Ājīvikas*, London, 1951.

Shivnath Basu, "Slavery in the Jātakas", *JBORS*, ix, 369-375.

S. K. Chakravorty, *A Study of Ancient Indian Numismatics*, Mymensingh, 1931.

Richard Fick, *The Social Organisation in North-East India in Buddha's time*, Calcutta, 1920.

Ivor Fiśer, "The Problem of the Seṭṭhi in Buddhist Jātakas", *AO*, xxii, 238-265.

U. N. Ghoshal, "The Status of Śūdras in the Dharmasūtras", *IC*, xiv, 21-27.

Ram Gopal, *India in Vedic Kalpasūtras*, Delhi 1959.

D. D. Kosambi, "Ancient Kosala and Magadha", *JBBRAS*, NS, xxvii.

B. C. Law, "Slavery as known to Early Buddhists," *Journal of the Ganganath Jha Research Institute*, vi, 1948, 1-10.

R. L. Mitra, *Indo-Aryans*, 2 Vols., Calcutta, 1881.

F. Max Müller, *The Hibbert Lectures* 1878, London, 1880.

B. C. Law, *India as Described in Early Texts of Buddhism and Jainism*, London, 1941.

R. N. Mehta, *Pre-Buddhist India*, Bombay, 1939.

J. J. Meyer, *Uber das Wesen der altindischen Rechtsschriften und zehr Verhaltnis Einander und zu Kauṭilya*, Leipzig, 1927.

Rodolf Mondolfo, "Greek Attitude to Manual Labour" *Past and Present*, No. 6.

Oldenberg, *Buddha, His Life, His Doctrine, His Order*, Tr. from German Hoey, London, 1882.

W. Rahul, *What the Buddha Taught*, Badford, 1959.

T. W. Rhys Davids, *Buddhist India*, London, 1903.

G. R. Sharma, *The Excavations at Kauśāmbi* (1957-59), Allahabad, 1960.

R. S. Sharma, "Development of Productive Forces and its Social Implications in India in the First Millennium B.C. With special reference to the Age of the Buddha".

Paper presented to International Conference on Development of Productive Techniques and their Consequences for Social Formation, Berlin, G.D.R. November, 1978.

" " "Material Milieu of the Birth of Buddhism", *Das Kapital Centenary Volume*, Delhi, 1967.

Narendra Wagle, *Society at the Time of the Buddha*, Bombay, 1966.

A. K. Warder, *Indian Buddhism*, Varanasi, 1970.

W. L. Westermann, *The Slave System of Greek and Roman Antiquity*, Philadelphia, 1955.

CHAPTER V

STATE CONTROL AND THE SERVILE ORDER

(*c*. 300—*c*. 200 B.C.)

ORIGINAL SOURCES

Texts

Arthaśāstra of Kauṭilya, Ed. and Tr. R. P. Kangle, Bombay, 1960-65. Ed. R. Shamasastry, 3rd edn., Mysore, 1924 (unless otherwise stated refs. in this work refer to this text).

Tr. R. Shamasastry, 3rd edn., Mysore, 1929. Ed. with comm. by T. Gaṇapati Śāstrī, 3 vols., Trivandrum, 1924-25. Ed. J. Jolly and R. Schmidt, Vol. i, Lahore, 1924. Tr. R. Shamasastry, 3rd edn., Mysore, 1929. Tr. *Das altindische Buch vom Welt und Staatsleben*, J. J. Meyer, Leipzig, 1926.

Commentaries

Jayamaṅgalā (runs up to the end of the BK. I of the *AŚ* with gaps), Ed. G. Harihara Sastri, *JOR*, xx-xxiii.

Pratipada-pañcikā by Bhaṭṭasvāmin (on BK. II from sec. 8), Ed. K.P. Jayaswal and A. Banerji-Sastri, *JBORS*, xi-xii.

Naya Candrikā by Mādhava Yajva (on BKs. VII-XII), Ed. Udayavīra Śāstrī, Lahore, 1924.

A Fragment of the Kauṭilya's Arthaśāstra alias Rājasiddhānta with the fragment of the commentary named Nītinirṇīti of Āchārya Yogdhama alias Mugdhavilāsa, Ed. Muni Jina Vijaya, Bombay, 1959.

Inscriptions

Inscriptions of Aśoka, Ed. E. Hultzsch, *CII*, i, Oxford, 1925.

Foreign Accounts:

J. W. McCrindle, *Ancient India as Described in Classical Literature*, Westminster, 1901.

,, ,, *Ancient India as Described by Megasthenes and Arrian*, Calcutta, 1926.

,, ,, *Ancient India as Described by Ktesias the Knidian*, London, 1882.

SECONDARY WORKS

K. V. Rangaswami Aiyangar, *Indian Cameralism*, Madras, 1949.

N. C. Bandyopadhyaya, *Kauṭilya or an Exposition of his Social and Political Theory*, Calcutta, 1927.

Bernhard Breloer, *Kauṭilīya-Studien*, 3 vols., Bonn, 1927-34.

Keith Hopkins, *Conquerors and Slaves*, Cambridge, 1978.

P. L. Narsu, *The Essence of Buddhism*, Madras, 1912.

Eva Ritschl and Maria Schetelich, *Studien zum Kauṭilīya Arthaśāstra*, Berlin, 1973.

I. J. Sorabji, *Some Notes on the Adhyakṣa-pracāra BK. II of the Kauṭilīyam Arthaśāstram*, Allahabad, 1914.

Thomas R. Trautmann, *Kauṭilya and the Arthaśāstra*, Leiden, 1971.

CHAPTER VI

CRISIS IN THE OLD ORDER

(*c.* 200 B.C.—*c.* A.D. 300)

ORIGINAL SOURCES

Texts

Āraṇyaka Parva of Mahābhārata, Ed., V.S. Sukthankar, Critical Edn., Vol. III, pt. I; Vol. IV, pt. II, Poona, 1942.

Dramas of Bhāsa: *Avimāraka*, *Bālacarita*, *Pañcarātra* and *Pratimānāṭaka*, Ed. T. Gaṇapati Śāstrī, Trivandrum, 1912-15.

Divyāvadāna, Ed. E. B. Cowell and F. A. Neil, Cambridge, 1886.

Lalita Vistara, Ed. S. Lefmann, 2 vols., Halle, 1902-1908.

Mahābhāṣya of Patañjali, Ed. F. Kielhorn, 3 vols., Bombay, 1892-1909.

Mahāvastu, Ed. E. Senart, 3 vols., Paris, 1882-97.

Manu Smṛti or Mānava Dharmaśāstra, Ed. V. N. Mandlik, Bombay, 1886. Tr. G. Bühler, *SBE*, xxv, Oxford, 1886.

Milindapañho, Ed. V. Trenckner, London, 1928. Tr. T. W. Rhys Davids, *SBE*, xxxv-xxxvi, Oxford, 1890-4.

Paṃnavaṇā Sūtra (with the comm. of Malayagiri), 2 vols., Banaras, 1884.

Saddharmapuṇḍarikasūtra with N. D. Mironov's readings from Central Asian MSS., Ed. N. Dutt, Calcutta, 1952. Tr. H. Kern, *SBE*, xxi, Oxford. 1884.

Yuga Purāṇa, Ed. D. R. Mankad, Vallabhavidyanagar, 1951.

Inscriptions

Lüder's List of Inscriptions, *EI*, x.

SECONDARY WORKS

G. L. Adhya, *Early Indian Economics: Studies in the Economic Life of Northern and Western India c.* 200 BC.-300 A.D. Bombay, 1966.

R. C. Agrawala, "Position of Slaves and Serfs as depicted in the Kharosthi Documents from Chinese Turkestan",

IHQ, xxix, 1953, 97-110.

K. V. Rangaswami Aiyangar, *Aspects of the Social and Political System of Manusmṛti*, Lucknow, 1949.

„ „ *Rājadharma*, Madras 1941.

Tan Chang, "Ancient China's Quest for Indian Products," *The Sunday Statesman*, Magazine Section, 6 April 1969.

E. W. Hopkins, *The Mutual Relations of the Four Castes according to the Mānavadharmaśāstram*, Leipzig, 1881.

G. F. Ilyin, "Śūdras und Slaven in den altindischen Gesetzbuchern", *Sowjetwissenschaft* (Berlin), 1952, No. 2., pp. 94-107.

K. P. Jayaswal, *History of India*, 150 A.D. *to* 350 A.D., Lahore, 1933.

B. B. Lal, "Examination of some Ancient Indian Glass Specimens", *AI*, Vol. viii, 1952-5.

Michael Loewe, "Spices and Silk: Aspects of World Trade in the first Seven Centuries of the Christian Era," *JRAS*, 1971, 166-79.

Sir John Marshall, "*Taxila*", ii, Cambridge, 1951.

B. N. Puri, "Some Aspects of Economic Life in the Kuṣāṇa Period", *IC*, xii.

A. D. Pusalker, *Bhāsa—A Study*, Lahore, 1940.

R. P. Singh, "Artisans in Manu", *Proceedings of the 32nd Session of Indian History Congress*, Jabalpur, 1970, Vol. i, 102-117.

D. A. Suleykin, "Fundamental Problems of the Periodisation of Ancient India", *Medieval India Quarterly* (Aligarh), i, No. 3-4, 46-58.

W. W. Tarn, *The Greeks in Bactria and India*, Cambridge, 1938.

E. H. Warmington, *The Commerce between the Roman Empire and India*, Cambridge, 1928.

R. E. M. Wheeler, *Rome beyond the Imperial Frontiers*, Pelican Series, 1955.

CHAPTER VII

PEASANTHOOD AND RELIGIOUS RIGHTS

(*c.* A.D. 300—*c.* 600)

ORIGINAL SOURCES

Texts

Amarakośa or *Nāmaliṅgānuśāsana* of Amara with the comm. of Bhaṭṭakṣīrasvāmin, Ed. A. D. Sharma and N. G. Sardesai, Poona, 1941.

Bṛhaspati Smṛti (this text has been followed), Ed. K. V. Rangaswami Aiyangar, *GOS*, lxxxv, Baroda, 1941. Tr. J. Jolly, *SBE*, xxxiii, Oxford, 1889.

Bṛhat Kalpasūtra and *Original Niryukti* of Sthavira Ārya Bhadrabāhu Svāmin and a Bhāṣya by Saṃghadāsa Gaṇi Kṣamaśramaṇa with a commentary begun by Malayagiri and completed by Kṣemakīrti, 6 vols., Bhavnagar, 1933-42.

Bṛhat Saṃhitā of Varāhamihira with Hindi Tr., Durga Prasad, Lucknow, 1884.

Bṛhat Saṃhitā of Varāhamihira with the comm. of Bhaṭṭotpala, 2 parts, Ed. Sudhākara Dvivedī, Banaras, 1895-7.

Jambudvipaprajñaptiḥ with the comm. of Śānticandra, Bombay, 1920.

Jayākhya Saṃhitā, Ed. Embar Krishnacharya, *GOS*, liv, Baroda, 1931.

Kāmandakiya Nītisāra, Ed. R. L. Mitra, *BI*, Calcutta, 1884. Tr. M. N. Dutt, Calcutta, 1896.

Kāmasūtra of Vātsyāyana with the comm. *Jayamaṅgalā* of Yaśodhara, Ed. Gosvami Damodar Shastri, Banaras, 1929.

Kātyāyana Smṛti on Vyavahāra, Law and Procedure, Ed. with reconstituted text, tr., notes and introduction by P. V. Kane, Bombay, 1933.

Laṅkāvatāra Sūtra, Ed. Bunyiu Nanjio, Kyoto, 1923. Tr. D. T. Suzuki, London, 1932.

Mālavikāgnimitra of Kālidāsa, Ed. P. S Sane, G. H. Godbole and H. S. Ursekar, Bombay, 1950.

Mṛcchakaṭika of Śūdraka, Ed. and Tr. R. D. Karmarkar, Poona, 1937. Tr. R. P. Oliver, Illinois, 1938.

Nārada Smṛti with extracts from the comm. of Asahāya, Ed. J. Jolly, Calcutta, 1885. Tr. J. Jolly, *SBE*, xxxiii, Oxford, 1889.

Narasiṃha Purāṇa, 2nd Edn., Bombay, 1911.

Nāṭyaśāstra of Bharata Muni with the comm. of Abhinavagupta,

Ed. Manavalli Ramakrishna Kavi, 3 vols., *GOS*, Baroda, 1926-54. Tr. Manomohan Ghosh, Calcutta, 1950.

Pañcatantra in its oldest recension, the Kashmirian, entitled *Tantrākhyāyikā*, Ed. J. Hertel, *HOS*, xiv, Harvard, 1915. The text in its oldest form, Ed. F. Edgerton, Poona, 1930 (References are made to this text).

Piṇḍaniryuktiḥ of Bhadrabāhu Svāmī, Bombay, 1918.

Raghuvaṃśa of Kālidāsa, Ed. Raghunatha Nandargikar, Bombay, 1891.

Theragāthā Aṭṭhakathā (*Paramattha Dīpanī*), the comm. of Dhammapāla, Ed. F. L. Woodward, 2 vols., PTS, London, 1940-52.

Yājñavalkya Smṛti with Vīramitrodaya and Mitākṣarā, Chaukhamba Sansk. Series, Banaras, Saṃvat, 1986.

Vajrasūcī of Aśvaghoṣa, Ed. and Tr. Sujitkumar Mukhopadhyaya, Santiniketan, 1950.

Vimāna-Vatthu Aṭṭhakathā, (pt. IV of the *Paramattha Dīpanī* of Dhammapāla), Ed. E. Hardy, PTS, London, 1901.

Viṣṇudharmottara Mahāpurāṇa, Bombay, Vikrama Saṃvat, 1969.

Viṣṇu Smṛti or *Vaiṣṇava Dharmaśāstra* (with extracts from the comm. of Nanda Paṇḍita), Ed. J. Jolly, *BI*, Calcutta, 1881. Tr. J. Jolly, *SBE*, vii, Oxford, 1880.

Chinese Sources

Samuel Beal, *Travels of Fah-hian and Sung-Yun* (Tr.), London, 1869.

H. A. Giles, *The Travels of Fa-hsien or Record of Buddhistic Kingdoms* (Tr.), Cambridge, 1923.

James Legge, *A Record of Buddhistic Kingdoms* (being an account of the Chinese monk Fa-hien's Travels) Tr., Oxford, 1886.

T. Watters, *On Yuan Chwang's Travels in India*, Ed. T. W. Rhys Davids and S. W. Bushell, 2 vols., London, 1904-5.

Muslim Sources

Edward C. Sachau, *Alberuni's India* (Tr. & Ed.), London, 1888.

Inscriptions

J. F. Fleet, *Inscriptions of the Early Gupta Kings*, CII, iii, London, 1888.

SECONDARY WORKS

J. N. Banerjea, *The Development of Hindu Iconography*, Calcutta, 1941.

R. G. Basak, "Indian Society as pictured in the Mṛcchakaṭika", *IHQ*, v.

R. G. Bhandarkar, *Vaiṣṇavism, Śaivism and Minor Religious Sects*, Strassburg, 1913.

H. C. Chakladar, *Social Life in Ancient India*, Calcutta, 1929.

H. T. Colebrooke, *A Digest of Hindu Law* (p. 252, fn. 5).

V. R. R. Dikshitar, *The Gupta Polity*, Madras, 1952.

E. W. Hopkins, *The Religions of India*, London, 1895.

„ „ *The Great Epic of India*, New Haven, 1901.

E. W. Hopkins, *Ethics of India*, Yale University Press, 1924.

E. W. Hopkins, *Epic Mythology*, Strassburg, 1915.

G. F. Ilyin, "Osobennosti Rabstva v drevnei Indii", *Vestnik drevnei istorii* (Moscow-Leningrad), 1 51, No. I, pp. 33-52.

D. N. Jha, *Early Indian Feudalism: A Historiographical Critique*, Presidential Address, Section I: Ançient India, Indian History Congress, 40th Session, Waltair, 1979.

B. Jowett (Tr.), *The Republic* (of Plato), New York, 1946.

A. B. Keith, *The Sāṃkhya System*, Oxford, 1919.

D. D. Kosambi, "The Working Class in the Amarakośa", *JOR*, xxiv, pp. 57-69.

B. C. Law, *Heaven and Hell in Buddhist Perspective*, Calcutta and Simla, 1925.

S. K. Maity, *The Economic Life of Northern India in the Gupta Period*, Calcutta, 1957.

R. C. Majumdar and A. S. Altekar, *The Gupta-Vākāṭaka Age*, Lahore, 1946.

R. C. Majumdar and A. D. Pusalkar, *The Classical Age*, Bombay, 1954.

Motichandra, *Bharatiya Veśa-bhūṣa* (p. 247, fn. 6).

E. P. O. Murray, "The Ancient Workers of Western Dhalbhum", *JRASB*, III Series, vi, 79-104.

M. A. Murray, *The Splendour that was Egypt*, London, 1949.

R. B. Pandey, *Hindu Sanskaras*, Banaras, 1949.

R. N. Nandi, "Aspects of Untouchability in Early South India," *Indian History Congress, Proceedings of the Thirty-fourth Session*, i, Chandigarh, 1973, 120-25.

D. R. Patil, *Cultural History from the Vāyu Purāṇa*, Poona 1946.

K. S. Ramaswami Sastri, *Studies in Rāmāyaṇa*, Baroda, 1944.

H. C. Raychaudhuri, *Early History of the Vaiṣṇava Sect*, Calcutta, 1920.

R. N. Saletore, *Life in the Gupta Age*, Bombay, 1943.

A. M. Sastri, *India as seen in the Bṛhat-Saṃhitā of Varāhamihira*, Delhi, 1969.

R. S. Sharma, "Decay of Gangetic Towns in Gupta Times.", *Journal of Indian history*, Golden Jubilee Volume, 1973, 135-50.

,, ,, *Indian Feudalism : c.* 300-1200, Calcutta, 1965.

,, ,, "Indian Feudalism Retouched," *The Indian Historical Review*, i, No 2, 1974, 320-30.

,, ,, The First Devraj Chanana Memorial Lecture, 1969: *Social Changes in Early Medieval India* (*c.* A.D. 500-1200), Delhi, 1969.

Vivādacintamani (p. 254, fn. 11).

D. C. Sircar, *Studies in the Society and Administration of Ancient and Medieval India*, i, Calcutta, 1967.

S. J. Tambiah, "From Varṇa to Caste through Mixed Unions," in Jack Good (Ed.), The Character of Kinship, Cambridge, 1973.

B. S. Upadhyaya, *India in Kālidāsa*, Allahabad, 1947.

K. J. Virji, *Ancient History of Saurashtra*, Bombay, 1952.

J. Ph. Vogel, *Antiquities of Chamba State*, Pt. I, Calcutta, 1911.

B. N. S. Yadav, *Society and Culture in Northern India in the Twelfth Century*, Allahabad, 1973.

INDEX

(Sanskrit, Pāli and Prākrit Words)

A

B

* All the terms have been italicised here, although some appear in Roman in the text.

GENERAL INDEX

(It also includes Sanskrit and Pāli words, especially names of castes, peoples and books, which are in general use)